In the Shadow of Race

IN THE SHADOW OF **RACE**

Jews, Latinos, and Immigrant
Politics in the United States

VICTORIA HATTAM

The University of Chicago Press
Chicago and London

Victoria Hattam is chair of and associate professor in the Department of Political Science at the New School for Social Research. She is the author of *Labor Visions and State Power: The Origins of Business Unionism in the United States.*

The University of Chicago Press, Chicago 60637
The University of Chicago Press, Ltd., London
© 2007 by The University of Chicago
All rights reserved. Published 2007
Printed in the United States of America

16 15 14 13 12 11 10 09 08 07   1 2 3 4 5

ISBN-13: 978-0-226-31922-3   (cloth)
ISBN-10: 0-226-31922-9   (cloth)
ISBN-13: 978-0-226-31923-0   (paper)
ISBN-10: 0-226-31923-7   (paper)

Library of Congress Cataloging-in-Publication Data

Hattam, Victoria Charlotte.
    In the shadow of race: Jews, Latinos, and immigrant politics in the United States / Victoria Hattam.
        p.   cm.
    Includes bibliographical references and index.
    ISBN-13: 978-0-226-31922-3 (cloth: alk. paper)
    ISBN-10: 0-226-31922-9 (cloth: alk. paper)
    ISBN-13: 978-0-226-31923-0 (pbk.: alk. paper)
    ISBN-10: 0-226-31923-7 (pbk.: alk. paper)
    1. United States—Race relations—Political aspects. 2. Ethnicity—Political aspects—United States. 3. Jews—United States—Politics and government. 4. Hispanic Americans—Politics and government. I. Title.
    E184.A1H37   2007
    320.973089—dc22

                                                         2007011060

♾ The paper used in this publication meets the minimum requirements of the American National Standard for Information Sciences—Permanence of Paper for Printed Library Materials, ANSI Z39.48-1992.

To My Family
Tom, Emily, and Robert Graham

CONTENTS

FIGURES

PREFACE

When discussing my research over the past several years, I discovered many colleagues simply presumed I am an advocate of ethnicity, the assumption being that we write about what we like. This is not the case here. I began this book because I saw dangers lurking in the current embrace of ethnicity as the preferred language of difference to that of race. So let the reader be forewarned; this is not simply a defense of ethnic difference over that of race. In fact, I advocate holding on to race because it has long been the language for addressing issues of power and inequality in the United States. But nor are older conceptions of race sufficient when it comes to twenty-first-century politics—they are too tightly linked to notions of descent. Thus, the central claim of the book is to stress the importance of reworking *both* our current languages of race *and* ethnicity as a necessary precondition for reinvigorating progressive politics in the United States.

A note on method might also clarify the aim of the project. I deliberately focus on public discourse rather than private talk. No doubt James Scott is right—hidden transcripts abound that might have been explored more effectively through private correspondence and personal papers.[1] But my task is a different one. Even though public discourse is inevitably constrained and, as such, offers only a partial view of politics, what is said in public carries a special weight because it sets the terms of political engagement.

My central preoccupation has been to map the contours, history, and political effects of public talk on matters of ethnic and racial difference in the United States. In doing so, I attend to what can—and cannot—be said within prevailing languages of ethnicity and race in order to identify the frontiers of change.

Throughout the book, I follow present-day conventions in which different racial terms are capitalized differently. The term *white* is almost always lowercase, while other ethnic and racial groups are capitalized: Blacks, Latinos, Hispanics, Jews. I considered capitalizing *white* throughout the book to draw attention to whiteness as a racial formation. But I decided that the unequal stylistic treatment of the words is part and parcel of the cultural and political terrain in which the lowercase indicates the taken-for-grantedness that comes with whiteness. Thus, I adhere to the capitalization conventions, even as I seek to analyze and change them. Generally, I use the term *Latino* rather than *Hispanic* throughout unless the sources themselves refer to Hispanic.

I have accrued many debts in writing this book. I have had several excellent research assistants at the New School for Social Research: Alexandra Budabin, Evan Daniel, William Gordon, Matthew Gritter, and Dan Mulcare. Andrea Carlá did a wonderful job constructing the tables presented in appendix A and in preparing the manuscript for final submission. I would also like to give a special thanks to Nancy Shealy, who has made working at the New School a pleasure.

Several government officials helped me identify and understand the significance of key research materials. Claudette Bennett (Census), Arthur R. Cresce (Census), Suzann Evinger (Office of Management and Budget; OMB), Juanita Tamayo Lott (Census), David Pemberton (Census), Susan Schechter (formerly OMB, now Census), Miriam Smith (Immigration and Customs Enforcement), and Katherine Wallman (OMB) were all enormously generous with their time and expertise. I could not have written the book without their assistance. I wrote the first substantive chapters while I was a National Endowment for the Humanities fellow at the Institute for Advanced Study in Princeton. I am very grateful for that wonderful year to think and write. I would especially like to thank Joan Scott and Michael Walzer for their support and Marcia Tucker for her research expertise.

I have presented pieces of the argument at a number of conferences and university colloquia and have benefited greatly from comments and criticisms in these sessions. I would like to thank participants in the APD seminar at University of California, Berkeley; the Twentieth-Century Politics and Society Workshop at Columbia University; the Race and

Racial Ideology Workshop at the University of Chicago; the Industrial Relations Seminar at MIT; the Conference on Legacies of Colonization and Decolonization and the Integration of Immigrants in Europe and the Americas; the Race and American Political Development Conference at the University of Oregon; the State and Ethnic Definitions Conference at Oxford University; the Race, Inequality, and Politics Seminar at Yale University; and the political science departments at the Johns Hopkins University, Oberlin College, University of Pennsylvania, and Rutgers University.

Many colleagues and friends have shaped the project through discussion. Others have provided invaluable comments on draft chapters: Peter Agree, Margo Anderson, Talal Asad, Alan Brinkley, Cathy Cohen, Josh DeWind, Janice Fine, Eric Foner, Oz Frankel, Joshua Freeman, Norm Fructer, Paul Frymer, Gary Gerstle, Sealy Gilles, Tim Gilles, Andreas Kalyvas, Riva Kastroyano, Ira Katznelson, Ina Kerner, Desmond King, Heather Lewis, Robert Lieberman, Richard Locke, Uday Mehta, James Miller, Mae Ngai, Joel Perlmann, Michael Piore, David Plotke, Adolph Reed, David Roediger, the late Michael Rogin, Louise Rosenblatt, Thaddeus Russell, Adam Sheingate, Rogers Smith, Ann Snitow, Bob Vitalis, Katherine Wallman, Dorian Warren, and Aristide Zolberg.

This book would never have seen the light of day without the support of John Tryneski at the University of Chicago Press. He has the perfect mix of patience and intellectual engagement; from our very first conversation, his support for this project has been an enduring inspiration. I would also like to thank both Rodney Powell and Lisa Wehrle, who carried the manuscript though the production process with unusual care. I greatly appreciate their flexibility, skill, and dedication.

But the intellectual wellsprings for this project have come from three rather different conversations, each of which has lasted for several years and two of which are still in motion. The first was a reading group on identification and politics that I convened at the New School for Social Research. The lines of argument we explored over many years together provided the intellectual foundations for the book and infuse all of the chapters that follow. We were joined at two workshops by faculty from the Ideology and Discourse Analysis program at the University of Essex. Our discussions there—including our disagreements—about poststructuralism, identification, and politics were invaluable. Long-term participants in the reading group were Kevin Bruyneel, Edmund Fong, Joseph Lowndes, George Shulman, and Priscilla Yamin. Participants in the workshops were Jason Glynos, David Howarth, Courtney Jung, Ernesto LaClau, Uday Mehta, the late Deborah Mitchell, Anne Norton, Aletta

Norval, Yannis Stavrakakis, and Linda Zerilli. I am indebted to conversations with all.

A second exciting intellectual exchange has taken place in the Prewitt Census Working Group. With the aid of a MacArthur Foundation planning grant, Ken Prewitt convened a committee to track the census race categories after Census 2000. We have met two or three times a year for several years to discuss issues of racial classification in the United States. At times, we met on our own; at other times, Prewitt invited members of relevant advocacy groups, academics, and government officials to join us. The sessions have given me a much richer sense of the politics of racial classification than I could have obtained through research alone. Members of the group are Reynolds Farley, Jennifer Hochschild, David Hollinger, Ian Haney López, Melissa Nobles, Kenneth Prewitt, Mathew Snipp, and Kimberly Williams. For the most part, we have pursued our respective book-length projects, but we also came together to contribute to an issue of *Daedalus* "On Race" published in 2005. I especially want to thank Ken Prewitt for including me in this important scholarly exchange.

Over the last four years, I have also participated in the American Literature Monthly Colloquium at New York University. The workshop was initially convened by Ross Posnock and George Shulman as a means of establishing an interdisciplinary exchange between scholars of American literature and political theory. It has been a terrific group. Conversational threads from our monthly discussions of race and politics have flowed into this book. The members of the colloquium include Aliyah Abdur-Rahman, Alyson Cole, Edmund Fong, Tanya Friedel, Jennifer Gaboury, Robert Gunn, Tom Jacobs, Megan Obourn, Cyrrus R. K. Patell, Shireen R. K. Patell, Ross Posnock, Lindsay Reckson, George Shulman, and Dan Skinner.

Three friends have been essential to my scholarly life. Conversations with Anne Norton, George Shulman, and Stephen Skowronek over the last twenty years have shaped my view of politics at every level. I could not have written this book without them.

Finally, my deepest thanks go to my family: Tom, Emily, and Robert Graham. They have listened patiently to arguments from the book and lived with a zillion boxes of photocopies all over the house. Most important of all, they have taught me about the pleasures and possibilities of identification. I dedicate this book to them—with love and gratitude.

Languages of Race—Politics of Difference

If you want to understand *how race works* in American politics and society, you would do well to attend to ethnicity. Considering race and ethnicity together is critical because ethnic identification has long been used as a counterpoint to race—a counterpoint that establishes the boundaries and meaning of race. By repeatedly contrasting ethnicity with race, American discourse sets in play a relational dynamic between the two terms that produces a quite particular conception of race. My point is *not simply to add* ethnicity to discussions of race, nor to show that many groups have suffered discrimination in American history—although that is certainly the case. Rather, I want to use the category of ethnicity to gain a new angle of vision. By seeing where the boundaries of race have been drawn, and by examining what has been designated as *not* race, one can identify key aspects of American race politics that remain obscured when we consider race by itself.

Debates over Jewish identity and Latino identity across the twentieth century reveal how certain characteristics typically have been linked with ethnicity and others with race. I examine academic journals, government documents, political speeches, and popular essays to show how, time and again, ethnicity is tied to culture, plurality, malleability, and equality. In contrast, race is seen as homogeneous, fixed, and hierarchical—repeatedly tied to body and blood. Although notions of race and ethnicity both address questions of difference, they do so differently, with each invoking quite distinct associations. Depending on which aspect of difference one wants to foreground or whom one identifies with, one is drawn into languages of ethnicity or race. Issues of power and inequality are more readily expressed in a descent-based language of race; issues of plurality and inclusion are the terrain of ethnicity.[1] Words are much more than weapons to be deployed, tools to be used for ends established in some other realm. Language is the ground of politics: it mediates our relation to the world. Identities and interests are fashioned through words. Hence, much is at stake in the words we use, in the associative chains and discursive fields we inhabit.[2] The terms *ethnicity* and *race* anchor two distinct languages of difference. I have come to see that—in the United States—race is almost always linked to power and inequality while ethnicity is used to convey openness and plurality. *Put simply, the central argument of the book is that where race rhetoric goes, race politics follows.* The core chapters of the book trace the shifting relation between words and politics that accompanied the invention of ethnicity as a different kind of difference to that of race.

Perhaps the notion of "chains," as shown in figure 1, suggests too linear a conception of linguistic association that does not do justice to the play of words; hence many refer to discursive *fields* rather than *chains*. Certainly linguistic associations move in many directions. We do not choose the words we use one at a time; they come linked together in

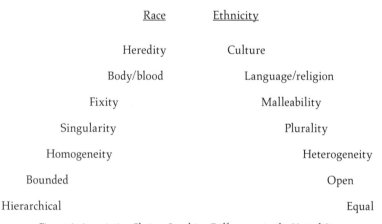

	Race	Ethnicity
	Heredity	Culture
	Body/blood	Language/religion
	Fixity	Malleability
	Singularity	Plurality
	Homogeneity	Heterogeneity
	Bounded	Open
	Hierarchical	Equal

Figure 1: Associative Chains: Speaking Differences in the United States

patterns or associative chains. The connections are neither fixed nor logi-cally derived, but are forged through culture, practice, and time. One might refer to fields rather than chains; either way, I want to attend to the discursive traditions, conventions, or habits of speech within the play of words.

But there is something else important in figure 1. There is a constitu-tive relation at work. In text after text I have found that the meaning of ethnicity is established by contrasting ethnicity with race. The terms *ethnicity* and *race* not only evoke quite distinct associations; there is also an implicit comparison between the two chains of association. I have come to see this comparative dynamic as enormously consequential; it secures the meaning of both terms. The central task of the book is to document and theorize the race-ethnicity distinction, to track changes in it over time, and to analyze its political effects. Throughout my research I have found a deep-seated reluctance to collapse ethnicity into race by adopting race as the single classificatory scheme. Rather the race-ethnicity distinction has persisted for almost a century structuring the meaning and terms of political engagement between immigrants and Blacks. Whether it will continue to do so is the question at hand.

The race-ethnicity distinction emerged over a century ago when chang-ing conceptions of hereditary created a political opening that leading New York Zionists and a handful of bureaucrats in the southwestern states be-gan to exploit. Between 1915 and 1935, scholars, government officials, and public intellectuals began to specify Jews and Mexicans as ethnic groups rather than races. A disparate array of sources reveal that Jews and Mexi-cans were treated as different kinds of social solidarities to those of race. The race-ethnicity distinction was formally codified by the federal govern-ment on May 12, 1977, when the Office of Management and Budget (OMB) promulgated Statistical Policy Directive 15, which mandated that both ra-cial and ethnic categories to be used by all federal government departments and agencies when collecting racial and ethnic data in the United States. Directive 15 stipulated that Hispanics/Latinos were an ethnic group and not a race, thereby institutionalizing the race-ethnicity distinction that lies at the heart of the U.S. classification system. These categories, with minor revisions, remain the operative ethno-racial taxonomy in the United States today.[3] Each of these research sites is quite spectacular; taken to-gether they reveal the amazing ways in which ethnicity and race have been used to constitute each other.[4] I trace the formation of the race-ethnicity distinction both over time and place, the assumption being that the mean-ing of ethnicity was established during the process of category formation.

Sharpton and Obama and the Rhetorics
of Racial and Ethnic Difference

Before delving into the history of the term *ethnic* and its relation to race, I want to prefigure my argument through a contemporary vignette in which we glimpse ethnic and racial discourses at work. Think back for a moment to the Democratic Party convention in Boston in the summer of 2004—specifically to Barack Obama's and Al Sharpton's speeches there. Both speeches were powerful and compelling—for many, they were the highlight of a rather lackluster convention. Each offered very different views of race. Their differences, I contend, reflect long-standing rhetorical traditions operative in the United States. Sharpton spoke in the classic language of racial difference while Obama positioned himself as the son of an immigrant and drew on the language of ethnicity for his account of difference in the United States. Analyzing both the Sharpton and Obama speeches allows us to glimpse these discursive traditions in action and to consider both the *possibilities* and *limits* they set for progressive politics in the United States.

Sharpton spoke forcefully and directly about the murderous rage of American racism. The "promise of America" has not been reached, Sharpton declared, because of the failure to redress the persistent racial inequalities that continue to structure the life chances of African Americans. Even in this short speech, Sharpton invoked the classic civil rights touchstones beginning with Crispus Attucks (an African American and the first person to die in the Revolutionary War); Fannie Lou Hamer and the Mississippi Freedom Party; James Earl Chaney, Andrew Goodman, and Michael Schwerner (the three civil rights activists killed on June 21, 1964, during the Mississippi Freedom Summer); Martin Luther King Jr. and the March on Selma; the Reverend Jesse Jackson; *Brown v. Board of Education*; and finally, Ray Charles. It was Sharpton at his best, a powerful orator, invoking a strong civil rights tradition as a means of holding America accountable for its history of slavery and racism. He reminded all who were willing to listen of the chasm that persists between the promise and reality in American politics when it comes to race.[5]

In addition to placing issues of racial inequality front and center, Sharpton also took direct aim at President George W. Bush by rebutting his recent appeal to African American voters asking that they consider shifting their support from the Democratic to the Republican Party.[6] Sharpton refused Bush's offer in no uncertain terms:

Mr. President, the reason we are fighting so hard, the reason we took Florida so seriously, is our right to vote wasn't gained because of our age. Our vote was soaked in the blood of martyrs, soaked in the blood of Goodman, Chaney and Schwerner, soaked in the blood of four little girls in Birmingham. This vote is sacred to us.

This vote can't be bargained away.

This vote can't be given away.

Mr. President, in all due respect, Mr. President, read my lips: Our vote is not for sale.[7]

As is often the case with Sharpton, not all welcomed his intervention at the convention. He ran over his allotted time, speaking for twenty minutes rather than six. Kimberly Crenshaw has documented the media's dismissive response in which CNN and *New York Times* commentators quickly declared Sharpton to be "off message." One commentator even suggested that he had "hijacked" the convention—a rather inflammatory remark in the post-9/11 United States. Another commentator declared Sharpton's remarks to have been "incendiary." Few reported what Sharpton said; most marginalized him as a wild man out to divide and upset. But for others, Sharpton was the only one willing to speak truth to power by addressing issues of racism and discrimination directly.[8]

But note also that Sharpton's powerful condemnation of American racism rested on a rather narrow conception of race. Sharpton's account of racism and civil rights was framed almost *exclusively* in relation to African Americans. He made no mention of Indian removal, Chinese exclusion, Japanese internment, or the numerous forms of American conquest and imperial expansion that have accompanied American nation building. No names were included that might resonate for these groups. Sharpton drew the boundaries of race tightly, leaving little or no room for coalition building across the race-immigration divide.

Enter Barack Obama. Like Sharpton, Obama also is a gifted orator, but his speech offered a rather different view of race. At the outset, he claimed his mixed-race and immigrant status: as a child of a Black African father and white American mother, he nevertheless identifies as Black and wants to represent Blacks politically. To do so, he embraces an expansive notion of race in which immigrants and African Americans are positioned as allies rather than competitors. For Obama, racial identification is not simply a matter of descent—it is a political identification, a way of positioning oneself in the United States.

This aspect of Obama's political persona I find compelling since it offers a way of advancing an antiracist politics that is open to many. Not only is it more accurate historically—to encompass a broad range of discriminatory practices as part and parcel of American nation building—but it also changes the political arithmetic in the present. Advocating a broad conception of race makes it easier to forge alliances across various racialized groups without equating one with another. Certainly not all groups suffered in the same way, and it is important to recognize the pernicious legacy of slavery and Jim Crow as a central force in American history. But we also need to be mindful of how we narrate the past; focusing exclusively on slavery and ignoring other forms of racism that accompanied American nation building can isolate African Americans from potential political allies in contemporary struggles. Opening up conceptions of race, as Obama does, lays the ground for the more inclusive antiracist politics that I want to embrace. But that is not all that Obama offered at the Democratic Party convention.

Note how Obama's more capacious conception of race was coupled with an assimilationist politics in the service of American nationalism. Unity out of difference was the theme he returned to throughout his speech. Obama's touchstones were equally familiar, but resonated quite differently from those used by Sharpton: Lincoln, the Declaration of Independence, Pearl Harbor and Patton's army, the GI Bill and FHA loans, and "E pluribus Unum. Out of many, one." Throughout he positioned himself as a hybrid figure, himself "a common dream, born of two continents," an instantiation of unity out of difference. Where Sharpton refused Bush's appeal to African Americans to consider voting Republican, Obama stressed political unity over division as an alternative strategy for Democratic Party building.

> Now even as we speak, there are those who are preparing to divide us, the spin masters, the negative ad peddlers who embrace the politics of anything goes. Well, I say to them tonight, there is not a liberal America and a conservative America—there is the *United* States of America. There is not a Black America and a White America and Latino and Asian America—there's the *United* States of America.[9]

Obama went on to challenge the pundits who would "slice-and-dice our country into Red States and Blue States," thereby jettisoning the principal metaphor that has been used to convey the sense that deep divisions exist within America today. Obama stood before the convention asking that Americans *overcome* their differences whether racial, political, or of some other kind.

What are we to make of these two quite different views of race? Which should we embrace? Why? And with what political effects? The speeches capture in microcosm two conceptions of difference offered within American politics today: racial inequality and ethnic pluralism. Certainly both Obama and Sharpton addressed the Democratic Party convention as leaders of the African American community, but they spoke of race in very different terms. Obama stood before the convention and claimed the mantle of immigrant along with the associated traits of open and malleable conceptions of race. But note how he hitched this expansive conception of difference to American nationalism. Unity—lack of division—is offered as central to the vitality of American democratic life. Sharpton, on the other hand, fixed his eye on inequality and exclusion, which he tied to a narrower, descent-based conception of race.

Some might object to hinging so much on two short convention speeches in which the forum itself might well shape the performances therein. Obama, in particular, may have toned down his racial appeal, so as not to compromise his very real presidential prospects in years ahead. Sharpton, on the other hand, was less constrained; he has long accepted his role as outsider and critic. If anything, Sharpton's role as critic fuels rather than diminishes his political position. Obama is positioned differently. He has much to lose by a misstep on the national stage. Perhaps he speaks differently in other venues.

Obama has engaged issues of inequality more directly elsewhere, but even when out of the spotlight, I see continuities rather than breaks with his convention themes. Take his speech at the National Press Club on April 26, 2005, when he reflected on Social Security and FDR's legacy in the United States. The speech is revealing and worth quoting at length.

> Think about the America that Franklin Roosevelt saw when he looked out the windows of the White House from his wheelchair—an America where too many were ill-fed, ill-clothed, ill-housed, and insecure. An America where more and more Americans were finding themselves on the losing end of a new economy, and where there was nothing available to cushion their fall.
>
> Some thought that our country didn't have a responsibility to do anything about these problems, that people would be better off left to their own devices and the whims of the market. Others believed that American capitalism had failed and that it was time to try something else altogether.

But our President believed deeply in the American idea.

He understood that the freedom to pursue our own individual dreams is made possible by the promise that if fate causes us to stumble or fall, our larger American family will be there to lift us up. That if we're willing to share even a small amount of life's risks and rewards with each other, then we'll all have the chance to make the most of our God-given potential.

And because Franklin Roosevelt had the courage to act on this idea, individual Americans were able to get back on their feet and build a shared prosperity that is still the envy of the world.[10]

Certainly Obama addresses inequalities more explicitly here than he did at the 2004 Democratic convention. References to FDR's wheelchair and to Depression-era Americans being "ill-fed, ill-clothed, ill-housed, and insecure" draw attention to issues of disability and class. But note how Obama attributes the systemic economic failures of the 1930s to individual misfortune—the Depression is cast as a moment when "fate causes us to stumble or fall." And the New Deal response is reduced to private assistance in which the "American family [was] there to lift us up." Public policy has morphed into private action. And what of race? It has disappeared. Obama's positions taken here are symptomatic of the dangers inherent in the language of ethnicity, which has little or no traction when it comes to asymmetries of power.

During an interview with Jodi Enda in *The American Prospect* in February 2006, Obama spelled out what sort of Democrat he wished to be. "Where I probably can make a unique contribution is in helping to bring people together and bridging what I call the 'empathy deficit,' helping to explain the disparate factions in this country and to show them how we're joined together, helping bridge divides between black and white, rich and poor, even conservative and liberal." He wants to unite rather than divide. "The story that I'm interested in telling is how we can restore that sense of commitment to each other in a way that doesn't inhibit our individual freedoms, doesn't diminish individual responsibility, but does promote collective responsibility." While Obama's vision does not preclude race, it is not at all clear that empathy will be sufficient to redress the persistent inequalities that fuel division.[11]

The Obama-Sharpton comparison allows us to glimpse contemporary ethnic and racial discourses at work. Each offers quite different views of race—views that resonate deeply with the American habit of contrasting ethnicity with race, immigrants with Blacks. Linguistic chains associated with the two terms both shape and constrain the politics of difference in the United States.

This book explores the political history behind Obama's and Sharpton's words. I trace the cultural and political processes that produced the rather different views of difference on the Democratic Party convention floor. The history behind the distinction is an amazing one, stretching back to arguments over heredity in the late nineteenth century through contestation over census classification in the early twenty-first century. Jews and Mexicans were the key operative groups; how they identified culturally and politically, and how they were viewed by others, established ethnicity as different from race.

Boundary Anxieties: Are the Jews a Race? Are Mexicans White?

The central theoretical task of the project has been to conceptualize the relation between ethnicity and race. Early on in the project I drew on feminist scholarship and viewed the race-ethnicity relation as a constitutive *opposition*, but soon found that opposition did not quite capture the dynamics at work here. There is a way in which race and ethnicity are understood as proximate terms, with a family resemblance one to the other, that differs from gender. The notion of *constitutive distinction* secured through shifting associative chains seemed closer to the mark, capturing the ways in which race and ethnicity are *at once* similar *and* different—repeatedly coupled, yet rarely collapsed into a single term.[12] The paradoxical sense of proximity *and* difference between ethnicity and race helps explain an anxiety that permeates many ethnicity texts over where to draw the boundary between ethnicity and race. The similarities continually threaten to swamp the distinction, leading one political figure after another struggling to secure the race-ethnicity distinction by asking: Are Jews a race? Are Mexicans white? Whether it be late nineteenth-century social science discussions of race, New York Zionists' essays published in the *Menorah Journal*, testimony before the 1911 Dillingham Immigration Commission, government classification schemes, or mayoral elections in New York City—all try to establish whether Jews and Mexicans are a race; if not, what sort of group are they? Much rides on whether the distinction can be sustained: if it falters, the meaning of both terms is breached.

I am not the first to analyze these debates; there are extensive literatures on both Jewish and Latino identity in the United States. But to my knowledge, few look across the two groups; each is dealt with separately as discrete phenomena rather than being viewed as a set. As a consequence, the boundary questions that both groups raise have been obscured.[13] Moreover, when considering the racial status of Jews or Latinos, most scholars simply come down on one side or the other: Jews are really white; Mexicans are really not white; or some other position. The central impulse in most accounts has been to *resolve* the ambiguity, to argue for a stable racial location for both groups. When presenting my research over the past several years, I continually encountered this desire to settle matters when one person after another suggested that I look at one source or another to establish definitively where Jews and Mexicans really stood. Over the years I dutifully looked, only to find that the issue was never settled.[14]

Gradually, I came to see that this was the wrong question to ask. Something else was going on here. What was most striking about these arguments was their anxious obsessive quality and their constant repetition. As I see it, the task is to hold on to the uncertainty *and* to understand its wellsprings. I think what fuels these anxious debates is the difficulty and importance of distinguishing ethnicity from race in any systematic fashion. If ethnics, whether Jews or Mexicans, can be subsumed within existing race categories as either Black or white, then race would be sufficient to accommodate all. The race-ethnicity distinction would disappear along with its generative cultural and political effects. Thus, how one resolves the racial status of Jews and Mexicans goes to the core of race politics in the United States. At issue is whether to distinguish ethnicity from race, thereby either reinscribing or destabilizing the meanings of both.

Ethnic Politics in a Racial Polity

What difference does it make how we talk? What is at stake in distinguishing ethnicity from race? Let me signal up front four ways in which the language of ethnicity and the identifications it entails serve to shape and constrain race politics in the United States. First, I have found time and again, both among New York Zionists in the 1910s and 1920s and Mexican Americans in the post–civil rights era, that ethnic identifications frequently work to reproduce biologized notions of race. Even when race itself is not at issue, the effect remains so long as the distinction between ethnicity and race is in place. Every time ethnicity is linked to culture *and* distinguished from race, then the discursive structure itself suggests that race is rooted in something else—most often the presumption being to body and blood. I have come to understand why the numerous critiques of the scientific basis of racial difference have had so little traction in popular understandings of race. A large part of the difficulty, I argue, lies in the discursive reproduction of biologized conceptions of race day in, day out, in which every utterance linking ethnicity with culture, malleability, and pluralism serves to reproduce hereditary notions of race as fixed and singular. Scientific arguments to the contrary are undercut by the micropolitics of everyday talk in which ethnicity is distinguished from race.[15]

Second, I have come to understand the task of forging broad antiracist coalitions to be discursively constrained. There has long been the tantalizing promise of a Black-Brown coalition in which immigrants and Blacks might join forces to contest American racial hierarchies on a broad front. This political promise has been fueled by demographic shifts occurring since the 1960s in which nonwhites are a majority of the population in fifteen of the twenty largest cities. The nation as a whole is projected to become a majority nonwhite by 2050, as can be seen in national-, state-, and city-level data are provided in tables 1–3 in appendix A.

The New York and Los Angeles mayoral elections in 2001 and 2005 captured the emerging political potential when two Latino candidates, Ferdinand Ferrer and Antonio Villaraigosa, tried to reposition Latinos alongside rather than against Blacks. But such coalitions have been difficult to build and even more difficult to sustain. The root of the problem lies in the ways in which ethnic difference has been continually positioned against race. Certainly, institutional and economic factors also divide immigrants and Blacks, but these divisions do not precede discourse. On the contrary, identities and interests are themselves the products of discursive formations. We will see how ethnicity has served to reinscribe, rather than challenge, the enduring inequalities that accompany racial difference.

Third, contemporary issues of Latino identification in general and Mexican American identification in particular are hotly contested, with disagreements being deeply embroiled in the race-ethnicity distinction. How Latinos position themselves, and are positioned by others, is currently up for grabs. The federal government quite formally designates Latinos to be an ethnic group and not a race. But some commentators assume Latinos are white, while still others believe Latinos are a race.[16] How Latino identifications play out in the decades ahead is of considerable political import and might even tip the balance of political power between the Republican and Democratic parties, the logic being that Latinos who identify as white are assumed to be more receptive to Republican appeals, while those who identify as "people of color" are assumed to lean Democratic. To be sure, linkages between race and party are not logically entailed; they have changed in the past and will no doubt change again. But at least since the New Deal, the Democratic Party has been the home to the majority of "nonwhites"—whether this will continue is the question on the table.[17]

Even if most Latinos remain loyal Democrats, with no substantial defection to the Republican Party, what sort of Democrats will they be? Will they side with the more centrist Democratic Leadership Council, backing away from race-based policy reform, or will they continue to advocate a civil rights agenda? The future contours of American party politics are intimately tied to *internal struggles* within Latino communities as to whether to identify by ethnicity or race, or find some new way to reconfigure the two. Which way Latino identifications are leaning is unclear and is likely to *remain* so for some time. But the political stakes are so high that many are trying to plot the trend lines.[18]

Finally, although I consider the race-ethnicity distinction to be deep and enduring, it is not set in stone. In fact, my interest in ethnicity stems from the fact that its relation to race seems to be changing right now. Increasingly, it seems that discourse of ethnicity is winning out. Over the last two decades, discussions over affirmative action policy have morphed into debates over the merits of multiculturalism and, more recently still, to the benefits of even more diffuse notions of diversity. Civil rights politics of the 1960s has been eclipsed—questioned by many as a viable tradition to draw on for advancing an antiracist politics in the decades ahead. Specialists and nonspecialists alike increasingly opt for *ethnicity* as an omnibus term to refer to differences of all kinds.

My research makes clear the high price we will pay for shifting *from* a discourse of race *to* ethnicity—namely, the elision of the persistent group inequalities in the United States. Let us assume that group-based discrimination persists in the decades ahead; how might we most effectively describe and challenge group inequities that continue to structure the life chances of many in the United States? Does it matter whether we speak of discrimination in terms of ethnicity or race? Although ethnicity offers a capacious conception of difference, it gives us little or no purchase on persistent asymmetries of power. The problem lies in the associative chains that permeate the discourse and continue to link ethnicity with pluralism and openness and race with inequality and power. Again, let me stress that the associative chains are not logically entailed—they are cultural presumptions forged through habit and time. But the words we use come with long discursive coattails, so that languages of race and ethnicity provide quite different resources for addressing persistent group inequalities in the United States.

To be sure, if the current shift to *ethnicity* as the preferred term were accompanied by significant improvement in group equality, then the political baggage of ethnicity might be diminished. But if the shift to ethnicity is a more superficial one in which the term *race* is dropped but significant group inequalities continue, and implicit comparisons between race and ethnicity linger in the associative chains, then the language of ethnicity will severely limit our ability to address persistent group inequalities and hierarchies in the decades ahead.

Ethnicity Rather than Whiteness or Collision

The contrasting rhetorics of race offered by Obama and Sharpton are by no means limited to the electoral arena. The race-ethnicity distinction pervades the academy as well. Race scholars, for want of a better term, usually attend to issues of power and inequality, but often do so by framing their accounts in Black and white. Slavery and its pernicious legacies are placed front and center, while broader histories of American racism often are set aside, relegated to different precincts of American scholarly life. To be sure, some have viewed American racism with a wide lens, but these are the exception rather than the rule.[19] Scholars of American *race* politics generally focus on the profound racial inequalities that continue to structure the life chances of African Americans, but they do so by deploying a rather narrow conception of race.[20]

Immigration scholars, on the other hand, tend to mirror Obama's vision, offering up broad conceptions of difference, but all too often they have a tin ear when it comes to issues of power, inequality, and racism as pervasive forces in the United States. The principal focus for most immigration scholars remains immigrant incorporation, in which they map the varied rates and patterns of immigrant accommodation. To be sure, few continue to advocate unidirectional views of assimilation; almost all now see immigrant incorporation as a dynamic and interactive process between host and immigrants. But even these more nuanced views of immigrant accommodation often ignore slavery as a framing condition of immigrant experience in the United States.[21]

Over the past decade, several scholars *have* tried to bridge this longstanding scholarly divide between those who address slavery/race, on the one hand, and those who focus on immigration/ethnicity, on the other.[22] But even those who have brought issues of race and immigration together have done so in ways that reproduce rather than challenge rhetorics of racial and ethnic difference. Two somewhat contradictory lines of argument have been put forward: The first, exemplified rather differently by David Roediger and Mary Waters, stresses the ways in which immigrants seek to avoid the ravages of American racism by *distancing* themselves from African Americans.[23] The other, argued most forcefully by Hugh Davis Graham and John Skrentny, sees the relation between immigrants and

Blacks as headed for a "collision course." The political magnet pulling them together, so the argument runs, is civil rights reform. While older affirmative action policies were targeted at historically disadvantaged groups, federal bureaucrats have extended civil rights remedies to immigrants and their descendants, thereby undermining the political legitimacy of civil rights reform across the board.[24]

Although much has been gained by these rich bodies of research, both fail to capture the central political dynamics of immigration and race. Both try to link histories of racism and immigration, but do so in ways that flatten out the distinctive positioning of ethnics. As a consequence, both misread the dynamics of contemporary ethnic and racial politics in the United States. Whiteness scholars have long argued that one immigrant group after another made a Faustian pact in which it secured their Americanness by becoming white. While there is much to admire in this work—it has transformed studies of immigration and race—I remain troubled by the way in which it echoes old assimilationist assumptions, only now attaching to them a different sign. Where older scholars viewed assimilation in a positive light as a desirable end, whiteness scholars see it as deeply problematic—as a crucial component of racial formation in the United States. Both see the same processes at work, but value the outcome in very different terms. Note how whiteness scholars look for similarities between race and ethnicity by tracking how one immigrant group after another became white; the central preoccupation has been to track the varied, but nevertheless persistent, assimilation of immigrant groups to the dominant racial order. The central social cleavage remains Black versus white. Immigrants understood all too well the benefits of whiteness; they identified and aligned with whites—if not immediately, then certainly over time.[25]

Waters offers a variant on the whiteness argument by focusing on the intra-racial politics between West Indian immigrants and African Americans. Like the whiteness scholars, Waters has found that West Indian immigrants and their children often try to avoid the horrors of American racism by distancing themselves from Blacks. Although the specific distancing mechanism is different—ethnicity rather than whiteness—the pattern of the argument is the same. In both, immigrants and their children try to distance themselves from Blacks. But note that Waters stops short of considering how immigrant identities help to *produce* the meaning of race as it is understood in the United States. The title of her book signals the problem: *Black Identities: West Indian Immigrant Dreams and American Realities* suggests that aspiring immigrants confront the fixity of American racial realities. In short, Waters fails to see the ways in which ethnic mobility is secured *by* reproducing a notion of race as fixed via descent. Immigrants do not simply distance themselves from race; the relation between the two terms is a constitutive one in which American immigrants unfix ethnicity by fixing race.[26]

"Collision course" views are especially problematic. These arguments view civil rights reform as a political magnet drawing immigrants *toward* Blacks as they seek to benefit from the hard-won political victories secured by African Americans. But these accounts ignore the long and multifaceted history of American racism and fail to see how it shaped mid-twentieth-century civil rights reform. Asians, Latinos, and Native Americans cannot simply be treated as new immigrants, gaining political advantage on the backs of Blacks. Many have been in the United States for centuries and have long been the objects of American racism. State bureaucrats did not simply extend civil rights to undeserving others; state policy had long recognized the multifaceted history of American racism by referring to "race, creed, color, and national origin" as grounds for redressing discrimination of many kinds.[27] By simplifying America's racial past, these scholars misread the present. Rather than trying to curb the extension of civil rights to non–African Americans, we need to retell the past in a broad frame and, in so doing, acknowledge that many groups have been subject to the long and bloody history of American racism.

What Is to Be Done?

What, then, are the current political options? Should we continue to distinguish ethnicity from race? Doing so allows us to identify different kinds of difference in the United States, but it also limits and constrains. Increasingly, I have come to see how our discursive conventions distort the past and circumscribe the present. In the end, I want to *refuse both* the Sharpton and Obama views of race, to refuse this oppositional twinning of race/power, on the one hand, and ethnicity/pluralism, on the other. I want to reconfigure the chains of equivalence now on offer. I want to hold on to both Sharpton's sense of racism and inequality while finding new ways of *aligning them with* Obama's more open, less descent-based conception of race.

Put differently, I want to keep a broad conception of race front and center without relinquishing Sharpton's astute sense of racism and inequality. Carving out the political space for such a position is not easy. Processes of resignification are not readily secured though programmatic reform. There is no ten-point program readily at hand. Although a diffuse and unwieldy task, it is what needs to be done. Without it, we are trapped in associative chains that make it difficult quite literally *to speak* the political position I wish to advance—namely, one that addresses the pervasive inequalities that structure life chances of immigrants and Blacks in the United States without tying them to descent-based conceptions of race.

I consider three domains in which the race-ethnicity distinction is currently being reworked in the hope that when faced with micro- and macropolitical choices in the years ahead, the implications of opting one way rather than another will be more readily apparent. No one domain will determine the outcome, but each will contribute to the direction of change.

An obvious place to start is with the *formal* ethno-racial taxonomy operative in the United States, since decisions made here will set the ethnic and racial categories for years to come. Both the OMB and the Census Bureau, discussed in chapter 5, are contemplating changing the official ethno-racial categories by formally removing the race-ethnicity distinction from within the federal classificatory system in the next two decades. But the possibilities for change, and for *extended public debate* over what sort of taxonomy to embrace, were cut short when Congressman José Serrano inserted a rider on the Census Bureau appropriations bill in 2005. In the short term, Serrano succeeded; the Census ethnicity and race categories will remain unchanged. But the underlying issues surrounding the complexity of Latino racial identification and the growing data-quality problems that they generate have not been addressed. If trends continue, these problems will increase.[28] Thus, Serrano's intervention offers a temporary solution at best. Even if one agrees with the outcome, Serrano's intervention is a political mistake. By attaching the rider to an appropriations bill, Serrano truncated debate over how to classify Latinos in the United States. As a consequence, an important opportunity to reconsider the U.S. ethno-racial taxonomy was lost.

But federal categories are not the only political front for the changing conceptions of ethnicity and race. Everyday speech practices are critical to the micropolitics of change. The possibilities for linguistic invention are amazing; new words appear and old ones are reinflected at a rapid pace. But shaping discursive practices in a particular direction is another matter. We have little capacity to orchestrate such microprocesses of change. But we can become more aware of the words we use, attending to the ways in which they either reinscribe existing notions of race and ethnicity or work to reorganize the associative chains. I hope to alert readers to the dangers of adopting a language of ethnic difference and to identify the opportunities to be had for resignifying American racial discourse in ways that allow us to combine more open conceptions of race with awareness of the persistent asymmetries of power.

Finally, another key avenue of change lies with political elites at all levels, from the grass roots to the White House. I take one of the principal tasks of self-appointed and elected political elites to be that of articulating chains of equivalence for others to consider. Most political figures simply recycle old equivalences; a few innovate. Most of the new recombinations fall flat, failing to resonate with others. But occasionally political elites crystallize nascent changes at hand, forging previously disparate elements into new political formations, bringing the emergent into being.[29] It is precisely in this context that Ferrer and Villaraigosa caught my attention. Both appeared to be rearticulating conceptions of Latino ethnicity and its relation to race. Even though both lost in 2001, the political opening they provided was thrilling.

Neither quite lived up to my expectations; both ultimately opted for evasion rather than reconfiguration. Nevertheless, the very possibility of rearticulating a different relation between immigration and race or Latino and Black is enormously important. Both made visible the very real possibility of repositioning Latinos within the prevailing ethno-racial taxonomy in the decades ahead. In so doing, they called into question the race-ethnicity distinction itself.

Reworking the associative chains is no silver bullet: disagreements will continue, and change will no doubt proceed in a dispersed and piecemeal fashion. But without dismantling the race-ethnicity distinction, efforts at building a robust antiracist coalition are likely to flounder. Strategic alliances will be built, but they will remain little more than marriages of convenience if we do not change the discursive traditions currently in place. Reconfiguring the associative chains is a prerequisite for building a robust antiracist coalition in the years ahead.

Architecture of the Book

The first substantive chapter maps nineteenth-century racial discourse before reference to ethnic groups appeared. By examining discussions of difference in the leading social science journals from 1890 through 1910, the chapter both recovers an earlier, rather different conception of race and traces its disarticulation into our more familiar twentieth-century notions of ethnicity, nation, culture, and race. Critics of Lamarckian conceptions of heredity in the late nineteenth century fueled changing conceptions of race. It was not until Lamarckian accounts of heredity had been displaced that biology was more clearly distinguished from social formations. Once Mendelian conceptions of heredity held sway, a narrower conception of race began to be tightly linked to descent. The emergence of ethnicity as a discrete social formation grounded in culture rather than blood is thus part and parcel of a larger late nineteenth-century social transformation centered on the disarticulation of social and biological processes into distinct phenomena. Attending to the larger context here alters how I understand issues of agency in subsequent chapters. I have come to appreciate the ways in which the emergence of ethnicity was nested within larger social transformations. This larger framing by no means diminishes the significance of the emergence of ethnicity as a new language of difference, but it does change my sense of the singularity and agency associated with the invention of ethnicity laid out in the chapters that follow.

Chapter 3 shifts to New York Zionists in the 1910s and 1920s and their efforts to articulate a conception of ethnicity as a distinct social formation to that of race. Almost *all* the leading intellectuals of the day wrote extensively about what it meant to be a Jew and an American in a little-known publication called the *Menorah Journal*. Several of the authors began to refer with increasing regularity to ethnic groups and loyalties and to specify the parameters of ethnicity. The list of contributors to the journal is stunning: Mary Antin, Charles Beard, Louis Brandeis, John Dewey, Felix Frankfurter, Roscoe Pound, Edward Sapir and Alfred Kroeber (both early students of Franz Boas), Horace Kallen, Randolph Bourne, Lewis Mumford, Norman Hapgood, G. Stanley Hall, Bertrand Russell, Hannah Arendt, and Charles Eliot, then president of Harvard. But that is not all; the leading international Zionists during the height of American Zionism also contributed essays. Finally, the journal allowed room for poetry and art by the likes of Marc Chagall, Pablo Picasso, Camille Pissarro, Thomas Mann, Lionel Trilling, Max Weber (the painter), and Israel Zangwill. All wrote about identification and politics. Taken together, they provide an amazing forum for exploring early twentieth-century conceptions of ethnicity in the United States.

In chapter 4, I turn to state classification of Jews and Mexicans in the 1930s through the 1950s. To what extent, I wanted to know, did leading state agencies operate with a notion of ethnicity as distinct from race? Did the state institutionalize Zionists' conceptions of ethnicity? If so, when and how? Initially, I had expected the Jewish story to dominate and Latino classification to follow. But research into classification of Mexicans on the southwest border quickly complicated a single origins story when it became apparent that classification of Mexicans also played a key role in the process of category formation. Moreover, the Mexican case is especially important because the creation of Spanish surname lists in five southwestern states (Arizona, California, Colorado, New Mexico, and Texas) were used to consolidate notions of ethnic difference within the state classificatory system. Jews had long resisted racial classification by the state, fearing that official designations of any kind could be turned to anti-Semitic ends. Classification of Mexicans followed a somewhat parallel path. Beginning with the Immigration and Naturalization Service in 1936, and adopted by the Census Bureau for the 1940 census, Mexicans in five southwestern states were identified by language and surname rather than race. This early designation of Mexicans as a distinct demographic group, united by language rather than race, established the precursors for Hispanics/Latinos ethnicity within the official ethno-racial taxonomy in the United States.

In chapter 5, I fast-forward to May 12, 1977, when the OMB promulgated Statistical Policy Directive 15. This short two-page document mandated the categories to be used by *all* federal agencies when collecting and disseminating data on race and ethnicity. I explore both the institutional origins of Directive 15, trying to understand why it was enacted in May 1977, as well as attending to the taxonomic structure of the Directive itself. Others have analyzed both the history and *racial* categories of Directive 15, but to my knowledge, no one has attended to the ways in which OMB incorporated the race-ethnicity distinction into the heart of the U.S. classificatory scheme.

Throughout the book I attend to politics broadly conceived, but in chapter 6 I turn to electoral and party politics directly by examining the New York City mayoral election of 2001. Democratic Party candidate Freddy Ferrer, of Puerto Rican descent, brought issues of Latino identification front and center, which enabled me to explore possibilities for coalition building between Latinos and Blacks. Moreover, the complex relations among highly visible Latino, Black, and white politicians—Ferrer, Al Sharpton, and Mark Green—made manifest the contested nature of race politics *inside* the Democratic Party and the place of Latinos within a broad-based civil rights coalition. The larger question here is where should Democratic candidates and the party as a whole stand on racial identification and politics in the twenty-first century? All of the democratic mayoral candidates in 2001 favored greater tolerance and equality in American life, but disagreed strongly on how this should be secured. The New York City election and its Los Angeles counterpart allow us to see dramatic fights over race politics being played out in a particular locale.

In chapter 7, I conclude by considering what is to be done. Since the American ethno-racial taxonomy is being reconfigured right now, how ought we negotiate immigrant and racial difference in the twenty-first century? I contemplate the political road ahead by considering the immigrant rallies that were held across the country on May 1, 2006.

In sum, I approach ethnicity from two vantage points: chapters 3 and 6 analyze ethnicity from the bottom up, from the ethnics' point of view, while chapters 4 and 5 consider state policy to view ethnic classification from above rather than below. Throughout I explore ethnicity with an eye to its political effects. Each chapter captures different aspects of the race-ethnicity relation; at no point do I find evidence of an assimilationist model at work in which ethnicity blends easily into race. One of the most striking things in writing this book has been the ways in which these very disparate research sites make clear the powerful echoes across time and place. The quite distinctive meaning of ethnicity in the United States is evident at every turn—even as it is also clearly reworked. It is this pattern of continuity *and* change that I have traced in the chapters that follow so that I might alert readers to both the political opportunities and pitfalls that await us.

From "Historic Races" to Ethnicity: 2
Disarticulating Race, Nation, Culture

If you open a popular or scholarly book written in the mid-nineteenth century, you will find innumerable references to race, but no references to ethnic groups or ethnicity. Moreover, the nineteenth-century conception of race will seem strange because of the ways in which it encompasses identities that we usually distinguish today. Nineteenth-century conceptions of race were expansive, often conflating notions of nationality, language, and culture under a general umbrella of race.[1] By 1924, racial discourse had changed. Scholars and laypeople alike began to distinguish race from language, culture, and nation, and it is from within this conceptual disarticulation that the term *ethnic* emerged. Examining the ways in which the social landscape was carved up conceptually and seeing how nineteenth-century conceptions of race gave way to a proliferation of different terms makes visible the large-scale social transformations that laid the groundwork for distinguishing ethnicity from race.

My task in this chapter was a difficult one: I wanted to capture enough of nineteenth-century racial discourse to serve as a counterpoint to racial discourse in later decades without turning the whole book into a treatise on nineteenth-century conceptions of race. My strategy has been to delimit my account of nineteenth-century racial discourse by focusing on elite discussions of race published in the leading social science journals in the last quarter of the nineteenth century and the first few years of the twentieth. An extensive survey of this kind would have been a daunting task a decade ago, but with the advent of JSTOR, an extensive electronic archive of scholarly journals, I was able to analyze all of the key journals from their inception up through World War I without too much trouble.[2]

The chapter proceeds in three parts. I first recount the quite different views of heredity that predominated in the nineteenth-century social science discussions of race when Jean-Baptiste Lamarck's notion of heredity prevailed. Fascinating as this aspect of recovery is, it is impossible for any one quotation, or set of quotations, to bear the weight of an era or to convey the very different view of race in vogue during the nineteenth century. The distinctiveness of the period comes alive more effectively via critiques of Lamarckianism in the 1890s. Somewhat paradoxically, it is the demise of Lamarckianism that helps to reveal its basic commitments; when the old orthodoxy begins to give way, several adherents argue more vociferously for Lamarckian views. In more hegemonic times, when particular understandings of heredity were more widely held, there was no need to specify assumptions in quite the same way; in moments of transition, however, many scholars began to lay out the basic tenets of the *old* order in an effort to fend off the new. Here I examine the response to August Weismann's critique of natural selection (1893–94) via the work of William Ripley and W. I. Thomas.[3]

Finally, I turn to scholarly discussions of Jews and immigrants where we see social scientists trying to rethink both race and nation in light of the break with Lamarck. The debate over whether Jews ought to be considered a race was waged in the scholarly journals between 1885 and 1913; the appearance of the question itself is further evidence that important conceptual changes were under way; twenty years earlier most would have agreed that the Jews were a race. Only once Lamarckian notions of heredity began to give way did the racial status of the Jews become a pressing question and the answer a means of specifying the boundaries of race. I conclude by turning to social scientists' increasing attention to the "immigration problem," which began as early as 1888 and continued with greater frequency up through the Depression. Again, I focus on how scholars framed the discussion rather than their substantive positions. Did they still refer to immigrants as races? If not, what categories were used to describe the changing face of America population at the turn of the century?

Lamarckian Conceptions of Race

From the mid-eighteenth through the end of the nineteenth century, elites spent considerable energy classifying the races of mankind. No one classificatory scheme dominated; rather, several were offered as the most effective means of ordering human difference. Immanuel Kant, Johann Blumenbach, Paul Broca, Louis Agassiz, Joseph C. Nott, Joseph-Arthur de Gobineau, and others all offered their own racial schemes before 1860, and the proliferation of racial discourse only intensified through the end of the century. In the United States, the institutionalization of the newly emerging social sciences between 1865 and 1906 fostered the proliferation via the creation of distinct disciplinary journals and the formation of academic departments, both of which provided new arenas for debating the nature and source of human difference. Although social science elites represent only a small segment of late nineteenth-century racial discourse, they allow us to grasp quite quickly just how different nineteenth-century views of race were from those we use today.

At first glance, I was struck by the centrality of race within the emerging social sciences; discussions of race were by no means limited to one or two isolated essays.[4] Although this comes as no surprise to anthropologists and sociologists, political scientists generally have paid little or no attention to the place of race in the origins of political science. Indeed, one recent scholarly article claimed that very few essays were published on race. I think the claim mistaken, resting on too narrow a conception of race and, as a consequence, overlooking the myriad ways in which notions of heredity and race inflect the entire social science project from soup to nuts.[5] George Stocking argued persuasively some time ago that all of the social science disciplines emerged out of the changing conceptions of race at the turn of the century, since it was only once notions of hereditary narrowed, and a clearer distinction was drawn between the biological and the social, that a separate realm of "the social" emerged for *social* scientists to examine. Thus, all of the social sciences are deeply implicated in changing conceptions of race.[6]

Interestingly, many key participants in these early race debates became presidents of their respective professional associations: Daniel G. Brinton was president of the American Association for the Advancement of Science (1895); W. J. McGee became president of the American Anthropological Society (1902–4); and Franz Boas presided over both associations in 1907–9 and 1931, respectively. Lester Frank Ward, Franklin Giddings, W. I. Thomas, Albion Small, E. A. Ross, Robert Park, and Ulysses Grant

Weatherly all were elected presidents of the American Sociological Society between 1906 and 1925. Paul Reinsch was president of the American Political Science Association in 1920; Horatio Hale was president of the American Folklore Society in 1893, and Ellsworth Huntington served as president of the American Association of Geographers in 1923 and of the Eugenics Society from 1934 through 1938. Finally, Simon Patten and William Ripley were both presidents of the American Economics Association in 1908 and 1933, respectively. All of these scholars contributed important essays to discussions of racial difference and were recognized by their peers as major figures in their respective disciplines.[7]

It would be a mistake, however, to overdraw disciplinary boundaries in the late nineteenth century since specific social science disciplines were only just being formed, and scholars in more than one discipline frequently held appointments that bridged both disciplines and institutions. In 1896, for example, Ripley's academic positions were described at the head of one of his essays: "Assistant Professor of Sociology and Economics in the Massachusetts Institute of Technology; Lecturer in Anthropogeography in Columbia University, New York."[8] Rather than thinking of racial discourse in disciplinary terms, I have found it more useful to follow debates and lines of research that frequently spilled over nascent disciplinary boundaries, establishing extensive debates over questions of racial difference.

Capacious nineteenth-century notions of race were rooted in the very different notions of heredity when Jean-Baptiste Lamarck's rather than Gregor Mendel's views of heredity prevailed.[9] One of the key distinguishing features of Lamarckianism was the notion of the heritability of acquired characteristics, which claimed that all human behavior could, over long periods of time, become habitual and ultimately heritable. Religion, language, nationality, and even institutions and social practices could become part of one's genetic makeup and, as such, could be passed on to future generations. Stocking summed up this feature of Lamarckianism as follows:

> Lamarckianism made it extremely difficult to distinguish between physical and cultural heredity. What was cultural at any point in time could *become* physical; what was physical might well *have been* cultural. Thus a widespread theory of the origins of instinct assumed that habits might become organized as instincts through the inheritance of acquired characteristics. Culturally conditioned behavior patterns would thus tend to become part of the genetic makeup of subsequent generations in the form of inherent tendencies or proclivities.[10]

Late nineteenth-century elites operated within a framework in which cultural and biological processes were considered to be deeply interrelated and were often viewed as two sides of the same coin.

Lamarckian notions of heredity had a direct influence on nineteenth-century notions of race; although scholars disagreed over the exact number of races, all adhered to the distinction between the "historic" and "natural" races.[11] Most agreed that there were at least three, and perhaps as many as five, natural races, each of which was thought to coincide with broad geographic territories and to correspond to the classic nineteenth-century color designations of Black, White, Red, and Yellow. Historic races, in comparison, were closer to what we now generally refer to as nations, so that the Americans, French, and Germans were all considered historic races, their once-heterogeneous populations having been forged into common bloodlines over long periods of time. Although historic races were never simply equated with the "pure" or "natural" races, they were considered distinct and coherent racial types.[12]

The concept of historic races presumed that environment, especially climate and geography, influenced racial formation, thereby raising questions as to whether Europeans could survive and maintain their superior racial character when colonizing the tropics. Ripley summed up the dilemma in his two-part essay on "Acclimatization,"[13] published in *Popular Science Monthly* in 1896:

> The modern problem plainly stated is this: First, can a single generation of European emigrants live? And secondly, living, can they perpetuate their kind in the equatorial regions of the earth? Finally, if the Aryan race is able permanently so to sustain itself, will it still be able to preserve its peculiar civilization in these lands; or must it revert to the barbarian stage of modern slavery—of a servile native population, which alone in those climates can work and live?[14]

The outlook for the colonizers was not very bright because the process of acclimatization forced the colonizers to "approach . . . the normal type of the natives."[15] After a rather lengthy discussion of the effects of climate on sexuality, marriage, and fertility, Ripley declared that Africa's future political destiny is likely "to be dominated by a remarkable fact—namely, the severe handicap against which the Teutonic stock, and especially the Anglo-Saxon branch, struggles in the attempt permanently to colonize the tropics." Ripley concluded that "the almost universal opinion seems to be that true colonization in the tropics by the white race is impossible."[16] The problem, at bottom, was that the Anglo-Saxons could not maintain their racial superiority in the tropics since white colonizers would themselves degenerate to the local racial norm.

Not all discussions of climate and geography were quite so dramatic, nor did they always invoke colonization so explicitly. But many social scientists made similar assumptions about the importance of environment for race. Daniel Brinton, one of the early founders of American anthropology who addressed questions of heredity and environment directly, made much the same argument: "Our late eminent colleague, Mr. Horatio Hale . . . argued once in my hearing that a colony of Germans located in Australia under the same conditions as the black tribes there, would in three generations become as degraded as they, and much like them in appearance."[17] Note how Brinton, and by implication Hale, drew little or no distinction between nationality and race; the Australian environment would eventually transform Germans into the same racial stock as the indigenous Australians. Brinton concluded his discussion of hereditary and environment by claiming that we must acknowledge "that acquired characters [sic] are surely and in certain cases uniformly transmitted to succeeding generations."[18]

In addition to climate and geography, one finds a quite *unfamiliar* discussion of "use" and "disuse" as important factors in heredity. Thus, particular racial features, and even more amorphous racial temperaments, could become hereditary traits through repetition. In 1901, for example, the anthropologist John Wesley Powell specified the "law of exercise" in which an organ that is used extensively tends to develop while those left idle will decay.[19] Arguments for changes in bodily form if occurring within a single lifetime are no different from our present-day assumptions of physical development; what distinguished late nineteenth-century thought from our own was that Powell and his contemporaries believed that once use brought about change, the change could be *passed onto subsequent generations as heritable traits*. Repetition led to habit, which in turn became instinctual, and eventually morphed into a heritable trait. One such example caught my eye; a noted English anthropologist, Joseph Jacobs, declared: "Australians, who have had no opportunity of pitting their wits against any other competing race, and have depended for their existence on the fleetness of their legs and the capacity of their stomachs to carry food from one orgy to another, have used their brains less than all other human races, and have the narrowest skulls of all."[20] Here "disuse" of the Australian brain leads to the development of "the narrowest skulls of all." Skeletal form was itself influenced and changed, according to neo-Lamarckians like Ripley and Jacobs, by use or neglect.

For Ripley, Powell, Jacobs, and other late nineteenth-century social scientists, no bright line separated culture and biology; rather, habit and skeleton were thought to be jointly formed. Even when they distinguished "social" and "organic" evolution, they continued to view both as two forms of a general unified law of human development. The tight link between the social and organic was not yet questioned; most social scientists operating within a Lamarckian frame looked for parallel developments undergirding social *and* biological change.[21]

Note that late nineteenth-century discussions of race did not refer to ethnicity or ethnic groups.[22] The discourse was framed in terms of *scientific* and *historic* races rather than our more familiar categories of *ethnicity* and *race*. To be sure, some of the same conceptual ground was covered by the terms *ethnic* and *historic race*, but they are not simply coterminous. They rarely, if ever, appeared in the same text. Rather, references to ethnic groups emerge as references to *historic races* declined. But the move from one to the other was not a simple exchange; the shift in terminology signaled much more than a change of words.

Tracking the shift from the language of "historic races" to that of ethnicity thus allows us to map shifts in complex assumptions about how the world worked, especially about how to understand the relationship among the environment, heredity, and race. Changes in terminology were far from superficial. They signaled and helped to produce our current-day assumptions about immigrant and racial difference in the United States. In this chapter, I track the changing languages of race in the last two decades of the nineteenth century. Documenting the disarticulation of *race* as the omnibus term for difference allows us to glimpse the larger social forces out of which the race-ethnicity distinction later emerged.

Before proceeding to the break with Lamarck, I want to underscore that Lamarckian notions of race by no means entailed a greater commitment to racial equality. As should be apparent from the quotations offered above, neo-Lamarckian notions of heredity went hand in hand with racial hierarchy, in which historic and natural races were ranked on a single normative scale ranging from barbarian to civilized—that is, from Black to white. Even Lester Ward, a staunch advocate of racial amalgamation who explicitly argued for a "utopia of ultimate race integration," nevertheless continually referred to the "superior" and "lower races."[23] Stocking summed up the link between Lamarckianism and racial inequality succinctly when he declared that "the assumption of white superiority was certainly not original to Victorian evolutionists; but the interrelation of the theories of cultural and organic evolution gave it a new rationale."[24]

Breaking with Lamarck: Disarticulating Race, Culture, and Nation

Perhaps the best way to recover Lamarckian assumptions about heredity is to attend to the breakdown of this view at the end of the nineteenth century when Lamarckianism began to lose ground. Once challenged, many scholars began to defend Lamarckian assumptions in ways that rarely occurred when Lamarckian notions of heredity were at their zenith and its underlying principles could be assumed. As with most major social transformations, the break with Lamarckianism was a gradual one, with early seeds of doubt being sown by publication of Charles Darwin's *Origin of Species* in 1859. But the concept of evolution itself proved to be quite malleable and was often combined with older Lamarckian notions of environmental change. Both shared a notion of adaptation, but differed as to the initial impetus for change. As long as this difference was not highlighted, discussions of evolutionary adaptation need not conflict with older Lamarckian notions of heredity.[25]

More direct challenges to Lamarckianism came near the end of the century with the Herbert Spencer–August Weismann debate over natural selection in 1893 and 1894, and then again with the rediscovery of Mendelian genetics in 1900.[26] Despite the powerful challenges offered by Weismann and Mendel, many scholars continued to defend older views— criticism itself did not dislodge late nineteenth-century commitments to the heritability of acquired characteristics. Both Brinton and Ward, for example, referred directly to Weismann's critique of Lamarckianism without relinquishing their Lamarckian assumptions. In his 1898 article on "heredity and environment," Brinton explicitly acknowledged the power of Weismann's critique, but went on to defend the heritability of acquired characteristics against Weismann's attack. Brinton clearly acknowledged that challenges to Lamarckianism were afoot, but set about defending the older views of heredity given the new work.[27] Ward also responded extensively to Weismann's critique and, like Brinton, responded to Weismann's challenge, at least initially, by rearticulating his commitment to Lamarckianism in 1891 and 1894.[28]

From the late 1890s through 1920, however, many scholars began to relinquish their Lamarckian assumptions and, in so doing, began to rethink the relation between the social and biological: a rethinking that had enormous consequences for prevailing views of race and for the emergence of ethnicity. Early signs of the break with Lamarck can be seen quite clearly by tracing the changing views of heredity and race within a particular scholar's work. Holding the author constant and examining his or her views of heredity and race *over time* helps to highlight the changes under way, changes that are often obscured when we move from scholar to scholar. William Ripley and W. I. Thomas provide excellent candidates as both wrote prolifically on race in the decades bracketing the turn of the century, and both changed their views of heredity in these same decades.

In his 1896 "Acclimatization" essays, Ripley adhered to classic Lamarckian notions of the heritability of acquired characteristics.[29] A year later, Ripley's views began to shift. In February 1897, Ripley published the first in a lengthy series of essays on "The Racial Geography of Europe," which appeared in *Popular Science Monthly* between February 1897 and May 1899. In each of these essays Ripley laid out his theory of race and applied it to a variety of situations; the essays were later compiled into his influential book, *The Races of Europe*, published in 1899. The view of race Ripley proposed was quite different from that advanced in his "Acclimatization" essays. The change is signaled in the very first essay entitled "Language, Nationality, and Race," in which Ripley explicitly called for the disarticulation of these terms. He defended his claim by reflecting on the disjunction between race, nation, and language:

> In the west, the formation of these boasted nationalities is so recent that it accords but slightly with the lines of physical descent. . . . Let us at the very outset avoid the error of confusing community of language with identity of race. Nationality may often follow linguistic boundaries, but race bears no necessary relation whatever to them.[30]

It is difficult to believe that this is the same man who but a year earlier wrote about the difficulty of colonizing the tropics due to the racial degeneration brought about by the influence of climate on racial type. Earlier the line between nationality and race had been a very porous one, with racial transformations accompanying geographic relocations, but now Ripley was beginning to articulate a sharper boundary between race and nation. At least for Ripley, then, we can date the break with Lamarck quite precisely; his views shifted between 1896 and 1899, as evident in the quite different arguments Ripley offered in the essays published in each of these years.

We can see Ripley beginning to distinguish heredity from environment in essay number thirteen of "The Racial Geography of Europe," which is entitled "Modern Social Problems." Here, Ripley again argued forcefully for the separation of race and culture:

> The whole matter simmers down to a decision between environment and race. . . . We may discover what are the distinctive social peculiarities of

the three races whose history we have been outlining (Teutonic, Alpine, and Mediterranean); and we may form a definite idea of the class of remedies necessary to meet the peculiar needs of each community; for it is quite obvious that social evils due to inherited tendencies require very different treatment from those which are of recent origin, the product of local circumstances.[31]

By suggesting that "inherited tendencies" and "local circumstances" produced distinct social problems in need of different solutions, Ripley broke with nineteenth-century race talk. Heredity and environment were no longer seen as interdependent processes as they had been in his "Acclimatization" essays; now they were seen as different problems requiring different solutions.

Ripley concluded the essay by insisting that the choice *"between race and environment . . .* is a matter of singular interest at this time."[32]

> A school of sociological writers, dazzled by the recent brilliant discoveries in European ethnology, show a decided inclination to sink the racial explanation up to the handle in every possible phase of social life in Europe. It must be confessed that there is provocation for it. So persistent have the physical characteristics of the people shown themselves, that it is not surprising to find theories of a corresponding inheritance of mental attributes in great favor. Yet it seems to be *high time to call a halt* when this "vulgar theory of race," as Cliffe-Leslie termed it, is made sponsor for nearly every conceivable form of social, political, or economic virtues or ills, as the case may be.[33]

The separation of race and environment had begun. Ripley himself remarked on the newness of the distinction. Throughout much of Ripley's work, and that of many other early social scientists, we see an acute sense of social sciences research breaking new ground. After carefully reviewing the correlations between racial types with divorce, suicide, and artistic talent, Ripley unambiguously concluded that "despite the geographical coincidence, that it is not the factor of race, but rather of social environment" that produces these correlations.[34]

Not surprisingly, the break with Lamarckianism did not happen cleanly in a short period of time, but rather occurred slowly and unevenly over two to three decades. Ripley's "The Racial Geography of Europe" essays, for example, contained aspects of Lamarckianism even as Ripley self-consciously called into question the heritability of acquired characteristics. But overall, the essays began to distinguish social, cultural, and political processes from heritable traits. Indeed, if one simply looks at the terms Ripley used to discuss the relationship of heredity and environment between 1896 and 1899, there is a distinct shift from the "Acclimatization" to "Social Problems" essays. In the former, he was at pains to identify the influences of environment on heredity, as if they were interdependent phenomena. In the latter, Ripley began to see heredity and environment in either/or terms and to insist that we needed to disarticulate these processes if we were to identify the appropriate solution to our social ills. By 1899, with the publication of *The Races of Europe* in book form, Ripley presented the relationship between heredity and environment in even more oppositional terms. Chapter 19, for example, is entitled "Social Problems: Environment *versus* Race," with the emphasis on the *versus* appearing in the original.[35]

In all, I see Ripley as a transitional figure between nineteenth- and twentieth-century views of race. At times, Ripley pieced together aspects of both worlds and, as a consequence, presented a somewhat inconsistent view of heredity and environment. The confusion is amplified if one reads *The Races of Europe* only in its book form. It was, in fact, largely a compilation of his essays ranging from 1895 through 1898. Each of the earlier essays was included, often with only minor revisions, and the inconsistencies were never fully worked through. As a consequence, Ripley's worldview is difficult to discern. But when viewed as distinct essays written *over time* during a period of intense debate and intellectual change, we see a progression from Lamarckian through more modern notions of heredity. To be sure, the break with Lamarck was never complete for Ripley, but this is not so surprising since when *The Races of Europe* was published in 1899, Mendelian genetics had not yet been rediscovered and very few scholars had completely rejected Lamarck. Nevertheless, Ripley's corpus makes evident a shift in racial discourse from a more unified account of race as a language encompassing many kinds of difference to a discursive field in which language, nation, and culture were considered quite different from race. This disaggregation of the nineteenth-century conception of race in the 1890s opened the way for the invention of ethnicity as a distinct social formation a quarter century later.

A similar shift in racial discourse can be seen in W. I. Thomas, one of the founders of the Chicago School of Sociology. Thomas's early essays reflect a classic Lamarckian interest in the relation between biological function and social relations; indeed, Thomas considered examining this relationship to be the principal task of the newly emerging "science of man."[36] Thomas's early 1890s essays trace the influence of instinct—especially in relation to food and sex—on the larger pattern of social relations. The key for Thomas was not to spend too much energy on measurement, as others had done, but to focus instead on *the relation* between physical measurement and the "developmental history of mind." To date, he lamented, anthropology and the other sciences of man have "been so absorbed in the preliminary task of collecting and classifying its materials that it has been able to do no more than approach its main task, the determination of the developmental relation of individual to race consciousness, and the relation of both to accompanying institutions and usages."[37] Measurement alone, Thomas argued, was not going to provide an agreed-upon system of classification nor enable us to understand the nature of mankind. Thomas's work contained little measurement and focused instead on tracking the illusive relationship between biological and cultural processes with particular attention to the difference between race and sex.

Thomas's two essays on the differences between the sexes, published a decade apart in 1897 and 1907, again allow us to track changing views of the relation between the biological and the social.[38] The very first sentence of Thomas's 1897 essay declared: "it is increasingly apparent that all sociological manifestations proceed from physiological conditions."[39] The key to sexual difference, Thomas agreed, lay in the sexes' different metabolic attitudes toward food:

> The determination of sex is a chemical matter, maleness and femaleness being solely expressions of a difference of attitude toward food. If such a connection can be traced between sex and nutrition it will afford a starting point for a study of the comparative psychology of the two sexes and for the investigation of the social meaning of sex.[40]

Thomas compared males and females to plants and animals and ultimately based all sexual difference in physiology. In this early essay, the social and biological were intimately intertwined; analyzing social relations quickly took him back to biology. After discussing sentiments, association, and culture, Thomas concluded that "the striking historical contrast and parallelism of the militant and industrial activities of society is a social expression of this sexual contrast. Man's katabolism predisposed him to activity and violence; woman's anabolism predisposed her to a stationary life."[41] Although there was no explicit discussion of heredity in this essay, or of the heritability of acquired characteristics, his assumptions that the physiological and sociological are closely linked are very neo-Lamarckian. As yet, there is independent realm of the social or cultural; the biological and the social are seen as deeply entwined.

By 1907, Thomas's views had changed. He offered quite a different view of sexual difference in his essay "The Mind of Woman and the Lower

Races." To be sure, Thomas did not simply abandon the links between the social and physiological; indeed, he opened the essays by reasserting the unity of mind and instinct: "the mind is a very wonderful thing, but it is questionable whether it is more wonderful than some of the instinctive modes of behavior of lower forms of life." [42] But Thomas went on to break with older views of heredity in two important ways. First, he explicitly questioned the use of brain weight as a means for establishing a hierarchical ranking of the races and argued instead that "the limits of variation between individuals in the same race are wider than the average difference between races. . . . There is also no ground for the assumption that the brain of woman is inferior to that of man. . . . Brains are, in fact, like timepieces in this respect, that the small ones work 'excellent well' if they are good material and well put together." [43] After discussing and dismissing arguments about the inferiority of the "lower races" as to their capacities for inhibition and abstraction, Thomas concluded that "in respect, then, to brain structure and the more important mental facilities we find that no race is radically unlike the others." Thomas asserted that the human mind is everywhere the world over essentially the same. Once we screen out the "local, incidental, and eccentric," we find similar laws and principles operating the world over. Racial hierarchy of a biological kind is gone, replaced with claims about the "homogeneous character of the human mind." [44]

With the physiological no longer identified as the source of human difference, Thomas turned to society and culture to explain the mind of woman and the lower races. In doing so, he first had to establish an *autonomous* social sphere that is not linked directly back to physiology. The move to distinguish culture and biology came in his discussion of progress in which he critiqued the "naive way we assume that our steps in progress from time to time are due to our mental superiority as a race over the other races, and to the mental superiority of one generation of ourselves over the proceeding." Instead, Thomas argued that "we are confusing advance in culture with brain improvement. . . . Culture is the accumulation of the results of activity, and culture could go in [sic] improving for a certain time even if there were a retrogression in intelligence." [45] Thomas began to disarticulate the brain and society, so that improvement in one was no longer presumed to lead to an advance in the other. In short, Thomas concluded that because "one race has advanced farther in culture than another does not necessarily imply a different order of brain, but may be due to the fact that in one case the social arrangements have not taken the shape affording the most favorable conditions for the operation of mind." [46]

Once Thomas delinked the biological and social, he was able to focus his attention more specifically on the social influences on the mind.

Home, school, and church now became his principal objects of study: "so-cial suggestion works marvels in the manipulation of the mind; but the change is not in the brain as an organ; it is rather in the character of the stimulations thrust on it by society." Society, not the brain, holds the key to understanding the differences between the sexes and races; and, as a consequence, the field of sociology, for Thomas, was born.

Thomas concluded his 1907 essay on a contemporary-sounding note:

> The world of modern intellectual life is in reality a white man's world. Few women and perhaps no blacks have ever entered this world in the fullest sense. To enter it in the fullest sense would be to be in it at every moment from the time of birth to the time of death, and to absorb it unconsciously and consciously, as the child absorbs language. When something like this happens, we shall be in a position to judge of the mental efficiency of woman and the lower races. At present we seem justified in inferring that the differences in mental expression are no greater than they should be in view of the existing differences in opportunity.[47]

Biology and sociology are finally split apart. Physiology is no longer seen as the basis of sexual and racial difference; they have been replaced by claims of a homogeneous human form that are given specificity by the institutions and social practices in particular locales. Lamarckian notions of the heritability of acquired characteristics have no place here; biological and social processes now are seen as independent forces that need to be analyzed on their own terms. They are no longer seen as two sides of the same coin.

By 1920, most scholars had broken with Lamarckian notions of heredi-tary and were insisting on the importance of distinguishing race from language, nation, and culture. Indeed, Madison Grant's *The Passing of the Great Race*, published in 1916, might well serve as a benchmark for the end of Lamarckianism and its concomitant notion of historic races. Grant began the book declaring that "it will be necessary for the reader to strip his mind of all preconceptions as to race [and] realize that race pure and simple, the physical and psychical structure of man, is something entirely distinct from either nationality or language."[48] Grant insisted that "fail-ure to recognize the clear distinction between race and nationality and the still greater distinction between race and language, the easy assumption that the one is indicative of the other, has been in the past a serious im-pediment to an understanding of racial values."[49] Thus, Grant warned that it is "necessary at the outset for the reader to thoroughly appreciate that race, language, and nationality are three separate and distinct things."[50]

Lamarckian notions of "historic races" are placed squarely in the past and are thought to have obscured "the racial basis of European history."[51]

Grant's break with Lamarck is especially telling because older Lamarckian notions of heredity had buttressed his political views by enabling him to disparage both immigrants and blacks as inferior races. When Grant began to distinguish race and nation, he had to elaborate new grounds for his anti-immigration politics. The fact that even he, too, abandoned Lamarckian views suggests just how pervasive the break was.

Rethinking Race and Nation: Are Jews a Race?

Once Lamarckian notions of heredity had begun to lose their hegemonic status in the 1890s, and scholars such as Ripley, Boas, Thomas, and others had begun to question the heritability of acquired characteristics, scholars also began to question whether groups that had been considered races under the old orthodoxy were, in fact, so, or if they were some other kind of social formation that ought to be distinguished from race. The Jews became the test case. How should scholars set the boundaries of race in a post-Lamarckian world? Ripley, Joseph Jacobs, Maurice Fishberg, Robert Bennett Bean, and Joseph Lipsky all published essays on the racial status of the Jews, most of which appeared in *Popular Science Monthly* between 1898 and 1913. How scholars classified Jews thus signaled where they stood vis-à-vis Lamarckianism; those who wanted to break with Lamarck, like Ripley and Fishberg, argued that Jews were *not* a race, but rather a different kind of social formation forged through cultural and political processes rather than descent. For Jacobs, Bean, and Lipsky, Jews were a race precisely because for them the social and biological remained intimately linked. In contrast to Ripley and Fishberg, they continued to adhere to broader nineteenth-century notions of heredity in which social solidarity mingled with physical notions of descent.

Ripley prompted the American debate over the nature and boundaries of race with publication of a two-part Supplement to "The Racial Geography of Europe." The Supplement, published in December 1898 and January 1899, focused specifically on the racial status of Jews. Ripley framed the issue as follows:

> How, bereft of two out of three of the essentials of nationality (language, tradition, and territory), has the Jew been enabled to perpetuate his social consciousness? Is the superior force of religion, perhaps abnormally developed, alone able to account for it all? Is it a case of compensatory development, analogous in the body to a loss of eyesight remedied through

greater delicacy of finger touch? Or is there some hidden, some unsus-
pected factor, which has contributed to this result? We have elsewhere
shown that a fourth element of social solidarity is sometimes, though
rarely, found, in a community of physical descent. That, in other words,
to the cementing bonds of speech, tradition, belief, and contiguity, is added
the element of physical brotherhood—that is to say, of race. Can it be that
herein is a partial explanation of the social individuality of the Jewish
people? It is a question for the scientist alone. *Race, as we constantly
maintain, despite the abuse of the word, really is to be measured only
by physical characteristics.* The task before us is to apply the criteria of
anthropological science, therefore, to the problems of Jewish derivation
and descent.[52]

After considering whether there was any basis for physical unity via discussion of stature, lung capacity, life expectancy, head form, hair color,
and shape of the eyes, nose, and chin, Ripley concluded: "The Jews are
not a race, but only a people, after all. In their faces we read its confirma-
tion, while in respect of their other traits we are convinced that such individuality as they possess—by no means inconsiderable—is of their own
making from one generation to the next, rather than as a product of an
unprecedented purity of physical descent."[53]

I want to underscore that breaking with Lamarck did not necessarily
signal a progressive politics. Even those who argued against Jews being
considered a race were by no means committed to notions of equality;
indeed there are strains of anti-Semitism running throughout the discussion as scholars frequently referred to the "Jewish problem" and wrote of
Jews as an "alien population" and a "peculiar people." Less ambiguously,
Ripley declared that the "recent anti-Semitic uprisings in Russia, Austria, and the German Empire" were not "to any great extent an uprising
against an existing evil, rather" they appeared to be "a protest against
a future possibility. . . . Germany shudders at the dark and threatening
cloud of population of the most ignorant and wretched description which
overhangs her eastern frontier. Berlin must not, they say, be allowed to
become a new Jerusalem for the horde of Russian exiles. That also is our
American problem. This great Polish swamp of miserable human beings,
terrific in its proportions, threatens to drain itself off into our country as
well, unless we restrict its ingress."[54] Rethinking heredity did not entail
greater tolerance toward Jews.

But Ripley's Supplement did not appear out of the blue; it was presented
as a critique of earlier scholars' work. In particular, Ripley referred dis-
paragingly to Joseph Jacobs, the very same Joseph Jacobs I quoted earlier,

who had written on the small size of the Australian skull.[55] In August 1899, Jacobs replied to Ripley with an essay entitled "Are Jews Jews?"[56]

Jacobs's opening paragraph sets up the debate concisely and is worth quoting in full.

> In the December [1898] and January [1899] numbers of Appleton's Popular Science Monthly Prof. William Z. Ripley concludes the remarkable series of articles on the Racial Geography of Europe, originally delivered as Lowell Institute lectures, by a couple of articles on the Jews. Strictly speaking, the articles might seem to have no right in the particular series in which Professor Ripley has included them, since their main object is to show that the Jews are not a race but a people, and have therefore no claim to be considered in the racial geography of any continent. But one can not regret that a daring disregard for logic has caused Professor Ripley to conclude his interesting series with the somewhat startling paradox that Jews are not Jews, in the sense of the word in which both their friends and their enemies have hitherto taken it. As Professor Ripley has been good enough to refer to me as having written with some authority on the subject, and as I have not been convinced by his arguments against the comparative racial purity of the Jews, I am glad of an opportunity to discuss the question, which is of equal theoretic and practical interest.[57]

Jacobs goes on to defend the "comparative racial purity" of the Jews by countering two of Ripley's arguments for racial "admixture" via discussion of intermarriage and Jewish physiognomy.

If one turns to history, Jacobs argued, one finds that, contra to Ripley's claim, there has been relatively little "admixture" of Jews and non-Jews over the last two thousand years. Jewish broad-headedness is not, as Ripley had argued, evidence of the dissipation of their original long-headed form. When countering Ripley, Jacobs offered a classic Lamarckian defense that Jewish broad-headedness was tied to brain use; extended use over time expanded their skulls and changed the classic shape of the Jewish head form:

> Every indication seems to point out that in races where progress depends upon brain rather than muscle the brain-box broadens out as a natural consequence. . . . From the nature of the sutures of the skull it is tolerably obvious that if brain capacity produces an enlargement of brain, and the consequent internal pressure on the skull will be lateral and tend to produce brachycephalism. The application of all this to the case of Jews seems obvious. If they had been forced by persecution to become mainly

blacksmiths, one would not have been surprised to find their biceps larger than those of other folk; and similarly, as they have been forced to live by the exercise of their brains, one should not be surprised to find the cubic capacity of their skulls larger than that of their neighbors.[58]

These physiological changes were not diminished by intermarriage, Jacobs continued, because the mixed "offspring have wandered away from the Jewish race and have not affected the more conservative remnant."[59] Those who intermarried, Jacobs concluded, left the group and thus did not diminish its racial purity.

Finally, Jacobs claimed that Ripley had not fully explained the "remarkable similarity of the Jewish physiognomy all the world over," which was further evidence of their "racial unity."[60] Jacobs then distinguished the "mere expression" and Jewish "features." Expression, for Jacobs, were the product of "social causes" while "features," which he specified as "Jewish nostrility" and "the Jew's eye," had "persisted throughout the ages [and] are themselves a striking proof of the absence of such admixture."[61] Jacobs concluded: "altogether I remain unconvinced by Professor Ripley's arguments as to any large admixture of alien elements among contemporary Jews as unvouched for by history, and not necessarily postulated by anthropology." Jacobs remained firmly convinced of the "racial purity" of the Jews.[62]

Another round of arguments over whether Jews were a race took place in 1902 when Fishberg followed Ripley's lead and argued against the racial homogeneity of Jews. Fishberg cited both Ripley and Jacobs in his text and, like Ripley, initially published a series of articles that subsequently provided the basis for a book-length project on the Jews.[63] Interestingly, Fishberg placed the term *race* in quotation marks and then set about demonstrating the parallel development between Jews and Christians within the same nation. Fertility, suicide, and stillbirths remained the same for Jews and non-Jews within the same national setting; significant differences appeared only when one looked at cross-national data. Thus, Fishberg concluded that "anthropological research has . . . revealed that there is no such thing as Jewish race, that ethnically Jews differ according to the country in which they happen to live, just as Catholics or Protestants in various countries differ from each other."[64]

A key element in Fishberg's argument for environment over race was his identification of religion as an alternative basis of solidarity to that of descent.[65] For Fishberg, unlike earlier Lamarckians, environmental factors were no longer seen as the basis for creating racial differences through the formation of "historic races"; he does not use such terms. For Fishberg, environmental influences are an alternative to, rather than a variant of, biological explanations. "Social factors" are now identified as being in tension with, or opposition to, heredity rather than being viewed—as earlier Lamarckians had done—as a pathway to heredity change.

One of the last gasps of Lamarckianism is seen in Robert Bennett Bean's 1913 discussion of the racial characteristics of the Jews, in which he insisted on the heritability of acquired characteristics. Most bizarrely, Bean claimed that the Jewish nose was a product of years of indignation that had passed from habit to heredity over time.[66] Before the outbreak of World War I, however, the tide had largely turned—Lamarckian notions of heredity no longer dominated social science discourse. By 1913, Bean was a minor voice, a vestige of an older race discourse that was fading from view. Most social scientists were operating within a Mendelian frame in which genetic notions of heredity buttressed a bright-line distinction between races and other kinds of social solidarity.

Rethinking the Nation: The "Immigration Problem"

The shift from Lamarckian to Mendelian notions of heredity not only shaped American social scientists' views of race; it also prompted many to rethink the nation. Once one disaggregated race, questions of what exactly bound the nation together became more difficult to answer. On what grounds, several scholars began to ponder, did national unity rest, and how could it be fostered or undermined? This new preoccupation with national solidarity was posed elegantly in 1894 by Richmond Mayo-Smith, a professor of political economy at Columbia University from 1883 to 1901 who published several essays on immigration in the *Political Science Quarterly*. Mayo-Smith opened his two-part essay on "Assimilation of Nationalities in the United States" by asking:

Who and what is an American?

We are familiar enough with the question whether nationality is determined by place, blood or allegiance. We are informed that originally it was determined by blood, that is by tribal relationship. . . . As nations acquired fixed abodes and territorial limits corresponded with the extent of political authority, residence in a country and allegiance to a sovereign became elements in the notion of nationality. An Englishman was ordinarily a man of English blood, living in England and owing allegiance to the King of England. A foreigner might, of course, live in England and not be an Englishman, just as an Englishman might live abroad and not lose his nationality. But such cases were exceptional; in the great mass, blood, residence and allegiance united to constitute nationality.[67]

But Mayo-Smith went on to declare that "the progress of events has gradually destroyed the simplicity and obviousness of this conception." The existence of confederated states and of colonialism, Mayo-Smith argued, had disrupted the unity of territory, blood, and political authority and had left the United States, in particular, with the historic task of fusing the "different elements" into one nationality.[68] How was national unity to be established and sustained?

Ultimately, Mayo-Smith was quite optimistic and concluded that the assimilating forces were powerful enough to forge an "ethnical unity" despite the disjuncture between place, blood, and nation.[69] But it is worth attending carefully to Mayo-Smith's account of the amalgamation process because it allows us to see the advent of the social as a distinct realm, more carefully delineated from heredity, body, and blood. Once a distinction was drawn between the biological and the social, many social scientists began to explore the nature and basis of nationality that heretofore had been subsumed under discussions of race.[70]

Post-Lamarckian anxieties over the status of national identities, however, were never solely academic concerns; anxieties also were fueled by recent mass migrations. Beginning in the late 1880s and running through the Depression, many social scientists such as Mayo-Smith, Henry Pratt Fairchild, Prescott Hall, Madison Grant, John Mitchell, and John R. Commons wrote extensively about what was increasingly referred to as "the immigration problem." Indeed, by 1927, American immigration history had become, at least in one scholar's eyes, a distinct subfield worthy of evaluation.[71] Interestingly, there was no reference to the older Lamarckian division between the natural and historic races; rather, immigrants were increasingly referred to as *foreigners* and *aliens* and, as such, began to be marked out as a distinct group requiring separate analysis from the races. For example, in an earlier essay published in 1888, Mayo-Smith wrote:

> According to the census of 1880 there were in the United States 6,679,943 persons of foreign birth, constituting 13 per cent of the whole population or 15.36 per cent of the native-born population. The comparison however is not a good one; for among the native-born are included the negroes of the South, who are as much an alien element in our civilization as are the foreign-born themselves. We must therefore compare the foreign-born with the native white population in order to get a fair idea of the strength of the foreign element. . . . Some may however object to this that

the colored people speak our language and have no other institutions and customs than those they have acquired here, so that they should be classed simply as a lower, rather than as an alien element in our civilization. I readily agree to this.[72]

Blacks, according to Mayo-Smith, did not fit with either the native or foreign-born and should not be collapsed in with the "foreign element."

Mayo-Smith elaborated his distinction between race and nationality in an 1894 essay when he explained that he excluded "the colored" from his discussion as they were "not so much alien" as they were "a peculiar element, separated from the rest of the community by an ineradicable mark." Mayo-Smith concluded that unlike foreigners, whom he went on to discuss at length, it was "impossible to predict how and when the negroes are to be assimilated to the white population of the United States."[73] As a consequence, Mayo-Smith set aside questions of slavery and its legacies when discussing immigration—a move that, we will see in the next chapter, is echoed by later ethnicity theorists. This separation of race from immigration, I will argue, has had an enormous impact on the parameters and dynamics of ethnic politics in the United States.

To be sure, questions of race by no means vanished altogether; Ripley continued to worry about "race suicide," in which he feared that the "future of Anglo-Saxon America" may go the way of the "American Indian and the buffalo" and disappear.[74] But for the most part, this was not the language within which questions of immigration were posed. Rather, a new discourse was emerging in which race and nation were being gradually teased apart and the immigrant problem treated as a distinct problem from that of race.[75]

Once a line had been drawn between race and nation, many social scientists, representing a fairly broad cross section of the political spectrum, set about specifying the *social* dimensions of the "immigration problem." Thus, we find John Mitchell and John R. Commons, both longtime advocates of American labor, agreeing with older race theorists such as Madison Grant and Prescott Hall that the recent immigration was having a deleterious effect on American workers and ought to be restricted. Even those who opposed restriction, such as William S. Bennett, often found themselves arguing on the same terrain as they tried to counter their opponents' claims about the social consequences of immigration.[76]

Political scientists and sociologists, in particular, began to focus on three aspects of immigration: class, politics, and assimilation. Commons, Mayo-Smith, and others set about documenting the changing class composition of the post-1880s immigration in order to claim that the lower class status of the recent immigrants was undermining American wages and ultimately would have a dangerous impact on the whole community.[77] Although immigration certainly brought about increased competition for American workers, it was a mistake, Mayo-Smith argued, to think that this would benefit the rest of society. On the contrary, he claimed that "such competition can in no sense be said to be desirable. It makes commodities cheaper, not by increased industry and ingenuity, but by reducing the civilization of the community. Such a result is not only wrong to our laboring class but it is suicidal to ourselves."[78]

The new immigration was also thought to be undermining the American political system as the recent immigrants no longer came from the same political tradition and thus were not suited to a system of self-government. Again Mayo-Smith captured the sense of political estrangement when he declared that new immigrants "can no longer speak of the constitution as the work of the Fathers except in an adoptive sense." This estrangement was acerbated for Mayo-Smith by the low naturalization and voting rates among the foreign-born.[79] Madison Grant, characteristically, put the issue more bluntly in his 1925 essay, "America for the Americans," in which he declared that "our institutions are Anglo-Saxon and can only be maintained by Anglo-Saxons and by other Nordic peoples in sympathy with our culture."[80] Grant went on to claim that the negative impact of immigration could already be seen in microcosm in "municipal governments where because of the well-known tendency of immigrants to crowd in cities, its first fruits have appeared." As a consequence, he argued, inefficiency and corruption abound due to the influence of the ignorant immigrant masses.[81]

Finally, immigration scholars almost always turned to questions of assimilation. Although they anticipated quite different outcomes, there was considerable agreement on the importance of assessing different immigrant groups' prospects for assimilating. Those most strongly opposed to immigration, such as Grant, began to make disparaging references to Israel Zangwill's melting pot and argued instead that immigrants were not dispersing throughout the nation but rather had a "tendency to form alien colonies in our midst." It was a short step from "alien colonies" to assertions of disorder and crime, which generally led many to conclude that the prospects of assimilation were indeed quite bleak.[82]

Whether social scientists ended up supporting or opposing immigration at the turn of the century, although of great consequence for American immigration policy at the time, is not my central concern. What I want to draw attention to in these early scholarly debates are the ways in which biology and culture, race and immigration, began to be distinguished from each other. The intellectual shifts that took place between 1880 and 1910, documented above, set the stage for the invention of ethnicity in decades hence. Put simply, the break with Lamarck, and the disaggregation of nineteenth-century conceptions of race that followed, provided the intellectual opening for New York Zionists and federal bureaucrats to construct a new category of ethnicity. Race was no longer an all-encompassing discourse that accounted for a wide range of human difference. Rather, social scientists now distinguished language, nation, and culture from race. Once nineteenth-century notions of race began to unravel, scholars, laypeople, and federal bureaucrats began to use the term *ethnic* not simply to refer to racial traits but as a new social category distinguished from, rather than equated with, race.

Finally, I want the reader to keep the changing conceptions of heredity in mind when reading the chapters that follow. Doing so helps temper, without negating, claims of agency by those who crafted the new category of ethnicity to which I now turn.

Fixing Race, Unfixing Ethnicity: 3
New York Zionists and Ethnicity

Much like its counterparts before and since, Progressive-era im-migration provoked considerable anxiety in the resident popu-lation. The combination of war and large-scale immigration led many Americans to call for immigration restriction and to demand that newcomers be assimilated through an extensive campaign of Americanization.[1] No one organization orchestrated the campaign; a myriad of private and government institutions championed the cause: the National Americanization Committee, the Bureau of Naturalization within the Department of Labor, the Bureau of Education within the Department of the Interior, school boards, unions (especially the United Mine Workers), chambers of commerce, philanthropic organizations such as the Young Men's and Young Women's Christian Associations, settlement houses, and, by no means least, patriotic associations such as the Daughters and Sons of the American Revolution and the Ameri-can Legion. In 1918, the National Americanization Committee compiled a list of organizations involved in Americanization in which they identified over a hundred organizations.[2] Moreover, the Americanization movement was buttressed at the presidential level by Theodore Roosevelt's and Woodrow Wilson's frequent anti-immigration appeals. Roosevelt's now famous attacks on the "hyphenates" in which he called instead for "100% Ameri-canism" were echoed by Wilson's albeit more muted calls for assimilation. Both rode the wave of nativist sentiment by questioning immigrants' wartime loyalties and pushing for immigration restrictions, which culminated in passage of anti-immigration laws in 1917, 1921, and 1924.[3]

Despite the enormous pressures to Americanize, not all immigrants readily assimilated to the dominant white population: some embraced or were forced to identify as nonwhites, while others resisted both of these positions and began to defend subnational identifications through the new language of ethnicity. Jewish immigrants, in particular, began to specify a distinctively ethnic identity and, as such, played a key role in the process of category formation. In chapter 4, we will see that they were not the only ones to craft a notion of ethnic difference, but they were some of the earliest to do so, and they left an extensive paper trail behind them. On reflection, it makes sense that Jews in particular coined the term *ethnicity* since their diasporic origins raised questions of group loyalty and national belonging differently than for other immigrant groups. Many immigrants negotiated competing loyalties by hyphenating national origins with American identity, hence the proliferation of Irish-Americans, Italian-Americans, Polish-Americans. But for Jews, there was no single national identifier to put on the left side of the hyphen since their national origins were not coincident with being Jewish. Indeed, many Jews had fled persecution at home and had no special desire to hold on to their territorial places of origin; they were especially receptive, then, to identifying by ethnicity rather than nation. They might have negotiated the competing loyalties by hyphenating religion and identifying as "Jewish-Americans," but fears of anti-Semitism and constitutionally mandated separation of church and state in the United States made such a move problematic. The omnibus term *ethnicity* offered a way out of these complexities, and many Jews began to refer with increasing regularity to ethnic groups and loyalties. Horace Kallen, Isaac Berkson, and Julius Drachsler all began to refer to Jews as an *ethnic group* and to discuss the dilemmas posed by *ethnic loyalty*. In so doing, they began to construct a new discourse of ethnic difference in which they eschewed the twin polls of assimilation and cultural separatism.[4] To be sure, as Werner Sollors has pointed out, the noun *ethnicity* did not become commonplace until the 1940s and 1950s, thus underscoring the point that Jewish intellectuals' efforts to specify a distinctive cultural position for ethnic groups in the 1910s and 1920s were the early precursors to the more general shifts in American discourse in subsequent decades.[5]

Fortunately, we can recapture debates over Jewish identification through the Harvard Menorah Society (established in 1906) and the

Intercollegiate Menorah Association (established in 1913), and through their official publication. The first Menorah Society was established in 1906 by Horace Kallen, Henry Hurwitz, Abraham Simon, and several other Jewish students at Harvard University. The Harvard Menorah Society quickly attracted a substantial following; by 1911–12, it had enrolled 230 members. The society met regularly two or more times a month during the academic year and regularly invited a distinguished list of speakers to address its meetings, including Jacob Schiff, Jacob de Haas, Charles Eliot, Joseph Jacobs, Horace Kallen, Stephen Wise, Mordecai Kaplan, and Louis Brandeis.[6] In January 1913, the association went national with the founding of the Intercollegiate Menorah Association and the creation of the *Menorah Journal* as the association's official publication. Two years later, thirty-five colleges and universities across the country had established Menorah Societies and affiliated with the Intercollegiate Menorah Association. The Menorah Association was eventually headquartered in New York at 63 Fifth Avenue. The *Journal* was published continuously from 1915 through 1961 under the editorship of Hurwitz as a means of advancing, as the masthead declared, "the Study and Advancement of Jewish Culture and Ideals." When Hurwitz died in 1961, publication of the *Journal* was suspended. A single valedictory issue, dedicated to Hurwitz, was published in 1962, and the Menorah Association officially dissolved in 1963.[7]

The high point for the *Menorah Journal* was the interwar years when leading intellectuals of the day contributed essays arguing over identification and politics in general and over what it meant to be a Jew and an American in particular. The list of contributors is stunning: Mary Antin, Louis Brandeis, Felix Frankfurter, Roscoe Pound, Charles Beard, Bertrand Russell, Edward Sapir and Alfred Kroeber (both students of Franz Boas), Horace Kallen and Randolph Bourne (early cultural pluralists), Isaac Berkson, Lewis Mumford, Norman Hapgood (editor of *Harper's Weekly*), Waldo Frank (editor of *Seven Arts*), Cecil Roth, G. Stanley Hall, Alvin Johnson, Hannah Arendt, John Dewey, Charles W. Eliot, and Harry Wolfson. Moreover, most leading Zionists of the period also contributed: Theodor Herzl, Richard Gotteil, Chaim Weizmann, Schmarya Levin, Jacob de Haas, Jacob Schiff, Martin Buber, Max Heller, Julian Mack, and Mordecai Kaplan. But that is not all. The journal was broadly conceived and allowed considerable space for poetry, drama, and art and included works by Pablo Picasso, Marc Chagall, Camille Pissarro, Max Weber (the painter), Thomas Mann, Israel Zangwill, and Lionel Trilling. It was an amazing forum in which issues of subnational identification and politics were debated at the highest levels. It was here that reference to ethnic groups and loyalties first appeared.

Interestingly, the *Menorah Journal* became the site of a high-powered intellectual exchange precisely at the moment when American universities and magazines were closing their doors to Jews.[8] Whatever the cause, the journal provided an amazing forum for Jews and non-Jews, Zionists and non-Zionists to engage questions of subnational identification and loyalty to the nation. I have come to think of the *Menorah Journal* as a neglected counterpoint to the New Negro; both seem to have provided broad-ranging forums for renegotiating ethnic and racial identities in the first half of the twentieth century. Even though there was no single editorial position offered, most of the contributors began to defend dual, and even plural, identifications. To be sure, not all contributors advanced this view. A few, such as Isaac Mayer Wise and Bernard Rosenblatt, continued to advocate the importance of immigrant assimilation, albeit of rather different kinds, while others, such as Jacob Schiff and Zalman Yaakov Friederman, heralded the importance of religious identification. But they remained the minority; most of the *Menorah* essays advanced hyphenation of some kind as the most promising means of reconciling conflicting identifications.[9]

The remainder of the chapter examines the writings of five early ethnicity theorists: Louis Brandeis, Horace Kallen, Alfred Kroeber, Maurice Fishberg, and Isaac Berkson. All five of these writers' contributions to the *Journal* provide a rare opportunity for tracing the process of category formation. All of these authors, and others besides, began to carve out a new position within American culture and politics that eschewed the twin polls of assimilation and separatism. Jews, they argued, could remain firmly rooted in both their distinctive cultural identification without calling into question their loyalty to America. By looking more closely at these early arguments in *defense of immigrant difference,* we can see the emergence of ethnicity as a distinctive identification in which hyphenation was not only tolerated but hailed as one of the cornerstones of American cultural and political life. As such, the *Menorah* writers turned upside down Roosevelt's and Wilson's attacks on hyphenated Americans when they claimed that hyphenation, and eventually pluralism, was *the* distinctive mark of being American.

Before looking at these early ethnicity essays, let me prefigure the argument that follows. To understand more precisely what sort of an identity is being fashioned here, we need to attend to the ways in which ethnicity was continually positioned against older notions of difference, especially those of race. By reading race and ethnicity together, we can see how the meaning of ethnicity was established relationally, how the meaning of each is secured through its relation with the other. Finally, my interest in ethnicity and its relation to race is driven by a concern for politics: by a desire to understand where likely political alliances might be forged, on what terms, and to what ends. In the final section of the chapter, I anticipate the larger political argument of the book by examining Horace Kallen's relationship with Alain Locke. Their friendship enables us to see in microcosm both the promise and the limitations of ethnic identification as it was crafted by New York Zionists in the interwar years.[10]

Ethnicity, Not Whiteness: Zionism, Group Loyalty, and National Belonging

The seven years from 1914 through 1921 often are viewed as the high point of American Zionism, but exactly what it meant to be a Zionist in the United States during this period is not altogether clear. During the war, many American Jewish intellectuals both inside and outside the movement began to specify more carefully what Zionism meant for American Jews. The once small and fragmented Zionist movement was transformed when membership exploded—increasing by almost twentyfold.[11] But war changed more than membership figures when the declaration of war in Europe split the World Zionist Organization Executive apart. Shmarya Levin (a member of the World Zionist Executive who was then visiting in New York) called an "Extraordinary Conference" of all American Zionist groups in the hopes of forming an emergency organization to carry out the work of the World Zionist Organization during wartime. The "Extraordinary Conference of Representatives of American Zionists" met at the Hotel Marseilles in New York on August 30, 1914. One hundred and fifty delegates attended and established the Provisional Executive Committee for General Zionist Affairs that was to continue the work of the world Zionist movement.[12] The Provisional Executive Committee raised an emergency fund of $200,000, and Louis D. Brandeis accepted the chairmanship, which quickly brought the movement new visibility and prestige.[13]

Even though Brandeis ultimately was forced out of power in 1921, his influence at home was more lasting; his views on group loyalty and national belonging laid out the key parameters of American ethnicity as a new social formation. Although central to the process of category formation, neither Brandeis nor any other figure single-handedly configured American notions of ethnicity; the preceding chapter made clear just how many forces were in play in the shift from "historic races" to ethnicity. But Brandeis and other early American Zionists gave definition, specificity, and political authority to the more diffuse transformations at hand.

Many of the players engaged in the *Menorah* debate went on to hold positions of considerable power and prestige in the United States and, as such, helped shape the contours of ethnicity for decades to come.[14]

Brandeis's Zionism: Anti-Assimilationist Nationalism

After assuming the chairmanship of the Provisional Zionist Executive Committee on August 30, 1914, Brandeis delivered several important speeches in which he began to lay out his vision of American Zionism. He returned repeatedly to three themes. First, Brandeis spoke of the dangers of assimilation and of the importance of maintaining group loyalty, particularity in the face of wartime pressures to Americanize. In addition, Brandeis reversed his earlier attacks on hyphenated identities and began to argue instead that subnational identifications were in no way inconsistent with loyalty to the nation. Finally, Brandeis moved quickly from arguments about hyphenation and plurality to rethinking the nation, in general, and America, in particular. Brandeis was not content to make hyphenated loyalties tolerable, but frequently advanced the stronger claim in which the very plurality of identifications was seen as *the* defining feature of the American nation. What distinguished America from other democracies, Brandeis, Kallen, Dewey, and others began to claim, were the ways in which it was plural through to the core.[15]

In several of his interwar speeches, Brandeis made plain his anti-assimilationist stance as he and other Zionists, such as Solomon Schechter and Julian Mack, explicitly claimed Judaism to be "a bulwark against assimilation."[16] In his speech entitled "A Call to the Educated Jew," which was initially delivered at an Intercollegiate Menorah Association Conference and subsequently published in the first issue of the *Menorah Journal* in January 1915, Brandeis declared assimilation to be "national suicide." He went on to buttress his anti-assimilationist claims through a quite explicit defense of group particularity, which he argued could be most effectively sustained through the creation of a Jewish homeland in Palestine.[17] Brandeis concluded the essay with a rather romanticized account of the decline of the immigrant communities and identified Zionism as the best means of reestablishing this special immigrant "spirit." "The ghetto walls are now falling. Jewish life cannot be preserved and developed, assimilation cannot be averted unless there be reestablished in the fatherland a center from which the Jewish spirit may radiate and give to the Jews scattered throughout the world that inspiration which springs from the memories of a great past and the hope of a great future."[18] Paradoxically, then, Jewish particularity could be sustained in the United States only by establishing a national homeland in the future to be from.

Later that same year, Brandeis argued against assimilation in a speech on "The Jewish Problem—And How to Solve It":

> We recognize that with each child the aim of education should be to develop his own individuality, not to make him an imitator, nor to assimilate him to others. Shall we fail to recognize this truth when applied to whole peoples? . . .
>
> While every other people is striving for development by asserting its nationality, and a great war is making clear the value of small nations, shall we voluntarily yield to anti-Semitism, and instead of solving our "problem" end it by ignoble suicide? Surely this is no time for Jews to despair. Let us make clear to the world that we too are a nationality striving for equal rights to life and to self-expression.[19]

Again Brandeis linked assimilation with national suicide and defended group difference, in general, and Jewish identity, in particular, as vital to both the health of American democracy and to Jewish self-expression.

Brandeis's anti-assimilationist claims would be less remarkable if it were not for recent whiteness scholarship that frequently equates ethnicity with assimilation, albeit with an important innovative twist from earlier work. David Roediger, Matthew Frye Jacobson, Gary Gerstle, and many others have found an intriguing, but I believe misguided, way of linking ethnicity and race. When immigrants assimilated, so the argument runs, they identified not only culturally and politically, but racially as well by siding with the dominant population and becoming white—hence the host of monographs on how the Irish, Germans, Italians, and Jews became white. Although I agree that it is crucial to examine the interrelations between immigration and race, because how immigrants position themselves or are positioned by others will set the broad contours of American political life, I think whiteness scholars have too readily collapsed ethnicity back into whiteness. By flattening ethnicity and equating it with whiteness, these scholars have misunderstood the constitutive relation between the two terms and misread ethnic politics as well.[20] As I read him, Brandeis was not on the road to whiteness; there is no equivocation in his anti-assimilationist appeals. Indeed, most of those who wrote in the *Menorah Journal* advanced variants on this same anti-assimilationist theme as they tried to carve out some space for subnational identities against the prevailing policies of Americanization.[21] If Brandeis and his allies were not trying to assimilate, then, exactly what kind of an identification were they constructing? How were they positioning themselves within American culture and politics? How did their defense of Jewish difference intersect the discourse and practice of racial inequality?

Brandeis further elaborated his vision of American Zionism by arguing for the viability of hyphenated and indeed even plural identifications. Loyalties were not zero-sum and could be multiplied without undermining one's commitment to any particular attachment.

> Let no American imagine that Zionism is inconsistent with patriotism. Multiple loyalties are objectionable only if they are inconsistent. A man is a better citizen of the United States for being also a loyal citizen to his state and to his city; for being loyal to his family, and to his profession or trade; for being loyal to his college or his lodge. Every Irish-American who contributed towards advancing home rule was a better man and a better American for the sacrifice he made. Every American Jew who aids in advancing the Jewish settlement in Palestine, though he feels that neither he nor his descendants will ever live there, will likewise be a better man and a better American for doing so. . . . There is no inconsistency between loyalty to America and loyalty to Jewry.[22]

One can hardly imagine a more explicit defense of plural loyalties as central to American democracy. The synergistic relationship among multiple loyalties has been taken up by subsequent ethnicity theorists and seems to belie critics' claims that early advocates of ethnicity conceived of it in rather "pure" terms.[23]

Having vigorously defended subnational identification, it was but a short step to rethinking the nation. Brandeis put his position succinctly in his speech on "The Rebirth of the Jewish Nation" delivered shortly after being elected chairman of the Provisional Executive Committee.

> My approach to Zionism was through Americanism. In time, practical experience and observation convinced me that Jews were by reason of their traditions and their character peculiarly fitted for the attainment of American ideals. Gradually, it became clear to me that to be good Americans, we must be better Jews, and to be better Jews, we must become Zionists.[24]

In some literal sense, this was true for Brandeis. He was born on November 13, 1856, into a secular household in Louisville, Kentucky, never observed Jewish holidays, never went to synagogue or Hebrew school, and turned to Zionism only at the age of fifty-eight. Why he did so has been the subject of some scholarly debate. Some have tried to identify family precursors to his Zionist turn in his uncle, Dembitz, whom Brandeis sought to honor by changing his middle name. Shapiro gives an interest-driven account in which Brandeis turned to Zionism to further his political career, while others look to the influences of Jacob de Haas and Horace Kallen as intermediaries who made Zionism resonate for Brandeis.[25] No doubt the truth is a complex mix of motives that need not be settled here. Rather than speculating about motives, I want to explore just what kind of Jewish identity Brandeis began to craft.

As we have seen in the previous quotation, Brandeis himself readily acknowledged his prior distance from Judaism and made no effort to reinvent a religious past for himself. Rather, Brandeis asserted that his "approach to Zionism was through Americanism"—that is, it was through his understanding of and commitment to "American ideals" that he came to Zionism. Brandeis made ethnic particularity not only compatible with loyalty to the nation but argued that it was essential for maintaining America's core ideals. Plurality was not just an aspect of American culture and politics, but was one of the defining features of the American national polity. American democracy thrived, Brandeis and his allies claimed, precisely because of the vigorous articulation of group particularity and difference. Plural identifications, as many political scientists would later claim, were the life force of a healthy democracy.

During the first quarter of the twentieth century, Brandeis was not the only one to defend an anti-assimilationist and plural view of America; ideas of hyphenation were somehow "in the air." John Dewey, Randolph Bourne, Horace Kallen, and W. E. B. Du Bois immediately come to mind, but many made related arguments. Henry Hurwitz, the editor of the *Menorah Journal;* Solomon Schecter, president of the Jewish Theological Seminary; Judge Julian Mack; and Norman Hapgood, the influential editor of *Harper's Weekly,* also advanced similar views in these same decades.[26] Although these concerns remained the minor voice in the nation as a whole, they were advanced by many intellectuals in a variety of locations who wanted to challenge the dominant drive for immigrant assimilation. It is difficult, and for my purposes unnecessary, to determine more precisely who influenced whom. I simply want to draw attention to the ways in which Zionism raised questions of group loyalty and national belonging in new and immediate ways, which led many Jewish intellectuals to articulate a distinctive vision of American nationalism that sought to *embrace and work to sustain* rather than assimilate Jewish difference.

But Brandeis's defense of American Zionism was not yet a fully fledged argument for ethnicity; in fact, Brandeis did not use the term *ethnic,* but rather continued to speak in terms of Jewish particularity. That is, Brandeis did not generalize from the Jewish experience to make more general claims about the nature and importance of ethnic difference for American democracy. But some of Brandeis's contemporaries did make just such an extension: Horace Kallen, Isaac Berkson, and Julius Drachsler all referred to ethnic groups and loyalties. Interestingly, it is precisely at the moment of moving from Zionism to a more general defense of group difference that Kallen, Berkson, and Drachsler all introduced the term *ethnic* to refer more generally to a plurality of subnational identifications. All three published essays in the *Menorah Journal,* and Kallen in particular had been a founding member of the larger *Menorah* movement.[27] All three authors referred to *ethnic groups, ethnic types,* and *ethnic loyalties* and went to considerable lengths to specify exactly what they meant. Moreover, their various efforts to specify how they were using the term *ethnic* often led to extended discussions about the ways in which ethnic identification was and was not like existing conceptions of race.[28]

Constitutive Distinctions: Horace Kallen, Fixing Race, Inventing Ethnicity

Kallen is not as well known as some other Progressive-era intellectuals, but his reputation has been enjoying something of a renaissance as many scholars have begun to view his theory of "cultural pluralism" as an important precursor to multiculturalism.[29] Kallen was born in Germany in 1882, immigrated to the United States as a child in 1887, grew up in Boston in an Orthodox Jewish household (which he initially rejected), and went to Harvard as an undergraduate and to Oxford in 1907–8. On returning to the United States, he became involved in the early Zionist movement and went on to write extensively about both Zionism and cultural pluralism. He taught initially at Princeton and then at the University of Wisconsin, where he resigned his position over a freedom of speech matter in 1918. He moved in 1919 to the New School for Social Research, where he taught until his retirement in 1970. Somewhat surprisingly, there is no recognition of his presence at the New School today.

Kallen contributed seven essays to the *Menorah Journal* between 1915 and 1948; in all he elaborated a defense of Jewish identity as central to American democracy.[30] Not surprisingly, his *Menorah* essays were directed at fellow Jews as Kallen sought to specify what the most salient aspects of a "Jewish life" were. The common theme running throughout was the importance of making Jewish identity a "living faith" tied to living communities in the present, rather than to the moribund study of the past. Kallen was especially interested in specifying institutional and social practices that undergirded Jewish life and that gave the Jewish communities their "contemporary relevancy." In one essay, he reflected on the "Judaistic economy" and considered all of the trades and employment relations tied to Jewish life; in another, he critically assessed the three dominant rabbinical training schools and lamented the curriculum offered in each. Throughout he tried to transcend internal divisions among different strands of Judaism and argued instead that he wanted to "integrate the diversities of American Jewry into a stable creative force in American life."[31]

Kallen spelled out his views on Jewish identity in his famous two-part essay, "Democracy versus the Melting Pot: A Study of American Nationality," published on February 18 and 25, 1915, in the *Nation*. To this day, the essay is known for its powerful defense of immigrant difference in the United States. America, Kallen argued, was no longer a homogenous population as it had been in colonial times; successive immigration of Irish, Germans, Scandinavians, Jews, Poles, and Bohemians were turning America into a "commonwealth of nationalities." The question facing the nation was "how to get order out of this cacophony" of immigrant voices? How to govern such a diverse people?[32]

Striving for "unison" was a mistake, Kallen claimed, as it reduced the rich variety of ethnic communities to a "sameness" that could be achieved only through force or cultural imperialism.[33] Instead, Kallen extended the musical metaphor and suggested that America strive for "a multiplicity in a unity, an orchestration of mankind."[34]

The orchestra became a favorite metaphor for Kallen; it captured both the sense of unity and difference that was central to his cultural pluralist vision. Kallen ended the "Melting Pot" essay by stating:

> As in an orchestra, every type of instrument has its specific timbre and tonality founded in its substance and form; . . . so in society each ethnic group is the natural instrument, its spirit and culture are its theme and melody and the harmony and dissonances and discords of them all make the symphony of civilization.[35]

Kallen, like Brandeis, advanced an anti-assimilationist politics in which he argued that it was neither desirable nor inevitable for immigrants to become fully American. Moving beyond Brandeis, Kallen began to disaggregate the process of assimilation and to argue that immigrants needed to assimilate economically and politically, but should maintain their distinctive cultural traditions as a way of avoiding the stultifying weight of industrialization with its "ready-made clothes, factory-made goods, [and] refrigerating plants," all of which were seen as vehicles of Americanization, and as such ought to be resisted through the cultivation of robust immigrant communities with distinctive immigrant cultures.[36] The homogenizing effects of industrialization were further reinforced for Kallen by the oppressive political climate of World War I, in which issues of loyalty to the nation were paramount—remember, this is when Teddy Roosevelt and Woodrow Wilson wanted to "swat the hyphen."[37]

Current-day assessments of Kallen's work have been caught up in debates over multiculturalism, specifically over whether his pluralist vision might serve as a resource for contemporary race politics. Some celebrate his defense of cultural pluralism as an alternative, a more plural American nationalism, while others remain skeptical of Kallen's pluralist vision as a resource for contemporary race politics.[38] John Higham and Werner Sollors, in particular, have offered powerful critiques of Kallen's work in which they quite rightly note that Kallen allowed no place for African Americans within his pluralist pantheon. Certainly it is the case that Kallen's orchestra had no place for African Americans; they were not seen as having any special timbre or tonality. Indeed, in his 1924 book, *Culture and Democracy*, Kallen explicitly relegated discussion of African Americans to a footnote in which he stated: "I do not discuss the influence of the negro upon the esthetic material and cultural character of the South and the rest of the United States. This is at once too considerable and too recondite in its processes for casual mention. It requires separate analysis."[39] The Higham/Sollors reading of Kallen in which they underscore the absence of African Americans from his federation of nationalities has been largely accepted, and Kallen is generally known for his silence on race today.[40]

Although Higham and Sollors are correct in noting that Kallen does not include African Americans in his pluralistic vision, they *misread him* when they say that he is silent on race. The first claim is certainly true, but it does not sustain the second. In fact, when I went back to Kallen's essay, I was amazed to see how much he discusses race. The essay is filled with references to "whites," "negroes," "Anglo-Saxons," and "white stock," especially in the first half of the essay. How, I began to wonder, has Kallen's essay become known for its silence on race? Why have all of the explicit racial referents been ignored?

The answer, I want to suggest, lies in the quite particular ways in which Kallen deployed race so that the text itself simultaneously invoked and displaced race. If we look more closely, we see that there was an explicit and implicit comparison running throughout the essay between ethnicity and race in which race served as a counterpoint to ethnicity. Moreover, the comparison served to foreground ethnicity by displacing race. When I looked closely, I noticed that Kallen almost always invoked racial terms in two quite specific contexts, namely, when discussing the colonial era and the American South. By limiting discussions of race to the past and the South, Kallen repeatedly linked race to images of *homogeneity* at the nation's founding and "south of Mason and Dixon's line," both of which he wanted to contrast with the quite different culture and politics in his own time and place, namely, New York in 1915.[41] For example, Kallen began the fourth paragraph of the essay by declaring:

> In 1776 the mass of white men in the colonies *were* actually, with respect to one another, rather free and equal. I refer not so much to the absence of great differences in wealth, as to the fact that the whites were *like-minded*. They were possessed of ethnic and cultural unity; they were homogeneous with respect to ancestry and ideals.[42]

Note the chains of equivalence created by Kallen: race is linked to homogeneity of several kinds—like-mindedness, ethnic and cultural unity, and homogeneity of ancestry and ideals. The colonists, according to Kallen, were a uniform lot, derived from Anglo-Saxon stock who, by virtue of being here first, became "the measure and the standard of Americanism that the newcomer is to attain."[43] Kallen began to create two quite distinct associative chains in which particular qualities are aligned with ethnicity and others with race so that the two terms began to designate different kinds of difference throughout the essay. To be sure, the notion of "ethnic unity" was mixed with Kallen's discussion of race—the distinctions between race and ethnicity are not cleanly drawn. But Kallen almost always introduced notions of racial difference as a counterpoint to, rather than as a synonym for, ethnic difference. Indeed, I have come to see that Kallen introduced discussions of race early in the essay as a means for staging his principal concern—immigration in the Northeast.

A little later, Kallen again coupled race and homogeneity when describing the culture and politics of the South:

> South of Mason and Dixon's line the cities exhibit a greater homogeneity. Outside of certain regions in Texas the descendants of the native white stock, often degenerate and backward, prevail among whites, but the whites as a whole constitute a relatively weaker proportion of the population. They live among nine million negroes, whose own mode of living

tends, by its mere massiveness, to standardize the "mind" of the proletarian South in speech, manner, and the other values of social organization.[44]

Again, languages of racial stock and explicit reference to the "negro" were linked to standardization of the mind; racial differences between whites and Blacks were seen by Kallen as flattening out the social contours of the South. Race, for Kallen, was positioned as singular, fixed, and homogeneous—different in all of these respects from his preferred notion of ethnic difference.

When Kallen counterposed ethnicity with race, it is important to note that he did not define ethnic difference only against slavery and the consequent degradation of African Americans, as whiteness scholars would have it. Rather, Kallen and other early ethnicity theorists tried to distance themselves from *both* Blacks *and* whites; ethnic difference was not simply a way station on the road to whiteness, but rather was positioned as a quite different axis of difference altogether that could not be collapsed back into race. Kallen, Berkson, and other ethnicity theorists began to refer to "ethnic groups and loyalties" as a way of defending immigrant difference in nonracial terms. Ethnic groups were indeed different from whites, but the difference was not based on race. Kallen sought to distinguish Jews from *both* Blacks and whites.[45]

The distancing of ethnicity from race that we see in Kallen's 1915 essay was no fleeting coincidence, but was, I have come to believe, constitutive of the category itself. One is an ethnic, in the American context, to the extent that one's difference is configured in nonracial terms. Ethnic difference, for Kallen, could not be accounted for within the older languages of race; those discourses might have worked for the colonial era and for the South, but they were of little or no use in capturing the pressing questions that accompanied Progressive-era immigration in the Northeast. Kallen responded by inventing new associative chains.

Immediately after discussing the homogenized character of the founding and the South, Kallen turned to his central preoccupation of the essay—immigration. Once he began this discussion in earnest, issues of race gradually disappeared. Kallen used race to mark the distinctiveness of the immigration problem as *new*, as something that had emerged in cities in "the East" in "the last two decades."[46] Social transformations taking place within northern cities, which remained Kallen's central concern, cannot be adequately addressed, Kallen implied, through existing languages of race. Thus, Kallen invoked racial difference precisely to underscore the quite distinct notion of difference that had emerged with the influx of nationalities in recent decades. As a consequence, the *text itself* simultaneously invoked and displaced race. By tying race to the past and to the South, Kallen drew readers' attention away from race and its associations to homogeneity and descent. The pressing issue for Kallen was that of immigrant difference, which he argued could best be addressed through notions of ethnicity and cultural pluralism—precisely the themes that the essay is known for today.

Looking back over Kallen's writings in the interwar years, I see two chains of equivalence being created: race is repeatedly equated with heredity, fixity, homogeneity, and hierarchy, while ethnicity gets linked with culture, especially language and religion, which are seen as malleable, plural, and egalitarian. In short, Kallen began to fix notions of race in order to unfix notions of ethnicity. The contrast between the two was used to generate the meaning of both. I began to understand why it has been so difficult to dislodge biologized notions of race when they are reproduced discursively day after day; even when race is not being discussed explicitly, the implication that race is tied to body and blood remains so long as a distinction persists in the discursive chains. For Kallen, ethnicity was not a stepping-stone on the way to whiteness. He was more deeply invested in ethnic difference than this allows. Ethnic pluralism was a desirable end that ought to be actively nurtured and sustained. But Kallen's pluralist vision was secured at a heavy price in which ethnic difference served to reproduce biologized notions of race.

Similarly, if we look more closely at Kallen's invocation of nationality and ethnic difference, we see that these terms also were being used in quite particular ways. Kallen began his discussion of nationality and ethnic types by first countering claims that "economic division" was in some way fundamental. Rather, Kallen argued that economic inequalities simply cross cut rather than abolished ethnic divisions, leaving the primacy of nationality in place: "The fact is that similarity of class rests upon no inevitable external condition, while similarity of nationality is inevitably intrinsic. Hence the poor of two different peoples tend to be less like-minded than the poor and the rich of the same peoples."[47] Having dispensed with class conflict, Kallen went on to elaborate his views on the nature and political consequences of national and ethnic difference.[48]

Throughout the essay, however, as Sollors has noted, Kallen frequently linked discussions of nationality with claims of inheritance through phrases such as "common ancestry," "national inheritances," and nationality being "inevitably intrinsic."[49] Sollors rightly stressed the essentialized nature of many of Kallen's arguments about nationality in which descent shaped the cultural content of national difference.[50] As Kallen famously claimed:

> Men may change their clothes, their politics, their wives, their religions, their philosophies, to a greater or lesser extent: they cannot change their grandfathers. Jews or Poles or Anglo-Saxons, in order to cease being Jews or Poles or Anglo-Saxons, would have to cease to be. The selfhood which is inalienable in them, and for the realization of which they require "inalienable" liberty, is ancestrally determined, and the happiness which they pursue has its form implied in ancestral endowment.[51]

At one point Kallen referred to our "psychosocial inheritance," surely a sign that he had not yet clearly distinguished biological from cultural processes. Ethnicity and culture, although distinguished from race, were not always completely unhinged from descent. His repeated use of the term *natio* captured the slippage:

> At his core no human being, even in "a state of nature," is a mere mathematical unit of action like the "economic man." Behind him in time and tremendously in him in quality are his ancestors; around him in space are his relatives and kin, looking back with him to a remoter common ancestry. In all these he lives and moves and has his being. They constitute his, literally, *natio*.[52]

The concept of *natio* allowed Kallen to draw all sorts of national traits and characteristics into the web of national inheritance. Indeed, it is difficult to see what might fall beyond the bounds of *natio* as it was specified here.

But Kallen's discussion of *natio* quickly bled into his argument about the social and cultural bases of immigrant difference. In fact, Kallen never fully succeeded in disarticulating culture and descent in the 1915 essay; indeed, distinctions between the two remain ambiguous to this day. But his *effort* to do so is evident throughout the text. Certainly, *natio* is frequently tied to ancestry, but Kallen also used the term to capture a view of nationality as linked to "spirit" and "consciousness."[53] Moreover, Kallen often associated this social side of *natio* with the importance of religion and language as markers of group difference, both of which he readily acknowledged can be changed but ought not be, if we are to avoid the stultifying effects of standardization and homogenization that accompany industrialization.

> It is the shock of confrontation with other ethnic groups and the feeling of aliency [sic] that generates in them an intenser self-consciousness,

which then militates against Americanization in spirit by reinforcing the two factors to which the spiritual expression of the proletarian has been largely confined. These factors are language and religion. . . . It [religion] becomes a principle of separation, often the sole repository of the national spirit, almost always the conservator of the national language and of the tradition that is passed on with the language to succeeding generations. Among immigrants, hence, religion and language tend to be co-ordinate: a single expression of the spontaneous and instinctive mental life of the masses, and the primary inward factors making against assimilation.[54]

Here Kallen clearly saw ethnic identification as a social formation, fueled by immigrant encounters with other ethnics rather than by ancestral endowment. Only when immigrants came into contact with Americans and other ethnic groups did they develop a retrospective sense of ethnic difference.[55]

Kallen's desire to position cultural identification as an alternative to both race and nation is signaled in the phrase he chose to identify his position—*cultural pluralism*—and in the title of his book—*Culture and Democracy*. Both suggest that cultural difference became for Kallen the alternative axis of difference to those of race and nation. To be sure, notions of descent were never fully vanquished, but for the most part, Kallen invoked the language of ethnic difference to underscore the social basis of immigrant difference, which cannot be captured adequately through existing languages of race or nation.

For Kallen, Jews became the quintessential ethnics precisely because they had no shared nationality to anchor their group identity, yet they continued to cohere as a group:

> They [the Jews] do not come to the United States from truly native lands, lands of their proper *natio* and culture. They come from lands of sojourn, where they have been for ages treated as foreigners, at most as semi-citizens, subject to disabilities and persecutions.[56]

In the absence of any strong national identification, Kallen continued, Jewish immigrants did not simply assimilate into the dominant population, but anchored their sense of community and collective identity by other means. Thus, Kallen noted that "the Jewish quarter in New York city" is "far more autonomous in spirit and self-conscious in culture" than other immigrant groups.[57] Jews became for Kallen the model ethnics, their "unity" not simply a product of ancestral endowment but rooted in their shared beliefs and ideals. Whenever Kallen used the term *ethnicity*, he usually did so to de-link culture and heredity. To be sure, the distinction was not always cleanly drawn, but there was a constant thread positioning ethnic difference against race—whether Black or white.

Are Jews a Race? Kroeber and Fishberg on Ethnicity and Race

Kallen was not alone in defining ethnicity against race; indeed, almost all the early ethnicity theorists made a similar move when trying to specify the nature of ethnic identification. If anything, many of Kallen's contemporaries addressed the relationship between race and ethnicity more directly when they posed the question of whether Jews were a race. As we have seen in chapter 2, this question had been debated for some time, at least since the 1898 publication of William Ripley's essays on the question in *Popular Science Monthly*. These same questions resurfaced in the *Menorah Journal* when Alfred Kroeber, Maurice Fishberg, and others tried to specify the racial location of the Jews and, in so doing, revealed how the emerging category of ethnicity was founded on maintaining the distinction between race and immigrant difference.[58] By looking more closely at how Kroeber and Fishberg deployed the terms of race and ethnicity in their *Menorah Journal* essays, we see how they, too, continually fixed race in order to unfix ethnicity. But, unlike Kallen, both Kroeber and Fishberg addressed the racial status of the Jews directly in order to spell out what they took to be the differences between the two.

Unlike many other early ethnicity theorists, Kroeber was neither an immigrant nor a Jew. He was born in 1876 in Hoboken, New Jersey, moved to Manhattan at an early age, and lived at Madison and 78th and then at 316 West 89th. Although born in the United States, his childhood was immersed in German immigrant culture. His father's first language was German, his mother was bilingual, they spoke German at home, and Kroeber was home-schooled by a German tutor until the age of seven. Kroeber thus grew up within a late nineteenth-century German-American community in which there was, as yet, little or no distinction drawn between German Jews and German gentiles. That division gained saliency only with the outbreak of World War I. His maternal grandparents were Protestant and Catholic, and he was baptized a Lutheran. His mother joined "Ethical Culture," where Felix Adler, an agnostic rabbi, led a part-gentile congregation.[59]

In 1892, at the age of sixteen, Kroeber entered Columbia University, where he studied with Franz Boas and went on to become Boas's first PhD student. Upon finishing his dissertation in 1901, Kroeber moved to San Francisco to join the Berkeley anthropology department; he remained at

Berkeley from 1901 through 1946. In addition, he directed the anthropological museum there from 1925 to 1946. According to Clifford Geertz, Kroeber was one of the last anthropologists to cover the discipline's four fields by conducting original research in physical, archaeological, linguistic, and social/cultural anthropology. He carried out his fieldwork primarily in the American Southwest, Mexico, and Peru.[60] Although his *Menorah Journal* essay lay outside his principal research areas, he adopted a classic Boasian analysis of the *in*consequential link between race and culture, which he used to secure Jewish particularity as a different kind of social solidarity from that of race.

Kroeber's essay "Are the Jews a Race?" opened with an explicit discussion of what he considered race to be:

> All members of a race are born with certain common features and traits which they cannot lose. Nor can the race become divested, except in small degrees and after lapse of ages, of its special qualities. It may dilute and wash itself out by intermixture with other races. It can be supplanted by a new and higher type. But for all practical purposes, it is unalterable. Only as the geologist reckons time does race alter.
>
> It is among those rare things in the world which may be broken and destroyed, but which cannot be bent.[61]

Right from the outset, Kroeber presented race as something "unalterable," as something enduring and unbending. Or, as he put it a little later in the essay:

> Heredity is the great conservative factor, the forever steadying fly-wheel of race. And if heredity means anything, it means permanence, repetition of the same, generation after generation.
>
> What is individual in us may therefore be distinctive; but what we owe to race is inevitable, fixed before our birth, and ineradicable. What human minds acquire, they receive from education, from environment. What human minds inherit from their race is instinctive and unalterable. The leopard cannot change his spots.[62]

It is important to note that this view of race as permanent and unchanging marks a quite dramatic change from Lamarckian conceptions of race examined in chapter 2, where the heritability of acquired characteristics assumed a quite plastic notion of race as changing along with environmental conditions. The incessant effort to fix race evident in many of these early ethnicity essays speaks to the difficult task of positioning ethnic difference against a moving target, namely, the changing conceptions of race. Remember, this is when notions of race were also shifting along with the changing views of heredity—hence the early ethnicity theorists' anxious efforts to fix race.

Kroeber ended his discussion of race by asking, "By these tests, are the Jews a race?" At first glance, Kroeber's analysis appears somewhat perplexing since he began his essay by carefully specifying the racial location of Jews, only to go on in the remainder of the essay to argue that Jews were not a race. What are we to make of these apparently contradictory arguments? Why and in what ways were Jews simultaneously raced and not raced for Kroeber? It is worth looking carefully here as Kroeber provided an extended discussion of the proximate yet distinct relationship between ethnicity and race. At the outset, Kroeber took care to specify the racial status of the Jews:

> Physically, as judged by measurements and anatomical examination, the ancient Jews and their modern descendants in the Orient were one in all essentials, with Phoenicians, Arabs, Syrians, Egyptians—yes, even with Greeks, Italians, and Spaniards. Even today, physical anthropology recognizes only one racial type among all the nations that fringe the shores of the Mediterranean Sea.[63]

However, Kroeber quickly went on to specify that "the expert in the field of comparative human anatomy does not speak of an Italian race, nor an Egyptian race, nor a Spanish race, nor an Arab, nor a Moroccan, nor a Jewish race. To him all these nationalities together form only a single unit, the Mediterranean race, one of the main branches of the Caucasian stock."[64] Experts, Kroeber made clear, no longer conflate race and nation and then went on to ask how this shift in social categories effected the social location of Jews.

Early in the essay, Kroeber stipulated that Jews are members of the Mediterranean race, itself a subset of Caucasians, but as the essay progresses, it becomes clear that this racial classification is of little consequence since it cannot explain what makes Jews Jews because it does not distinguish Jews from all the other groups along the shores of the Mediterranean Sea. Race becomes a set of background conditions that have little bearing on his immediate intellectual preoccupation, namely, how to understand and sustain *Jewish* solidarity in the United States. Addressing questions of Jewish particularity required a different set of arguments, all of which began from the assumption that whatever it was that made Jews cohere as a group, it was not their race. The remainder of the essay shifted the focus from racial classification to Jewish identity per se; here Kroeber argued forcefully against the importance of Jews being considered a race.

To establish that Jewish identity ought *not* be defined in terms of race, Kroeber asked, "Is the Jew a recognizable type the world over?" And answered: "If the Jew were everywhere the same, if he formed, physically, a true race, then the Polish Jew should be long-headed like his fellow Jew of Africa. But the Polish Jew resembles, instead, the Polish Gentile, and is short-headed!"[65] Kroeber speculated briefly on the cause of the national variability of Jews and suggested that it might be due to either environment or intermarriage, and concluded that "in any event, whatever the cause, the fact remains that throughout the civilized world the Jew, *in his body*, is essentially the same with the Gentile of the same country."[66] The reasons for the variation was of little interest to Kroeber; what mattered was the fact that the Jewish body varied across nations. Variation in itself was taken as evidence that Jews were not a race, which was presumed to manifest itself in stability of type over time and place. Malleability and change were thought to signal collective identifications that must be of a nonracial kind.

There is no logical necessity to Kroeber's account; he might have embarked on a more direct attack on the coherence of racial classification of all types. Others did so in these same decades. But this is not the line of argument that Kroeber pursued. Instead, he limited his critique of race to its insufficiency as a descriptor for Jews while leaving racial classification of other kinds unchallenged.[67]

Kroeber concluded the essay asking, "If, then, the Jew is not a race, what is he?" His answer, much like Kallen's before him, looked to the social basis of Jewish identification as a counterpoint to race and nation:

> If, then, the Jew is not a race, what is he? For over two thousand years he has not formed a nation in the political sense. For nearly as long he has not been a geographical unit. For the same period he has not even possessed the unifying bond of a common language, except for ritual purposes. Only one thing is common to Jews of the past and present and to all Jews of today—their faith.
>
> The Jew, then, is a group, a caste, in the better sense of the word, held together by religion. Hence the emphasis is justified which the Jew always has laid and still lays on his faith. . . . Their future as Jews, therefore, is clearly and indissolubly bound up with Jewish belief and worship; but their future as human beings is in no sense limited or predestined by any bonds or race, but lies in themselves as individual men, and in their ideals and character.[68]

For Kroeber, Jewish people were a distinct social formation, a collectivity bound by religious faith. Being Jewish, for Kroeber, was different from other collectivities rooted in race and nation. Unlike Kallen, he did not as yet articulate this social solidarity in terms of ethnicity; he did not generalize in this essay from Jews to ethnicity per se. Nevertheless, the opposition between the social basis of Jewish particularity and the hereditary differences of race and nation was clear. Kroeber, like Kallen, fixed race to unfix ethnicity. Jews, Kroeber claimed, are "in no sense limited or predestined by" race. Being Jewish, for both Kroeber and Kallen, was a cultural and social phenomenon that cannot be captured adequately by reference to heredity and racial difference.

A better sense of the distinctive conception of ethnicity being advanced by Kallen and Kroeber is seen when contrasted with Franz Boas's views in these same decades. Boas, too, was trying to think through the difference between immigrant groups and races; he published several papers on the subject in 1911, 1912, and 1913. Moreover, Boas was commissioned to explore the racial status of immigrant groups at length by the Dillingham Commission and authored one of the forty-two volumes in the Commission's final report. Indeed, this was a subject to which Boas returned throughout his career. Unlike Kallen and Kroeber, Boas did not invoke the "fly-wheel" of race to construct ethnicity; rather, he set about contesting the cultural and political significance of race for *both* immigrants *and* African Americans. The general thrust of his argument was to insist on the "instability of human types" and the insignificance of race as a determinant of cultural and mental faculties for all groups. The contrast with Kroeber and Kallen is instructive; it highlights how readily the early ethnicity theorists invoked biologized conceptions of race to construct ethnicity.[69]

Kroeber was not the only one to contemplate the racial status of Jews. As we have seen in chapter 2, many were interested in figuring out whether Jews were a race and, if they were not, what sort of social solidarity they entailed. Interestingly, several key figures from the debates over heredity discussed in chapter 2 reappear in the pages of the *Menorah Journal* debating the racial status of Jews. Maurice Fishberg, for example, was one of the key participants in the extended social science discussions of Jews and race; both his *Popular Science Monthly* essays and his extensive monograph, *The Jews: A Study of Race and Environment* (1910), had established him as an expert on the racial status of the Jews.[70] In 1920, he published an essay in the *Menorah Journal* entitled "Assimilation: A Statement of Facts by a Scientist." The *Journal* editors heralded Fishberg's contribution as the "first discussion . . . after a silence of eight years" from this noted "authority on the anthropology and pathology of the Jews."[71]

After laying claim to his professional authority as a "scientist," Fishberg undertook an explicit discussion of the racial status of Jews. There was no doubt for Fishberg that the Jews were themselves "whites" and, as a consequence, had no trouble "assimilating with their fellow-men of other faiths," unlike "Negroes" whom "cannot be rendered white merely by speaking English, becoming Christians etc." According to Fishberg, Jews could assimilate into the "white population" as the old barriers to assimilation, especially the Sabbath and dietary laws, no longer maintained sufficient degrees of "social separation."[72]

Although Fishberg explicitly located Jews as white, he nevertheless distinguished ethnicity from race, but he did so rather differently from Kallen and Kroeber. The constitutive distinction comes into focus when we look at the principal anxiety that fueled the essay, namely, the rapid rate of Jewish assimilation: indeed, the object of the essay was to find some means of avoiding what Fishberg saw as the "threatening extinction of the Jew." Fishberg's conclusion linked this anxiety with ethnic difference:

> The Jews who have given thoughtful consideration to this matter have finally recognized that assimilation is more dangerous to the Sons of Jacob than persecution. They realize that under present conditions, when the Jews assimilate linguistically and socially, and wipe away the differences which have existed between them and the non-Jews among whom they live, it is becoming almost impossible to remain within the fold as a minority.[73]

Racial assimilation, for Fishberg, was tantamount to extinction. If Jews continued to identify as "white," as Fishberg claimed they had been doing at alarming rates, then they would cease to exist. Ethnic particularity and their distinctive group identity could be sustained, Fishberg argued, only if Jews found an alternative point of identification to that of race.

Fishberg's ultimate question—in some sense, the whole point to his essay—was to figure out how to avoid the current high rates of assimilation by specifying just such an alternative identification for Jews to embrace.

> We have seen above that in fact only strict adherence to the tenets of the faith keeps the Jew within the pale, and that the least deviation is likely to prove disastrous. But we have also pointed to the fact that under modern industrial conditions it is economically difficult, if not impossible, to keep the Sabbath. It is also economically costly, and socially difficult, to adhere

to the dietary laws. These separatist tenets of Judaism disregarded, assimilation and especially intermarriage is inevitable.[74]

In conclusion, Fishberg stated that "the outlook for Jewry in Europe and America is not very bright." What was to be done to halt the devastating effects of assimilation if religious practices and faith could not suffice? The final paragraphs of the essay, which no doubt were the impetus for submitting it to the *Menorah Journal*, offered the hope that Zionism might provide the critical opportunity for preserving Judaism as a bulwark against assimilation.

In sum, race and ethnicity were twinned differently for Kroeber and Fishberg than they were for Kallen. Kroeber and Fishberg engaged the racial location of Jews directly rather than simply positioning race as a boundary condition of ethnicity, as Kallen did when tied race to the colonial era and the South. But even as Kroeber and Fishberg racialized Jews, they continued to distinguish ethnicity from race, albeit in slightly different terms. For Kroeber, Jews were members of the Mediterranean race, but this tells us nothing whatsoever about what makes them Jews; to understand Jewish particularity, we must look beyond the notion of race. Similarly, while Fishberg expressly declared Jews to be "white," as long as race remains the principal point of identification, their very existence as Jews cannot be sustained. Only by providing alternative grounds of identification, perhaps through Palestine, is there any prospect for sustaining their identity as a distinct ethnic group. Thus, at the very moment Fishberg located Jews in terms of race, their Jewish particularity began to erode.

Even though Kroeber and Fishberg engaged race overtly and at length, the constitutive opposition between race and ethnicity can be seen at work. The two categories and their respective identifications were used repeatedly by the authors to position one against the other. For all three writers, if one is raced, then one is not an ethnic. Conversely, if one is an ethnic, then one's racial identification recedes. There is a constitutive distinction between the two terms that was not the product of logical necessity since the two terms have had a quite different relation to each other in other times and places. Rather, beginning in the 1910s and 1920s, we can see the race-ethnicity distinction being socially constructed by key figures within the New York Zionist movement.

"The Great War" and Ethnic Identification

The Great War both fueled and challenged the emergence of ethnicity as a new social category. Isaac Berkson, Julius Drachsler, and Horace Kallen all published monographs and essays in the early 1920s that explicitly used the language of ethnic difference in defense of immigrant cultures as essential to American democracy.[75] The specter of war hung over all of these writings, having made apparent the horrific consequences of nationalism both at home and abroad. Not only had national rivalries fueled the war itself, they had also provoked an intense American nationalism at home—a nationalism that was threatening the very existence of ethnic groups, and as such, these early ethnicity theorists claimed, was endangering the health of American democracy.[76] Although all three authors continued to position ethnic difference as social, malleable, and plural, the counterpoint of homogeneity and fixity shifted somewhat from that of race to nation. Or, to be more specific, race in terms of slavery and its legacies faded while discussions of nationality were moved center stage, linked to heredity, and positioned as the principal opposition to ethnicity. Indeed, much of the time race and nation were simply conflated, tied together through the language of inheritance. Although the terms of race and nation changed, the constitutive distinction with ethnicity remained; ethnicity was still positioned as cultural and mobile in contrast to race and nation, which were repeatedly presented as enduring and homogenous, fixed by heredity.[77]

Berkson is a particularly interesting figure for my purposes since he went further than any of the *Menorah* writers in unhinging ethnicity from race and nation through his "community theory" of ethnic groups. Moreover, he explicitly critiqued Kallen's claim that whatever else we change, we cannot change our grandfathers. In place of Kallen's lingering essentialism, Berkson offered a theory of ethnic difference rooted in "community" and "culture" as opposed to descent:

> The community theory insists on the value of the ethnic group as a permanent asset in American life. It differs from the "Americanization" and "melting pot" theories in that it refuses to set up as an ideal such a fusion as will lead to the wiping out of all ethnic distinctions. Furthermore, it regards a rich social life as necessary for the development of the culture of the foreign group. In the "federation of nationalities" theory, which is pivoted on the identity of race, the argument is primarily that "we cannot change our grandfathers." The community theory, on the other hand, makes the history of the group, its esthetic, cultural, and religious inheritance, its national self-consciousness, the basic factor. *The change of emphasis from race to culture* brings with it a whole series of implications, arising from the fact that culture is not inherited but must be acquired through some educational process. The difference is crucial. A community

of culture possible of demonstration becomes the ground for perpetuating the group, rather than an identity of race, questionable in fact and dubious in significance.[78]

Note the associative chains created here between "ethnic distinction," "culture," and "history," on the one hand, and "fusion," "inheritance," and "race," on the other. Inheritance becomes the means of linking race and nation in opposition to the cultural and historical production of ethnicity.

Once ethnicity was unhinged from descent, Berkson argued, it provided a much-needed means of reworking American nationalism and its associated policies of Americanization. Rather than perpetuating notions of "tribal" nationalism, ethnicity would drive home the "multiple cultural allegiances" embedded within the American nation and, as such, would lead "to an emphasis upon the international elements in each nation" rather than to "national separation" and "provinciality."[79] "International ties" promote an "international vision" in which we can gain much needed "perspective" that might even prevent war.

> A double allegiance, it should be noted, is something other than twice a single allegiance. The knowledge of an additional language and culture means not only a personality richer by so much. It means rather what an additional dimension does in spatial relations; it gives perspective. It opens the mind to a new concept—there are other nations than one's own. The change of view is of significance not only for the additional nationality for which the interest is aroused, but for the whole mental outlook. It prevents the mind from falling into the natural tendency of imagining that one's own culture is the only culture worthy of the name, and one's own countrymen the only real humans. Interest in another nationality must go far toward giving one an international, as opposed to a provincial, outlook. Differences are seen more readily in their proper proportion; it is understood that humanity can speak in other languages, express itself in other arts, exist in other physiognomies.[80]

Here Berkson provided as elegant an account of twentieth-century notions of ethnic pluralism as I have seen, in which subnational identifications are seen as generative of a desirable democratic political disposition.

Having declared ethnicity to be a social formation, Berkson, like Fishberg, was well aware that relinquishing claims to ancestry and descent brought with it a set of vulnerabilities. The break with heredity meant that the survival of the ethnic groups was no longer guaranteed, and Jews

came face-to-face with the prospect of, to use Berkson's terms, "disinte-
gration" and "extinction."

> The danger of disintegration is undoubtedly real, especially if there is
> more than a formal religious adherence in mind. To some thinkers the
> fate of the Jews in democratic countries, wherever they form a minority
> of the population (and they do so practically everywhere), is inevitable
> extinction.[81]

Ethnic groups, for Berkson, were not self-reproducing but had to be sustained politically through cultural institutions whose task was to actively
cultivate a sense of group identity. Educational institutions, Berkson argued, were especially important to this process of group renewal. Interestingly, Berkson spent his entire professional life in just such an institution
when working as executive director of the Central Jewish Institute in New
York and as supervisor of schools and extension activities of the Bureau of
Jewish Education.[82]

It is worth returning to Kallen, where we can see with particular clarity the repositioning of nationality in the wake of the war by comparing
his 1915 essay with *Culture and Democracy*, published in 1924. The book
was actually a compilation of essays written between 1914 and 1923 and
included, unchanged, his 1915 essay. Kallen specified that two of the chapters had been written in 1923: "the postscript—to be read first," which
was entitled "Culture and the Ku Klux Klan," and chapter 3 on "'Americanization'—and the Cultural Prospect." Neither of these, in contrast
with the 1915 essay, framed questions of immigrant difference against
the racial formations of the colonial era and the South; now the impact of
the Great War moved center stage, bringing with it the dangers of nationalism at home and abroad. The war, Kallen argued, displaced existing divisions of class and property as the central dynamics of American politics
and replaced it with the growing nativism of the American-born. Kallen
declared that "towards the end of the first decades of the century,"

> [e]thnic contrasts began to be made, cultural comparisons, sociological
> special pleas. Before these beginnings could run their course in public dis-
> cussion, generating their appropriate anti-bodies of argument in the blood
> of public opinion and terminating without danger to the health of the
> body-politic, the Great War came up, dividing the land, intensifying and
> focalizing passions, and finally, with America's entry therein, converting
> this whole, relatively smooth, slow process of change into a thing rapid,
> sudden, explosive and—dangerous.[83]

The war, according to Kallen, heightened tensions over recent immigra-tion and "transformed . . . the growing uneasiness of the native-born . . . from an unconsciousness strain into a conscious repulsion." The shift in political climate at home made it all the more important to defend im-migrant difference against the onslaught of nativist sentiment and policies, a defense that Kallen attempted through his calls for "cultural pluralism."[84]

Having centered the war and questions of nationality, what happened to questions of race? What role, if any, was left in Kallen's pluralism for redressing the long-standing legacy of slavery? The short answer is very little—references to slavery and race virtually disappear. Throughout the book, Kallen referred to the Civil War and the "negro" on only one or two occasions and generally cast the entire discussion in terms of "wealth and power," not slavery. Kallen reduced the Civil War to class-based politics in which the central conflict hinges on question of property. This older politics, Kallen then went on to declare, was being displaced by ethnic and national divisions:

> Only with respect to the Negro was there a steady and cumulative an-tagonism, and that is due as much, perhaps, to the negro's having been property and to the holding over of the traditional attitude toward private property in private feeling and public policy.[85]

Slavery was equated with class politics and then set aside as a thing of the past. There was no room in this account for thinking of the endur-ing power of racial inequality as a cornerstone of American political and social life.

Kallen's postscript on the Klan is especially interesting precisely for the ways in which it reworked race and nation, for the ways in which Kallen showed how racial hatred has morphed into nativism against the foreign-born:

> The Klan, indeed, is the concretion, sublimate, and gratification of the passions in play since the coming of the Great War. . . . Its membership is recruited from every class and every station in the United States that con-siders itself "native, white and Protestant." Its animating hate extends to everything that, like Jew, Catholic or negro, is a variant from this type by traditional opinion, or that, like views of minorities upon religion, politics, economics, manners or morals, is a variant from the conventional type by recorded utterance or act.[86]

Note how Kallen blended notions of race and nation. Nationalism became the means of "fusing the anarchic diversity of these many objects of hatred into a single hieroglyph to be described as 'seeking in an insidious but powerful manner to undermine the fundamentals of the Nation.'"[87] Reference to Negroes, whites, and Anglo-Saxons were gone, replaced by racialized accounts of nationality and nativism, which Kallen presented as the antithesis of his cultural pluralism. Thus, even as nationality was racialized in the wake of war, the nonracial conception of ethnicity was maintained.

Ethnic Politics in a Racial Polity

If ethnic groups are not to be considered races, as many Zionists and cultural pluralists argued, then where did this leave them politically? How were ethnics positioned in terms of race politics? In many ways, the remainder of the book explores this question, especially chapter 6, but I want to prefigure the political possibilities and limitations of ethnic identification via Kallen's relationship with the noted African American scholar Alain Locke. The two first met at Harvard, went on to Oxford the same year, and stayed in touch in subsequent decades while both were living in New York. Their friendship allows us to glimpse the dynamics of ethnic politics in microcosm.

In a 1972–73 interview with Sarah Schmidt, Kallen recounted that he coined the term *cultural pluralism* in 1906 out of discussions with Locke when he was Locke's section leader at Harvard.[88]

> It was in 1906 that I began to formulate the notion of cultural pluralism, and I had to do that in connection with my teaching. I was assisting both Mr. [William] James and Mr. [George] Santayana, and I had a Negro student named Alain Locke, a very remarkable young man, intelligent, poetic, very sensitive, who insisted that he was a human being and that his color ought not to make any difference. So we had to argue out the question of how the differences did make differences, and in arguing out those questions the formulae, the phrases developed—"cultural pluralism," "the right to be different."[89]

Kallen and Locke maintained a significant relationship in the ensuing decades; they were both at Oxford in 1907–8, and Locke contributed essays both to a volume edited by Kallen and Sidney Hook in 1935, and to a Festschrift honoring Kallen on his sixty-fifth birthday (1947). There is much evidence of interaction between the two in New York over the decades.[90]

After graduating from Harvard, Locke became the first African American Rhodes scholar. He went off to Oxford in 1907, only to find that other American Rhodes scholars from the South refused to invite him to the traditional Thanksgiving dinner held at the American Club in Oxford. Kallen, in support of Locke, refused to attend the dinner and wrote to Barrett Wendell, Locke's English professor at Harvard, to ask him to intervene with the other Rhodes scholars on Locke's behalf. Wendell refused to do so. Sollors went back to the Kallen/Wendell correspondence and found Kallen's letters to be filled with racist language: at one point Kallen referred to Locke as "Little Locke, the yellow boy who took English 42"; at another, Kallen stated explicitly: "As you know, I have neither respect nor liking for his race—but individually they have to be taken, each on his own merits and value, and if ever a negro was worthy this boy is."[91] What are we to make of these remarks? How should we read them? In what sense are they indicative of Kallen's views on race?

Sollors, it seems to me, made the wrong move when reflecting on this correspondence when he suggested that Kallen's letters to Wendell provided the smoking gun for finally identifying Kallen's racial prejudice. Sollors used the letters to explain Kallen's supposed silence on race and to question his pluralist commitments. I think that this is the wrong question to ask, whether Kallen was a racist; it is the wrong question on two grounds. First, it frames the issue of racism too narrowly as an individual matter—as a question of whether Kallen was racially prejudiced—and in so doing diminishes the larger cultural processes at work. Second, it continues to pose too stark a choice in which we must view ethnicity in either/or terms—as either fully emancipatory or in fact repressive and exclusionary. I want to resist the temptation to resolve the ambiguity that resides at the heart of ethnic identification and to acknowledge instead the simultaneity of its emancipatory and exclusionary aspects.

For me, the Oxford incident captured this ambiguity at the heart of ethnic identification and politics perfectly. It is certainly true that Kallen's correspondence was stunning and underscored his failure to fully embrace racial equality. Yet, it is also the case that Kallen did intervene on Locke's behalf; he did boycott the dinner so that he could stand with Locke. But it is also the case that Kallen could defend Locke only on the basis of individual merit rather than as a fully entitled member of his pluralist polity. Locke got included, but never on equal terms. After the Thanksgiving incident, Kallen organized a series of afternoon teas through which Locke was to be introduced to fellow students, but the efforts at integration were always partial at best. Thus, we see Kallen negotiating the contradictory impulses of pluralism and exclusion that I have suggested reside at the core of cultural pluralism.

Kallen could never fully engage questions of racial inequality; never fully embrace Locke as an equal, precisely because of his intense personal investment in ethnic identification that grounded both his political and intellectual work throughout his life. Kallen's ethnicity, I have tried to show, was constructed against race when he strove to fix race in order to unfix ethnicity. This specification of ethnicity as different from race made it difficult for Kallen to support Locke in anything but an ambivalent fashion, because doing so called into question the very distinction that secured his own identity as an ethnic. The Kallen-Locke relation thus captured in microcosm the tensions that pervade much ethnic and racial politics in the United States on a larger scale.

Kallen's deep investment in the race and ethnicity distinction—in ethnicity as a different kind of difference to that of race—helps explain why cultural pluralists and cultural anthropologists never really engaged intellectually or politically with each other. The disjunction between the two was signaled early on by the lack of intellectual engagement between Kallen and Boas. Even though both wrote extensively on immigrant difference, their projects were never aligned. The disconnect is even more telling given the clear evidence that they knew each other and each other's work. The lack of engagement stemmed, I believe, from their very different conceptions of ethnic and racial difference.

Even a cursory glance at Kallen's life and work suggests that he certainly knew of Boas's intellectual project critiquing biological notions of race in these same decades. Kallen referred explicitly to Boas in *Culture and Democracy*, and Randolph Bourne, a fellow pluralist, was a student of Boas's at Columbia, while Edward Sapir and Alfred Kroeber both contributed to the *Menorah Journal* that Kallen had helped to establish as the Menorah Association's principal publication. Finally, Kallen was a panelist in an NAACP forum on "Africa and World Democracy" held in Carnegie Hall on January 6, 1919. Sitting on the panel alongside Kallen were James Weldon Johnson, then field secretary of the NAACP, and W. E. B. Du Bois. The forum was subsequently published under the auspices of the NAACP.[92] It seems clear that Kallen was aware of the arguments being advanced in anthropology and elsewhere against biologized notions of race and yet made little or no effort to address, or connect, these concerns to his own work. Kallen's hereditary notion of race seems all the more deliberate and purposeful, rather than an act of casual omission.

Cultural pluralists were never willing to really deconstruct race as a category, but rather used it to anchor ethnicity, while the cultural anthropologists, especially Boas and his students, made deconstruction of the category of race their central intellectual problematic. Thus, while both groups engaged parallel issues concerning the nature, extent, and tolerance of difference in the United States, they ultimately talked past each other because of their very different views of race. After all, if one is an ethnic in the United States because one is not raced, because one's difference is *not* figured in racial terms, then deconstructing the category of race also calls into question the category of ethnicity. The early ethnicity theorists' acceptance of racial difference—indeed, their efforts to reify the category as a contrast to ethnicity—made it difficult to challenge the color line without simultaneously undermining ethnicity as well. Most of those identifying as ethnics found the price too high and opted instead for a defense of greater tolerance and plurality in American culture and politics in a form that reinscribed rather than contested biologized views of race.

Are Jews a Race? Are Mexicans White? 4
The State and Ethnicity

In the 1910s and 1920s when New York Zionists and cultural pluralists began referring with some regularity to ethnic groups and loyalties, they were, as yet, a minor voice within American culture and politics. Although men such as Louis Brandeis, Horace Kallen, Isaac Berkson, and Julius Drachsler clearly began to articulate the parameters of ethnicity, they were by no means the only ones to craft the new category. We need to look beyond the pages of the *Menorah Journal* to see when and how the term *ethnic* garnered more general acceptance and authority in society at large.

There is, however, no single moment or one location of discursive codification; the term *ethnic* gained traction slowly on many fronts. Certainly, social relations and cultural practices within immigrant communities were key; ethnic particularity was embodied quite literally on the streets in New York. The work of Deborah Dash Moore, Hasia Diner, and Arthur Goren has paved the way here by documenting the social relations and cultural practices of New York Jewish life. In addition, we have seen how Jewish particularity was sustained by the creation of new institutional forms; the Bureau of Jewish Education where Berkson worked is a classic case in point, as were the creation of Hebrew schools and Jewish advocacy groups, both of which gave definition and structure to collective identities in ways that helped Jewish particularity to endure.[1]

Although I have no doubt that changes in prevailing social practices and the emergence of ethnic institutions were critical for ethnicity to take hold, I want to consider the role of the state in category formation. My point is not that the state initiated or controlled the emergence of ethnicity; in fact, the state frequently followed discursive shifts initiated elsewhere. Nevertheless, state policy provides a wonderful vehicle for tracking the process of category formation because of the elaborate paper trail that usually accompanies state action. By examining categories used on bureaucratic forms, in statutory provisions, in congressional testimony, and in executive orders, we can begin to reconstruct the politics that surrounded state codification of ethnicity. To this end, this chapter considers two different policy domains in which issues of ethnic and racial classification came to the fore. I look first to Census Bureau classification of Progressive-era immigrants, and then turn to imperial expansion and the dilemmas of racial classification on the Mexican border.

Although I consider census categories and border politics to have played formative roles in establishing the parameters of ethnicity, I do *not* consider either of these policy domains to provide the originary moment of category formation. Indeed, I have come to think of a quest for origins as an impossible task. No single origin story, no one executive order, no one statute or court case secured ethnicity as a new category within state policy and administrative practice. If one were to shift the focus to other bureaucracies or related policy domains, other venues for mapping the emergence of ethnicity would quickly emerge. The Immigration and Naturalization Service (INS), Ellis Island, or the Border Patrol were equally implicated in the changes I trace here.[2] The two policy domains discussed below nevertheless illustrate the forces in play. In both locations, the state not only legitimated ethnicity as a legal category, but did so in ways that repeatedly sought to establish a distinction between ethnicity and race. How this relationship is cast, how ethnicity is positioned in relation to race, continues to beset federal policy and racial politics to this day.

Ethnicity and the Census

Ever since the very first census in 1790, the American state has counted and classified by race. Even though racism has been a constant force in American society and politics, the *form* that racism has taken varies from one era to the next. Racism is a constant, but the content and boundary conditions of the term *race* are not. Key shifts in the meaning of race can be seen in questions asked on decennial census forms. Numerous scholars have examined the changing racial classifications and, in so doing, have noted the enumeration of mulattos, quadroons, and octoroons in 1850–70, 1890, and 1910–20; the varied inclusion of nationalities as races; the shift from enumerator to self-identification in 1970; and, most recently, the introduction of a multiple race check-off in 2000.[3] Although more attention needs to be paid to nineteenth-century shifts in the race question from slave, through color, to race—we should not simply assume that these different terms carried the same meaning—nevertheless, there is a sense in which a race question of one form or another has been on every census since 1790.

In contrast, census scholars have paid much less attention to ethnicity. What I want to consider here is the precise ways in which the census responded to changes in immigration flows. What categories did the census use to classify immigrants? How did the census classify immigrants in terms of race? When did the census adopt the language of ethnicity? I am certainly not the first to consider such questions. Reynolds Farley, Ira Rosenwaike, and others have written on related matters for some time. For the most part, however, issues of "nativity," as they were known, have been considered separately from race, as distinct aspects of census classification. I want to consider ethnicity and race together so that I can attend to the quite particular ways in which the Census Bureau conceptualized the boundary between the two. In short, how, when, and why did the census distinguish ethnicity from race and nation?[4]

Looking back over two hundred years of census questions, I have been struck by the responsiveness of the census to prevailing social and political conditions, whether it be recognition of the Fifteenth Amendment in 1870 or attention to work and unemployment during the 1930 census. The issue of immigration is no exception; we see that census questions changed quickly in an effort to track the ebb and flow of immigration. As early as 1820, the census began to count the number of "foreigners not naturalized," and by 1850 had introduced a question on "place of birth," no doubt in response to the great wave of Irish and German immigration at midcentury. By 1870, the census added a question as to whether the respondent's "father or mother were of foreign birth," which enabled the Bureau to track second-generation immigrants who had themselves been born in the United States but whose parents were foreign-born. By 1900, the census introduced a general heading of "nativity," under which questions on place of birth were located, and one labeled "citizenship," which included questions on respondents' year of immigration to the United States and whether they had naturalized. Finally, under the heading of "education," respondents were asked whether they spoke English. Thus, as immigration increased in the decades bracketing 1900, census questions concerning immigrant status and characteristics proliferated.[5]

Much was at stake in these question changes because census categories played a critical role in shaping immigrant status in the United States. Mapping changes in the size and composition of the immigrant population was not simply an act of description; acts of classification also established the ground rules through which immigrants' interests and identities were formed. The census thus helped to *produce* the very identities it sought to record. The pressing question for many in the 1890s and early 1900s was how to distinguish, and thus monitor, the differential impact of what became known as the "old" from the "new" immigration. The first wave of immigrants at midcentury had come largely from western Europe, especially Germany and Ireland, while second-wave immigrants originated in southern and eastern Europe, principally from Italy, Russia, Romania, and Bohemia. This shift in immigration from west to south and east was seen by many as considerably more than a change in geographic origins. For men such as Henry Cabot Lodge, Madison Grant, Charles Davenport, Prescott Hall, and their allies in the Immigration Restriction League, southern and eastern European immigrants represented a threat to the racial composition and social cohesion of the nation and, as such, required more stringent immigration restrictions.[6] At a minimum, many agreed that the demographic changes under way had to be monitored carefully through a more fine-grained system of state classification.

The Census Bureau, and other government bureaucracies as well, had to decide how best to classify immigrant groups. What classificatory scheme ought to be used? Or more specifically for the Census Bureau, what questions ought to be added to capture the new social phenomena at hand? In 1850, the question about place of birth was sufficient for monitoring newly arriving immigrants, but by 1890 these same questions seemed increasingly inadequate. The problem lay in the growing disjunction between race and nation that accompanied conquest, war, and increasing immigration flows. Place of birth did not distinguish Russian Jews from other Russian immigrants, nor Bohemians from other immigrants from Austria, nor the Irish as a distinct subset of immigration from the United Kingdom. Many both inside and outside the Census Bureau wanted to fine-tune the classificatory scheme so as to enable the state to identify newly arriving immigrants by more than place of birth.

Given the enormous number of immigrants entering the United States in the last two decades of the nineteenth century, it is no surprise that the 1910 census in particular brought questions of immigrant classification to a head. Census takers, politicians, and relevant stakeholders argued over how best to track changes in immigration.[7] The U.S. Immigration Commission tried to shape the debate by constructing a comprehensive racial taxonomy for the Census Bureau to use in 1910. Joel Perlmann has already completed a masterful analysis of the Immigration Commission hearings in which he argues that the question on the table was whether racial classification could be effectively extended to new immigrants, especially Jews. While the Commission ultimately failed in its larger ambition to set the terms used within the federal statistical system, the Commission hearings, as Perlmann has shown, provide a fascinating glimpse into late nineteenth- and early twentieth-century views of race.[8] My own analysis operates through a slightly different lens. The Commission's extensive discussion of race also revealed key forces shaping the emergence of ethnicity as a distinct social category to that of race. Specifically, we see how the category of ethnicity helped to resolve the boundary problems inherent in racial classification in an age of mass migration. By resolving problem cases, the emerging category of ethnicity actually shored up racial classification during this period of massive population change. Specifically, we will see that the precursor to ethnic classification within the decennial census emerges from a political impasse between immigration restrictionists and Jewish advocates over where to set the boundaries of race and from within state classification of Mexican Americans in the Southwest.

Once again the racial status of Jews was front and center; how Jews were classified became the limiting case for establishing the boundaries of race. Many of the Commission hearings probed whether Jews were a separate race; if not, what was the basis of their group identity? And perhaps most importantly for the Commission, how should the state classify Jewish immigrants? Many scholars of Jewish immigration have focused on divisions within the Jewish community, especially between Zionists and reform Jews, but when considering the racial location of Jews, I have been struck by the remarkable unity among Zionists and reform Jews; both saw racial classification as a problem, both sought a way forward that would avoid racial classification and yet sustain Jewish particularity. Both wanted recognition of Jewish difference in nonracial terms. Jews' reluctance to be classified by race was at odds with the widely shared desire to monitor the demographic changes at hand. Solving this impasse, we will see, laid the groundwork for state recognition of ethnicity.

After much political debate, Zionists and reform Jews, as well as immigration restrictionists such as Henry Cabot Lodge, reached a political settlement in which language was accepted as the appropriate marker of Jewish difference. The Census Bureau introduced "mother tongue" as an additional form of immigrant classification to that of race. The mother tongue compromise thus provided a critical step toward state recognition of ethnicity as a distinct social category to that of race. The process of state codification of ethnicity was not completed for several decades, but struggles over census classification in 1910 reveals state policy in formation.

The U.S. Immigration Commission: Limiting Race, Codifying Ethnicity

The U.S. Immigration Commission was established on February 20, 1907, charged with making a "full inquiry, examination, and investigation by subcommittee, or otherwise, into the subject of immigration." The committee of nine was chaired by Senator William P. Dillingham (R-Vt.), included three senators (including the longtime immigration restrictionist Henry Cabot Lodge), three members from the House of Representatives, and three presidential appointees.[9] Senator Dillingham presented the Commission report to the Senate on December 5, 1910, and the forty-two-volume report was printed the following year. Much of the Commission's work focused on the economic status of immigrants via a detailed inventory of the impact of immigration on leading industrial sectors; volumes 6 through 25 went industry by industry documenting the deleterious impact of immigration on everything from meatpacking, through glass and leather manufacturing, to agriculture. Three volumes of the Commission report directly engaged questions of immigrant classification: volume 5 provided a *Dictionary of Races or Peoples*; volume 38 reported a study led by Franz Boas entitled *Changes in Bodily Form of Descendants of Immigrants* in which questions of stability of immigrant types was examined and found wanting; and volume 41 contained *Statements and Recommendations Submitted by Societies and Organizations Interested in the Subject of Immigration*, many of which focused on issues of immigrant classification.[10]

The Dillingham Commission in many ways made manifest the early twentieth-century preoccupation with the dramatic increases in immigration. Interestingly, no one testifying before the Commission questioned the importance of monitoring the impact of immigration; those who favored a more open immigration policy simply argued for a more positive evaluation of immigrant contributions, but did not protest the act of classification itself. The disagreement was not over whether to monitor, but over what system of *classification* ought to be used. Should the federal government record immigrants by nationality, language, religion, race, or some combination? Deciding which categories to employ was no easy task since the categories themselves were still in formation; especially uncertain was the boundary between race and nation. Before commissioners could decide whether to classify immigrants by race or nation, they first had to determine what they, and other stakeholders, understood these distinctions to entail. Were the Irish or the Jews a race, a geographic designation, or a political affiliation? Engaging such questions quickly brought participants face-to-face with the task of specifying what they understood a race to be. Inevitably, borderline cases became the locus of contention, and hence the question of the racial status of Jews once again took center stage. Whether or not the Immigration Commission was going to classify Jews as a race was seen by many as establishing the very parameters of race. Classification of the Jews became a litmus test for securing the boundaries of race.

Similar debates over the nature and limits of race had been in circulation in other venues for at least two decades, as we have seen in chapter 2. Academics had spent considerable time and energy arguing over the nature of race via extended discussions of the racial status of Jews, as had several contributors to the *Menorah Journal*. The Dillingham Commission raised these same questions in a different arena—now they were raised in the hallways of political power rather than in the pages of scholarly and popular journals. Although several key figures appear in all three venues, the spheres of influence of social science journals, the *Menorah* movement, and the Dillingham Commission were rather different. Because the Commission operated with the official imprimatur of the state, it carried a special authority, an authority that was further enhanced by the Commission's ambition to import its classificatory scheme into the 1910 census, thereby instantiating the Commission's taxonomy at the heart of the federal classificatory system.[11] Thus, much is at stake in the Commission's conception of immigration and race. Recapturing the political struggles it engendered enables us to see just how contested were the boundaries of race. More important for my purposes is the solution reached to negotiate this political debate—namely, the addition of language or "mother tongue," as it was known, to the census as an additional marker of group difference. The "mother tongue" compromise laid the groundwork for state classification by ethnicity. Later in the chapter we will see that similar issues were being negotiated in the Southwest over the racial status of Mexicans. For the Dillingham Commission, however, the focus was on how to classify immigrant Jews.

Classification Gone Wild:
The Dillingham Commission and Race

When reading volume 5 of the Commission's report, entitled *The Dictionary of Races or Peoples,* I was struck by the rather fantastical effort to classify all the peoples of the world. The volume is 150 pages long and contains 562 separate entries. To be sure, some of the entries refer to other headings, but even allowing for the rather extensive cross-referencing, the *Dictionary* provides a massive project of classification. Although impressive in many regards, the *Dictionary* was certainly neither an elegant nor a parsimonious document. Rather, its contribution, or authority, is garnered from its aspiration to completeness. Every imaginable grouping was given due consideration. But thoroughness and scope notwithstanding, the overall impression left by the *Dictionary* was a sense of confusion and a rather obsessive desire to map and master the demographic encounters around the world.

The frenetic aspect of the classificatory scheme under construction is seen in the numerous tables and maps placed throughout the volume. Consider, for example, the table entitled "Comparative Classification of Immigrant Races or Peoples,"[12] reproduced as figure 2, in which the *Dictionary* tried to square the classic nineteenth-century racial classificatory schemes of Brinton, Keane, and Ripley into a single frame. The effort was at once impressive and unworkable. Although all the pieces are accommodated, the end result was so complex, and key entries so contested, that it never gained currency.

The *Dictionary's* textual entries were even more complex than the tables and maps. The entry for "Hebrew, Jewish, or Israelite" is a perfect case in point; the *Dictionary* authoritatively located the Jews as a subgroup within the Caucasian race, but the definition never quite held. No sooner had Hebrews been classified than qualifications began to appear and the orderly classification started to unravel. The entry for Hebrew ran for two full pages and began with a discussion of Hebrews and language. It then moved on to declare:

> Physically the Hebrew is a mixed race, like all our immigrant races or peoples, although to a less degree than most. This has been fairly well demonstrated by recent studies, notwithstanding the earlier scientific and present popular belief that they are a pure blood.[13]

COMPARATIVE CLASSIFICATION OF IMMIGRANT RACES OR PEOPLES.

Based on Brinton (cf. Keane).			People.	Ripley's races, with other corresponding terms.
Race.	Stock.	Group.		

Caucasian-----	Aryan----	Teutonic-------	Scandinavian:
			  Danish----------------
			  Norwegian-----------
			  Swedish--------------
			German (N. part)--------
			Dutch--------------------
			English (part)-----------
				I. TEUTONIC
				
				H. Europæus (Lapouge).
				Nordic (Deniker).
				Dolicho-leptorhine (Kohlmann).
				Germanic (English writers).
				Reihengräber (German writers).
				Kymric (French writers).

		Lettic---------	Flemish---------------- Lithuanian--------------	
		Celtic---------	Scotch (part)------------ Irish (part)-------------- Welsh-------------------	Part Alpine.

		Slavonic-------	Russian-----------------
			Polish------------------
			Czech:
			  Bohemian------------
			  Moravian------------
			Servian------------------
			Croatian----------------
			Montenegrin------------
			Slovak------------------
			Slovenian---------------
			Ruthenian--------------
			Dalmatian--------------
			Herzegovinian----------
			Bosnian----------------
				II. ALPINE (OR CELTIC).
				
				H. Alpinus (Lapouge).
				Occidental (Deniker).
				Disentis (German writers).
				Celto-Slavic (French writers).
				Lappanoid (Pruner-Bey).
				Sarmatian (von Holder).
				Arvernian (Beddoe).

		Illyric--------- Armenic-------	Albanian---------------- Armenian---------------	
		Italic----------	French------------------ Italian (part)------------ Roumanian------------- Spanish----------------- Spanish-American------ Mexican, etc------------- Portuguese--------------	Part Alpine. Part Mediterranean. III. MEDITERRANEAN. H. Meridionalis (Lapouge). Atlanto-Mediterranean and Ibero-Insular (Deniker). Iberian (English writers). Ligurian (Italian writers).
		Hellenic------ Iranic---------	Greek------------------ Hindu------------------ Gypsy------------------	Part Mediterranean. Part Teutonic.
	Semitic---	Arabic--------- Chaldaic-------	Arabian---------------- Hebrew---------------- Syrian------------------	Part Mediterranean.
	Caucasic---------------- Euskaric----------------		Caucasus peoples-------- Basque------------------	Doubtful.
Mongolian----	Sibiric----	Finnic----------	Finnish---------------- Lappish----------------- Magyar---------------- Bulgarian (part)---------	
		Tataric-------- Japanese------ Mongolic------	Turkish, Cossack, etc----- Japanese, Korean-------- Kalmuk-----------------	
	Sinitic----	Chinese--------	Chinese---------------- East Indian (part, i.e., Indo-Chinese)------ Pacific Islander (part)---- East Indian (part)--------	
Malay-------			Negro------------------	
Ethiopian-----				
American---- (Indian)			American Indian--------	

Figure 2: "Comparative Classification of Immigrant Races or Peoples," from *Dictionary of Races or Peoples* (1911).

The *Dictionary* continued in classic late nineteenth-century fashion to discuss the persistence of the "Jewish nose" and other facial characteristics, and finally turned to the "social solidarity" of the Jews:

> The social solidarity of the Jews is chiefly a product of religion and tradition. Taking all factors into account, and especially their type of civilization, the Jews of today are more truly European than Asiatic or Semitic. The classification of the Bureau of Immigration separates the Hebrews from Semites and places them in the Slavic grand division of the Aryan family, although, as is explained above, they are not Aryan. Nine-tenths of the Jewish immigrants to the United States come, however, from Slavic territory.[14]

A bewildering entry. The *Dictionary* did little or nothing to clarify the racial status of the Jews. Notions of language, physical features, religion, and tradition were all offered up as grounds for Jewish solidarity, but it was precisely the relationship, or priority, to be awarded to each of these features that was being hotly debated by Jews and non-Jews alike. By including all of the competing definitions in its entry, the *Dictionary* evaded the political issue at hand, namely, whether the Jews were a race.

Although many colleagues have suggested that the *Dictionary* be taken as a definitive account of the racial status of the Jews circa 1910, I do not find this a useful way to read the text. Rather than settling matters, the *Dictionary* simply folded conflicting definitions into the entry and provoked considerable protest on the heels of publication. The appearance of classificatory coherence was fleeting—an effort to stabilize an increasingly disorderly world. The appearance of stability was soon shattered when a host of Jewish organizations and individuals contested the Commission's classificatory scheme and protested its use as the basis for immigrant classification in the upcoming 1910 census.[15]

Simon Wolf, the longtime leader of the Union of American Hebrew Congregations, and Julian Mack, vice president of the American Jewish Committee and president of the League for the Protection of Immigrants, both testified before the Commission on December 4, 1909, and called into question the Commission's elaborate classificatory scheme.[16] The Commission hearings contained several quite extraordinary exchanges between senators Dillingham and Lodge, on the one hand, and Wolf and Mack, on the other, in which they argued over whether the Jews were a race and over *which* classificatory scheme was the most appropriate one for the Commission to embrace. The extended exchanges made clear the considerable uncertainty over what constituted a race.

There are many echoes here to the academic debates mapped in chapter 2 in which we saw the disarticulation of nineteenth-century notions of race via the specification of nationality, language, and culture as distinct social phenomena from that of race. Several documents submitted to the Commission, as well as testimony given before it, referred explicitly to the very same men who dominated the academic discussions of race: Joseph Jacobs, Maurice Fishberg, William Ripley. All were established authorities on questions of the Jews and race; all were cited in the Commission reports.[17]

Both Wolf and Mack argued forcefully against the Immigration Commission and Census Bureau considering Hebrew as a racial classification. Both Wolf and Mack pondered how to classify Jews once one rejected race. Several different lines of argument were offered during the hearings as commissioners, and those testifying before them, struggled to articulate the nature of Jewish solidarity and its relation to race. Wolf and Mack had to elaborate their views of Jewish identity against persistent opposition and interrogation from Lodge, who was incredulous that neither Wolf nor Mack considered the Jews to be a race. Lodge countered Wolf and Mack's arguments throughout by asserting that he had always assumed the Jews to be a race.

Early in the testimony, Lodge pushed Wolf to clarify in what ways he considered the term *Hebrew* to designate a religious affiliation rather than a race. The following exchange captures the flavor of their extended debate:

> *Senator Lodge:* Do you mean to deny—I want to understand your position—that the word "Jew" is a racial term? . . . How would you classify Benjamin Disraeli? Was he a Jew?
>
> *Mr. Wolf:* He was born a Jew.
>
> *Senator Lodge:* No, he was not born a Jew, for he was baptized in a Christian church.
>
> *Mr. Wolf:* He was born of Jewish parents, and subsequently at a certain age was baptized.
>
> *Senator Lodge:* He was baptized as a Christian. He then ceased to be a Jew?
>
> *Mr. Wolf:* Yes; religiously he ceased to be a Jew.
>
> *Senator Lodge:* Ah! Religiously. He was very proud of the fact that he was a Jew, and always spoke of himself that way. Did the fact that he changed his religion alter his race?[18]

Wolf responded in classic intellectual fashion by asking Lodge to read a pamphlet that he, Wolf, had written for the board of delegates for the

Union of American Hebrew Congregations in 1904. Lodge accepted the pamphlet but wanted to continue the argument then and there.

The pamphlet Wolf handed to Lodge during the hearing laid out the particular difficulties in state classification of Jews and was reprinted in the Commission's final report. Wolf spelled out the classificatory dilemma as follows:

> I have never for a moment swerved from the opinion that, first, the Jew at present has no nationality other than that to which he has sworn allegiance and to which he owes obedience; second, the Jew, as an immigrant, should not be classified as belonging to a race, because he does not land as a Jew, but comes as a native of the country in which he was born; third, that if this question is to be treated from a scientific point or ethnological standpoint, then all immigrants should be treated uniformly so as to give the benefit of the classification to the world at large; fourth, but that if the classification is religious, then I most solemnly protest, as it is contrary to the spirit and genius of our institutions, and the Government is assuming functions that were never contemplated in the Constitution of the United States, the administrative functions are political and not religious.[19]

The difficulty confronting both the commissioners and Jewish advocates was that each of the classificatory frames on offer was fraught when applied to Jews: religion was not an option given the constitutionally mandated separation of church and state, nationality did not work given the diasporic origins of the Jews, and race was undesirable because it opened the door both to anti-Semitism and the stigma of race.

Commission discussions were not limited to the racial status of Jews; they ranged over a number of immigrant groups. The problem, most agreed, lay in the emerging disjunction between race and nation, which was making it increasingly difficult to identify "races and peoples" by nationality alone. In the past, so the analysis went, there had been a congruence between race and nation that enabled one to extrapolate from one to the other, but changes in territorial boundaries and increased population flows had disrupted the congruence, making nationality an inadequate guide to racial composition of immigrants arriving in the United States. Lodge laid out the problem when probing Wolf on the viability of classifying by nationality alone.

> *Senator Lodge:* How are you going to define the nationalities? We must make it the same for everybody. Are you going to classify a Hungarian as an Austrian?

Mr. Wolf: The Hungarians, as far as their allegiance is concerned, under present conditions are undoubtedly Austrians. They are Hungarians, of course. Hungary is a separate and distinct Kingdom.

Senator Lodge: How would you classify those coming from the 17 Provinces of Austria—men of utterly different races, historically speaking? We classify the Croatians, the Bohemians, according to the race they represent in Austria. We classify them according to their race, not according to their allegiance. We classify none of them according to allegiance or religion.

Mr. Wolf: I am aware of that.

Senator Lodge: The Irish are a perfect illustration of that. They are not classified according to their religion. They are British subjects.

Mr. Wolf: Certainly.

Senator Lodge: But we classify them as Irish because they are Irish, and undoubtedly there is a great deal of mixed blood in Ireland—English, Scotch, and Welsh blood.

Mr. Wolf: That is altogether geographical, and so with respect to the 17 Austrian Provinces.

Senator Lodge: The Irish are not classified geographically. An Irishman is classified as an Irish immigrant wherever he may come from.

Mr. Wolf: You seem to forget—and you certainly are sufficiently versed in the history of all people and especially the people I represent to know—that when a Jew is spoken of a Jew in faith is meant.

Senator Lodge: Not at all.

Mr. Wolf: And the race has absolutely nothing to do with it.

Senator Lodge: There is where we start off with a vast difference. I deny that this classification is according to religion.

Mr. Wolf: It should be.

Senator Lodge: It is purely a racial classification, and I used the illustrations I did to establish that.

Shortly thereafter Julian Mack continued to press the classification of Irish immigrants:

Senator Lodge: Is there an Irish Nation?

Mr. Mack: They want to be very strongly. They would resent being called Englishmen.

Senator Lodge: They would, and I would resent it if I were an Irishman.

Mr. Mack: You would have to call them Great Britainers. You have never used that term. Therefore you say Scotsmen, Englishmen, Welshmen, Irishmen. But that is geographical.

Senator Lodge: An Irishman is classified as an Irishman no matter where he comes from.

Mr. Mack: No matter whether he believes in home rule or not.

Senator Lodge: No matter what country he comes from—whether Australia or Canada.

Representative Bennett: Eight came from Belgium, 30 from France, 1 from Germany.

Mr. Mack: They probably were not subjects of those countries.

Senator Lodge: You do not know that. It is a pure assumption.

Mr. Mack: I do not know that. But you do not know the contrary.[20]

If an Irishman was classified as Irish no matter which country he immigrated from, then what does this tell us about state classification? Were the Irish a race? If not, what made them cohere as a social group regardless of their immediate political allegiance?

The Commission hearings made clear the enormous difficulty the state faced when classifying many immigrant groups—especially Jews, but other groups as well. No single taxonomy seemed adequate to the task; neither race nor nation worked, and religion was prohibited due to the constitutional separation of church and state. Thus, the Immigration Commission and Census Bureau faced a very real dilemma when constructing an effective and constitutionally admissible classificatory scheme. What was the state to do? What classificatory scheme should it pursue? It was difficult to see a way forward. All of the standard axes for classifying peoples were blocked. The Commission hearings closed without any agreement being reached by the likes of Lodge and Dillingham, on the one hand, and Wolf and Mack, on the other.

One option, offered by both Wolf and Mack, was simply to classify by political allegiance; hence Jews would be designated as citizens of the nations from which they came, or if second-generation immigrants, then as citizens of the United States. Mack was especially perturbed that the Commission was distinguishing second-generation Jews from other Americans—classifying foreigners was one thing, but census categories were quite another since the census was used to classify those at home. Mack put his concerns as follows:

Mr. Mack: Your classification, for the purposes of your work, is not merely of those coming in. You are classifying the Americans. You are classifying the American children in the schools racially. You would call my child in the school racially a Jew. I would call my child in the school racially an American.

Representative Bennett: You are mistaken about that.

Mr. Mack: So I am informed.[21]

Rather than suffer the dangers and ignominy of race-based classification, Mack was willing to forgo state recognition of Jewish particularity in favor of equitable treatment of all Americans by national origin in which religion was left as a private matter. But other Jewish advocates such as Wolf, along with immigration restrictionists such as Lodge and Dillingham, did not agree. Although motivated by very different concerns, Lodge, Dillingham, and Wolf all wanted some way of specifying what it was that made Jews Jews. But by the close of the hearings, there was no agreement on what the system for classifying Jews should be. The Commission hearings ended at an impasse: there seemed to be no way to square the circle by classifying Jews in ways that *both* recognized their particularity but did not resort to race.

Avoiding Race, Constructing Ethnicity

What exactly was it about racial classification that Wolf and Mack so desperately wanted to avoid? Two issues emerged from the Immigration Commission Reports: anti-Semitism and Chinese exclusion. Interestingly, at no point did either Wolf or Mack discuss the African American in their testimony. Let me first consider what they said and then turn to what they ignored. At one point, Wolf laid out the dangers of racial classification at length.

> *Mr. Wolf:* The reform element in the United States and throughout the world, that class which has not been living in Russia and Roumania under medieval conditions, is decidedly on the lines I have indicated; that is, that we are citizens of the country in which we reside, and we have been fighting in every possible way against the idea of founding a Jewish state.
>
> It is under all circumstances the only course for the Government of the United States to pursue, to ignore the action taken by Russia and Roumania, who recognize the Jew racially and who confer no rights or privileges upon him as a citizen; in short, they do not recognize him. Therefore the tabulating of the Jew as such [as a race], especially coming from those countries, is simply strengthening the hands of the people who have oppressed him in other countries.[22]

For the United States to classify by race, according to Wolf, simply played into the hands of European anti-Semitism. Indeed, the specter of anti-Semitism was evident throughout much testimony given before the Commission. Wolf and Mack both explicitly and implicitly saw any form of state classification as a problem precisely because it could be too easily turned to anti-Semitic ends.[23]

A second and somewhat unexpected fear apparent in the Immigration Commission reports was seen in the discussion of Chinese exclusion as a dangerous precedent for Jewish immigration to the United States. Max Kohler, Abram Elkus, and Commissioner Bennett all raised the concern explicitly when discussing whether to classify the Jews as a race. All referred to the case of Chinese exclusion, spelling out the ways it paralleled current discussions of how to weigh race and nation for Jewish immigrants. By passing the 1882 Chinese Exclusion Act, they argued, the U.S. government used race to trump nationality. No matter where Chinese immigrants arrived from, no matter where they were currently living, no matter what their past or present political affiliations, they were classified by race and prevented from entering the United States. A Chinese immigrant was always classified as Chinese regardless of competing geographic and political identifications. The possible parallels with Jews were obvious: the Chinese Exclusion Act served as a dangerous precedent should the Immigration Commission and Census Bureau classify Jews as a race.[24]

The most notable silence in the Commission hearings was the absence of any discussion of African Americans in these lengthy debates about race. There was no discussion of slavery or Jim Crow—no mention of African Americans at all. Whiteness scholars have shown time and again that such absences ought not be taken at face value.[25] Is that the case here? For the most part, Wolf and Mack have very European conceptions of race in which the disjunction between race and nation and the dangers of anti-Semitism loomed large, while questions of slavery and Jim Crow were never broached. But their allusions to Chinese exclusion showed a familiarity with American racism that made their silence on Blacks telling.

No doubt the desire to avoid the degradation and very real material consequences of American racism played an important part in Wolf and Mack's opposition to racial classification of Jews. But the evasion of racism does not fully account for Wolf and Mack's position. After all, securing Jewish whiteness surely would have been the best protection against the ravages of American racism. Yet Wolf and other Jewish advocates did not argue for Jewish whiteness; they were *not* willing to forgo Jewish particularity. Rather, they tried to negotiate American racism by insisting that Jews be classified in terms other than race. Wolf and Mack offered another version of the Alfred Kroeber and Maurice Fishberg arguments discussed in chapter 3 by looking for ways to capture Jewish particularity without invoking race. Being classified as white would have left Jewish identity in a precarious position since it did not distinguish Jews from all the others subgroupings within the grand division of the Caucasian race. White racial classification by the state did not satisfy questions of Jewish identity for either Wolf or Mack. The task, as they conceived it, was to find a way of specifying Jewish particularity without classifying Jews as a race.

The Census Bureau Compromise: "Mother Tongue" as the Marker of Ethnic Difference

The Immigration Commission's preferred policy outcome was the classification of immigrants via the adoption of a forty-cell taxonomy of races or peoples.[26] However, its efforts to have this classificatory scheme imported into the 1910 census failed, due largely to the intense opposition from various Jewish organizations.[27] But the Commission was not easily deterred and looked for other ways to distinguish new immigrants from those who had come before. Ultimately, an amendment to the Census Act was adopted stipulating that the foreign-born would be enumerated according to their "mother tongue." Although by no means a perfect identifier, it enabled the principal stakeholders to satisfy some of their concerns. For the likes of Lodge and Dillingham, mother tongue enabled the federal government to distinguish the new immigrants from the old, and thus solved the problem of the increasing disjunction between race and nation. Now large national origin populations, such as those originating from Russia or Austria-Hungry, *could* be disaggregated into subnational groupings. To be sure, Lodge and Dillingham considered language to be a poor substitute for race, but it was infinitely preferable to relying on nationality alone, an option that they insisted generated demographic data that "would be useless."[28] Wolf and Mack also were willing to accept mother tongue since it allowed for some degree of group particularity while avoiding classification of Jews as a race. Wolf and Mack would have preferred religious identification, but given the constitutional prohibition against doing so and the deep division within the Jewish community over religion as the mark of group affiliation, they, too, accepted the introduction of language as the next best option.

Language thus became the compromise option, a way for all to agree on a classificatory scheme that allowed for a more fine-grained identification of new immigrant groups while avoiding the stigma and dangers of race. For Lodge and Dillingham, language served as a proxy for race—an imperfect proxy, but better than no proxy at all. For Jews, language became a way of signaling group difference while avoiding state classification by race. The shift to mother tongue marked a break with racial classification of Jews, and thus began the process of state recognition of ethnicity as a new social category that was not reducible to race.

By the time the mother tongue amendment had passed, it was too late for it to be included in the 1910 census as a separate question since the forms had already been printed. The only way of incorporating mother tongue information at this late date was by changing the instructions to enumerators. Just such a change was introduced specifying that language spoken was to be recorded alongside the existing question on place of birth. To save space, the instructions specified that country of birth might be abbreviated, "but the language given as the mother tongue should be written out in full." Moreover, the new instructions further specified that mother tongue was to be asked of all persons ten years old and over, *but only* for the foreign-born. Thus, Julian Mack's concern that the census would begin to make invidious distinctions among American citizens was averted by restricting collection of language spoken to those born abroad.[29]

The instructions to enumerators on the mother tongue item were extensive; ten entries elaborated exactly how language was to be recorded. The first instruction provided a list of forty-one "principal foreign languages spoken in the United States" and stipulated that enumerators were to "avoid giving other names when the one in this list can be applied to the language spoken."[30] In addition, the instructions made clear the importance of avoiding large national identifiers through a series of specific examples. For instance, paragraph 135 stated, "Do not write 'Austrian,' but write German, Bohemian, Ruthenian, Slovenian, Slovak, or such other term as correctly defines the language spoken." Similar stipulations were made for several national origin populations in which the appropriate subnational language options were laid out in detail.[31]

The introduction of mother tongue information in the 1910 census marked, I believe, the beginnings of state recognition of ethnicity. To be sure, foreign language was not then, and is not now, synonymous with ethnicity; there is considerable slippage between the two. Yet, the two are often associated. From 1910 on, notions of race were increasingly restricted to what Lodge and others referred to as the "grand divisions" or the "scientific" races,[32] while language became the marker of group difference of another kind. Interestingly, this change in the 1910 census parallels the cultural pluralists' discussions of ethnic groups and loyalties discussed in chapter 3. We see that both intellectuals and state officials were looking for ways to fit new immigrants into a comprehensive classificatory scheme. Doing so led both to articulate what have become the key parameters of ethnicity. As of 1910, however, the state had only begun the process of category formation; it would be several more decades until the process was complete. Indeed, I would argue that state designation of ethnicity was not fully articulated until 1977 when the Office of Management and Budget promulgated Statistical Policy Directive 15. But before considering Directive 15, it is important to consider another key factor in the process of category formation.

Not Just a Jewish Story: Imperial Expansion and Mexican American Ethnicity

It would be a mistake to conclude from the preceding discussion that we can safely equate ethnicity with immigration. Although immigration was certainly one of the state's principal concerns in the first quarter of the twentieth century, there is another strand of state policy that fueled ethnic category formation, namely, the long history of U.S. imperial expansion that forcibly brought new populations into the United States. Indian removal, land purchase, war, and conquest all were used to secure the borders of the U.S. nation; all brought new populations under U.S. jurisdiction and, in so doing, made racial homogeneity difficult to sustain. The southwestern border in general and the war with Mexico in particular are classic cases in point. The Treaty of Guadalupe Hidalgo, signed on February 2, 1848, added the present states of Arizona, Nevada, California, and Utah, and parts of New Mexico, Colorado, and Wyoming. Along with Texas, the treaty added 1,193,061 square miles to U.S. territory.[33] The treaty also specified that the peoples living in the ceded/annexed territories could remain Mexican citizens or, after a year, would become citizens of the United States. This stipulation had enormous consequences for border politics in the ensuing decades and was at odds with racial prerequisites that all U.S. citizens be white, which had been in force since 1790. By declaring those in the ceded territories to be eligible for U.S. citizenship, regardless of race, the treaty raised the possibility of an alternative avenue to U.S. citizenship that became a bone of contention in subsequent decades.[34]

The political opening provided by conquest was elaborated by the Texas district court in 1897 when Judge Maxey ruled favorably in the naturalization case of *In re Rodriguez*. The case brought the contradictions between the immigrant exclusion and imperial expansion into focus.[35] Ricardo Rodriguez, a citizen of Mexico, arrived in Texas on February 15, 1883; after a decade, he initiated proceedings to naturalize as a U.S. citizen, first by filing a declaration of intent on January 25, 1893, and finally by filing with the U.S. Circuit Court for the Western District of Texas, San Antonio, on May 11, 1896. The case was decided by Judge Maxey on May 3, 1897. The court had to decide whether Rodriguez was eligible to naturalize, and, if yes, on what grounds. When District Judge Maxey granted the application, thereby permitting Rodriguez to naturalize, his ruling ran counter to most racial prerequisite cases of the period. Ian Haney López has identified twelve naturalization cases between 1878 and 1909 that involved issues of racial qualification. Eleven claims were denied; *Rodriguez* was the only favorable decision.[36] Those denied the right to naturalize included applicants from China, Japan, Burma, Hawaii, and two mixed-race applicants. Thus, the *Rodriguez* decision was by no means typical of late nineteenth-century naturalization law, but it is nevertheless instructive on the limits of the Black-white binary when it comes to understanding the interplay of immigration and race in the United States.[37]

Even though Maxey allowed Rodriguez to naturalize, he did not consider Rodriguez to be white. Rodriguez's racial status, Maxey made clear, was not the issue at hand: "It is not necessary to enter upon a discussion of that question [race and naturalization]; nor is it deemed material to inquire to what race ethnological writers would assign the present applicant. If the strict scientific classification of anthropologists should be adopted, he [Rodriguez] would probably not be classified as white."[38] According to Maxey, Rodriguez's right to naturalize lay elsewhere, in the long tradition of political conquest and treaty provisions, rather than in his skin color or some other marker of race.[39]

One way to sum up *Rodriguez* is to see that, for Judge Maxey, imperial expansion, and the heterogeneity it entailed, trumped the exclusionist impulse behind immigration restriction. Maxey laid out the imperial origins of U.S. citizenship in no uncertain terms:

> A reference to the constitution of the republic of Texas and the constitution, laws, and treaties of the United States will disclose that both the republic and the United States have freely, during the past 60 years, conferred upon Mexicans the rights and privileges of American citizenship, not individually, it is true, but by various collective acts of naturalization.[40]

Later in his ruling, Maxey referred specifically to the Treaty of Guadalupe Hidalgo:

> It has been shown that Mexicans (and the term includes all Mexicans, without discrimination as to color) who remained in the ceded territory,

and who failed to declare their intention within one year to remain Mexican citizens, became, by virtue of the stipulations of the treaty of February 2, 1848, citizens of the United States. Whether Congress intended to include Mexicans in the expression "white male inhabitants," as employed in the territorial acts above mentioned, may admit of question. But it is entirely clear, whatever meaning may be attached to those words, that the language of the acts explicitly recognized Mexicans who remained in the ceded territory, and who did not renounce their Mexican citizenship within one year, as citizens of the United States, and conferred upon them the elective franchise, and the important and valuable right to hold office. It is equally true that by article 5 of the treaty between the United States and Mexico proclaimed June 30, 1854, known as the "Gadsden Treaty," Mexicans who remained within the territory ceded by Mexico to the United States in article 1 of the treaty, and who failed to renounce their Mexican citizenship within a year, became citizens of the United States.[41]

For Maxey, Mexican whiteness remained open to question, but Rodriguez's claim to U.S. citizenship did not. Thus, Judge Maxey allowed Rodriguez to naturalize on the basis of treaty provisions, rather than on considerations of race. The treaty provisions, and Maxey's extension of them to a Mexican immigrant, were at odds with U.S. naturalization law. The two areas of state policy led in different directions. Racial exclusion would have been more easily sustained had the United States abandoned its imperial ambitions. That, however, was never seriously contemplated by those in positions of power. Thus, the United States had to negotiate the contradictory consequences inherent in the twin policies of racial exclusion and territorial expansion. *Rodriguez* did not sit easily alongside the nation's increasingly racist immigration policy.

Although Judge Maxey's ruling was clear, a single legal judgment by no means settled the matter of how and on what terms to police the U.S.-Mexican border. George Sánchez, Mae Ngai, and others have documented the rather porous nature of the southwestern border in the first three decades of the twentieth century when passage back and forth across the border was a common occurrence.[42] Demand for low-wage agricultural and railroad workers was certainly part of the reason why the border was kept open. U.S. businessmen and their advocates were not averse to pressing their case in favor of Mexican exemptions from immigration restriction. Those testifying before the House Committee on Immigration and Naturalization in the spring of 1928 revealed the power of the emerging agro-business lobby. Four groups were represented at the hearings: politicians, immigration restrictionists, farmers, and representatives of larger agricultural producers, but it was the large producers who came out in force. Almost half of those testifying represented large southwestern agricultural businesses.[43]

The relative openness of the Mexican border in the first three decades of the twentieth century was buttressed by special provisions in U.S. immigration law. In the first quarter of the twentieth century, Congress passed a series of immigration laws in quick succession: 1903, 1907, 1917, 1921, 1924, 1929.[44] All sought to curb immigration into the United States via the introduction of head taxes, literacy tests, provisions against becoming a public charge, and, ultimately, through the adoption of national origin quotas.[45] Each new statute was harsher than the one before; taken together they have long been considered the high point of immigration restriction, with the pinnacle being the introduction of the national origin quota system enacted in 1924. A quick glance at immigration figures across the twentieth century shows a steep decline in absolute numbers in the decades from 1924 through repeal of the national origins system in 1952 (see table 1 in appendix A).[46]

What is interesting about each of these statutes is not only their repeated efforts to restrict immigration, but also the exemptions they contained. Each of these statutes included important provisions exempting, or greatly reducing, restrictions on immigrants from Mexico, Canada, and a handful of other nations.[47] Thus, even at the height of immigration restriction, these Western Hemisphere exclusions, as they became known, are worth considering at greater length. Continued discrimination against Mexicans despite the Western Hemisphere exclusions laid the groundwork for state classification of Mexicans and others from Latin America as an ethnic group rather than a race. Classification by ethnicity eventually enabled the state to reconcile the contradictory effects contained in the twin impulses of imperial expansion and whiteness as essential criteria for citizenship.

The very first provision of the 1903 statute exempted Mexicans and Canadians from the newly imposed head taxes, the prime instrument for restricting immigrant entry in these early years. Section 1 of the 1903 Immigration Act stipulated "that there shall be levied, collected, and paid a duty of two dollars for each and every passenger not a citizen of the United States, or of the Dominion of Canada, the Republic of Cuba, or of the Republic of Mexico, who shall come by steam, sail, or other vessel from any foreign port to any port within the United States, or by any railway or any other mode of transportation from foreign contiguous territory to the United States."[48] In addition, the 1903 statute contained a provision facilitating movement across the Canadian and Mexican borders, a provision that would be repeated and elaborated over the next four decades. Specifically, section 32 of the 1903 act stated:

> That the Commissioner-General of Immigration, under the direction or with the approval of the Secretary of the Treasury, shall prescribe rules for the entry and inspection of aliens along the borders of Canada and Mexico, so as not to unnecessarily delay, impede, or annoy passengers in ordinary travel between the United States and said countries, and shall have power to enter into contracts with foreign transportation lines for the same purpose.[49]

This same provision, word for word, was included in the 1907 law that also raised the head tax from two to four dollars, but again included a provision limiting the tax on those entering from Canada or Mexico.[50] In the first decade of the twentieth century, then, immigration restriction focused primarily on entry into northeastern seaports, while allowing easier crossing over the Mexican and Canadian borders.

The 1924 Immigration Act is generally considered the high-water mark of immigration restriction, but even here, when immigration restrictionists such as Henry Cabot Lodge won the day, Western Hemisphere exemptions were included in the law, greatly diminishing the statute's impact on the southwestern border. Before stipulating national origin quotas, the statute identified a set of "non-quota immigrants" in section 4, of which subsection c specified that "an immigrant who was born in the Dominion of Canada, Newfoundland, the Republic of Mexico, the Republic of Cuba, the independent country of Central or South America" was considered a non-quota immigrant under the statute.[51] The Western Hemisphere exclusion has received too little attention. Its import lies in the light it sheds on the unevenness of state policy toward different population groups.[52] This unevenness in state policy, as with debates over racial classification of Jews, provided the political ground on which a full-fledged distinction between ethnicity and race was built in subsequent decades. Interestingly, we will see that it was Mexicans in particular that the INS and Census Bureau designated as an ethnic group and not a race. They did so in part by capitalizing on the differential treatment of Mexicans in immigration statutes passed in the first three decades of the twentieth century.

The creation of the Border Patrol in the 1924 statute might suggest otherwise, perhaps signaling the introduction of a more uniform policing of the southwestern border. Sánchez, however, has argued convincingly that this was not yet the case. The Border Patrol was not in fact created to close the Western Hemisphere exclusions, but rather was intended to screen Chinese and Japanese immigrants entering the United States from Latin America. In 1924, Mexican immigration was not as yet the state's primary concern.[53]

Although Western Hemisphere exemptions were important, we should not assume that the border was free of racism. It was not. Immigration exemptions were quite compatible with persistent racism. Mae Ngai's brilliant account of southwestern border politics documents the intense racialization of border crossing, which involved "degrading procedures of bathing, delousing, medical-line inspections, and interrogation. The baths were new and unique to Mexican immigrants, requiring them to be inspected while naked, have their hair shorn, and have their clothing and baggage fumigated."[54] In addition to humiliating border crossings, Mexicans were subject to the massive repatriation policy of the 1930s in which 20 percent of the Mexican population of the United States was returned to Mexico, either through formal deportation or "voluntary" departures and repatriations. This racial expulsion, Ngai concludes, was "exceeded in scale only by the Native American Indian removals of the nineteenth century."[55]

Moreover, exemption from immigration restriction was not always a blessing; agricultural laborers were left with little or no protection from unions or the state. Porous borders meant a ready supply of cheap Mexican labor that made unionization difficult to impossible. These labor market conditions were made even more problematic when classic New Deal legislation excluded agricultural workers from their provisions.[56] Nor did legislative exemptions translate into social acceptance or integration on the U.S. side of the border. The standard practice in the Southwest was for housing, schools, and cultural institutions to segregate Mexicans from whites. Mexicans were permitted to enter the United States, but this by no means protected them from the harsh realities of racial discrimination in daily life.[57]

What are we to make of the contradictory impulses in which Western Hemisphere exemptions went hand in hand with intensely racialized border crossings?[58] How should we understand the *disjunction* between practice and policy along the Mexican border? What should we make of this difference in legislative provision and enforcement? It might be tempting to attribute the disjunction between legislative provisions and border policy to problems of implementation. Although this is no doubt part of the story, the contradictory and unstable status of Mexican immigrants within the American racial taxonomy is more pervasive and deep-seated than this suggests. In fact, evidence of Mexicans' ambiguous racial status pervaded elite debates over Mexican immigration. The disjunction was not restricted to differences between legislative provisions and border practices, but was manifest *within* elite debates over Mexican racial classification. If we look more carefully at elite debates over implementation of the 1924 Immigration Act, issues of Mexican liminality quickly become apparent; Mexican immigrants did not fit easily within the prevailing racial taxonomy and, as such, remained a source of anxiety and political instability for race-based immigration policy.

The Racial Liminality of Mexican Americans: Debating Western Hemisphere Exemptions

From 1928 through 1930, when the 1924 Immigration Act was still being implemented, Congress considered several bills aimed at repealing the Western Hemisphere exclusion. H.R. 10343 and H.R. 6465, for example, both sought to bring Mexican immigrants under national origin quotas. More important for my purposes, Congress held several hearings on Western Hemisphere immigration, and the Congressional Committee on Immigration and Naturalization submitted a report on March 13, 1930, distilling arguments advanced for and against revising the "non-quota" status of Mexican immigrants and others from the Western Hemisphere.[59] Both the report and the hearings that preceded it show how Western Hemisphere exemptions, and whether to maintain them, quickly raised questions about the nature and boundaries of race.

Writing for the majority, Albert Johnson spelled out why the Committee thought that Mexicans' non-quota status ought to be revoked by declaring that Mexicans are not like the population of the United States:

> Citizens of the United States do not go to Mexico because the bulk of the population there is of a different type, much of it not homogeneous with the general population of the United States. And it is for this reason primarily, that the United States should restrict heavily the flow of lower classes of the Mexican population into the United States. Caste exists and is recognized in Mexico. It is the peon type that has been sucked into the United States in large numbers since 1917, so that now the number of persons in the United States who were born in Mexico exceeds 1,000,000.[60]

Note first that Mexicans were distinguished from the more homogeneous U.S. population: Johnson, it seems, was anxious to distinguish Mexicans from whites. Note also how racial distinctions were buttressed by allusions to both class and revolutionary political orientation. In fact, the 1917 Mexican Revolution was invoked on several occasions when underscoring the dangers that followed Mexican immigration.[61]

Johnson also considered the "fecundity" of Mexicans to acerbate the immigration problem confronting the United States:

> It must be clear that the continuation of such a birth rate (or even considerably less) in California, New Mexico, Arizona, Texas, Utah, and Colorado, will in a comparatively short time change the complexion of the population of those States, and bring about a hyphenized, politically unstabilized, Latinized majority throughout the Southwest.[62]

Hyphenation and political instability were thought to follow from the Latinization of the Southwest, thereby diminishing the homogeneity of the United States.

The majority report frequently drew parallels between Mexicans and African Americans, again suggesting that many elites did not consider Mexicans white:

> The United States has to accept the conditions which the introduction of African slaves has already created; has to recognize the rights of the population created from that migration, but should determine at once, with past experience for a guide, that it will not permit another race and color problem to erect its head by the slow processes of infiltration and differential fecundity.[63]

Those signing off on the majority report viewed immigration through the lens of slavery and, in so doing, positioned Mexicans as similar to African Americans. The comparison was further underscored by referring to slavery simply as an earlier "migration." Mexicans, for Johnson and his allies, were the new slaves. The policy choice confronting the nation, the report made clear, one that ought to be acted upon with all due haste, was the introduction of Mexican quotas so as to avoid repeating past mistakes by letting those of a different "race and color" into the nation.[64] Johnson concluded the discussion of Mexican immigration by endorsing the bill designed to repeal the non-quota status of Mexicans so as to ensure that "the white population in the great Southwest will not be under continued pressure to move farther and farther north into non-Mexicanized areas."[65]

Moreover, the report makes the links between territorial expansion and racial heterogeneity explicit. The following lengthy quote helps to convey the intercurrents among the "immigration problem," imperial expansion, and race.

> It is a major immigration problem which America faces in the growing Mexican immigration. Consider the southwestern part of the United States, and we find that in area more than one-fourth of our whole country was formerly a part of Mexico.
>
> This was acquired by the annexation of Texas, and by cession in 1845, 1848, and 1853. Into this newly acquired territory there was a migration of fine American pioneers, who took possession of the country, colonizing it and setting up law and order. During the last 10 years the racial problem has become acute in the Southwest. Here there have been established, as the demand for cheap labor increased, a great many Mexican immigrants who seem to be driving out the Americans.
>
> How will this situation ultimately work out? The Mexican peon, of course, as we know him, is of Mixed racial descent—principally Indian and Spanish, with occasionally a little mixture of black blood. The Mexican comes in freely because there is no quota against him, and during the last few years he has come here in such increasing numbers as almost to reverse the essential consequences of the Mexican War. *The recent Mexican immigrants are making a reconquest of the Southwest.*[66]

Johnson understood all too well how conquest led to racial mixing. Conquest was understood as tightly coupled with population change. But note that Johnson portrayed *American* conquest as a benign process accompanied by the migration of "fine American pioneers" who set about establishing "law and order," while Mexican immigration was seen in more threatening terms. Indeed, Mexican immigrants were portrayed as a powerful force, able to undo the Mexican War, and in so doing were changing the racial composition of the Southwest by introducing peoples of Indian and Spanish descent and even "a little mixture of black blood." Doing so was tantamount to a "reconquest of the Southwest"—a remarkable view of the power of immigration to redress the effects of imperial expansion.

Yet, the nonwhite status of Mexicans was far from secure. So much so that Johnson had to specify that "in various hearings relating to immigration from Mexico, the committee has found that facts presented are somewhat confused owing to the fact that Mexicans are frequently classified with the white race."[67] Johnson did not dwell on the whiteness of Mexicans, but the issue would not rest. Take, for example, the Congressional House Committee Hearings on H.R. 12382, held May 15, 1930. The Box bill, as it was known, again tried to introduce national origin quotas for Mexicans. At one point during the Committee hearings, Undersecretary of State Joseph P. Cotton and Congressman John L. Cable engaged in a fascinating exchange over the racial status of Mexicans.

> *Mr. Cable:* In the enforcement of the law have our officials given consideration to the provision of the immigration act of 1924 that debars any alien who is ineligible for citizenship?
>
> *Undersecretary Cotton:* I think they have. I think they have fully. You will realize that all of this Mexican immigration that came in there or in general comes in is white immigration.
>
> *Mr. Cable:* They are not Indians?
>
> *Undersecretary Cotton:* As a rule, they are classed as whites in the census figures.
>
> *Mr. Cable:* Then the departments followed the rulings of the Bureau of the Census in determining that Mexicans are of the white race?
>
> *Undersecretary Cotton:* They have followed that ruling. I do not know whether that is the only basis of ruling, but they have followed that ruling.
>
> *Mr. Cable:* The Supreme Court of the United States has held that an Indian is not eligible for citizenship, and it is my understanding that the Mexicans are of the Indian race and therefore could not be admitted.
>
> *The Chairman:* A preponderance of the Mexican race is Indian blood but not all of it.
>
> *Undersecretary Cotton:* Of course, when a man comes up it is a question whether the individual applicant is to be classed as white or Indian. However, generally speaking, the Mexicans are classed as whites.
>
> *Mr. Cable:* Do you know whether that is the reason for the reduction in the number admitted?
>
> *Undersecretary Cotton:* The reasons for the reduction in the number admitted are the alien contract labor law, the illiteracy test, and the element of "likely to become a public charge."[68]

Undersecretary Cotton declared Mexicans as a subset of the white race and used the authority of the Census Bureau to secure his claim. At first blush it seems as if a moment of clarity had settled upon this complex matter of Mexican classification. Cotton spoke definitively and seemed to have the backing of a reputable state bureaucracy to sustain his claim. The moment of clarity, however, was short-lived since precisely when Cotton invoked the Census Bureau to establish that Mexicans are white, the Census Bureau had, in fact, just classified Mexicans as a separate race.[69] The parallels with the *Dictionary of Races or Peoples* are striking.

Definitive claims as to the racial status of Jews and Mexicans were no sooner claimed than they quickly unraveled. The difficulty of fitting Mexicans into the extant U.S. Black-white binary was evident throughout.

In 1930, the Census Bureau classified Mexicans as a distinct race and included Mexican along with the other race categories within the census race question: white, Negro, Mulatto, Chinese, Japanese, Indian, Other. Census enumerators were instructed to "classify as 'Mexican' all persons of Mexican origin who were not definitely white, Negro, Indian, or Japanese," thereby classifying the "whole Mestizo group" as "nonwhite."[70] According to the Census Bureau's own account, the Mexican race category was added because of the increased interest in tracking the "Spanish-American and Mexican population" that had been "stimulated by the heavy immigration from Mexico during the decade of the twenties" in the wake of the Mexican Revolution.[71] Congressional hearings on Mexican immigration in 1928 and 1929 often referred to the political instability associated with the revolution and the dangers it harbored for northward migration: the fear lay both in the increased numbers coming to the United States as well as a concern that the political radicalism and instability would be carried north across the border. Tellingly, national immigration legislation in this same period also began to specify "anarchists" as undesirable immigrants.[72]

The new Mexican race category was short-lived. It quickly met with criticism from both sides of the border. The Mexican government protested classifying Mexicans as "nonwhites," in part, some have suggested, because doing so would call into question Mexican immigrants' right to naturalize as U.S. citizens. The Mexican government protest was echoed by the League of United Latin American Citizens (LULAC), which also protested to the Census Bureau that Mexicans ought to be classified as white. The Census Bureau quickly backed off and removed the Mexican race category from the race option for the 1940 census. A Mexican race category has never again appeared on the decennial census. From 1940 through the introduction of self-identification in 1970, instructions to census enumerators specified that Mexicans should be classified as white unless obviously of either Negro, Indian, or some other race.[73]

However, it is important to note that the Census Bureau did not leave matters there—with Mexicans being positioned securely as a subset of the white race. Rather, the Census Bureau continued to search for ways of capturing the particularity of Mexican difference without resorting to notions of black and white. Soon after dropping the Mexican race option, the Bureau introduced a series of questions that enabled the so-called Spanish population to be counted as a distinct subgroup tabulated by

Spanish surname rather than race. Initially, the separate Spanish population questions were used in five southwestern states (Arizona, California, Colorado, New Mexico, and Texas), but the questions eventually were used for the population as a whole, thereby creating another bureaucratic tributary establishing ethnicity as a distinct social category to that of race.

From the INS to the Census Bureau:
Spanish Surnames and Mexican Ethnicity

In 1936, the INS published *A Manual of Immigration Spanish*, which was to provide the Border Patrol with a Spanish language guide.[74] The manual was created by inspector George Lockwood of the Arizona INS, interpreter George Vanson of Ellis Island, and clerk Josephine Ortiz of Arizona. The 198-page manual was distributed to "officers and employees of the United States Immigration and Naturalization Service" to assist in the "performance of their duties." The manual was intended as a quick guide to the Spanish language via the provision of translations and phonetic pronunciation of relevant immigration questions, along with a quick guide to grammar and a vocabulary section. The preface to a later INS Spanish language manual spelled out the purpose of such publications, stating: "The primary purpose of this course in Spanish is to furnish the minimum essentials of Spanish grammar to Border Patrol trainees in a very short period of time."[75] Although the manuals do not tell us much about Border Patrol practices, they indicate the increased attention being paid in the mid-1930s to identifying, classifying, and counting the number of Mexicans crossing into the United States.

Interestingly, one of the sample questions on the very first page under the heading "Primary Manifest Questions" asked about race: "Of what race are you (not your nationality, but your race)?" A Spanish translation was then provided. Note how the question carefully distinguished race and nation. When the INS first asked immigration officers to list the "race or peoples" of those arriving into the United States in 1898, no such distinction was made. Rather, immigration officers were handed a long list in which races and nations were listed together as if equivalent subcategories within the classificatory scheme.[76] By 1936, sample questions in the Border Patrol manual made sure that immigration officers would distinguish race from nation when interrogating those entering into U.S. territory. For the most part, however, these manuals were designed as language training guides, aimed at facilitating interrogation of Spanish speakers by the Border Patrol.

Along with the Spanish language manual, the INS also published a supplement with the unwieldy title of *US Immigration and Naturalization Service Supplement to Manual of Immigration, Spanish—Spanish Personal Names*, which provided a list of Spanish surnames for Border Patrol officers to use when documenting the arrival of Mexicans into the United States. The same George Lockwood generated a list of six thousand Spanish surnames, which quite literally migrated to the Census Bureau, where it was updated and became the basis of Census Bureau efforts to count the Spanish-named and Spanish-speaking persons in the five southwestern states of Arizona, California, Colorado, New Mexico, and Texas.[77]

In addition to Spanish surname, the 1940 census began to "include tabulations on the white population of Spanish mother tongue."[78] Spanish had been included on the census language list ever since the mother tongue compromise had been introduced to resolve the political impasse of how to classify Jewish immigrants in 1910. But remember that in 1910, the mother tongue compromise specified that mother tongue was to be asked only of the foreign-born. In 1940 that changed. In a 5 percent sample in the southwestern states, the Census Bureau included Spanish mother tongue, but no longer restricted it to the foreign-born. In fact, the Census Bureau explicitly identified two different population streams in the Southwest: "Spanish-American, Spanish-Colonial, or Hispano group," as well as Mexican immigrants and their descendants.[79] The Bureau itself noted that direct immigration from Spain, the West Indies, and Central and South America was negligible, thereby suggesting that the key population to be counted were *non-immigrant Spanish speakers*. The 1940 census recorded 1,858,024 people of Spanish mother tongue in the 5 percent sample, or an estimated 1.4 percent of the population.[80] Thus the mother tongue question, which had been introduced to classify Jewish immigrants in 1910, was modified to count Spanish speakers in the Southwest.

Two key issues remain: What exactly was the relationship between Spanish surname, mother tongue, and racial classification? And how did the introduction of Spanish surname and mother tongue anticipate the creation of the census category Hispanic three decades later?

For the 1950 census, the Bureau introduced special training sessions for Spanish-surname coders, which is suggestive when it comes to understanding the relationship between surname, mother tongue, and race. The sessions included instructions on the characteristics of Spanish surnames and how to differentiate them from surnames in other Romance languages such as Portuguese, French, and Italian, along with "intensive study of lists of the most common Spanish surnames; practice exercises; and practice coding under close supervision." [81]

Once the count by Spanish surname was completed, the Bureau still had to decide how to record the data within the existing census taxonomy. Ultimately, the Bureau coded Spanish surname under the race question, although not as a separate race. Rather, the Bureau introduced the practice of coding Spanish surname in a way that both placed it *alongside existing race categories*, but at the same time made clear that it was not itself a race. The procedural history of the 1950 census laid out the complex coding procedure:

> White persons with Spanish surname are not a racial group, but separate information on these persons was needed for special studies. As a matter of convenience, they were identified in the column in which race was normally coded. This was done only in the five Southwestern States (Arizona, California, Colorado, New Mexico, and Texas). A list of common Spanish surnames was used as a guide. The coder also examined entries in State or country of birth (item 13) and parents' birthplace (item 25) for contributing information.
>
> Race entries were manually coded only for the 5 Southwestern States and the "mixed Stock" communities. For other areas, the operator punched the proper code on the punch card directly from the enumerator's entry. The code scheme was as follows:

Race	Schedule Entry	Code
White (except persons with Spanish Surnames in 5 Southwestern States)	W	1
Negro	Neg	2
American Indian	Ind	3
Japanese	Jap	4
Chinese	Chi	5
Filipino	Fil	6
Asiatic Indian, Korean, Eskimo, Malayan, Polynesian, Hawaiian, and "Mixed Stock" races (in selected counties)	—	7
White-Spanish surname (only in 5 Southwestern States)	W	0 [82]

Note how the census instructions first specified that white persons with a Spanish surname were not a race, yet the data was recorded under the race question, and that Spanish-surname responses were simultaneously recorded as white while being given a separate code to that of white. We might say that Spanish-surname peoples were thereby recorded as a subset of the white race: white and yet not simply white. Spanish surname was used again in the 1960 and 1970 decennial censuses. In fact, the Census Bureau maintains a Spanish-surname list today.[83]

The parallels with struggles over Jewish classification in 1910–11 are instructive. Recall how the *Dictionary of Races or Peoples* classified Jews as white while the Dillingham Commission hearings simultaneously made clear just how contentious and unstable such a designation was. So, too, with Mexicans in the Southwest. At times they were considered white and yet were repeatedly derided as racially inferior. The Census Bureau recorded the Spanish-surname population in the white-race column, yet specified that they were not white. The head begins to spin; the taxonomy wobbles. It is difficult to sustain the sense of a coherent and orderly mapping of race.

Rather than trying to arbitrate between these conflicting views of Mexican racial status, we need to place the unstable and contested status of Jewish and Mexican racial positioning front and center. The Dillingham Commission and Western Hemisphere hearings make clear the difficulty of locating Jews and Mexicans within the prevailing U.S. racial taxonomy. Instability and contestation were the hallmarks of most documents attempting to classify both Jews and Mexicans. Declarative claims to the contrary are best understood as positional claims within a larger struggle over how to classify Jews and Mexicans—the more unstable the location, the more authoritatively the designation had to be claimed. Note again the parallels with our earlier discussion—the Dillingham Commission's *Dictionary of Races or Peoples* definitively claimed Jews to be white, while the Lodge and Wolf exchange shows how far from settled such claims were.

Thus the INS and the Census Bureau's early efforts to classify Mexican Americans via the proxy of mother tongue and surname set in place the central features of what would become known as Hispanic ethnicity in the wake of civil rights reform. The mother tongue and surname proxies, much like the mother tongue compromise for Jews forty years earlier, enabled the state to classify both Jews and Mexicans as distinct subnational populations without invoking race. Jews and Mexicans were different, INS and Census Bureau records made clear, but it was a different kind of difference to that of race.

By proliferating different kinds of difference, men such as Lodge, Wolf, and Lockwood were able to stabilize existing forms of racial classification and hierarchy by absorbing problematic classificatory populations into the omnibus category of ethnicity. The difficulty of classifying Jews and Mexicans was not used to question racial classification per se. Rather, key state officials began to distinguish different kinds of difference as a way of accommodating Jews and Mexicans through the construction of ethnicity as a distinct social category to that of race. Ethnic difference thus became a way not only of mapping the increasingly heterogeneous population in the United States, but also served to shore up classification by race.

Latinos: The New Ethnics?
Rereading Statistical Policy Directive 15

Fast-forward from state classification of Jews and Mexicans in the first half of the twentieth century to issues of antidiscrimination policy today, and we see yet another tributary into the process of category formation. When you enroll a child in school, hire someone in a university, apply for a mortgage, read a newspaper, or fill out census forms, the chances are that the categories you use were established by a rather obscure government directive promulgated by the Office of Management and Budget (OMB) on May 12, 1977. The "Race and Ethnic Standards for Federal Statistics and Administrative Reporting," later known as Statistical Policy Directive No. 15, mandated categories to be used for the collection and dissemination of all race and ethnicity data by federal departments and administrative agencies. Although Directive 15 was officially limited to "Federal Statistics and Administrative Reporting," the Directive's categories quickly became the de facto standard for U.S. society at large. Indeed, the Directive might be seen as one of the most important and enduring legacies of the civil rights movement of the 1960s since it has set the terms of ethnic and racial classification for the past quarter century.[1] A copy of Directive 15 can be found in appendix B.

The initial impetus for the Directive was as a means of standardizing the categories used by government agencies when collecting and disseminating racial and ethnic data, a task that took on new significance with passage of numerous civil rights laws. The Civil Rights Act of 1964, the Voting Rights Act of 1965, the Fair Housing Act of 1968, the Equal Credit Opportunity Act of 1974, and the Home Mortgage Disclosure Act of 1975 required the federal government to monitor ethnic and racial discrimination in a variety of policy domains. To assess discriminatory practices, agencies first had to specify the relevant protected groups, which, in turn, required stipulating ethnic and racial categories. In short, federal agencies charged with enforcing antidiscrimination statutes had to determine which groups were to count as protected minorities. Throughout the late sixties and early seventies, numerous government bureaucracies established their own categories so as to comply with these new legislative mandates, but with little or no effort at coordinating or standardizing categories. This dispersed multi-agency process of data collection proved unwieldy, prompting efforts to standardize the collection and dissemination of federal race and ethnicity data via Directive 15.[2]

On first reading, the Directive appears to be quite straightforward. This concise two-page document specified that all federal agencies were to collect race and ethnic data in five categories: Black, white, American Indian or Alaskan Native, Asian or Pacific Islander, and Hispanic. When examined more closely, however, we see that in fact the Directive did *not* specify five parallel racial groups; rather, it specified four races and one ethnicity in ways that echoed arguments over classification of Jews and Mexicans in preceding decades. The four races were Black, white, American Indian and Alaskan Native, Asian and Pacific Islander. Hispanic was designated as an ethnicity, not a race. OMB thus codified the more dispersed and nascent practice of distinguishing ethnicity from race that had been in formation since the late nineteenth century by recommending that all federal departments and agencies "collect all race and ethnic data separately via a two-question format in which the four racial categories are presented in one question and ethnicity in another."[3]

Directive 15: Institutionalizing the Race-Ethnicity Distinction

Both Directive 15 and its revision in 1997 have been powerful forces leading us to distinguish ethnicity from race in the United States. Understanding how this is so requires that we explore both the specifics of the taxonomy itself and its complex origins. Interestingly, the Directive's four racial groups parallel the classic nineteenth-century color designations of black, white, yellow, and red. Note also that there was *no brown race* in the American ethno-racial taxonomy. "Hispanics," to use OMB's lexicon, were not considered to be a race but were designated instead as an ethnic group whose collective identity was independent of race.[4] According to the Directive, one was Hispanic because of one's "Spanish culture or origin, regardless of race." Exactly what this cultural heritage entailed was not at all clear; it was given no content except to say that it was independent of race. Hispanics were expected to check a race box in addition to ethnicity, again underscoring the Directive's presumption that race and ethnicity be considered separate phenomena. In the United States, Hispanic was considered to be an ethnic rather than a racial identification.[5]

The Directive strove for categorical symmetry by defining each of the ethno-racial categories in terms of origins. American Indians or Alaskan Natives were said to have "origins in any of the original peoples of North America"; Blacks to have "origins in any of the black racial groups of Africa"; whites to have "origins in any of the original peoples of Europe, North Africa, or the Middle East"; Hispanics to be persons of "Mexican, Puerto Rican, Cuban, Central or South American or other Spanish culture or origin, regardless of race." In addition, the Directive specified that American Indians or Alaskan Natives must maintain "cultural identifications through tribal affiliations or community recognition."[6] Yet, the symmetry was not sustained; subtle differences were revealed when OMB specified the origins of each of the major groups. Note, for example, that the category Black was the only one in which the Directive explicitly referred to race when it specified that a Black person had "origins in any of the black *racial* groups of Africa." For whites, the Directive referred to geography, not race—to Europe, North Africa, and the Middle East, not to whiteness.[7] Note also that American Indian/Alaskan Natives was the only group for which Directive 15 required that some form of cultural or tribal identification be maintained. For all other groups, identification was presumed, without active affiliation being called for. For Hispanics, shared cultural identification was *explicitly* unhinged from race.

Despite efforts to the contrary, no single variable was used to define racial groups. Rather, the Directive variously characterized race as origin, geography, nationality, culture, and cultural identification. Although the Directive differentiated ethnicity and race, the two were not positioned simply in opposition. Rather, it was as if the two identifications stand in a family relation to each other, at once similar and yet different. This complex relation can be seen in the Directive's rather intricate stipulations as to whether racial and ethnic data should be collected in separate or combined question formats. The Directive explicitly stated that the two-question format was preferred in which race and ethnicity were asked in separate questions, but allowed for the combined option to be used in which the one ethnic and four race categories were presented together.[8] But even when racial and ethnic data were asked in a single question, the Directive made clear that social phenomena were supposed to remain distinct. It was the *question format* that was combined, not race and ethnicity. Finally, note that Directive 15 also stipulated racial identifications to be mutually exclusive: respondents must select only one race. If you consider yourself to be of mixed race, you were asked to select the "category which most closely reflects the individual's recognition in his community."[9]

Intricate and arcane as the Directive is, I consider knowledge of the Directive to be required currency for understanding race politics in the United States today. This rather obscure document and the 1997 Revised Standards have mandated racial and ethnic categories for the past thirty years and, in doing so, have established the terrain on which ethnic and racial politics is waged. At the end of the chapter, we will see that Latino classification is being hotly debated today. The issue is not raised directly but is framed in terms of question format. Should OMB adopt the "combined format" in which the category Hispanic might be placed alongside of race, or should OMB and the Census Bureau continue to treat ethnic and racial identifications as separate phenomena, collecting data via the two-question format?

Almost as soon as the Directive was promulgated, groups began to protest its formulation and to call for revisions. OMB considered revising the Directive in 1988 but continued with the status quo.[10] Demands for change intensified as several groups, especially the emerging mixed-race movement, claimed that the Directive no longer reflected the increasing diversity of the U.S. population. In 1993, OMB initiated an extensive four-year-long review of the Directive that included several public hearings "hosted" by OMB in the spring and summer of 1993 and again in the summer of 1994. In addition, OMB asked the Committee on National Statistics of the National Academy of Sciences to convene a workshop to discuss issues surrounding category revision. In March 1994, OMB itself established a new Interagency Committee to Review the Racial and Ethnic Standards.[11] The extended review process considered several changes, including adding race categories for Hawaiians and those from the Middle East, addressing the issue of mixed race, as well as reconsidering a "combined question" format in which the federal government would cease distinguishing between race and ethnicity.[12]

In October 1997, OMB promulgated new standards for "maintaining, collecting, and presenting federal data on race and ethnicity," which replaced Directive 15. In the end, the 1997 revision made two important changes: the category of Native Hawaiian or Other Pacific Islander was added, thereby taking the race options from four to five; and mixed-race demands were accommodated by allowing individuals to "mark one or more" when answering the race question. The issue of adopting a separate Middle Eastern category was deferred. But the practice of distinguishing ethnicity from race was not changed. Thus the revised standards continue the long-standing practice in which "the federal government considers race and Hispanic origin to be two separate and distinct phenomena." The race-ethnicity distinction remains the formal taxonomic practice in the United States to this day.[13]

The Bureaucratic Origins of Directive 15

Why did Directive 15 designate "Hispanics" as an ethnic group and not a race? How, exactly, were the OMB categories created? By whom? And with what political effects? I answer these questions by beginning with the most immediate influences and then working back to more distant, but by no means less significant, forces. Specifically, I examine the Interagency Committee, whose report became the basis for Directive 15; second, I widen the lens to include the broader political context in which the Directive was drafted. Finally, I shift the analysis to early antidiscrimination initiatives that established a very broad conception of discrimination as the basis for federal antidiscrimination policy for the past six decades. I conclude by returning to contemporary political fights over the race and ethnic classification within the Census Bureau.

In April 1973, the Federal Interagency Committee on Education (FICE) met to discuss a report from the Subcommittee on Minority Education. FICE had been created by executive order in 1964 (updated in 1974) as a means of improving coordination of federal agencies in the area of education. More than thirty agencies participated in the Committee, which met on a monthly basis; much of the Committee's work was carried out by a series of subcommittees on issues such as graduate education, education and work, educational technology, and minority education. At its monthly meetings, FICE met to discuss and act upon particular subcommittee recommendations and to arrange for implementation. The April 1973 meeting was convened to discuss the minority education subcommittee report, *Higher Education for Chicanos, Puerto Ricans, and American Indians*, but before the discussion started, several members "stormed out" of the meeting, "livid over how it wrongly identified certain groups."[14] FICE nevertheless endorsed the subcommittee report and forwarded recommendations to then-secretary of the Department of Health, Education, and Welfare (HEW), Caspar Weinberger, recommending that the secretary "coordinate development of common definitions for racial and ethnic groups"—an idea that Weinberger endorsed.[15]

In June 1974, Weinberger appointed an Ad Hoc Committee on Racial and Ethnic Definitions to clarify issues of terminology and classification. The ad hoc committee was chaired by Charles E. Johnson Jr., assistant chief of the Population Division at the Census Bureau, along with twenty-four members drawn from several government departments and agencies, including Census, HEW, OMB, the Department of Housing and Urban Development (HUD), the Bureau of Labor Statistics, the Equal Employment Opportunity Commission (EEOC), and the U.S. Commission on Civil Rights.[16] Although the original FICE subcommittee report on minority education that had prompted debate over ethnic and racial classification had dealt only with "people of Spanish and American Indian origins," the Ad Hoc Committee on Racial and Ethnic Definitions determined that if it was to be effective, it needed to consider "a broad range" of classificatory terms.[17]

The ad hoc committee report drafted a comprehensive ethno-racial taxonomy that was, in its view, "an integrated scheme of terms and definitions, conceptually sound, which can be applied to cover major categories of race and ethnicity and be used by all agencies to help meet their particular requirements."[18] The Committee report allows us to recapture classification debates both through the deliberations it records and through the disjunction evident between the majority and minority positions. Both the Committee report and the differences between it and the Directive are instructive as to the politics of classification.

The instability of racial classification is immediately apparent in the classification of South Asians. In the ad hoc committee report approved on April 23, 1975, South Asians had been classified as Caucasian/White, noting that there was much discussion over the category Asian or Pacific Islander, specifically over "where to draw the geographic line—east or west of the Indian subcontinent. The decision was east, which limits this category to peoples with origins formerly called 'Oriental' and to 'natives of the Pacific Islands.'" The Committee recommended that South Asians "are Caucasian, though frequently of a darker skin color." Two years later, Directive 15 drew the geographic line differently when it classified people from the Indian subcontinent within the category Asian or Pacific Islanders. Thus, between April 1975 and May 1977, South Asians in the United States shifted from white to Asian; such are the vicissitudes of racial classification, even in the late twentieth century.[19]

The ad hoc committee also considered the possibility of creating a category "Other," so as to accommodate people of mixed race. But most ad hoc committee members opposed doing so because they thought it would "complicate a survey and add to its costs." We will see that the issues of mixed race and of the residual category of "some other race" were by no means settled with Directive 15. Both issues came back to plague processes of racial classification in the ensuing decades.[20]

My principal concern remains with Latinos: how did the ad hoc committee construct the category Hispanic? What alternatives were considered? And who were the key players? There were four Latinos on the ad hoc committee: Grace Flores from the Office for Spanish Surnamed Americans at HEW, Philip Garcia from HUD, Abdin Noboa-Rios from the National Institute of Education, and Paul Planchon from the Statistical Policy Division at the OMB. These four individuals—aided by the Committee's working group—were in some literal sense the immediate agents of the U.S. category Hispanic. The working group made recommendations to the Committee as a whole; taken together, they selected the governing term and specified that Hispanics were to be considered an ethnic group and not a race. Directive 15 largely ratified the Committee's report.[21]

The ad hoc committee considered several different terms for identifying this population, including *Spanish surname, Spanish language, Hispanos,* and *Latino.* Discussion as to terminology was contentious; there was no ready agreement within the Committee. Not surprisingly, the four Latino Committee members did not agree among themselves. Darryl Fear's interview with Grace Flores-Hughes (then Grace Flores) attributes the final designation of *Hispanic* to Flores and to her refusal to accept any other term.[22] Flores, a Mexican American, recalled preferring *Hispanic* because it "was better than anything I had been called as a kid. . . . It was hard eliminating all those terms. . . . I felt alone. But I was determined to stick to 'Hispanic.' We kept going back to Spain. We couldn't get away from it."[23] Both Latino and Spanish surnames, according to Flores, were too capacious and would have included others who had not been discriminated against. Moreover, Flores added, not everyone in the Spanish diaspora has a Spanish name, so she stuck to her position that *Hispanic* be the term used.[24]

Others on the Committee, such as Abdin Noboa-Rios, a native of Puerto Rico who was raised in the Bronx and Chicago, preferred the term *Latino.* Noboa-Rios recalled that others wanted to use the term *Hispano,* but lost out when the Committee recommended that *Hispanic* be adopted as the agreed-upon term. Although the Committee reached a decision, Noboa-Rios recalls, they remained sharply divided: "There was never any consensus in that group to the very end. . . . We came up with an agreement, but . . . there were some bad feelings. I know two people who didn't speak for up to a year after it was over."[25] For many, the term *Hispanic,* a term rarely used outside of the United States, was too closely tied to Spanish imperialism. Juanita Tamayo Lott—also a member of the ad hoc committee and its working group—suggested that the racial and national origin differences within the Committee replayed in microcosm the complex issues of reconciling recognition of Hispanics as a distinct social formation given the heterogeneity of the population encompassed by the term *Hispanic.*[26]

Whether Flores-Hughes's memory is accurate is difficult to assess. Perhaps she has exaggerated her role in the Committee; others do not remember her as such a forceful figure. For my purposes, however, Flores's role is not the issue. No one figure need be identified as the sole architect of the category Hispanic. What is clear is that the Ad Hoc Committee on Racial and Ethnic Definitions drafted the central operative features of the federal ethno-racial taxonomy and that the ad hoc committee's recommendations provided the blueprint for Directive 15. On April 23, 1975, FICE endorsed the ad hoc committee's report and recommended that the following steps be taken to implement it. First, FICE recommended that the Bureau of the Census field-test the five ethno-racial categories, review the results, and, if necessary, revise the categories. Once approved, the Committee chairperson would transmit the categories and procedural recommendations to the director of the OMB to be promulgated as the standard to be used throughout the federal government when collecting and reporting racial and ethnic data.[27]

The Government Accounting Office (GAO), HEW Office of Civil Rights, and EEOC all adopted the ad hoc committee categories for a trial period of at least a year. In August 1976, OMB and GAO convened another committee to assess the trial; the committee included members from OMB, GAO, the Department of Justice, the Department of Labor, HEW, HUD, the Bureau of the Census, and EEOC to review the field test. After minor revisions, the review committee proposed and circulated categories for agency comment. By September 1976, the categories became effective as the standard for "all record keeping and reporting" for federal agencies represented on the 1976 ad hoc committee. OMB drafted and again circulated the proposed categories for agency comment. After minor revisions, OMB promulgated Statistical Policy Directive 15 on May 12, 1977, thereby establishing uniform standards for the collection and dissemination of data on race and ethnicity for all federal government agencies. The Directive was posted in the *Federal Register* on May 4, 1978, and hence the rather varied citations one sees to Directive 15.[28]

Civil Rights Politics and Directive 15

While the bureaucratic history of Directive 15 is important, it tells only part of the story. To capture the larger forces in play, it is worth remembering that Directive 15 was forged at the very moment when issues of language discrimination and bilingual education were highly politicized issues. Recall that the immediate impetus for Directive 15 came from within the Federal Interagency Committee on Higher Education, specifically the subcommittee on minority education therein, which was considering the role of Chicanos, Puerto Ricans, and American Indians in higher education. Moreover, several other government initiatives ensured that the emerging federal taxonomy would disaggregate the "nonwhite" population and attend to issues of language discrimination. *Lau v. Nichols* is a classic case in point; the landmark Supreme Court case mandating bilingual education under Title VI of the 1964 Civil Rights Act was handed down on January 21, 1974, right as federal bureaucrats were drafting Directive 15. Even though *Lau v. Nichols* involved a class action suit on behalf of non-English-speaking Chinese students in the California public school system, the case established language discrimination as a central component of the civil rights agenda that was crucial to the designation of Hispanics as a protected minority.[29] Indeed, HEW was already enmeshed in issues of bilingual education, thereby making many HEW ad hoc committee members attuned to questions of discrimination against Asian Americans and Latinos as well as African Americans.[30]

Pressure for OMB to include Hispanics in Directive 15 was consolidated with passage of Public Law 94-311 on June 16, 1976, which required all federal agencies to collect and disseminate "economic and social statistics for Americans of Spanish origin or descent." Congress thus ensured that whenever the government was to count various population groups, Hispanics had to be included.[31]

The broad conceptions of discrimination captured in *Lau* and Public Law 94-311 were echoed in the work of the U.S. Civil Rights Commission, which also frequently included Mexican Americans in its purview. The Commission's Mexican American Education Study was especially impressive; it drew on survey data gathered by HEW in five southwestern states in the fall of 1968 to draft a series of reports in the early 1970s documenting the pervasive discrimination against Mexican Americans within the education system: "Ethnic Isolation of Mexican Americans in Public Schools of the Southwest," "The Unfinished Education: Outcomes for Minorities in the Five Southwestern Sates," "The Excluded Student: Educational Practices Affecting Mexican Americans in the Southwest," and

"Mexican American Education in Texas: A Function of Wealth." Taken together, they helped to document the pervasive discrimination against Mexican Americans within the education system.[32]

The Civil Rights Commission's discussion of Mexican Americans was not limited to education. After the 1970 census, the Commission issued a powerful critique of the Census Bureau's count of "Spanish-speaking persons" in its report entitled *Counting the Forgotten*. The report laid out a blistering attack on the Census Bureau on four fronts: the undercount of those who would later be designated as Hispanics; the inadequacy of the questions used to identify the Hispanic population; the insufficient provision of bilingual forms; and the dearth of Latino personnel at the Bureau itself. Reading the Civil Rights Commission reports makes clear that problems of discrimination against Mexican Americans were understood as *integral* to civil rights enforcement at the very moment that the ad hoc committee was drafting the federal ethno-racial taxonomy. Not surprisingly, then, the ad hoc committee framed issues of discrimination in broad terms.[33]

But antidiscrimination policy was not invented *de novo* with the civil rights movement; the federal government had begun to move on issues of discrimination much earlier. Where one begins the political clock here is unclear, but Franklin Roosevelt's Executive Order 8802, signed on June 25, 1941, seems an obvious place to start. The executive order prohibited discrimination by the national defense program and defense contractors on the basis of "race, creed, color, or national origin" and initiated a long series of executive orders aimed at antidiscrimination reform. Harry Truman, Dwight Eisenhower, John Kennedy, and Lyndon Johnson all followed the FDR blueprint when they, too, issued successive executive orders, all of which prohibited discrimination in these very same terms.[34] The mantra "race, creed, color, or national origin" quickly became a hallmark of national policy: American racism, federal policy makes clear, was never limited to race narrowly conceived. Although early antidiscrimination efforts were limited in scope, they are nevertheless instructive when trying to understand the category of ethnicity because they make plain the capacious view of discrimination at work, even in these early decades.[35]

There is an interesting story still to be told as to the origins of this broad conception of discrimination and its remedies within the New Deal. Why FDR framed Executive Order 8802 broadly, to my knowledge, is still not understood. How did state-level Fair Employment Practices Commissions conceptualize discrimination? Other scholars are working on these questions, and I eagerly await the results of their research.[36] In the meantime, it is clear that even as early as 1941, federal antidiscrimination policy was never limited to race narrowly conceived. Directive 15 codified long-standing, widely diffused assumptions about ethnicity as a distinct social formation and its quite particular relation to race.

Recovering the origins of Directive 15 allows us to see how broad conceptions of difference were incorporated into the burgeoning American antidiscrimination policy regime. Difference was not limited to race, but rather had long accommodated identities tied to creed and national origin. Directive 15 codified this capacious conception of difference by specifying ethnicity as a proximate yet distinct social category to that of race. OMB institutionalized a set of presumptions about the heterogeneous nature of difference in the United States in which ethnicity was given a place in the emerging ethno-racial taxonomy but was specified as different from race. The Directive and its 1997 revisions thus buttressed the race-ethnicity distinction by building it into the heart of the American statistical system. Since OMB standards establish our census categories as well, and the census in turn is the denominator for race and ethnic data of all kinds, the OMB categories have set the terms of racial and ethnic classification for American society at large.

Tempting as it is, I do not want to claim that I have uncovered the precise moment of category formation here. If we shift the focus from Directive 15 to the Fair Employment Practices Committee (FEPC), or to early ships' manifests at Ellis Island, or to the Immigration and Naturalization Service, as other scholars have done, we see similar issues being negotiated, albeit in slightly different ways.[37] The task is not to pinpoint the singular original moment; other sites will surely be discovered. What is clear is that Directive 15 codified and institutionalized the race-ethnicity distinction in the heart of the bureaucratic state.

Responses to OMB Classification

The story told thus far considers issues of category formation from the state's point of view: census questions, OMB categories, and executive orders all show how federal bureaucracies came to use ethnicity as well as race. But this is only part of the story; state action alone cannot determine whether the categories will take hold. To see whether bureaucratic categories have any traction, we need to consider issues of ethnic and racial *identification* as well. Did the category Hispanic resonate with those it sought to classify? Did it map readily onto existing social relations? Has the category's legitimacy changed over time? In short, how have Hispanics/Latinos viewed the OMB taxonomy over time?

In fact, the meaning of the term *Hispanic* is by no means settled; it remains highly contested. Immediately after Directive 15 was issued, it was unclear whether the category Hispanic would gain currency in anything other than formally mandated documents. Many questioned whether the pan-ethnic category of Hispanic corresponded with any actual social or political community at all. Martha Gimenez, for example, argued force-fully that analyzing pan-Latino political subjectivity is a fruitless task since no such entity exists. The category was a top-down invention, a product of OMB regulations rather than an expression of ethnic identity from below. The relevant identities, so critics claim, remained those of na-tion, language, class, and migration wave.[38]

The contested status of Hispanic ethnicity, and the pan-ethnic identifi-cation it sought to forge, does not mean that the category has had no pur-chase at all. In fact, there are signs that over time the category has taken hold. Some survey data and ethnographic studies as well suggest that third-generation Latino immigrants are more likely than their parents to identify as Latino or Hispanic, although the recent Pew/Kaiser survey found that this was not so.[39] But even the Pew/Kaiser poll found that the terms *Hispanic* and *Latino* are regularly invoked. When asked what terms do you *ever* use to describe yourself, respondents indicated that they were just about as likely to describe themselves by their own or their parents' country of origin as they were to use the terms *Latino* or *Hispanic* (88:81); when asked which is the *first or only* term they use to describe themselves, 54 percent specified country of origin, 24 percent identified *Latino/His-panic*, and 21 percent identified *American*. The Pew/Kaiser survey sug-gests that pan-ethnic identities are now regularly invoked as counterparts to national and racial classifications.[40]

But even as the term *Hispanic* gained currency, its meaning remained uncertain, especially in terms of the racial identifications. Decipher-ing Latino ethnic and racial identifications is an especially difficult task, Rodriguez and others have argued, because Latin American conceptions of race are quite different from those operating in the United States. In addition, Latino racial identification in the United States may well be changing; as Ian Haney López has suggested, we might well be witness-ing a process of racial formation. Census returns prove to be a surpris-ingly useful site for exploring the shifting ground of Latino identification. How to read census responses requires further explanation.[41]

Latinos and the U.S. Census: The Problem of "Some Other Race"

Since the OMB categories govern all federal agencies, it is OMB policy that sets the Census Bureau's terms. Therefore, we can get some sense of the response to OMB categories via the decennial census returns. In fact, a slight discrepancy between the OMB and census categories has produced a hotly contested bureaucratic fight over how to think about ethnicity and race. The particulars are dry, but the politics is not. It is worth wading through the bureaucratic details to grasp the issues at hand.

The ethnic and racial categories used by the Census Bureau, as with all federal departments and agencies, are governed by the 1997 revisions of Directive 15. However, the Census Bureau has sought, and been granted, permission to include a residual "some other race" category alongside the official OMB race options. The inclusion of "some other race" has come to play an important role in issues of Latino identification, especially in the last decade. In fact, 42.2 percent, or 14,891,303, Latinos checked "some other race," and 97 percent of those checking that category were Latinos.[42] What is more, the number of Latinos selecting "some other race" has increased dramatically over the last two decades. Up through 1980, "some other race" drew little attention because of the small numbers involved. Between 1980 and 1990, however, the numbers began to grow, and they have increased at a rapid clip since then.[43] For example, only 0.03 percent of the total population checked "some other race" in 1950, 0.10 percent in 1960, 0.30 percent in 1970, 3.0 percent in 1980, 3.9 percent in 1990, and 5.6 percent in 2000—almost a twofold increase in the period from 1980 to 2000.[44]

Scholars disagree over how to interpret the growing number of Latinos checking "some other race." Certainly, it reflects the difficulty that many Latinos have in locating themselves within the standard OMB race categories, and this difficulty is creating very real data quality problems for the Census Bureau. So much so that the Census Bureau has been considering dropping "some other race."[45]

The data quality problems surrounding the census race question are generated from the discrepancy between Census Bureau categories and those mandated by OMB. Because other government departments and agencies do not collect data under "some other race," census race data are not compatible with data collected by all other departments and administrative agencies. To reconcile the discrepancy, the Census Bureau *reallocates* respondents who selected "some other race" to one of five standard OMB race categories. The Census Bureau does so via a statistical process of imputation, which then generates the Modified Age, Race, and Sex file, or MARS file, which serves as the operative census data file for all federal departments and agencies.

But there is a further layer that complicates the data collected under "some other race." Although the Bureau reports that 97 percent of those selecting "some other race" were Latinos, this is misleading. In fact, the

Bureau does a preliminary reallocation of those selecting "some other race" to the standard OMB categories *before* it reports the raw data and certainly before the creation of the MARS file. The Bureau uses the 90 percent rule in which it reallocates "some other race" respondents to the standard categories if there is evidence that 90 percent or more of such respondents would generally identify by the relevant race category. Thus, if someone selected "some other race" and wrote in "German," they would be reallocated to white because the Bureau is confident that most Germans identify as white. But if someone selected "some other race" and wrote in "Mexican American" or "Latin American," the Bureau leaves the response as "some other race" because it is well aware that the racial identification of Latinos is a complex matter. Thus, the claim that 97 percent of those selecting "some other race" in the 2000 census were Latinos needs to be qualified since this figure itself reflects long-standing presumptions about the relation between race and nation. In fact, the Bureau reallocates many non-Latinos from "some other race" to the OMB race categories, but does not do so for Latinos because they do not fit easily into the official racial taxonomy now operative in the United States.[46]

The Census Bureau worries about imputation rates because of the data quality problems they generate. To ensure a high-quality census count, the Bureau tracks questions generating high imputation rates. "Some other race" ranks first on the list. Interestingly, the question with the next highest imputation rate is that of same sex and marriage; when members of a household select *both* same sex and married, the Census Bureau actually reallocates either respondent's sex or more often their marital status![47] One way to understand imputation rates is as a barometer of disjunctions between census questions and current social practices—when the two get misaligned, the Bureau initially reallocates the data. If high imputation rates persist or increase, the Bureau rightly senses a problem and seeks to change the question asked. Latino racial identification is the pressing case right now.

The Census Bureau is not happy with the current state of affairs; it does not want to reallocate respondents to categories that respondents themselves did not select. To get out of the imputation business, the Bureau has been considering removing "some other race" from the census form. Doing so, however, makes apparent the difficulty many Latinos face when trying to locate themselves within the OMB race categories, since you will remember there is no brown race in the American ethno-racial taxonomy. Removing "some other race" may well lead to a drop-off in response rate from Latinos on the race question, which in turn will create new problems since nonresponses are also subject to imputation by the Census Bureau.

Thus, the Bureau faces a dilemma. All agree that it is important to improve data quality by avoiding imputation. How to do so is the issue at hand. Removing "some other race" from the race question will diminish one source of imputation, but it may also increase the Latino nonresponse rate since the number of Latinos simply leaving the race question blank may also rise, which in turn will raise imputation rates in another form. The root of the problem lies in the inadequacy of the standard OMB race categories for many within the Latino population: many Latinos simply do not identify readily with the existing OMB race options and thus have selected "some other race" at ever increasing rates. The inclusion of "some other race" on the census form has provided a safety valve for many Latinos, enabling them to negotiate the American taxonomy by selecting the racial residual of "other." The prospect of removing this option may well politicize the Census Bureau's classification of Latinos as an ethnic group and not a race.

To see what the Census Bureau is doing with "some other race," I attended the Census Bureau's Race and Ethnic Advisory Committee (REAC) meetings in Crystal City, Virginia, on May 5 and 6, 2004.[48]

Enter the Bush Hispanics: Crystal City, Virginia, 2004

Race and Ethnicity Advisory Committees were established in the early 1970s as a means of ensuring minority populations and their advocates a voice in the census process. REAC meetings are free and open to the public. Observers cannot participate in the discussions but can attend any sessions. When arriving at Crystal City, I expected to see familiar civil rights advocacy groups in action. After all, when the first Race Advisory Committee was established, the Census Bureau director, Vincent Barabba, had approached Bobby Seale, the Black Panther leader, to serve on the committee. Seale agreed as long as the Census Bureau paid for his bodyguard. In the end, Seale did not take up the appointment because he had to go underground. I was well aware that times had changed but was not prepared for how much so.[49]

I was shocked, perhaps naively, to see that the 2004 committees had been influenced so dramatically by the Republican ascendance in the White House. What were once civil rights forums are now completely transformed. Gone are civil rights advocates, replaced by small entrepreneurs. The Hispanic advisory subcommittee was particularly fascinating.

All of the members were Latinos, but most with explicitly Republican ties. When giving their biographies at the beginning of the concurrent session on May 5, 2004, three of the nine committee members mentioned professional connections to George H. W. Bush, Pete Wilson, and Colin Powell. Six of the nine had been appointed since May 2003, and eight of the nine had been appointed since the election of George W. Bush in 2000.[50] My first reaction was to marvel at the Bush administration's capacity to appoint its own. After all, this is only an *advisory* committee. Given the enormous number of appointments to be made in a new administration, I would not have been surprised to see Democratic appointments lingering on. But that was not the case. There was almost no vestige of an old civil rights politics; few clearly Democrat-identified Committee members were left at all. One has to admire the speed and reach with which Bush Republicans used their powers of appointment to seize the reins of power.

The very first item up for discussion in the Hispanic advisory committee was the race question, specifically the proposed census pretests removing "some other race" for the 2010 census.[51] Much to my surprise, none of the committee members protested removing "some other race." Moreover, committee members clearly understood that eliminating "some other race" would likely mean that most Latinos would check "white" in 2010. No one seemed to see the likely increase in white identification as a problem, though the subcommittee chair, Carlos Chardón, has voiced discontent with the committee's position after the fact.[52] No members made a case for the importance of maintaining "some other race" during the session. Indeed, one committee member even stated that "the whole issue is for the census to give guidance to Hispanics as to where they belong." Another pondered the implications of removing "some other race" for civil rights reform: "If Hispanics are classified as Caucasians, might this jeopardize their civil rights claims?"[53] The committee accepted the need to drop "some other race," even though doing so would mean that most Hispanics would check "white" on future census forms.

Efforts to have Hispanics identified as white are not limited to the Census Bureau fights. A new advocacy group, the National Association for the Advancement of Caucasian Latinos (NAACL), has its own Web site and an elaborate program. Certainly a Web site alone does not make a movement for white racial identification among Latinos, and it is unclear how many are involved in the advocacy group or identify with its program. But it underscores the contested status of Latino racial identity beyond distinctions based on national origin.[54]

In Crystal City, I could see how the Census Bureau's concern for data quality, specifically its desire to avoid rising imputation rates, is dovetailing with the Bush appointments to the Hispanic advisory committee. For now, the issue of "some other race" has been forestalled through Representative José Serrano's actions. But the problem has been deferred, not resolved. In all likelihood, the data quality problems built into "some other race" will continue to grow. Is there another way for U.S. ethno-racial categories to be configured?

Rethinking Latino Ethnicity and Its Relation to Race

An alternative for OMB and the Census Bureau to consider is the possibility of *removing the distinction* between race and ethnicity from the federal statistical system by shifting to a combined-question format. This is an intriguing option in which Latino ethnicity would be placed alongside the standard OMB race categories in a single combined race-ethnicity question. A respondent might select Latino as either an ethnic or a racial identification, but the federal statistical system would no longer reify the distinction. You will recall that Directive 15 and the 1997 revision allow for such a combined-question format, although OMB specifies a preference for ethnic and racial data to be collected separately, especially where self-identification is concerned. But it is only a preference and not a requirement, and thus the combined format is a viable political option that requires only minimal changes in OMB guidelines for the Census Bureau to begin dismantling the race-ethnicity distinction, at least as it resides in the federal statistical system.

However, dismantling the race-ethnicity distinction by shifting to the combined option is not without serious dangers. Eliding the formal distinction between race and ethnicity might well lead to a false sense of equality in which Americans assume, to paraphrase Nathan Glazer, that we are all ethnics now. Combining ethnicity with race without simultaneously changing the social practices that continue to secure ethnic privilege by distinguishing ethnicity from race may only mask persistent ethnic and racial inequalities. Thus, while I think we should remove the formal distinction between race and ethnicity from the federal statistical system, we need to remain alert to, and seek to change, the complex ways in which ethnic advantage has long been secured by defining ethnicity against race. Changes in the taxonomy *alone* cannot redress the complex relation between ethnic and racial identification; the relational meaning of these two terms is deeply embedded in American society. Taxonomic changes can contribute to a reworking of these social categories, but formal changes need to be buttressed by a politics in which the meaning and social relations between ethnic groups and races shift as well. Formal taxonomic equality will be meaningful only if it is sustained by equitable social and political practices. To this end, we need to look beyond the federal government to see how the categories are being deployed and reshaped in other domains. The following chapter turns to New York City politics in an effort to assess whether Latino ethnicity is changing in other domains as well.

Shadowed by Race: **6**
Latinos in New York City Politics, 2001 and Beyond

What it means to be an ethnic in the United States is changing. Not only are the parameters of ethnicity being formally reconsidered by the state, but Latinos are refashioning ethnicity from below as well. Many Latinos are repositioning themselves within the American ethno-racial taxonomy by racializing their identities and aligning *with*, rather than *against*, Blacks. This ethnic repositioning is taking place in many locales, but it is most clearly visible in the classic immigrant cities of Los Angeles, San Diego, Miami, and New York, where demographic shifts are changing the political calculus for ethnics and Blacks. Once "nonwhites" approach the 50 percent mark, becoming white is no longer the only way to gain political power. The possibilities of building a successful Black-Brown coalition seem to grow by the day. Consider, for example, the mayoral candidacies of Antonio Villaraigosa, in Los Angeles, and Fernando Ferrer, in New York. Both ran as Democratic Party mayoral candidates in 2001; both sought to forge Black-Brown coalitions through racialized appeals to class; both tried to reposition Latinos' political subjectivity from that of white ethnics to members of a class-based racial alliance. Neither Villaraigosa nor Ferrer was elected in 2001, but their campaigns nevertheless signaled important changes under way.[1]

The question, then, is how, and on what grounds, are American Latinos identifying politically? How are they positioning themselves, and being positioned by others, within the American racial taxonomy? And what of their political identification? How will they line up within American party politics in the years ahead? Many believe, as I do, that how Latino identifications play out in the next two decades will be *the* critical site of political change, establishing where basic social cleavages will be drawn and political alliances made. If Latinos continue to identify primarily as white, or as white ethnics, as Orlando Patterson and others have suggested, then the central cleavage will continue to fall between Blacks, on the one hand, and whites allied with white ethnics, on the other. But if large numbers of Latinos break with the past by racializing their ethnicity, they may well shift the balance of power by forging a sizable coalition between Blacks and Latinos identifying as "people of color."[2] Which of these political positionings will win out is far from clear: Latinos do not agree over whom to support, or how to position themselves within the American ethno-racial taxonomy. Contestation and uncertainty are the order of the day, but how these contested identities sort out, which way the trends go, is the issue at hand.

Moreover, the contested status of Latino racial identification has enormous implications for party politics as well. Even though race and party never mirror each other directly, enduring links between race and party have been forged so that African Americans identify and vote solidly Democratic, at rates of 80 percent or better. Indeed, it is this seventy-year-long association between race and party that is now in question: will the growing number of Latino voters follow African Americans and identify with the Democratic Party? Or might Latinos be wooed successfully into the ranks of the Republican Party? Democratic and Republican Party activists clearly recognize the political opening and have been actively courting Latino voters for some time, anticipating that how Latinos come to identify politically will be of enormous consequence to the electoral fortunes on both sides of the partisan aisle.[3]

Even if the vast majority of Latinos continue to identify as Democrats, how they identify racially will have important consequences for what sort of party it will be. Will the Democratic Party continue to defend race-based policy reform, or will it shift its focus, as some have advocated, to race-neutral policy reform? How Latino Democrats identify racially will shape the substantive political commitments of the Democratic Party in decades to come.

To get a better sense of the changing conceptions of race and ethnicity currently under way, and the significance of these changes for Democratic Party politics, I turn to New York City, where struggles over ethnic identification are readily apparent. There are signs of change in national politics as well. George W. Bush and his Democratic rivals have made targeted appeals to Latino voters by running Spanish-language commercials, including Spanish segments in their speeches, and campaigning regularly in Latino communities, in an effort to court the Latino vote.[4] But for now, these trends are playing out with greater intensity at the local level and may well take some time to work their way through as a major factor on the national stage. To explore current changes in ethno-racial identification, I focus on the New York City mayoral election of 2001 as a harbinger of the political terrain ahead.

Before turning to Latinos in New York, a few cautionary remarks are in order. First, many question whether the pan-ethnic category of Hispanic/Latino corresponds with *any* social or political community. After all, the category was itself a top-down invention, a product of the Office of Management and Budget (OMB) regulations, rather than an expression of shared identity from below. As a consequence, many claim that analyzing pan-Latino political identity is a fruitless task since no such collective entity exists: the relevant identities remain those of nation, language, class, and migration wave.[5] Second, Latinos have not been especially politically active to date, with low rates of naturalization and voter registration limiting their political power. Whether Latinos will ever emerge as a political force is not certain.[6] Finally, even if we recognize Latinos as a group, albeit a deeply fractured one, deciphering shifts in Latino racial identifications is especially difficult because Latin American conceptions of race differ significantly from those operating in the United States. This disjunction in racial taxonomies makes it all the more difficult to interpret the political significance of racial identification of Latino immigrants in cities like New York.[7]

All that being said, there is considerable evidence that the pan-Latino identifications are taking hold, and even when the long-term patterns remain uncertain, the sheer size of the Latino population, which is now regularly identified as the largest and fastest growing minority in the United States, means that the stakes are too high to sit back and wait. Scholars and activists alike feel compelled to assess current trends.[8] Rodolfo de la Garza and others have argued that the extent of political openness has been overdrawn; in fact, the vast majority of Latinos, especially if one brackets Cubans, continue to identify with the Democratic Party with little evidence of a shift to the Republican Party.[9] On this telling, the Democrats have much to gain from increased Latino mobilization, which may well consolidate their electoral advantage in a number of important states.[10] The balance of power in Texas, New Mexico, California, Colorado, and Florida all might be determined by the shifting allegiances

of Latino voters in the years ahead. But the Democratic advantage is by
no means secure; the 2002 gubernatorial races in New York, Florida, and
Texas suggest that Democrats should not to be too complacent when assuming Latino support since many Latino voters helped elect Republican
governors in each of these states. The Texas case is especially worrisome
for Democrats since Tony Sanchez, a seventh-generation Mexican American, was soundly defeated by his Republican Party opponent, Rick Perry,
who obtained significant Latino support.[11]

Continued Democratic identification among Latinos notwithstanding,
the number of Latino Independents has grown over the last decade, suggesting that party attachments might be weakening, leading some Latinos to become swing voters. The 2002 Pew/Kaiser national survey of "The
Latino Electorate" showed 49 percent of Latinos identified as Democrats,
20 percent as Republicans, and 19 percent as Independents. But looking more closely still, we see a quite pronounced age differential when
it comes to party identification; those fifty-five and older identified
64 percent Democratic, 17 percent Republican, and 12 percent Independent, while those eighteen to twenty-nine identified 34 percent Democratic, 21 percent Republican, and 26 percent Independent. It is precisely
these *young* Latino Independents that the Republican Party so anxiously
courts. To date, Republican inroads have been small, but whether they
will remain so is the thing to watch.[12]

Democrats and Race: The New York Mayoral Election, 2001

The Democratic Party primary initially scheduled for September 11,
2001, was rescheduled for September 25 after the attack on the World
Trade Center. Four candidates were on the ballot: Mark Green, the early
front runner and the most liberal of the lot; Fernando Ferrer, his principal
rival, who if elected would have become the first Puerto Rican mayor of
New York; Alan Hevesi; and Peter Vallone (neither Hevesi nor Vallone
ever made a strong showing). Much to many New Yorkers' surprise, Ferrer came in first on primary day, having overtaken Green's initial forty-
point lead. Even though Ferrer beat Green by three percentage points, he
was five points shy of the required 40 percent needed to avoid a runoff
election, which was scheduled for October 11. Green won the runoff,
obtaining 52 percent of the vote to Ferrer's 48 percent. But Green went on
to lose the general election to the Republican candidate, Michael Bloomberg, on November 6, 2001. Green's eventual defeat surprised many
because registered Democrats outnumber Republicans by 4 to 1 in New
York City.[13]

The reasons for Bloomberg's victory are multiple and complex; many factors shaped voter choices, especially in the immediate aftermath of 9/11. My aim is not to provide a definite account of why Bloomberg won; rather, I want to use the mayoral election as a window onto internal Democratic Party politics on questions of race. Green and Ferrer, along with Al Sharpton, who became an important figure in the race, represent three contending modes of racial politics on offer within the Democratic Party today. Green, the classic liberal and Jew, has a long-standing track record on civil rights, but also was seen by many as arrogant and exclusionary— a white liberal speaking on behalf of others. Ferrer, on the other hand, tried to embody a sense of racial pluralism by mobilizing Blacks, Latinos, and liberal whites into a racially coded class-based alliance. Finally, the specter of Al Sharpton hung over the race, embodying a politics in Black and white, a politics fueled, many claimed, by racial polarization and division. Tracing both Ferrer's initial success and subsequent defeat reveals critical fault lines over race politics that continue to plague Democratic Party politics—fault lines that pivot critically on the ethnic and racial identification of Latinos.

Certainly, the Ferrer strategy of bringing together a multiracial and ethnic coalition within the Democratic Party is not new; it was the basis of Jesse Jackson's Rainbow Coalitions in 1984 and 1988, and the Harold Washington, David Dinkins, and Tom Bradley administrations in Chicago, New York, and Los Angeles, respectively. Indeed, one might say that forging a Black-Latino alliance with white liberals has been the principal counterpart to the more centrist strategy epitomized by Bill Clinton and the Democratic Leadership Council at the national level and by Mayor Ed Koch in New York City. One way of viewing Ferrer's campaign is as the latest effort at forging a progressive Democratic Party coalition—a strategy that has been in formation in New York City since the early days of the anti-Koch movement.[14] From this perspective, it is interesting to compare Ferrer's initial success and ultimate defeat with the earlier Koch-Dinkins, Dinkins-Giuliani, Giuliani-Messinger campaigns and to ponder, as John Mollenkopf has done, why such a liberal city as New York has had more trouble forging progressive coalitions than their Democratic Party counterparts in Los Angeles, Chicago, and Philadelphia.[15] But I leave this task to other scholars. I want to place Ferrer in a different frame.

Rather than comparing Ferrer with other New York City mayoral candidates over the last two decades, I want to contrast his campaign with other appeals to ethnicity across the twentieth century. In preceding chapters, I have shown how American cultural and political elites from the 1910s onward have repeatedly positioned ethnicity against race as cultural difference rather than the supposedly more bodily difference of race. In this chapter, I want to consider how Ferrer's conception of ethnicity differed from that advanced by Horace Kallen, Isaac Berkson, or Julius Drachsler before him, and to contrast Ferrer's view of Latino identity with that offered by OMB in 1977 when it designated Hispanics as an ethnic group and not a race. How did Ferrer's campaign seek to rework the long-standing American distinction between ethnicity and race? How did Ferrer's campaign seek to transform the American ethno-racial taxonomy through racially coded appeals to class? What, in short, do these broader historical comparisons reveal about the changing nature of American ethnicity in the mayoral campaign?

Freddy Ferrer and "the Other New York"

Ferrer's campaign was heralded by many as a timely effort at coalition building as Ferrer claimed that he would fight for those shut out of the Giuliani administration and the 1990s' dot-com economic boom. Ferrer appealed to those left behind by declaring that he would represent "the other New York":

> Let's talk about *the other New York*, the New York where most New Yorkers live, the New York where 1.1 million children, most of them black and Latino and Asian, poor and working class, attend public schools that are underfunded, that are overcrowded and increasingly staffed by teachers who lack proper training and credentials.[16]

Initially, Ferrer successfully invoked "the other New York" as a means of contrasting his campaign with the Giuliani administration:

> Undeniably, New York City has gotten better in so many respects in the last eight years, but I do not view the last eight years as an unalloyed success. Just as the New Yorkers who can't find a decent place to live at a price they can afford, or the parents of New York City public school children who are still deeply conflicted about their public schools, finding too many of those children trapped in schools that cannot succeed. Or the one out of four New Yorkers who has no health insurance and no decent and reliable access to health care. Or too many New Yorkers who find themselves on the wrong side of the divide of distrust with their own Police Department. Those are the things that need to change to bring this city to the very next level.[17]

Like many politicians, Ferrer frequently referred to his familial disadvantages; he grew up on Fox Street in the South Bronx when, as he put it, "it was *the* South Bronx." As a child he did not always have heat or hot water, at times had holes in his shoes, and had to learn to survive in a tough neighborhood.[18] Moreover, Ferrer referred regularly to his achievements as Bronx borough president, especially in the area of housing: he claimed to have generated more than sixty thousand new housing units to replace the infamous rubble and abandoned buildings with their decals in the windows depicting fake flowers and curtains so as to make passersby think that the buildings were inhabited. Ferrer framed his campaign at the first mayoral forum sponsored by the Village Independent Democrats on January 24, 2001:

> Let me tell you the reason why I am running, and it's really rooted in a lot of what I have been trying to do in the Bronx over the last 14 years as borough president. You might recall the circumstances under which I became borough president [recounts dilapidated conditions of the Bronx, including burned-out buildings with decals that made it look as if there were windows with window shades and flower pots]. . . .
>
> Let me fast-forward 14 years, 64,000 units of housing. Some home ownership, 2- and 3-family homes. Those apartment buildings with the pictures of the window shades and flower pots. Real windows, real window shades. Some real flower pots, and above all real people living on the inside. 64,000 of them.[19]

What political work was accomplished through the slogan "the other New York"? Who did it mobilize? And on what grounds?

Two aspects of Ferrer's campaign are especially important from my perspective. First, note that his Democratic Party opponents as well as political commentators quickly accused Ferrer of running a racially divisive campaign that many considered inappropriate, especially after September 11. But Ferrer stuck with his program, no doubt in large part because he needed to distinguish himself from his Democratic Party rivals, all of whom were white liberals. By emphasizing his Puerto Rican background and long-standing ties to the Bronx, and by declaring that he was going to speak for those who had been left out, Ferrer sought to mobilize African American and Latino voters through racially coded appeals to class.[20] One might say that Ferrer and his advisers adapted strategies of racial coding that had been used so effectively by Republicans in the 1980s and redeployed them to their own ends. Where George H. W. Bush had fostered white backlash in his presidential race with Michael Dukakis through racially coded Willie Horton ads, Ferrer used racially coded language as a means of *attracting* Black and Latino support—racial coding in reverse, if you will, in which they made *indirect* appeals to race while speaking directly about class.[21] Second, note how Ferrer tried to reposition Latino ethnicity. Unlike Kallen, Berkson, Kroeber, and Drachsler, Ferrer did *not* distinguish ethnicity from race as cultural difference rather than a difference of blood. Instead, Ferrer focused on issues of economic and racial exclusion, on what Latinos and African Americans might share, rather than on what drives them apart. Ferrer's appeal to "the other New York" tried to reposition Latinos alongside rather than against Blacks.

For Ferrer, poverty and race were two sides of the same coin; neither could be addressed effectively on its own. They were intimately connected. Linking race and class required reworking long-standing Democratic Party assumptions in which the two forms of inequality had been addressed at length sequentially, but rarely together. The New Deal had mobilized voters on the basis of class and had adopted an extensive policy agenda to remedy the most egregious economic inequalities, but classic New Deal policies made little or no effort to redress the color line.[22] Civil rights politics, at least in the retelling, is seen as politics attendant to race rather than class. Ferrer's campaign tried to put race and class back together by emphasizing how deeply entangled they are; neither can be remedied effectively if they are split apart. Attending to the *intersection* of race and class seemed to resonate with many voters, and certainly helped to distinguish Ferrer from his Democratic primary rivals, all of whom tried to build on, rather than criticize, the Giuliani administration.

Reworking the relation between race and class, however, was no easy matter; the more entangled the phenomena, the less clear the policy solution. When race and class were seen as discrete problems, it was easier to identify appropriate leverage points at which to direct public action, but when they are viewed as intricately connected, it becomes all the more difficult to cut the Gordian knot. During the campaign, Ferrer seemed caught in just this dilemma. While he successfully appealed to the simultaneity of race and class as it is lived in "the other New York," he was unable to craft a clear programmatic response, unable to craft a policy agenda that was tailored to redressing the complex *interactive* dynamic that has served to entrench racial and economic inequality as two sides of the same coin. Interestingly, Ferrer has pursued this intersectional vision with greater self-consciousness in the aftermath of the election. For example, Ferrer began an op-ed on education policy in *Newsday* this way:

> Last year when I ran for mayor, I spoke about the unmet needs of "the other New York." This New York is where economic class, race, ethnicity and geography intersect with dramatic consequences for everyone. I took

a lot of heat for saying this because it is sometimes difficult to think about differences when we want so desperately to unite as a city. But "the other New York" exists. . . . Its residents are the 1.1 million children—overwhelmingly working class and poor, black and Latino—who rely on a public school system that is failing to provide them with opportunities to succeed.[23]

The difficult task ahead, for Ferrer and other urban Democrats, was to fashion a policy agenda that matched their recognition of the simultaneity of economic and racial inequality. This was no easy task and something that few Democrats—old or new—have attempted.

Even though there is much to admire in Ferrer's campaign, I do not want to cast him as too heroic a figure by overdrawing the extent to which he took a strong position on questions of racial discrimination and racial inequality. He did not always do so. Most of the time, his appeals were more clearly framed in terms of class, with race left *implicit*. Ferrer's speeches, interviews, campaign debates, forums and roundtables, and campaign Web site reveal that Ferrer rarely took on questions of racial discrimination and inequality directly. Moreover, in the first mayoral debate on May 6, 2001, Ferrer was asked whom he would support in a hypothetical three-way race among Giuliani, Koch, and Dinkins. Ferrer evaded the question: he would not declare even hypothetical support for Dinkins. Eventually, the moderator cut Ferrer off, saying, "Right, OK, we get it, you want to dodge it," an equivocation that some have suggested led Dinkins to endorse Green shortly thereafter.[24] In addition, somewhat surprisingly, Ferrer did not make police brutality and racial profiling central to his campaign, even though both had become highly politicized issues after the two high-profile cases involving Abner Louima and Amadou Diallo from August 1997 through September 2002.[25] Throughout the campaign, Ferrer shifted back and forth from appeals to "the other New York" to advertisements that claimed that he would represent "all New Yorkers," thereby diminishing the sense that he would stand by those left out.[26]

Finally, several liberal icons such as former governor Mario Cuomo and Congressman Jerrold Nadler criticized Ferrer for flip-flopping on the death penalty and abortion, and for having overdrawn his role in revitalizing the Bronx. For critics, he was a political opportunist who would change his policy positions to win elections, thereby again casting doubt on the depths of his commitment to "the other New York."[27] But rather than dwelling on his limitations, we might see his campaign in a different light. When a political moderate like Ferrer is willing to make a racialized appeal to Latino voters, perhaps this shows just how much the mainstream political calculus had begun to shift. Ferrer no longer assumed that the only pathway to power was for Latinos to distance themselves from Blacks. Rather, Ferrer and his advisers sought to bridge rather than reinforce the race-ethnicity divide, thereby trying to build political alliances between Latinos and Blacks.[28]

Building the Coalition: Who Supported Ferrer?

Ferrer's efforts to forge a racially coded class-based coalition between Latinos and Blacks gained new credibility when African American and Latino political leaders organized a joint endorsement of Ferrer on August 17, 2001. All of those endorsing Ferrer at this carefully orchestrated event were clearly identified by the media as stalwarts from within the Democratic Party: Congressman Charles Rangel; Manhattan Borough president C. Virginia Fields; assemblymen Keith Wright and Adriano Espaillat; City Council members Bill Perkins, Philip Reed, Margarita López, and Guilermo Linares; Representative Nydia M. Velázquez; State Senator Olga A. Mendez. All had political authority through Democratic Party service. After this collective endorsement, the media began to portray Ferrer as both leading and building a Black-Latino alliance. The image was reinforced when Dennis Rivera, of the health-care workers' union 1199, composed largely of Black and Latino workers, also endorsed Ferrer on September 5, 2001. New York demographics *and* politics were increasingly portrayed in plural terms rather than Black and white.[29]

During this wave of endorsements, Ferrer's campaign gained momentum—suddenly it seemed that Ferrer might actually win.[30] Only one figure was missing from the fray; Al Sharpton had not yet endorsed anyone, and there was much speculation as to whether he, too, would back Ferrer's campaign. Initially, Sharpton's absence from the group endorsement on August 17 was explained by the fact that Sharpton was serving a ninety-day term in federal prison for trespassing during a protest of U.S. Navy bombing exercises on the Puerto Rican island of Vieques. After much anticipation, Sharpton eventually backed Ferrer on August 27, 2001. At this point, Ferrer already had the momentum; Sharpton was merely joining the ascending coalition. But things changed quickly once Sharpton appeared. His endorsement of Ferrer set in motion a racial dynamic that shaped the last six weeks of the campaign.

The primary, rescheduled because of September 11, was eventually held on September 25. What had begun as a cakewalk for Green ended up being a hotly contested campaign in which Green saw his forty-point lead disappear and Ferrer come out ahead on Election Day. Ferrer defeated

Green in the primary by four percentage points (35 to 31), while the three other Democratic Party candidates split the remaining votes. Black voters broke 52 percent to 34 percent for Ferrer over Green; Hispanics/Latinos voters chose Ferrer 72 percent to 12 percent; and whites opted for Green over Ferrer 40 percent to 7 percent, with the remaining white voters going to Hevesi and Vallone. Interestingly, there was a considerable class differential in Ferrer and Green support; union members voted 41 percent to 27 percent for Ferrer over Green, and those whose income was $29,999 or less supported Ferrer over Green by twenty points or more. Voters at the other end of the income scale, $75,000 and up, went for Green over Ferrer by twenty points or better. Ferrer's appeal to "the other New York" seemed to have worked; there was much excitement at the possibility of Ferrer becoming the first Puerto Rican mayor of New York.[31]

Although he won the primary, Ferrer did not have the 40 percent required for an outright win, and a runoff was scheduled between Ferrer and Green for October 11. The runoff campaign was nastier than the primary: where Green had been relatively restrained in the earlier race, now he took off the gloves hoping that "the mean Mark Green" could differentiate himself from his opponent.[32] Since there were few programmatic differences between the two Democratic contenders, both the Green campaign and the media increasingly made race the wedge issue. Even though Green had a long track record of supporting civil rights and consumer protection, and had a more progressive stance on both the death penalty and abortion, there was something in Green's demeanor, in his arrogance and assumptions about power, that signaled to many that his administration would involve a progressive politics in which white liberals would speak on behalf of racialized others. Green signaled his whiteness at several points in the campaign, at first by relying almost exclusively on an all-white kitchen cabinet, and through his equivocation over whether he had sought an endorsement from Al Sharpton. After not securing Sharpton's support, Green denied that he had ever tried to court Sharpton, an equivocation that many believe hurt Green with Black voters. More telling still, after 9/11 Green ran an attack ad calling Ferrer "borderline irresponsible" and "racially divisive." The ad ended with a voice asking, "Can we afford to take a chance?"[33]

Most notoriously, after losing to Ferrer in the primary, the Green campaign worked to inflame white racial fears via anonymous automated telephone calls the night before the runoff in which voters were told to go to the polls to stop Ferrer giving Sharpton "the keys to City Hall" and through the distribution of leaflets inflaming fears of Sharpton's power within a Ferrer administration. One of the leaflets included a *New York*

Post cartoon (initially published on October 4, 2001) in which Ferrer is shown, knees bent, kissing Al Sharpton's rear. Text was added to the cartoon urging voters to go to the polls or else "Al Sharpton will be our next mayor." Both the phone calls and flyers were targeted at the outer boroughs in an effort to mobilize white voters through their racial fears.[34]

It is important to remember that it was Green, the longtime advocate of civil rights, who played the race card. We see how readily white liberals could simultaneously advocate civil rights principles while benefiting from white racist fears.

As if all this were not enough, after winning the runoff, Green continued to alienate many nonwhite voters with his botched efforts at rapprochement with the Ferrer campaign. The hope had been to reunite the party behind a single candidate, thereby strengthening Green's hand in the general election. But reconciliation was not easily secured. On all accounts, the meeting did not go well, and during a heated exchange, Green is reported to have said to Ferrer organizers, "I don't need you to win, I need you to govern." This response resonated with unfavorable images of Green as embodying whiteness, arrogance, and power—as one reporter put it, Green is "the Great White Hope" of the New York Democratic Party.[35]

On Election Day, the vast majority of white voters, 83 percent, backed Green over Ferrer, thereby returning New York politics to Black and white. Gone was the possibility of Ferrer's ethnic racialization in the service of building a multiracial and ethnic coalition. As one commentator put it, Green's runoff strategy was clear: "Get whites to turn out against Ferrer by raising the specter of a Sharpton takeover of City Hall."[36] Once Green's liberalism was tied to whiteness, choosing one meant embracing the other. The specter of Al Sharpton came to dominate the racial dynamics of the campaign, symbolizing the dangers of race-based political mobilization for many New Yorkers.[37]

I do not recount Green's race baiting because it is especially remarkable. In many ways, such tactics *have* become standard fare—the everyday practices of negative campaigning, especially when white liberals are running against nonwhite rivals. The issue is not the uniqueness of the New York election; nor do I want to claim that these tactics decided the outcome. Rather, the New York primary is useful because it stages in no uncertain terms the competing strategies *within* the Democratic Party over how the Left should address racial inequality today. The New York mayoral election makes clear both the stakes therein and the treacherous road ahead.

Al Sharpton and Specters of Racial Excess

Within days of Ferrer's primary victory, the racial dynamics of the mayoral campaign changed. Once Sharpton entered the fray, Ferrer began to lose his political authority; he was increasing portrayed as a diminutive figure, overshadowed physically and politically by Al Sharpton. Increasingly, Ferrer was seen as politically ineffective, as having lost control of his campaign, which was now depicted as being in the hands of extra Democratic Party forces. Gone were discussions of coalition building between Blacks and Latinos or of the new immigration and its impact on New York politics. Instead, commentators increasingly focused on Ferrer's supposedly dependent relationship with Sharpton and began to read the election as a rerun of older racial politics that dominated in the decades between the 1960s and Dinkins's administration (1989–93). Sharpton's endorsement quickly raised images of intense racial conflict that were reminiscent for many of the intense racial conflict during the Crown Heights riots and Red Apple boycott, both of which had polarized New Yorkers into opposing racial camps.[38]

Sharpton, unlike the other African Americans who endorsed Ferrer, was not subject to the disciplining forces of the Democratic Party organization. Media coverage repeatedly implied that no one would be containing Sharpton's influence within a Ferrer administration. Commentators anxiously began to ask whether Sharpton would have a veto over the next police commissioner—indeed, would he be given the keys to city hall? Ferrer's effort to rework the race-ethnicity distinction was eclipsed as political debate was increasingly cast as Black and white. Discussions of Black-Latino coalition building virtually disappeared—overshadowed by Sharpton's symbolic presence.[39]

This shift in Ferrer's image from coalition builder to political pawn was captured most vividly by a series of Sean Delonas cartoons run in the conservative *New York Post* the week before the Democratic Party runoff.[40]

Taken together, the cartoons are remarkable, offering one image after another of Sharpton as the embodiment of racial excess and Ferrer his pawn. In each, Sharpton is enormous, even grotesque, at times balloon-like, as if about to explode, an inflated body with receding head, swallowed up quite literally by his own gigantic girth. Along with his size, Sharpton's clothes appear to be out of control, always disheveled and bursting at the seams. In four of the six cartoons, Delonas included little puffs of gas emanating from Sharpton's rear as if to suggest that he is in some literal sense full of hot air and an odoriferous presence to boot. In most

Figure 3: Sean Delonas, *New York Post*, October 3, 2001. Reprinted with permission from the NEW YORK POST, 2006, Copyright, NYP Holdings, Inc.

Figure 4: Sean Delonas, *New York Post*, October 5, 2001. Reprinted with permission from the NEW YORK POST, 2006, Copyright, NYP Holdings, Inc.

Figure 5: Sean Delonas, *New York Post*, October 7, 2001. Reprinted with permission from the NEW YORK POST, 2006, Copyright, NYP Holdings, Inc.

Figure 6: Sean Delonas, *New York Post*, October 10, 2001. Reprinted with permission from the NEW YORK POST, 2006, Copyright, NYP Holdings, Inc.

Figure 7: Sean Delonas, *New York Post*, October 11, 2001. Reprinted with permission from the NEW YORK POST, 2006, Copyright, NYP Holdings, Inc.

of the cartoons, Ferrer is shown as a tiny, scrawny figure, powerless, and ineffectual alongside the oversized Al. Two of the cartoons underscore the point, depicting Ferrer as a puppet and Sharpton as the puppeteer. Sharpton, Delonas keeps suggesting, was now calling the shots, with Ferrer merely serving as his mouthpiece.

Attending to the racial dynamics of Sharpton's endorsement helps explain why Ferrer got an unexpected bounce when he refused to go along with Mayor Giuliani's demand that he be granted special dispensation for an unprecedented extended term—a special request given the unique circumstances facing the city after 9/11. Unlike his Democratic rivals, Ferrer refused to agree to Giuliani's demand and, at least temporarily, countered the image of himself as a political pawn.[41] For the most part, however, the specter of Sharpton hung over the campaign as Ferrer was cast again and again as a diminished figure alongside an oversized Sharpton.

The Queering of Al Sharpton

The *Post* cartoon of October 4, 2001, that the Green campaign circulated in the outer boroughs to generate white support, shows Sharpton bending over, oversized as usual. Ferrer with bended knees is kissing Sharpton's

Figure 8: Sean Delonas, *New York Post*, October 4, 2001. Reprinted with permission from the NEW YORK POST, 2006, Copyright, NYP Holdings, Inc.

rear, while Sharpton says, "You're the best Freddy, the very best!!!"[42] Ferrer again is positioned as the one trying to please, though here sexual overtones are thrown into the mix, suggesting that the alliance between them lies beyond prevailing heterosexual norms.

In fact, issues of sexuality and cross-dressing are recurring tropes in Sharpton cartoons; take, for example, the Jim Sleeper article in Salon.com entitled "The Joker" in which he attacks Sharpton, as many have done, of playing "race-card politics." To underscore the point, a cartoon is placed at the head of the essay in which Sharpton appears on the face of a playing card dressed as a Joker, clothed in leotard and harlequin hat, with arm outstretched and bent at the wrist.[43]

Perhaps the most spectacular was the *Village Voice* cover from its April 16–22, 2003, issue in which Sharpton is seen getting a "makeover."[44] Sharpton appears in profile, pink curlers in his hair, with several unattached hands applying lipstick, blush, powder, and spray to his face and hair. The accompanying article, "The Makeover of Al Sharpton," is about Sharpton's 2004 presidential run. Although the text is somewhat favorable, the graphic is hardly a pinup poster for a serious presidential figure. By casting Sharpton as a feminine figure—as emotive, unproductive, and consumed with his appearance—the media served to marginalize and discredit.

What is going on here? What exactly does the specter of Sharpton signify in the New York election? What is it that makes Sharpton such a con-
troversial figure? Who was purveying these images? And to what political
effect?

The *New York Post* cartoons of Sharpton were by no means the first,
nor will they be the last; Sharpton is someone cartoonists love to draw.
While researching this chapter, I began collecting images of Sharpton;
once I began looking, I found that Sharpton iconography abounds, so
much so that after a short time I began to feel as if I were inhabiting
a Sharptonesque version of Spike Lee's *Bamboozled*. Sharpton, it seems,
has come to symbolize for many the dangerous consequences that follow
a certain kind of race politics. Beginning with the Howard Beach protests
in late 1986–87, and especially since the Tawana Brawley episode of late
1987–88, Sharpton has been a figure of both awe and disdain.[45] As one
of the more sympathetic profiles put it: Sharpton is "a riddle: a peculiar
synthesis of courage and opportunism, a mind-bending hybrid of Jesse
Jackson, James Brown, and Don King—with elements of Marcus Garvey,
Father Divine, and George Wallace thrown in."[46] Since the mid-1980s, the
leading general circulation magazines, newspapers, and online journals
such as the *New York Times*, the *National Review*, the *Village Voice*, the
New Yorker, the *Economist*, the *Nation*, *Esquire*, *Gentleman's Quarterly*,
New York Press, *New York Magazine*, the *American Prospect*, Slate,
and Salon.com all have run profiles of Sharpton.[47] Indeed, almost any
discussion of post–civil rights politics in New York inevitably comes back
to Sharpton; activists and commentators alike seem compelled to comment on Sharpton as a means of signaling where they stand. For many,
Sharpton embodies political practices beyond the pale, although exactly what it is about Sharpton that remains out of bounds is not easily
characterized.

As is often the case with major political figures, Sharpton is a complex and compromised figure whose actions have turned many potential
supporters away. Most notably, Sharpton has been accused of being an
FBI informant and of having ties to the Mob.[48] When confronted with
these accusations, at times Sharpton has denied their validity, while on
other occasions he has acknowledged providing information to the FBI
concerning known drug dealers, while denying that he acted as a political informant.[49] Such accusations certainly raise serious questions about
Sharpton's credibility as political activist on the Left. But even assuming
these allegations to be true, they do not quite put the issue of Sharpton to
rest. They do not fully explain the intense emotions that Sharpton continues to arouse, nor do they account for the persistence of Sharpton as an

Figure 9: Stanley Martucci and Cheryl Griesbach, *Village Voice*, April 16–22, 2003.
Reprinted with permission of Griesbach/Martucci.

Figure 10: Joseph Salina, *Village Voice*, April 16–22, 2003. Copyright Joseph Salina.
Reprinted with the artist's permission; may not be reproduced without his consent.

iconographic figure. There is a dynamic in play here that is worth attending to because it foregrounds important racial fault lines that continue to
plague the American Left.

Sharpton, Race, Power, and Division

Since the mid-1980s or before, Sharpton has been depicted as a fantastical
figure, as both literally and figuratively larger than life. Almost all the
commentary in the mainstream and Left media has been negative; critics
focus repeatedly on two aspects. On the one hand, Sharpton is repeatedly dismissed as a "charlatan," "clown," "joker," "showman," and "buffoon," whose political antics play into the emotions of the masses and the
sensationalist impulses of the news media. Despite all the posturing, so
it is said, Sharpton is ultimately politically ineffective, delivering little
or nothing to his constituents except for the cathartic emotional appeal.[50]
Characterizations of Sharpton also repeatedly draw attention to his appearance, referring incessantly to his "inflatable hair do," "considerable
girth," "gaudy gold medallions," and infamous jogging suits, all of which
are used to underscore his lack of professionalism and to position Sharpton as operating beyond prevailing political norms.[51]

However, many of these traits, including the gold medallion and perhaps even his hair, might be described in more positive terms in which
they are seen as evidence of Sharpton's past political achievements and
enduring commitment to civil rights reform. After all, the "gaudy medallion" is in fact a Martin Luther King medal awarded to Sharpton, and the
hairdo was modeled after James Brown, to whom Sharpton made a promise that he would wear his hair in this style until Brown died.[52] *Ebony*
magazine alone offers a more sympathetic account of Sharpton's hairdo,
underscoring the slant that infuses more mainstream media views:

> In 1981, Brown was invited to the White House to meet Ronald Reagan,
> who, at the time, was considering a national Martin Luther King Jr.
> holiday. Brown told Sharpton he wanted him to come along. But before
> he took Sharpton to the White House, he first took him to his hairdresser,
> who permed Sharpton's Afro. "He said, 'I want [Reagan] to see a younger
> version of me when he sees you,'" Sharpton recalls. "After I did it, he
> said he wanted me to keep my hair like that until he died, as our bond. So
> that's how I ended up with this hairstyle. Later, it became a trademark for
> me. But people never understood that it is a personal thing between James
> and me. Even when he got into trouble and went to jail, he would call me
> every other day and say, 'Rev., you holding up with your hair?'"[53]

By refusing to identify the medallion correctly as a civil rights award, commentators played into depictions of Black consumption as tasteless and undisciplined. As for his hairdo, one might consider it evidence of Sharpton's capacity to keep his promise rather than vain excess. All the attention to his weight, hair, and medallion keeps the focus on appearance rather than substance. Visuals have been particularly effective means of dismissing Sharpton as a serious political figure; even the rather thoughtful assessment of Sharpton's presidential bid was accompanied by the dramatic illustration by Joseph Salinas in which Sharpton is depicted as having morphed into a circus tent.[54] Why, I want to know, does the media portray Sharpton as a figure of ridicule and excess? Why is he feminized and thereby cast as an ineffective or inappropriate political leader?

But there is another side to portraits of Sharpton. Alongside characterizations of him as an ineffective showman, the media also casts him as a dangerous and powerful figure. Here the emphasis is on his "race baiting," his "one-note racial analysis," and his "hatemonger[ing]," through which Sharpton is seen as perpetuating a "politics of protest and victimhood" and "racial violence."[55] The role of racial "rabble-rouser" and "agent provocateur" is usually portrayed with ominous overtones in which Sharpton is seen as stirring up intense feelings of racial hatred and division, at times being portrayed as a "racial arsonist" and even as New York's Osama bin Laden.[56] Interestingly, the Republican National Committee produced a "backgrounder" on Sharpton during the spring of 2000 entitled "Al Sharpton: A Chronology of Hate," which the renown Republican adviser Mary Matalin said described Sharpton as "a professional monger of racial hatred."[57] But liberals, as much as conservatives, denounce Sharpton as a "demagogue." Take Jim Sleeper, who has critiqued Sharpton's politics on numerous occasions. In one of his many commentaries, Sleeper declares Sharpton to be the "impresario of racial grievance. His unspoken motto: 'I am excluded, therefore I am.'"[58] Sharpton is clearly a charged figure, at once politically ineffective *and* dangerous—an apparently discordant mix of claims that will resonate for many feminist theorists who have long identified a similar dynamic for the category woman.

One of the most troubling aspects of Sharpton's racial politics has been the ways in which Sharpton seems to play fast and loose with the truth. In fact, some have argued that Sharpton operates with a double standard when it comes to judicial practice for Blacks and whites. The *Economist* summed up the issue as follows:

> Mr. Sharpton's problem is that too many people regard him as radioactive. He is indelibly remembered for championing Tawana Brawley, the black

15-year-old who falsely alleged that she had been raped and abused by six white men. Mr. Sharpton was more interested in "riling up the masses" than in pondering the truth of her accusations.[59]

Questions of character lay at the center of the Tawana Brawley episode, since it seemed to many that Sharpton and his advisers compromised the truth, leading one journalist to declare it Sharpton's Chappaquiddick.[60] This willingness to bend the truth has reinforced the notion that Sharptonesque politics fosters racial division in which Blacks and whites are held to different standards.

The dangers inherent in Sharpton's alleged loose commitment to the truth is perhaps best captured by his frequent critic Jim Sleeper:

> Sharpton himself never claimed that blacks' history of oppression in America exempted them from transracial legal standards of truth-telling. But his tactics, by equating dubious charges of racism with genuine cases of racial violence, strengthened notions about a separate black reality, unknowable to whites and subversive of the fragile bases for interracial dialogue.[61]

It is but a short step from such notions of "a separate black reality, unknowable to whites," to claims of double judicial standards that were raised during both the Rodney King and O.J. Simpson trials. How, Sleeper asks, can we sustain a vibrant civic culture in the face of such deeply felt division? The final liberal lament is that Sharpton encourages an undesirable "victimhood" politics in which Blacks are encouraged to view everything in terms of racial inequality and exclusion. This so-called race-card politics is said to promote narrowly conceived identity concerns rather than helping to sustain a shared civic culture that might provide the basis for greater racial integration rather than division.[62]

Sharpton has countered such claims directly. When asked whether he was an ambulance chaser, again implying that he was inflaming racial tensions, Sharpton replied that he is *the* ambulance, not the chaser. His actions make visible, Sharpton claimed, the enduring fact of American racism. In several interviews, Sharpton has argued that we need to distinguish more carefully between him and the context; we should not simply attribute the divisiveness that accompanies many of his political actions to his power or misdeeds. We need to understand the reactions as a product of deep-seated racial antagonisms that his presence reveals. Sharpton makes the case most effectively for distinguishing between himself and his *political effects* when discussing the controversy over the Howard

Beach protest that he organized in December 1986 during which onlookers shouted racial slurs and commentators berated Sharpton for fueling racial antagonism. Sharpton responded to accusations that he was race baiting, saying:

> What they're really saying is I should accept we can't walk in Howard Beach . . . to go out there is not exposing racism but I'm fanning the flames. Like I went out there and taught the people in Howard Beach to use the N-word.[63]

Those who blame the racial conflict on Sharpton himself, Sharpton continued, "want to deny that racism exists, and don't want someone to pull the covers off. I knew that all I had to do is walk down the street in Bensonhurst and they would prove the case. And how did I know it? Because I grew up in New York and I knew where I was. What did I do to exacerbate that? Get off a bus and walk down the block?"[64] From Sharpton's perspective, he did not provoke racial hatred and division. He simply made visible the deep-seated racism that was already there, his presence staging rather than producing the intense racial hatred that whites do not want to acknowledge.

It is difficult, and most likely impossible, to ever distinguish clearly between Sharpton's political opportunism from his efforts to draw attention to the persistent racism and racial inequality in New York; impossible to separate completely the man from his political effects. Dissecting Sharpton's motives, which have so preoccupied the media to date, seems largely beside the point. We would do better, I believe, to address the equally important but largely unasked question of who exactly is invoking these images of Sharpton the "racial arsonist" so as to inflame threats of racial antagonism and excess?

It is crucial to remember that it is *not* Ferrer's Republican rivals who capitalized on the specter of Sharpton, *nor* Sharpton's rivals within the African American community, although he certainly has critics there.[65] Rather, the source of racial antagonism came from *white liberals*, from the Green campaign, who were willing to use racial hatred to win. In the immediate aftermath of the campaign, several Ferrer advisers protested the race baiting of the Green campaign. Roberto Ramirez, Ferrer's chief adviser, lodged a formal complaint to the Democratic Party National Committee chairman, Terry McAuliffe, objecting to Green's racially charged campaign. Ramirez denied that this was just another instance of negative campaigning, saying, "The use of race is the issue here . . . it is wrong and it should not be tolerated." In an interview with the *Village Voice*,

Ramirez clarified his point: "I don't believe Mark stereotyped Freddy. . . . But I believe he capitalized on the stereotyping. His campaign saw an opportunity and didn't stand up against it." [66] Bill Lynch—a longtime Democratic Party activist, a vice chairman on the Democratic National Committee, former deputy mayor, and Ferrer adviser—also denounced Green's race baiting, not just in terms of the Green campaign but as symptomatic of the deeply embedded racism within the Democratic Party.[67]

Interestingly, a few months after the election, the *Economist* captioned an article on Sharpton with the phrase "every white bigot's favourite black," thereby stating what is rarely acknowledged, namely *whites' investment in promoting the specter of Al Sharpton the race baiter.*[68] Similarly, David Axelrod, a Ferrer consultant, made the same point: "I've covered and I've participated in over twenty urban political campaigns in which minority candidates were running—invariably, in the end, somebody says 'can we afford to take a chance?'" This is the classic way, Axelrod continued, that white candidates undercut the authority of their Black competitors.[69]

Moreover, it is worth remembering exactly what Sharpton had done to provoke all this havoc—he had simply endorsed Ferrer, nothing more. Sharpton's actions alone cannot account for the emotional intensity of the reactions he aroused. The mere appearance of Sharpton, let alone any direct association with him, set off a firestorm. The intensity of the reaction suggests that something else other than the routine politics of political endorsement was at work.

We will never know how the racial dynamics of the New York mayoral election would have played out absent the events of September 11, 2001. First, the election itself had to be rescheduled from September 11 to September 25. But the principal candidates' electoral fortunes also were shaped in more indirect ways; Giuliani's enormous popularity in the wake of the attacks on the World Trade Center greatly enhanced his endorsement for the Republican Party nominee, Michael Bloomberg. Moreover, Bloomberg's business background suddenly became an asset rather than a liability when attention shifted from his lack of public service to his capacity to run a tight fiscal administration—something most agreed was going to be necessary once the full extent of the economic fallout from the attacks became more clear. Bloomberg went on to win the general election and to serve as mayor of New York City. Even though the final outcome of the New York election was overdetermined, making it difficult to specify the impact of race in the election, the "Sharpton effect" in the election is symptomatic of wider concerns over the place of racial identification within the American Left.

Resignifying Ethnicity, Reconfiguring Democratic Party Politics

What does the 2001 New York mayoral election suggest about future patterns of ethno-racial politics in the United States? What do the *New York Post* cartoons, and the specter of Al Sharpton they evoke, tell us about racial politics within the ranks of the Democratic Party today? Perhaps the most important thing to underscore is the contested nature of racial identifications during the campaign. Ferrer, I have argued, tried to rework Latino political subjectivity via a racialized notion of class—a strategy that required reworking the long-standing conception of American ethnicity as different from race. Ferrer's campaign, although never explicitly articulated as such, implied a major reconceptualization of American ethnicity in which he sought to racialize Latino ethnicity in the hopes of forging a class-based alliance *with* Blacks. By appealing to "the other New York," Ferrer's campaign challenged, rather than reinforced, the constitutive distinction between ethnicity and race.

If we look across the broad sweep of the twentieth century, comparing Ferrer to other cultural and political elites who have identified as ethnics, we can see how dramatically he was trying to reconfigure what it means to be an ethnic in the United States. Where the OMB Statistical Policy Directive 15 codified earlier cultural pluralists' notions of ethnicity as a distinctive kind of social solidarity from that of race, Ferrer neither defined himself nor his fellow Latinos in terms of their Spanish origins and culture. Nor did he try to appeal to Latinos as a distinct racial group to that of Blacks. Rather, Ferrer's central concern was to link Latinos and Blacks together by addressing the diminished life chances of "the other New York"—both Latino and Black.

Resignifying the term *ethnic* is no easy task; any such transformation is a multifaceted endeavor that cannot be accomplished by a handful of individuals or a single political campaign. Yet, it is in micropolitical struggles, such as the Ferrer campaign, where alternative conceptions of race and politics are put forth and from which we can begin to question prevailing assumptions and political alliances. In so doing, we can open up a wider range of political possibilities for the Left to consider. It is within this larger context that I see Ferrer undertaking the crucial task of reworking ethnicity and its relation to race. Changing demographic realities of the last four decades are clearly on the side of increased racial heterogeneity and coalition politics; the extensive post-1965 immigration has made it increasingly difficult to see American politics exclusively in Black and white. We can expect many more such attempts at reconfiguring the prevailing ethno-racial categories and politics in New York and in other gateway cities around the United States.

But we should *not* be too optimistic—changes in the ethno-racial taxonomy are being met with resistance. Not all agree that the race-ethnicity distinction should go. The New York election revealed intense divisions within the Democratic Party ranks over questions of race. Once Ferrer became a contender, once he won the initial primary, we have seen how quickly the Green campaign *and* the media deployed old racial stereotypes to inflame white voters' racial fears. Grotesque images of Al Sharpton quickly appeared, playing on old racial tropes in which Blacks are depicted as powerful, excessive, and out of control. As soon as it looked like Ferrer might actually win, his main *Democratic* rival worked hard to reposition Sharpton as simultaneously ineffectual and dangerous—as a longtime advocate of racial separatism and division. The cartoons were supposed to remind those contemplating supporting Ferrer of the pernicious consequences that would surely follow if one embraced Ferrer's racially coded political appeals.

Interestingly, the Los Angeles mayoral election held that same year followed a remarkably similar course where Villaraigosa's insurgent campaign also went down to a narrow defeat. There are important differences between the Los Angeles and New York elections, most notably that one of Villaraigosa's Democratic primary rivals, Jim Hahn, had a distinctive relationship with African American voters due to his father's legendary civil rights work. Nevertheless, the parallels are striking. As the race tightened, Hahn, like Green, resorted to race baiting. Just before Election Day, Hahn ran an ad in which Villaraigosa is shown several shades darker, "alongside images of a razor cutting cocaine and a crack pipe being held to a flame." The voice-over reminded voters that Villaraigosa had written a letter to the Clinton White House supporting the clemency appeal of Carlos Vignalia, a convicted drug dealer.[70] Harry Pachon, president of the Tomas Rivera Policy Institute, summed up the attack ads as "the old equation of Latino equals drug dealer equals criminal class."[71] When faced with very real political challenges, both Hahn and Green inflamed white voters' racial fears to close out their campaigns. Again, let me stress that my point is not to claim that these racist appeals determined the outcome; they were one of many factors at work. But the New York and Los Angeles elections provide an important opportunity for examining splits within the Democratic Party over race.

Both Ferrer and Villaraigosa used remarkably similar strategies: neither appealed to race directly, and both focused on enduring economic and political inequalities, which they, and many voters, understood to be deeply implicated in American racial stratification. By offering racially coded appeals to class, Ferrer and Villaraigosa addressed issues of enduring inequality *without* relying *directly* on racial appeals.[72] Thus, they opened the door to racial politics, but stopped short of a head-on engagement with race. This strategy was simultaneously politically invigorating and limiting. Assessing its strengths and limitations is critical when determining the best way forward in race politics now.

Although neither Ferrer nor Villaraigosa advocated a simple return to the race-based identity politics of the 1960s, both initially benefited from the racial identifications that their campaigns evoked. Both appealed to race, but differently from civil rights politics of decades past. The question posed was not whether to appeal to race at all, but on what terms to do so? A racial politics of what kind? A racial politics to what end? Rather than taking racial identifications for granted or dismissing race-based politics out of hand, Ferrer and Villaraigosa invoked racial identifications as an aid to mobilization, while simultaneously revising our assumptions about the boundaries of race by rearticulating its relationship to both ethnicity and class.

Both Ferrer's and Villaraigosa's more oblique racial appeals had considerable advantages—especially early on in their campaigns when they were able to simultaneously acknowledge the persistence of racial inequality without having to defend race-based political appeals—in the end, the racial coding left each one vulnerable to his white liberal opponents. By avoiding explicit discussions of race, both Ferrer and Villaraigosa relinquished control of the debate; by making ambiguous and indirect racial appeals, they no longer framed the terms of their own racial identifications and political positions. Ultimately, both campaigns were easily whipsawed by racist appeals that played on long-standing scripts that neither Ferrer nor Villaraigosa had the time or wherewithal to counter.

No doubt some readers might counter that Ferrer and Villaraigosa avoided direct racial appeals precisely because race-based identity politics has been shown to be a political liability. That was exactly the lesson, many have argued, that Democrats were supposed to have learned from the 1960s, namely, that race-based political mobilization provokes a conservative backlash that we are still living with today.[73] It was precisely the pitfalls associated with race-based politics that Ferrer and Villaraigosa were trying to avoid, trying to find a way around, by deploying racially coded appeals to class.

What lessons, then, should we draw from the fact that even indirect engagements with race met with such strong reactions from rival Democratic candidates and white liberal voters? Two quite different reactions might be envisioned. On the one hand, we might imagine that both Ferrer and Villaraigosa will back away from race politics even more completely than they have in the past, denuding their campaigns of all references to race. One can hardly blame them; having been burnt by racial attack ads and circulars, they might assume that the only way to protect themselves from such racist attacks is to deemphasize race even more thoroughly than before. On the other hand, it is by no means clear that this would provide them the necessary protection, and it would surely defer the necessary engagement with the difficult task of acknowledging and remedying the enduring racial stratification in the United States. Rather than trying to avoid or move beyond race, I see a different lesson. Instead of backing away from racial appeals, Ferrer, Villaraigosa, and other Democratic Party candidates might have done better had they made their challenge of the race-ethnicity distinction explicit and buttressed it with a more thoroughgoing defense of their position. Adopting such a strategy would not have been easy, but it would have armored them against white racial backlash in advance.

Postscript: Ferrer and Villaraigosa in 2005

Both Ferrer and Villaraigosa ran again in 2005. This time Villaraigosa won, becoming the first Latino mayor of Los Angeles in over one hundred years, while Ferrer's campaign never really got off the ground. What lessons had each taken from his earlier defeat in terms of ethnic and racial identification? Even though Villaraigosa won and Ferrer lost, both campaigns were disappointing. Both stopped short of using their political visibility to rearticulate the meanings of ethnicity and race; both were even more evasive on racial issues than they had been the first time around. Both seemed to have responded to their 2001 defeats by moving to the center in classic Downsian fashion in the hopes of appealing to sufficient number of white middle-class voters to bring them to power.[74]

Ferrer's centrist drift got him into trouble early in the campaign when he addressed the Sergeants' Benevolent Association on March 15, 2005, and declared that the 1999 shooting of Amadou Diallo had not been a crime. Rifts quickly emerged in the Black-Brown coalition as one African American political leader after another denounced Ferrer's remarks and threw support behind the African American candidate, Virginia Fields.[75] This particular incident was symptomatic of a more general trend, signaled by Ferrer's campaign slogan, which claimed that he would be "the mayor for all New Yorkers, for a change." The contrast with 2001 was immediate. Four years earlier he had run as the mayor for "the other New York." His critical edge had been dropped, and he never mounted a serious challenge to Bloomberg.[76]

Although Villaraigosa won, from my perspective his campaign was also disappointing since he did little to articulate his own or his campaign's position on issues of racial discrimination, inequality, or ethnic and racial identification. Like Ferrer, evasion seemed to be the order of the day, so much so that his official campaign Web site made no mention of civil rights at all. Race politics of all kinds was gone, replaced by animal rights and environmental reform. I have nothing against such issues but am bothered by the way in which they displaced race. They are safer issues, ones that will not antagonize middle-class whites. The result is a progressive politics that ignores the central structural inequalities of our time. Similarly, his campaign Web site referred to the San Fernando Valley, while completely ignoring Watts and South Central. Presumably, Villaraigosa took a classic low profile on race, hoping that doing so would increase his chances of getting elected. And the strategy paid off. He won. But winning is not everything. In terms of building the political foundations for an enduring antiracist politics in Los Angeles, his victory was a pyrrhic one. By avoiding issues of racial identification and inequality, by alluding to them only indirectly, Villaraigosa failed to articulate the new associative chains needed to sustain a Black-Brown coalition. As soon as difficult policy choices must be made, as surely they will, his electoral coalition will most likely split apart, rift through with distrust and political antagonism that will only help to perpetuate Republican rule.[77]

7

Dismantling the Race-Ethnicity Distinction:
Reconfiguring Race, Power, and Descent

In the United States, we distinguish ethnicity from race—both formally within the federal classificatory system and more informally in our social practices. The distinction is a generative one that establishes the meaning of both terms. In doing so, it sets in play a dynamic relation that pervades ethnic and racial politics in the United States. Like new shoes, I see these dynamics everywhere. I have shown how time and again each term conjures up quite different associations in which race is repeatedly tied to body and blood and, as such, is generally viewed as fixed, singular, and hierarchical. In contrast, ethnicity is seen as rooted in cultural difference—especially in terms of language and religion—and, as such, is understood as malleable, plural, and equal. These associative chains permeate the institutional and cultural fields, reproducing in a quotidian fashion the quite different meanings of ethnicity and race.

The race-ethnicity distinction was created slowly over many decades and locales. No one moment marked a clear beginning; no one group served as the architect of ethnicity. Rather, several disarticulated changes contributed to the process of category formation. My task has been to identify key forces in play and to map their divergent and contiguous courses, showing when and how these disparate processes came together and specifying their political consequences.

Perhaps the most visible moment of category formation was the Office of Management and Budget's promulgation of Statistical Policy Directive 15 on May 12, 1977. The Directive mandated the racial and ethnic categories all federal agencies had to use when collecting and disseminating ethnic and racial data. The Directive specified quite clearly that racial and ethnic data were best collected separately, thereby helping to ensure that the race-ethnicity distinction would endure. Important as the Directive was in formalizing the race-ethnicity distinction within America's ethno-racial taxonomy, it would be a mistake to consider it *the* moment of category formation. The Directive is best understood as codifying and institutionalizing more diffuse understandings that had been in circulation for decades.

To map the invention of ethnicity, we need to attend to the micropolitics of category formation: to the early writings of New York Zionists in the 1910s and 1920s, to debates within the 1911 Dillingham Immigration Commission, and to the classification of Mexicans by the Immigration and Naturalization Service (INS) and the Census Bureau on the southwestern border in the 1930s and 1940s. In each, cultural and political elites tried to distinguish immigrants and races by specifying ethnicity as a distinct social formation. Moreover, I have argued that these actions were themselves embedded in changing conceptions of heredity that swept the academy in the last quarter of the nineteenth century. The process of category formation was a long and multifaceted one. Although I consider all of the forces identified above to have played a vital role, I do not claim to have documented all of the factors in play. In fact, I consider such definitive aspirations to belie the complexity of large-scale historical change. What I *have* done is identify several moments in this important historical formation, moments that enable us to see the category in formation and to track the political effects of repeatedly distinguishing ethnicity from race.

The Current State of Play—Is the Race-Ethnicity Distinction Still in Force?

Although I have argued that the race-ethnicity distinction has been a central force in shaping American race politics for almost a hundred years, it is also the case that the distinction is not as robust as it once was. Indeed, at moments, it seems to be crumbling beneath our feet. One might well ask whether the constitutive distinction examined in this book has the same significance today as it did in decades past. Perhaps the distinction was a matter of importance in the 1970s and 1980s, but is it a force to be reckoned with today? In media sources today, the terms *ethnicity* and *race* are used more interchangeably than in the past, making the distinction seem less stable than a quarter century ago. Take, for example, a 2005 *New York Times* article on hate crimes in the city. The article uses numerous terms to monitor trends in hate crimes: *anti-ethnic, anti-Hispanic, anti-religion,* as well as *anti-Black,* all appear. But interestingly, the summary graphic is headed "anti-ethnic crimes over time." This example is only one of many. There is a way in which the terms *race* and *ethnicity* seem especially unstable right now, thereby calling into question the significance of the long-standing race-ethnicity distinction.[1]

There also appears to be a strange inversion taking place in which the more omnibus term *race,* which dominated in the nineteenth century when Lamarckian notions of hereditary held sway, is being replaced by *ethnicity* as the omnibus term of choice today. At times it seems that ethnicity is becoming the more politically correct way to refer to differences of all kinds, including race. I do not question that the languages of race and ethnicity are changing—I have no vested interest in maintaining the distinction between the terms *ethnicity* and *race.* On the contrary, I hope it is now apparent that I believe the distinction is in many ways a pernicious one. It was the sense that the race-ethnicity distinction was being reworked that made me write this book. I wanted to understand how the terms *ethnicity* and *race* had worked in the past so that I might better appreciate the opportunities for change now. What difference, I wanted to know, does it make if we do, or do not, distinguish ethnicity from race? How do the taxonomies we use shape our politics?

The historical analysis presented above should alert readers to the potential dangers inherent in relying on *ethnicity* as the preferred term. At issue is the status of the associative chains set in place over the past hundred-odd years: if the shift to ethnicity signals a thorough dismantling of the race-ethnicity distinction, then racial and ethnic identities, and the politics they entail, might indeed be changing in a beneficial fashion. But what if the change is a more superficial one in which the term *race* has been dropped, but the chains of equivalence remain largely intact? Perhaps the term *ethnic* is gaining greater currency, but this does not necessarily mean that the associative chains have changed. If the chains of equivalence remain largely intact, then old meanings (in which ethnicity is used to fix race) will persist, the only difference being that the meanings will now be conveyed implicitly rather than through more direct comparisons between ethnicity and race.

How deep the present-day changes are will depend on whether the race-ethnicity distinction lingers in the associative chains. As yet, it is difficult to assess the depth of change, but few would contest that change is at hand. I want to conclude by considering the recent immigrant rallies of 2006 to see how the analytic lens might be used to understand this recent site of change.

Immigrant Rallies, May Day 2006

In March and April 2006, a number of immigrant rallies were held across the country; on May 1, these demonstrations culminated in a national day of protest—"The Day Without Immigrants." Seventy cities held May Day immigrant rallies; in the largest turnouts in Los Angeles and Chicago, over a million protestors took to the streets. The visuals were stunning, press coverage extensive, and future rallies likely.[2] What just happened here?

The immediate catalyst for the spring protests was passage of H.R. 4437—"The Border Protection, Anti-Terrorism, and Illegal Immigration Control Act" passed by the House of Representatives on December 16, 2005, by a vote of 239 to 182. The "Sensenbrenner bill" as it is sometimes known, after its sponsor Representative Jim Sensenbrenner (R-Wis.), is said by many to be the harshest piece of anti-immigration legislation in almost a century. Three of the bill's provisions have framed the current debate: criminalizing of undocumented immigrants and individuals and organizations that assist them, mandating employer verification of workers' legal status, and securing the U.S.-Mexican border by building a wall and improving electronic surveillance.[3] The law-and-order rhetoric has gained considerable traction, leaving moderates in both political parties with little room to maneuver. The legislative alternative put forward by John McCain and Edward Kennedy in the Senate continues to stress border control, while adding a guest worker program and pathways to citizenship. No one in Congress is calling for amnesty, pure and simple.

The spring rallies were directed quite explicitly at the U.S. Congress and at blocking H.R. 4437. Rally organizers hoped that a massive turnout would make plain the impossibility of enforcing the criminalization and deportation provisions while showcasing the substantial contribution of undocumented workers to the U.S. economy. On both counts, organizers hoped to change the larger political climate of early twenty-first-century immigration reform.[4]

This mix of legislative action and grassroots mobilization is making immigration one of the most salient political issues of the decade. The political significance is magnified by the unstable alignment of immigrant politics and party identification. Indeed, immigration may well emerge as a wedge issue of a volatile kind since both the classic Republican and

Democratic coalitions do not cohere when it comes to immigration. Economic conservatives want more open borders, along with the cheap labor that follows, while social conservatives want to enforce law and order and border control. The Democratic Party is split as well; many liberals support more open borders as an extension of their long-standing commitment to diversity and civil rights, while labor leaders and some civil rights advocates fear that immigrants will undercut hard-earned working conditions and civil rights.[5]

These tensions are not new; the very same divisions pervaded Progressive-era immigration reform. Nor can the scale of recent immigration account for this particular moment of politicization; massive legal and illegal immigration has been the order of the day for the past four decades. So why politicization of immigration now? Perhaps it is a symptom of George W. Bush's vulnerability on other fronts in which Sensenbrenner and other conservatives sense that there is a political opening to be exploited by raising the issue of illegal immigration. Whatever the reasons, old tensions have come to the fore and have made immigration policy a hot political issue for all concerned.

To date, two themes have dominated the coverage of the legislative debate and May Day rallies: class competition and national identity. Who wins and who loses with large-scale mass immigration into the United States? Do immigrants, especially undocumented workers, lower wages, take jobs, or drain resources from those already living in the United States, as some claim? The Day Without Immigrants was intended to reframe the economic debate by making visible the myriad ways in which Americans have come to rely on undocumented labor. Sensenbrenner himself tries to avoid the reach of such arguments by making sure that both his Wisconsin and Washington housekeepers are American or naturalized citizens and by washing his car himself so to avoid hiring undocumented workers. On May Day, photos of shuttered-up stores and rotting food conveyed the impact of the boycott. But for the most part, the economic aspect of the Day Without Immigrants took backstage to the protest itself. It was the marches, the presence of large numbers in the streets, that got the media attention.[6]

The massive May Day rallies led many to ask what does it mean to be an American in a land of immigrants? Cartoons and placards both during and after the rallies used Pilgrims and Native Americans to question the distinction between citizen and foreigner. In a similar vein, a Chicago placard declared, "The First Immigrants Arrived in 1492," and another pictured an Aztec asking, "Who's the Illegal Alien, Pilgrim?" The old question of what it means to be an American was again front and center.[7]

Figure 11: Christo Komarnitski, "A Day Without Immigrants," politicalcartoons.com, May 3, 2006. Copyright 2006 Christo Komarnitski. All rights reserved. Reprinted with permission.

Important as the class and identity themes are, they do not capture what I take to be the most significant aspects of the rallies, namely, their role in reconfiguring the subnational political alliances between immigrants and Blacks. One might have expected a replay of the *New York Post* cartoons of 2001, in which Sean Delonas so effectively exploited white anxieties over Black-Latino coalition building. But if any such images appeared, they did not make a splash. How, then, did the immigrant rallies intersect with the race-ethnicity distinction laid out in this book? What were the racial politics conveyed by the Day Without Immigrants? Did participants and organizers seek to blur the boundary between race and ethnicity? How exactly did the immigrant rallies signify in terms of race?

Reworking the Race-Ethnicity Distinction: Realigning Power and Descent

One of the most striking features of the May Day rallies has been the inadequacy of older languages of race and ethnicity for describing the immigrant protests. The long-standing cultural practice of distinguishing African Americans from immigrants—race from ethnicity—that I have mapped throughout the book seems to miss the mark. Something else is going on here. New political possibilities are emerging that older discourses cannot quite capture.

The political changes at hand are seen most easily by recalling the Sharpton-Obama Democratic Party convention speeches from 2004 with which I open the book and comparing them to the speeches, visuals, and commentary associated with the May Day events of 2006. Remember how Obama linked a more open and plural conception of race to American nationalism and called for unity over division, while Sharpton raised issues of power and inequality, but tied them almost exclusively to descent-based conceptions of racial difference. Sharpton and Obama, I argue in chapter 1, were drawing on long-standing discursive traditions in which race is the language of power and inequality, which—in the United States—typically is tied to descent, while ethnicity is the language of cultural difference and, as such, is positioned as plural and more malleable than race. The contrast with the immigrant rallies could not be sharper. The May Day rallies certainly raised issues of power, inequality, and opposition, but began to reconfigure the associative chains. Asymmetries of power were no longer voiced in terms of race-based conceptions of descent. *Viewed through my analytic lens, the most important shifts to watch at the rallies—and interpretations of them—are the ways in which issues of dissent and descent are being realigned.*

The visual images of hundreds and thousands of immigrants marching in the streets on May 1 signaled the shift; immigrants were giving voice to persistent inequalities in ways that have not been the case for ethnic politics in decades past. Tellingly, the shift was made by connecting immigration politics to an earlier tradition of civil rights protest. Jesse Jackson put it succinctly, claiming that the May Day rallies aimed to build "a bridge and not a wall"—to connect race and immigration politics in ways that typically had not occurred before.[8]

The very act of taking to the streets signified politically as a "show of strength," as an effort to redress persistent inequalities through dissent and opposition.[9] Guri Sadhwani, executive director of the New York Civic Participation Project, an umbrella organization for several progressive unions and community organizations, captured the mood:

> There isn't necessarily unilateral consensus around which bill is the best bill, but there is a real consensus about preventing—and sending a strong

signal against—anti-immigrant bills, and that's what you see in the streets. People are really pissed off.[10]

The Reverend Lewis Logan II, the pastor at Bethel AME Church in South Los Angeles, declared: "A power more powerful than Katrina has been unleashed here," while Ron Powell, the president of the United Food and Commercial Workers, claimed that "by standing together, our message cannot be ignored." Time and again the demonstrators are described as displaying a newfound strength aimed at reframing the policy debate.[11]

An important aspect of this claim to power was immigrants' willingness, especially the undocumented, to make themselves *visible* on May 1. Not all agreed that this was the right strategy; some feared reprisals, others division. But on the day, large numbers were willing, as so many commentators remarked, to "come out of the shadows." Visibility generally has not been associated with ethnic politics in the past; assimilation and incorporation are best secured by forgoing political visibility, opposition, or dissent.[12]

But power through numbers was not all that was important on May 1. A deeper political significance lay in the ways in which attention to asymmetries of power were *unhinged* from race-based conceptions of descent. The visuals from May 1 were striking precisely because of their multiethnic or multinational cast. Flags from all over Latin America and around the globe were waved high; some were even stitched together into an enormous patchwork multinational banner as seen on LA's Wilshire Boulevard. Mexican flags certainly predominated, but many other nationalities were represented. The presence of immigrants from Africa and the Caribbean made the line between immigration and race incoherent. Again, what was striking was the sense that the rallies were establishing new political ground—something politically significant was in the works. The significance, I suggest, lies in immigrant protestors' efforts to breach the old race-ethnicity distinction by addressing issues of inequality and power without relying on the language of descent.[13]

Both Jesse Jackson and Al Sharpton spoke at the New York May Day rally in Union Square; both spoke directly and forcefully to the race-immigrant distinction; both urged that old divisions be bridged. Throughout his speech, Jackson tried to position immigrants and African Americans as allies by identifying commonalities rather than differences: "We are a nation of people brought here by force and volunteer labor, but always cheap and under exploitative conditions."[14] Slavery and immigration are linked together in new associative chains.

For African Americans we were too long undocumented and without legal protections. Two hundred and forty-six years without citizenship. And then second class citizenship for another 100 years. And now we are threatened with the loss of voter protection in New Orleans: Iraqi Americans had more voter protection to vote in the Iraq election than Katrina survivors have to vote in New Orleans.[15]

Here Jackson reconfigured typical associations by linking slavery with the *undocumented*. Perhaps most powerfully, Jackson ended his speech by repeating the May Day chant, "Si se puede [Yes we can]," and then followed it with "We shall overcome," thereby connecting two quite different political moments. Throughout this speech and on many other occasions, Jackson has tried to forge new political alliances by offering up new associations. This is not a new strategy for Jackson to pursue—he has been at it for years. What is different now is the increased resonance of his claims.[16]

Sharpton also addressed the race-immigration division, but as is his want, he zeroed in on antagonism and division:

As the fate of 11 million so-called illegal immigrants hangs in the balance, some African-Americans have questioned the prominent role that myself and others have been playing in the debate, suggesting that our focus on immigration reform will compromise the unfinished battle for true racial equality.

The tensions are real. . . .

I have little doubt that what registers in the news media is the tip of the iceberg. Discussions are surely even more searching and intense at African-American kitchen tables around New York and across the country.

Yet these concerns aren't just misplaced—they're dead wrong, and worse, they give credence to a dangerous right-wing attempt to divide two communities in equal need of passionate and effective representation.

It is past time for all African-Americans to understand that our interests and those of immigrants are not at odds. In fact, more often than not, they are one and the same.

Is there some merit to the argument that low-income workers have lost jobs to undocumented immigrants and would face still stiffer competition if more were to legalize? Of course. . . .

Those truly concerned about economic fairness would be better off targeting businesses that exploit and underpay illegal immigrants to the detriment of American workers. We should look at corporations that actively engage in outsourcing American jobs. We should be criminalizing the businessmen who profit, not making the victims who are ill-paid suffer twice.[17]

Sharpton, like Jackson, aimed to diminish the race-ethnicity distinction by first acknowledging the tensions and then arguing for connections. But the claim of African Americans' and immigrants' interests being "one and the same" seems premature. The political connections need to be forged in ways that allow for identifications across the ethnicity-race divide. Neither Sharpton nor Jackson are quite able to make the pitch in which alliances are built without unity being presumed. Nevertheless, both the speeches and the rallies themselves are indicative of the new political possibilities afoot.[18]

Jackson and Sharpton were perhaps the most visible, but certainly not the only ones trying to bridge the race-ethnicity divide. Numerous organizers and activists from a myriad of organizations big and small worked to build the Day Without Immigrants by linking together labor, community, and civil rights organizations into a broader coalition. Collaboration does not always come easily, especially given the long history attached to the race-ethnicity distinction. Many have made a conscious political effort to build alliances between immigrants and Blacks, rather than being drawn into a politics of division. One of the most moving aspects of the May Day commentaries has been the personal testimonies from several African Americans in which they voiced both their sense of loss and displacement, alongside their support of immigrant mobilizations. One participant at the San Francisco May Day rally reflected on the complex mix of identifications and difference with particular subtlety and is worth quoting at length:

> At this week's "Dia Sin Immigrantes/Day Without Immigrants" march in San Francisco, I saw a beautiful, exciting and hopeful vision of the future of this country.
>
> I also caught a glimpse of a familiar past, fading away. And I shed a few tears for both. . . .
>
> Deep inside, I was grieving for my own people. I wished that my beloved African-American community had managed—somehow—to retain our own sparkling sense of faith in a magnificent future. There was once a time when we, too, marched forward together. There was a time when we, too, believed that America's tomorrow held something bright for us . . . and for our children.
>
> But those dreams have been eaten away by the AIDS virus, laid off by down-sizers, locked out by smiling bigots, shot up by gang-bangers and buried in a corporate-run prison yard. . . .

My feelings of solidarity quickly trumped my sorrows. Thousands of people were standing up, here, and across the United States, for their right to live and work in dignity in this country. . . . And just as non-Blacks had supported our freedom movement in the last century, I was determined— as a non-immigrant—to give my passionate support to this righteous cause.

The blogger goes on to describe in some detail the sense of displacement marchers felt during the event, especially when it came to Spanish chants. Eventually the sense of dislocation is resolved as follows:

I decided instead to just walk cheerfully along, clapping in time with the drummers. But even some of the Latin rhythms were unfamiliar, strangely syncopated. I couldn't always find the beat. Suddenly, I was filled with sympathy for all those a-rhythmic white folks whom I used to make fun of at Black rallies. . . .

In the end, despite feeling somewhat out of place, I was absolutely thrilled to see my sisters and brothers taking the future into their own hands.[19]

The play of emotions here is quite amazing. Moments of pleasure and identification are quickly mixed with a sense of difference and disidentification. I am especially intrigued by the way optimism for future possibilities is tempered by a sense of loss. Indeed, I think it is precisely this delicate balance between difference *and* identification that needs to be fostered as the ground of political transformation in which a progressive politics is built on identifications across difference. Nor should Blacks be the only ones contemplating the current political moment as one of both possibilities and loss; white liberals ought to engage in a parallel yet rather different act of self-reflection rather than simply lamenting the displacement of past identifications and movements whether on the basis of class or racial politics from a different time and place.[20]

But not all progressives supported the rallies. And of those who did, not all advanced the transformative possibilities that I have identified here. Perhaps the most surprising to me were Antonio Villaraigosa and Ferdinand Ferrer, neither of whom advocated the realignment of power and descent that I take as the most potent political possibility offered by these events. Ferrer, the Puerto Rican New York City mayoral candidate in 2001, was nowhere to be seen; he did not speak at Union Square, and the Drum Major Institute Web site has nothing on the rallies.[21] As for Villaraigosa, he played a more visible role since he is now mayor of Los Angeles. But his interventions also served to undercut rather than foster the realignment of power and descent. When addressing the Los Angeles rally, Villaraigosa urged demonstrators to "wave the American flag. It is the flag of the country that we are all proud of and want to be part of. Don't disrespect the traditions of this country."[22] But why an either/or frame? Why so stark a choice between the flags? At most rallies, protestors held up more than one, an American flag in one hand and a Mexican flag in another. There was a way in which the visuals from many of the rallies signaled a multivocality that Villaraigosa's remarks ignored. On a second occasion, later that same May, Villaraigosa again came up short when the president of Mexico, Vicente Fox, was visiting Los Angeles; Villaraigosa preemptively refused to discuss U.S.-Mexican immigration, claiming that it "was a federal matter and out of his hands."[23] An evasive comment at best; certainly Villaraigosa missed an opportunity to shape immigration politics in the United States. He missed an important moment to realign power and descent. His refusal to engage the issue is reminiscent of an older assimilationist politics in which many immigrants were forced to declare that they were indeed 100 percent American.

Whether we will look back on the Day Without Immigrants as a key moment in dismantling the race-ethnicity distinction remains uncertain. We need to wait for the dust to settle. What is clear is that the rallies have confused, troubled, or scrambled existing associations in which race and immigration have been channeled into different discursive and political traditions. New associative chains, and the political alliances they enable, are information. The current moment is one of possibilities. Whether and in what ways the race-ethnicity distinction is reinforced or reconfigured is of enormous consequence; it will set the parameters of progressive politics in the United States for decades to come.

APPENDIX A

TABLE 1

U.S. Demographics: Race, Hispanic Origin, and Foreign-Born Population, 1900–2005
(absolute number in thousandths and percentage of total population)

Year	Total Popula-tion	White Total N	White Total %	White Alone, Not Hispanic N	White Alone, Not Hispanic %	Black or African American N	Black or African American %
1900	75,994	66,809	87.9	NA	NA	8,833	11.6
1910[4]	91,972	81,731	88.9	*81,364*	*88.4*	9,827	10.7
1920[5]	105,710	94,820	89.7	*94,120*	*89.0*	10,463	9.9
1930[6]	122,775	110,286	89.8	108,864	*88.6*	11,891	9.7
1940[7]	131,669	118,214	89.8	116,530	*88.4*	12,865	9.8
1950	150,697	134,942	89.5	NA	NA	15,042	10.0
1960	179,323	158,831	88.6	NA	NA	18,871	10.5
1970[8]	203,211	177,748	87.5	169,615	83.5	22,580	11.1
1980	226,545	188,371	83.1	180,256	79.6	26,495	11.7
1990	248,709	199,686	80.3	188,128	75.6	29,986	12.1
2000	281,421	211,460	75.1	194,552	69.1	34,658	12.3
2005[9]	288,378	215,333	74.7	NA	NA	34,962	12.1

N: absolute number; NA: not available; X: not applicable; —: less than 0.1%.

[1] For 2000 and 2005, it refers to Asian alone. For this period the following data on Native Hawaiian and Other Pacific Islander are available: 2000: 398—0.1%; 2005: 397—0.1%.

[2] For the year 2000 and 2005, it refers to American Indian and Alaska Native.

[3] 1950–1990 sample data.

[4] Hispanic origin refers to the population of Mexican origin. Data are estimates. These estimates are in italics.

[5] Ibid.

[6] Hispanic origin refers to tabulation on race category for Mexican. Percentages are estimates. These estimates are in italics.

[7] Hispanic origin based on the white population of Spanish mother tongue. Data shown are based on 5% sample data. Percentages are estimates. These estimates are in italics.

[8] Hispanic origin defined as population of Spanish origin based 5% sample data. Data based on 15% sample are also available in which Hispanic origin is defined as population of Spanish language and population of Spanish heritage. Data regarding population of Spanish language: White Alone, Not Hispanic: 169,023—83.2%; Hispanic Origin or Latino: 9,589—4.7%. Data regarding population of Spanish heritage: White Alone, Not Hispanic: NA—NA; Hispanic origin or Latino: 9,294—NA.

[9] Data based on 2005 American Community Survey.

Asian and Pacific Islander[1]		American Indian, Eskimo, and Aleut[2]		Some Other Race		Hispanic Origin or Latino (of Any Race)		Foreign Born (of Any Race)[3]	
N	%	N	%	N	%	N	%	N	%
114	0.2	237	0.3	X	X	NA	NA	10,341	13.6
146	0.2	265	0.3	X	X	367	0.3	13,515	14.7
182	0.2	244	0.2	X	X	700	0.6	13,920	13.2
264	0.2	332	0.3	X	X	1,422	1.1	14,204	11.6
254	0.2	333	0.3	X	X	1,861	1.4	11,594	8.8
321	0.2	343	0.2	48	—	NA	NA	10,347	6.9
980	0.5	551	0.3	87	0.2	NA	NA	9,738	5.4
1,538	0.8	827	0.4	516	0.3	9,072	4.5	9,619	4.7
3,500	1.5	1,420	0.6	6,758	3.0	14,608	6.4	14,079	6.2
7,273	2.9	1,959	0.8	9,804	3.9	22,354	9.0	19,767	7.9
10,242	3.6	2,475	0.9	15,359	5.5	35,305	12.5	31,107	11.1
12,471	4.3	2,357	0.8	17,298	6.0	41,870	14.5	35,689	12.4

Table compiled by Andrea Carlá. Data for years 2000 and 2005 from "American Fact Finder," U.S. Bureau of the Census, http://factfinder.census.gov (accessed December 14, 2006); data on race in the United States for years 1900–1990 in Campbell J. Gibson and Kay Jung, "Historical Census Statistics on Population Totals by Race, 1790 to 1990, and by Hispanic Origin, 1970 to 1990, for the United States, Regions, Divisions, and States," Working Paper Series No. 56 (Washington, DC: U.S. Bureau of the Census, Population Division, September 2002), http://www.census.gov/population/www/techpap.html (accessed December 14, 2006); data on foreign-born population for years 1900–1990 in Campbell J. Gibson and Emily Lennon, "Historical Census Statistics on the Foreign-Born Population of the United States: 1850–1990," Population Division Working Paper No. 29 (Washington, DC: U.S. Bureau of the Census, Population Division, February 1999), http://www.census.gov/population/www/techpap.htm (accessed December 14, 2006). Percentages on Hispanic origin in 1910, 1920, 1930 estimated by the author.

TABLE 2

U.S. State Demographics: Race, Hispanic Origin, and Foreign-Born Population in 2000 (percentage of total population)

		Percentage of Population								
		White								
State[1]	Total Population in 1,000s	Total	White Alone, Not Hispanic or Latino	Black or African American	Asian	Native American, Indian, and Alaska Native	Hawaiian and Other Pacific Islander[2]	Some Other Race	Hispanic Origin or Latino (of Any Race)	Foreign Born
Puerto Rico	3,808	80.5	0.8	8.0	0.2	0.4	—	6.8	98.8	2.9
Hawaii	1,211	24.3	22.8	1.8	41.6	0.3	9.4	1.3	7.2	17.5
District of Columbia	572	30.8	27.7	60.0	2.7	0.3	0.1	3.8	7.9	12.9
New Mexico	1,819	66.8	44.6	1.9	1.1	9.5	0.1	17.0	42.1	8.2
California	33,871	59.5	46.6	6.7	10.9	1.0	0.3	16.8	32.4	26.2
Texas	20,851	71.0	52.4	11.5	2.7	0.6	0.1	11.7	32.0	13.9
Mississippi	2,844	61.4	60.7	36.3	0.7	0.4	—	0.5	1.4	1.4
New York	18,976	67.9	61.9	15.9	5.5	0.4	—	7.1	15.1	20.4
Maryland	5,296	64.0	62.0	27.9	4.0	0.3	—	1.8	4.3	9.8
Louisiana	4,468	63.9	62.5	32.5	1.2	0.6	—	0.7	2.4	2.6
Georgia	8,186	65.1	62.6	28.7	2.1	0.3	0.1	2.4	5.3	7.1
Arizona	5,130	75.5	63.8	3.1	1.8	5.0	0.1	11.6	25.3	12.8

Nevada	1,998	75.2	65.2	6.8	4.5	1.3	0.4	8.0	19.7	15.8
Florida	15,982	78.0	65.4	14.6	1.7	0.3	0.1	3.0	16.8	16.7
New Jersey	8,414	72.6	66.0	13.6	5.7	0.2	—	5.4	13.3	17.5
South Carolina	4,012	67.2	66.1	29.5	0.9	0.3	—	1.0	2.4	2.9
Alaska	626	69.3	67.5	3.5	4.0	15.6	0.5	1.6	4.1	5.9
Illinois	12,419	73.5	67.8	15.1	3.4	0.2	—	5.8	12.3	12.3
North Carolina	8,049	72.1	70.1	21.6	1.4	1.2	—	2.3	4.7	5.3
Virginia	7,078	72.3	70.1	19.6	3.7	0.3	0.1	2.0	4.7	8.1
Alabama	4,447	71.1	70.2	26.0	0.7	0.5	—	0.7	1.7	2.0
Delaware	783	74.6	72.4	19.2	2.1	0.3	—	2.0	4.8	5.7
Oklahoma	3,450	76.2	74.0	7.6	1.4	7.9	0.1	2.4	5.2	3.8
Colorado	4,301	82.8	74.4	3.8	2.2	1.0	0.1	7.2	17.1	8.6
Connecticut	3,405	81.6	77.4	9.1	2.4	0.3	—	4.3	9.4	10.9
Arkansas	2,673	80.0	78.5	15.7	0.8	0.7	0.1	1.5	3.2	2.8
Michigan	9,938	80.2	78.5	14.2	1.8	0.6	—	1.3	3.3	5.3
Washington	5,894	81.8	78.9	3.2	5.5	1.6	0.4	3.9	7.5	10.4
Tennessee	5,689	80.2	79.1	16.4	1.0	0.3	—	1.0	2.2	2.8
Massachusetts	6,349	84.5	81.8	5.4	3.8	0.2	—	3.7	6.8	12.2
Rhode Island	1,048	85.0	81.8	4.5	2.3	0.5	0.1	5.0	8.7	11.4
Kansas	2,688	86.1	83.0	5.7	1.7	0.9	—	3.4	7.0	5.0
Oregon	3,421	86.6	83.5	1.6	3.0	1.3	0.2	4.2	12.5	8.5

(continued)

Table 2 continued

State[1]	Total Population in 1,000s	White Total	White Alone, Not Hispanic or Latino	Black or African American	Asian	Native American, Indian, and Alaska Native	Hawaiian and Other Pacific Islander[2]	Some Other Race	Hispanic Origin or Latino (of Any Race)	Foreign Born
					Percentage of Population					
Missouri	5,595	84.9	83.7	11.2	1.1	0.4	0.1	0.8	2.1	2.7
Ohio	11,353	85.0	84.0	11.5	1.2	0.2	—	0.8	1.9	3.0
Pennsylvania	12,281	85.4	84.0	10.0	1.8	0.1	—	1.5	3.2	4.1
Utah	2,233	89.2	85.2	0.8	1.7	1.3	0.7	4.2	9.0	7.1
Indiana	6,080	87.5	85.8	8.4	1.0	0.3	—	1.6	3.5	3.1
Wisconsin	5,363	88.9	87.2	5.7	1.7	0.9	—	1.6	3.6	3.6
Nebraska	1,711	89.6	87.3	4.0	1.3	0.9	—	2.8	5.5	4.4
Idaho	1,293	91.0	88.0	0.4	0.9	1.4	0.1	4.2	7.9	5.0
South Dakota	754	88.7	88.0	0.6	0.6	8.3	—	0.5	1.4	1.8
Minnesota	4,919	89.4	88.1	3.5	2.9	1.1	—	1.3	2.9	5.3

Wyoming	493	92.1	88.8	0.8	0.6	2.3	0.1	2.5	6.4	2.3
Kentucky	4,041	90.1	89.2	7.3	0.7	0.2	—	0.6	1.5	2.0
Montana	902	90.6	89.4	0.3	0.5	6.2	0.1	0.6	2.0	1.8
North Dakota	642	92.4	91.7	0.6	0.6	4.9	—	0.4	1.2	1.9
Iowa	2,926	93.9	92.6	2.1	1.3	0.3	—	1.3	2.8	3.1
West Virginia	1,808	95.0	94.5	3.2	0.5	0.2	—	0.2	0.7	1.1
New Hampshire	1,235	96.0	95.1	0.7	1.3	0.2	—	0.6	1.7	4.4
Vermont	608	96.8	96.2	0.5	0.9	0.4	—	0.2	0.9	3.8
Maine	1,274	96.9	96.5	0.5	0.7	0.6	—	0.2	0.7	2.9

Table compiled by Andrea Carlá. Data from "American Fact Finder," U.S. Bureau of the Census, http://factfinder.census.gov (accessed December 14, 2006).

[1] States ranked in order of smallest percentage of "White Alone, not Hispanic or Latino" population.

[2] A dash (—) represents less than 0.1%

TABLE 3

U.S. City Demographics: Race, Hispanic Origin, and Foreign-Born Population in 2000 of Twenty U.S. Largest Cities (percentage of total population)

City	Total Population in 1,000s	White		Black or African American	Asian	American Indian and Alaska Native	Native Hawaiian and Other Pacific Islander	Some Other Race	Hispanic Origin or Latino (of Any Race)	Foreign Born (of Any Race)
		Total	White Alone, Not Hispanic or Latino							
New York City (NY)	8,008	44.7	34.9	26.6	9.8	0.5	0.1	13.4	27.0	35.9
Los Angeles (CA)	3,694	46.9	29.7	11.2	10.0	0.8	0.2	25.7	46.5	40.9
Chicago (IL)	2,896	42.0	31.3	36.8	4.3	0.4	0.1	13.0	26.0	21.7
Houston (TX)	1,953	49.3	30.7	25.3	5.3	0.4	0.1	16.5	37.4	26.4
Philadelphia (PA)	1,517	45.0	42.4	43.2	4.5	0.3	0.0	4.8	8.5	9.0
Phoenix (AZ)	1,321	71.1	55.7	5.1	2.0	2.0	0.1	16.4	34.1	19.5
San Diego (CA)	1,223	60.2	49.3	7.9	13.6	0.6	0.5	12.4	25.4	25.7
Dallas (TX)	1,188	50.8	34.5	25.9	2.7	0.5	0.0	17.2	35.6	24.4

Percentage of Population

City									
San Antonio (TX)	1,144	67.7	31.8	6.8	1.6	0.8	0.1	19.3	58.7	11.7
Detroit (MI)	951	12.3	10.4	81.6	1.0	0.3	0.0	2.5	5.0	4.8
San Jose (CA)	894	47.5	36.0	3.5	26.9	0.8	0.4	15.9	30.2	36.9
Indianapolis (IN)	781	69.1	67.4	25.5	1.4	0.3	0.0	0.2	3.9	4.6
San Francisco (CA)	776	49.7	43.5	7.8	30.8	0.4	0.5	6.5	14.1	36.8
Jacksonville (FL)	735	64.5	62.1	29.0	2.8	0.3	0.1	1.3	4.2	5.9
Columbus (OH)	711	67.9	66.8	24.5	3.4	0.3	0.1	1.2	2.5	6.7
Austin (TX)	656	65.4	52.8	10.0	4.7	0.6	0.1	16.2	30.5	16.6
Baltimore (MD)	651	31.6	30.8	64.3	1.5	0.3	0.0	0.7	1.7	4.6
Memphis (TN)	650	34.4	33.2	61.4	1.5	0.2	0.0	1.5	3.0	4.0
Milwaukee (WI)	596	50.0	45.3	37.3	2.9	0.9	0.1	6.1	12.0	7.7
Boston (MA)	589	54.5	49.4	25.3	7.5	0.4	0.1	7.8	14.4	25.8

Table compiled by Andrea Carlá. Data from "American Fact Finder," U.S. Bureau of the Census, http://factfinder.census.gov (accessed December 14, 2006).

TABLE 4

New York City Demographics: Race, Hispanic Origin, and
Foreign-Born Population, 1900–2005

(absolute number in thousandths and percentage of total population)

Year	Total Popu- lation	White		White Alone, Not Hispanic		Black or African American		
		Total						
		N	%	N	%	N	%	
1900	3,437	3,369	98.0	NA	NA	60	1.8	
1910	4,766	4,669	98.0	NA	NA	91	1.9	
1920	5,620	5,459	97.1	NA	NA	152	2.7	
1930[4]	6,930	6,589	95.1	NA	NA	327	4.7	
1940[5]	7,454	6,977	93.6	*6,863*	*92.1*	458	6.1	
1950	7,891	7,116	90.2	NA	NA	747	9.5	
1960	7,781	6,640	85.3	NA	NA	1,087	14.0	
1970[6]	7,894	6,048	76.6	*5,053*	*64.0*	1,668	21.1	
1980	7,071	4,294	60.7	3,668	51.9	1,784	25.2	
1990	7,322	3,827	52.3	3,163	43.2	2,102	28.7	
2000	8,008	3,576	44.7	2,801	34.9	2,129	26.6	
2005[7]	7,956	3,499	44.0	NA	NA	2,011	25.3	

N: absolute number; NA: not available; X: not applicable; —: less than 1,000; –: less than 0.1%.

[1] For 2000 and 2005, it refers to Asian alone. For this period the following data on Native Hawaiian and Other Pacific Islander are available: 2000: 5—0.1%; 2005: 3—less than 0.1%.

[2] For the year 2000 and 2005, it refers to American Indian and Alaska Native.

[3] 1950–1990 sample data.

[4] Hispanic origin refers to tabulation on race category for Mexican.

[5] Hispanic origin based on the white population of Spanish mother tongue. Data shown are estimates based on 5% sample data. These estimates are in italics.

[6] Hispanic origin defined as population of Spanish origin based on 5% sample data. Data based on 15% sample are also available in which Hispanic origin is defined as population of Spanish language and population of Spanish heritage. Data based on 15% sample: White Alone, Not Hispanic: 4,969—62.9%; Hispanic Origin or Latino: 1,278—16.2%. Data on White Alone, Not Hispanic are estimates. These estimates are in italics.

[7] Data based on 2005 American Community Survey.

Asian and Pacific Islander[1]		American Indian, Eskimo, and Aleut[2]		Some Other Race		Hispanic Origin or Latino (of Any Race)		Foreign Born (of Any Race)[3]	
N	%	N	%	N	%	N	%	N	%
6	0.2	—	–	X	X	NA	NA	1,270	37.0
5	0.1	—	–	X	X	NA	NA	1,944	40.8
7	0.1	—	–	X	X	NA	NA	2,028	36.1
12	0.2	—	–	X	X	2	–	2,358	34.0
17	0.2	1	–	X	X	*121*	*1.6*	2,138	28.7
21	0.3	2	–	4	0.1	NA	NA	1,860	23.6
43	0.6	3	–	7	0.1	NA	NA	1,558	20.0
94	1.2	9	0.1	73	0.9	1,202	15.2	1,437	18.2
231	3.3	11	0.2	749	10.6	1,406	19.9	1,670	23.6
512	7.0	27	0.4	852	11.6	1,783	24.4	2,082	28.4
787	9.8	41	0.5	1,074	13.4	2,160	27.0	2,871	35.9
922	11.6	33	0.4	1,355	17.0	2,221	27.9	2,915	36.6

Table compiled by Andrea Carlá. Data for years 2000 and 2005 from "American Fact Finder," U.S. Bureau of the Census, http://factfinder.census.gov (accessed December 14, 2006); data on race 1960–1990 from Campbell J. Gibson and Kay Jung, "Historical Census Statistics on Population Totals by Race, 1790 to 1990, and by Hispanic Origin, 1970 to 1990, for Large Cities and Other Urban Places in the United States," Working Paper No. 76 (Washington, DC: U.S. Bureau of the Census, Population Division, February 2005), http://www.census.gov/population/www/techpap.html (accessed December 14, 2006); data on foreign-born population 1900–1990 from Campbell J. Gibson and Emily Lennon, "Historical Census Statistics on the Foreign–Born Population of the United States: 1850–1990," Population Division Working Paper No. 29 (Washington, DC: U.S. Bureau of the Census, Population Division, February 1999), http://www.census.gov/population/www/techpap.html (accessed December 14, 2006).

Directive No. 15

Race and Ethnic Standards for Federal Statistics and Administrative Reporting

As adopted on May 12, 1977.

This Directive provides standard classifications for recordkeeping, collection, and presentation of data on race and ethnicity in Federal program administrative reporting and statistical activities. These classifications should not be interpreted as being scientific or anthropological in nature, nor should they be viewed as determinants of eligibility for participation in any Federal program. They have been developed in response to needs expressed by both the executive branch and the Congress to provide for the collection and use of compatible, nonduplicated, exchangeable racial and ethnic data by Federal agencies.

1. Definitions

The basic racial and ethnic categories for Federal statistics and program administrative reporting are defined as follows:

a. American Indian or Alaskan Native. A person having origins in any of the original peoples of North America, and who maintains cultural identification through tribal affiliations or community recognition.

b. Asian or Pacific Islander. A person having origins in any of the original peoples of the Far East, Southeast Asia, the Indian subcontinent, or the Pacific Islands. This area includes, for example, China, India, Japan, Korea, the Philippine Islands, and Samoa.

c. Black. A person having origins in any of the black racial groups of Africa.

d. Hispanic. A person of Mexican, Puerto Rican, Cuban, Central or South American or other Spanish culture or origin, regardless of race.

e. White. A person having origins in any of the original peoples of Europe, North Africa, or the Middle East.

2. Utilization for Recordkeeping and Reporting

To provide flexibility, it is preferable to collect data on race and ethnicity separately. If separate race and ethnic categories are used, the minimum designations are:

a. Race:

—American Indian or Alaskan Native
—Asian or Pacific Islander
—Black
—White

b. Ethnicity:

—Hispanic origin
—Not of Hispanic origin

When race and ethnicity are collected separately, the number of White and Black persons who are Hispanic must be identifiable, and capable of being reported in that category.

If a combined format is used to collect racial and ethnic data, the minimum acceptable categories are:

American Indian or Alaskan Native
Asian or Pacific Islander
Black, not of Hispanic origin
Hispanic
White, not of Hispanic origin.

The category which most closely reflects the individual's recognition in his community should be used for purposes of reporting on persons who are of mixed racial and/or ethnic origins.

In no case should the provisions of this Directive be construed to limit the collection of data to the categories described above. However, any reporting required which uses more detail shall be organized in such a way that the additional categories can be aggregated into these basic racial/ethnic categories.

The minimum standard collection categories shall be utilized for reporting as follows:

a. Civil rights compliance reporting. The categories specified above will be used by all agencies in either the separate or combined format for civil rights compliance reporting and equal employment reporting for both the public and private sectors and for all levels of government. Any variation requiring less detailed data or data which cannot be aggregated into the basic categories will have to be specifically approved by the Office of Management and Budget (OMB) for executive agencies. More detailed reporting which can be aggregated to the basic categories may be used at the agencies' discretion.

b. General program administrative and grant reporting. Whenever an agency subject to this Directive issues new or revised administrative reporting or recordkeeping requirements which include racial or ethnic data, the agency will use the race/ethnic categories described above. A variance can be specifically requested from OMB, but such a variance will be granted only if the agency can demonstrate that it is not reasonable for the primary reporter to determine the racial or ethnic background in terms of the specified categories, and that such determination is not critical to the administration of the program in question, or if the specific program is directed to only one or a limited number of race/ethnic groups, e.g., Indian tribal activities.

c. Statistical reporting. The categories described in this Directive will be used at a minimum for federally sponsored statistical data collection where race and/or ethnicity is required, except when: The collection involves a sample of such size that the data on the smaller categories would be unreliable, or when the collection effort focuses on a specific racial or ethnic group. A repetitive survey shall be deemed to have an adequate sample size if the racial and ethnic data can be reliably aggregated on a biennial basis. Any other variation will have to be specifically authorized by OMB through the reports clearance process. In those cases where the data collection is not subject to the reports clearance process, a direct request for a variance should be made to OMB.

3. Effective Date

The provisions of this Directive are effective immediately for all *new* and *revised* recordkeeping or reporting requirements containing racial and/or ethnic information. All *existing* recordkeeping or reporting requirements shall be made consistent with this Directive at the time they are submitted for extension, or not later than January 1, 1980.

4. Presentation of Race/Ethnic Data

Displays of racial and ethnic compliance and statistical data will use the category designations listed above. The designation "nonwhite" is not acceptable for use in the presentation of Federal Government data. It is not to be used in any publication of compliance or statistical data or in the text of any compliance or statistical report.

In cases where the above designations are considered inappropriate for presentation of statistical data on particular programs or for particular regional areas, the sponsoring agency may use:

> (1) The designations "Black and Other Races" or "All Other Races," as collective descriptions of minority races when the most summary distinction between the majority and minority races is appropriate;

(2) The designations "White," "Black," and "All Other Races" when the distinction among the majority race, the principal minority race and other races is appropriate; or

(3) The designation of a particular minority race or races, and the inclusion of "Whites" with "All Other Races," If such a collective description is appropriate.

In displaying detailed information which represents a combination of race and ethnicity, the description of the data being displayed must clearly indicate that both bases of classification are being used.

When the primary focus of a statistical report is on two or more specific identifiable groups in the population, one or more of which is racial or ethnic, it is acceptable to display data for each of the particular groups separately and to describe data relating to the remainder of the population by an appropriate collective description.

[FR Doc. 95-20787 Filed 8-25-95; 8:45 am]
BILLING CODE 3110-01-P

Source: Office of Management and Budget, Statistical Policy, *Federal Register* 60, no. 166 (August 28, 1995): 44692–93.

NOTES

Preface

1. *Domination and the Arts of Resistance: Hidden Transcrips* (New Haven, CT: Yale University Press 1990).

Chapter 1

1. For politics as processes of forming and reforming chains of equivalence, see Ernesto Laclau, *Emancipation(s)* (New York: Verso, 1996); and Victoria Hattam and Joseph Lowndes, "Ground Beneath Our Feet: Language, Culture and the Micro-Politics of Change," in *Formative Acts: American Politics in the Making*, ed. Stephen Skowronek and Matthew Glassman (Philadelphia: University of Pennsylvania Press, 2007).

2. Many have argued forh the importance of language in shaping politics, though they theorize the relation in quite different ways. For the inherent limits of signification, see Judith Butler, *Gender Trouble: Feminism and the Subversion of Identity* (New York: Routledge, 1990); Judith Butler, *Bodies That Matter: On the Discursive Limits of Sex* (New York: Routledge, 1993); Laclau, *Emancipation(s)*; Anne Norton, *Reflections on Political Identity* (Baltimore: Johns Hopkins University Press, 1988); Slavoj Zizek, *The Sublime Object of Ideology* (New York: Verso, 1989); Yannis Stavrakakis, *Lacan and the Political* (New York: Routledge, 1999). For attention to the historicity of language, see J. G. A. Pocock, *Politics, Language, and Time: Essays on Political Thought and History* (Chicago: University of Chicago Press, 1989); J. G. A. Pocock, *The Machiavellian Moment: Florentine Political Thought and the Atlantic Republican Tradition* (Princeton, NJ: Princeton University Press, 1975); J. G. A. Pocock, *Virtue, Commerce, and History: Essays on Political Thought and History, Chiefly in the Eighteenth Century* (Cambridge: University of Cambridge Press, 1985); Quentin Skinner, "Meaning and Understanding in the History of Ideas," *History and Theory* 8, no. 1 (1969): 3–53; and Bernard Bailyn, *The Ideological Origins of the American Revolution* (Cambridge, MA: Harvard University Press, 1967). For genealogical analysis of key words, see Ray-

mond Williams, *Keywords: A Vocabulary of Culture and Society* (New York: Oxford University Press, 1985).

3. The OMB promulgated Statistical Policy Directive 15 on May 12, 1977. The Directive mandated ethnic and racial categories to be used for the collection and dissemination of all race and ethnicity data by federal departments and administrative agencies. For official notification of Directive 15, see *Federal Register,* vol. 43, no. 87 (May 4, 1978): 19269–70. Directive 15 can be accessed electronically, as an appendix to "Standards for the Classification of Federal Data on Race and Ethnicity," *Federal Register,* vol. 59, no. 110 (June 9, 1994): 29834–35, at http://www.whitehouse.gov/omb/fedreg/notice_15.html.

4. Note that distinguishing ethnicity from race is a particularly American practice. In many other countries the two terms are used interchangeably, thereby generating a quite different topography for racial politics than in the United States.

5. For the text of Sharpton's speech to the Democratic National Convention on July 26, 2004, see the *New York Times,* July 27, 2004.

6. President Bush had delivered a speech at the NAACP on July 20, 2006, where he appealed to African Americans to reconsider their Democratic Party affiliation.

7. Sharpton, "Democratic National Convention Speech."

8. For Crenshaw's analysis of the media response to Sharpton's speech, see Kimberle Williams Crenshaw, "Sharp Tongues for Sharpton," *Nation,* August 6, 2004.

9. Barack Obama, "Remarks to the Democratic National Convention," text of speech reprinted in the *New York Times,* July 27, 2004 (emphasis in convention delivery).

10. Barack Obama, "A Hope to Fulfill" (remarks, National Press Club, Washington, DC, April 26, 2005), http://obama.senate.gov/speech/050426-_a_hope_to_fulfill/index .html.

11. Jodi Enda, "Great Expectations," *American Prospect,* February 2006, 24. For other recent critiques of Obama, see Alexander Cockburn, "They Should Have Hissed Barack Obama," *Nation,* April 24, 2006, 10; and Alexander Cockburn, "Obama: As He Rises, He Falls," *Nation,* May 8, 2006, 9.

12. Feminist literature is enormous. See especially Joan Scott, *Gender and the Politics of History:* (New York: Columbia University Press, 1999) chaps. 3, 4; Butler, *Bodies That Matter;* and Linda M. G. Zerilli, *Feminism and the Abyss of Freedom* (Chicago: University of Chicago Press, 2005).

13. For Jewish historiography, see Hasia Diner, *Lower East Side Memories: A Jewish Place in America* (Princeton, NJ: Princeton University Press, 2000); Hasia Diner, *Jews in America* (New York: Oxford University Press, 1999); Deborah Dash Moore, *At Home in America: Second Generation New York Jews* (New York: Columbia University Press, 1981); and Arthur Goren, *New York Jews and the Quest for Community: The Kehillah Experiment, 1908–1922* (New York: Columbia University Press, 1970). For discussion of Jews and racial classification in the United States, see Joel Perlmann, "'Race or People': Federal Race Classifications for Europeans in America, 1898–1913," Working Paper Number 320 (Levy Economics Institute, Bard College, January 2001). For Latinos and race in the United States, see Clara Rodriguez, *Changing Race: Latinos, the Census, and the History of Ethnicity in the United States* (New York: New York University Press, 2000); Ian Haney Lopez, "Hispanics and the Shrinking White Majority," *Daedalus* (Winter 2005): 42–52; Victoria Hattam, "Ethnicity and the American Boundaries of Race," *Daedalus* 134, no. 1 (2005): 61–69; Orlando Patterson, "Race by the Numbers," *New York Times,* May 8, 2001, Op. Ed. section; Clara Rodriguez and Hector Cordero-Guzman, "Placing Race in Context," *Ethnic and Racial Studies* 15,

no. 4 (1992): 523–42; and the excellent series of essays in "Race and Racism in the Americas, I–III," *NACLA: Report on the Americas* 34, no. 6 (2001); 35, no. 2 (2001); 35, no. 6 (2002). For survey data on Latinos racial identifications, see Pew Hispanic Center/Kaiser Family Foundation, *National Survey of Latinos: The Latino Electorate* (Washington, DC: Pew Hispanic Center and Henry J. Kaiser Family Foundation, 2002).

14. Several scholars do recognize the ambiguous racial location of Mexicans, but even they usually frame the problem as a classification issue generated from the lack of fit between the U.S. taxonomy and those it sought to classify. But this is to treat the issue simply as a question of application, as if the issue is simply how to implement the classificatory scheme on hand. See Peter Skerry, *Mexican Americans: The Ambivalent Minority* (Cambridge, MA: Harvard University Press, 1993); and Rodriguez, *Changing Race.*

15. For a critique of the biological basis of race, see Anthony Appiah, "The Uncompleted Argument: Du Bois and the Illusion of Race," in *"Race," Writing, and Difference,* ed. Henry Louis Gates Jr. (Chicago: University of Chicago Press, 1986).

16. For federal classification of Latinos as an ethnicity, see Directive 15. For Latinos as white, see Patterson, "Race by the Numbers"; and the National Association for the Advancement of Caucasian Latinos Web site, http://www.whitehispanic.com. For Latinos and race, see the excellent series of essays in "Race and Racism in the Americas, I–III."

17. For work connecting immigration and race, see Philip Kasinitz, *Caribbean New York: Black Immigrants and the Politics of Race* (Ithaca, NY: Cornell University Press, 1992); Matthew Frye Jacobson, *Whiteness of a Different Color: European Immigrants and the Alchemy of Race* (Cambridge, MA: Harvard University Press, 1998); Mae Ngai, "The Architecture of Race in American Immigration Law: A Reexamination of the Immigration Act of 1924," *Journal of American History* 86, no. 1 (1999): 67–92; Claire Kim, "The Racial Triangulation of Asian Americans," *Politics and Society* 27, no. 1 (1999): 105–38; Charles Hirschman, Philip Kasinitz, and Josh De Wind, eds., *The Handbook of International Migration: The American Experience* (New York: Russell Sage Foundation, 1999); Mary C. Waters, *Black Identities: West Indian Immigrant Dreams and American Realities* (Cambridge, MA: Harvard University Press, 1999); Desmond King, *Making Americans: Immigration, Race, and the Origins of the Diverse Democracy* (Cambridge, MA: Harvard University Press, 2000); John Skrentny, ed., *Color Lines: Affirmative Action, Immigration, and Civil Rights Options for America* (Chicago: University of Chicago Press, 2001); Nancy Foner and George Fredrickson, eds., *Not Just Black and White: Historical and Contemporary Perspectives on Immigration, Race, and Ethnicity in the United States* (New York: Russell Sage Foundation, 2004); Mae Ngai, *Impossible Subjects: Illegal Aliens and the Making of Modern America* (Princeton, NJ: Princeton University Press, 2004); and David R. Roediger, *Working Toward Whiteness: How America's Immigrants Became White. The Strange Journey from Ellis Island to the Suburbs* (New York: Basic Books, 2005).

The classic shift in race and party identification is that of African Americans who were initially tied to the party of Lincoln, but became stalwarts of the New Deal and Great Society coalitions. See James Sundquist, *Dynamics of the Party System: Alignment and Realignment of Political Parties in the United States* (Washington, DC: Brookings, 1973).

18. Census 2000 identified Latinos as the largest minority in the United States, at 12.5 percent of the national population. See Elizabeth M. Grieco and Rachel C. Cassidy, *Overview of Race and Hispanic Origin: Census 2000 Brief* (Washington, DC: U.S. Department of Commerce, Economics and Statistics Administration, U.S. Census Bureau, 2001). Moreover, Latinos are now the largest minority in twenty-three of the fifty states. See Matt Barreto, Rodolfo O. de la Garza, Jongho Lee, Jaesung Ryu, and

Harry P. Pachon, "Latino Voter Mobilization in 2000: A Glimpse into Latino Policy and Voting Preferences" (Claremont, CA: Tomas Rivera Policy Institute, September 2002), 1. Latino party identification is a hotly contested in both the academy and politics. For Latinos as a possible boon to the Republican Party, see Tamar Jacoby, "Republicans and Their Amigos: GOP No Longer for the Gringos-Only Party," *Weekly Standard,* November 25, 2002; Mireya Navarro, "Pataki's Success Among Latinos Worries Some Democrats," *New York Times,* November 9, 2002, Metro section, B1; Will Lester, "Political Parties Court Hispanic Vote," Associated Press, March 14, 2003; "Gov Eyes More Latino Support, but Budget Plans Spark Major Debate," *Newsday,* March 9, 2003; and Lizette Alvarez, "Hispanic Voters Hard to Profile, Poll Finds: Mixture of Beliefs Helps Make Latinos an Attractive Swing Bloc," *New York Times,* October 4, 2002, National section, A20. For the stability of Latinos' Democratic Party identification, see Barreto et al., "Latino Voter Mobilization in 2000."

19. See Ronald Takaki, *A Different Mirror: A History of Multicultural America* (Boston: Little, Brown, 1993); and Ngai, *Impossible Subjects.*

20. See George Fredrickson, *The Black Image in the White Mind: The Debate on Afro-American Character and Destiny, 1817–1914* (New York: Harper & Row, 1972); Winthrop D. Jordan, *The White Man's Burden: Historical Origins of Racism in the United States* (New York: Oxford University Press, 1974); Cathy Cohen, *The Boundaries of Blackness: AIDS and the Breakdown of Black Politics* (Chicago: University of Chicago Press, 1999); and Michael C. Dawson, *Black Visions: The Roots of Contemporary African-American Political Ideologies* (Chicago: University of Chicago Press, 2003).

21. For arguments about assimilation, see Richard Alba and Victor Nee, *Remaking the American Mainstream: Assimilation and Contemporary Immigration* (Cambridge, MA: Harvard University Press, 2003); and Russell A. Kasal, "Revisiting Assimilation: The Rise, Fall, and Reappraisal of a Concept in American Ethnic History," *American Historical Review* 100, no. 2 (1995): 437–71. For the classic analysis of assimilation, see Milton Gordon, *Assimilation in American Life: The Role of Race, Religion, and National Origins* (New York: Oxford University Press, 1964).

22. See especially Skrentny, ed., *Color Lines;* Waters, *Black Identities;* and Hugh Davis Graham, *Collision Course: The Strange Convergence of Affirmative Action and Immigration Policy in America* (New York: Oxford University Press, 2003).

23. See David Roediger, *The Wages of Whiteness: The Making of the American Working Class* (New York: Verso, 1991); David Roediger, *Towards the Abolition of Whiteness: Essays on Race, Politics, and Working Class History* (New York: Verso, 1994); and Waters, *Black Identities.*

24. The phrase "collision course" is taken from Graham, *Collision Course.* See also John Skrentny, *The Minority Rights Revolution* (Cambridge, MA: Harvard University Press, 2002).

25. The whiteness literature is now enormous, but for influential works see James Baldwin, "On Being White . . . and Other Lies," *Essence,* April 1984, 10–12; Richard Dyer, "White," *Screen* 29, no. 4 (1988): 44–65; Toni Morrison, "Unspeakable Things Unspoken: The Afro-American Presence in American Literature," *Michigan Quarterly Review* 28, no. 1 (1989): 1–34; and Roediger, *Wages of Whiteness.* See also Richard D. Alba, *Ethnic Identity: The Transformation of White America* (New Haven, CT: Yale University Press, 1990); Toni Morrison, *Playing in the Dark: Whiteness and the Literary Imagination* (New York: Vintage Books, 1993); Karen Brodkin Sacks, "How Did Jews Become White Folks?" in *Race,* ed. Stephen Gregory and Roger Sanjek (New Brunswick, NJ: Rutgers University Press, 1994); Roediger, *Towards the Abolition of*

Whiteness; Noel Ignatiev, *How The Irish Became White* (New York: Routledge, 1995); Ian Haney Lopez, *White by Law: The Legal Construction of Race* (New York: New York University Press, 1996); Michael Rogin, *Blackface, White Noise: Jewish Immigrants in the Hollywood Melting Pot* (Berkeley: University of California Press, 1996); George Lipsitz, *The Possessive Investment in Whiteness: How White People Profit from Identity Politics* (Philadelphia: Temple University Press, 1998); Matthew Frye Jacobson, *Whiteness of a Different Color: European Immigrants and the Alchemy of Race* (Cambridge, MA: Harvard University Press, 1998); and Gary Gerstle, *American Crucible: Race and Nation in the Twentieth Century* (Princeton, NJ: Princeton University Press, 2001). For my assessment of the enormous contribution and theoretical innovations advanced by these scholars, see Victoria Hattam, "Whiteness: Theorizing Race, Eliding Ethnicity," *International Race and Working Class History* 60 (Fall 2001): 61–68.

26. Waters, *Black Identities.*

27. See Victoria Hattam, "The 1964 Civil Rights Act: Narrating the Past, Authorizing the Future," *Studies in American Political Development* 18 (Spring 2004): 60–69; and John D. Skrentny's response, "Policy Making Is Decision Making: A Response to Hattam," *Studies in American Political Development* 18 (Spring 2004): 70–80. For a recent debate of these issues, see Stephen Steinberg, "Immigration, African Americans, and Race Discourse," *New Politics* 10, no. 3 (2005): 1–14; and responses in the following issue. See also the debate over Steinberg's essay in "Do Immigrants Block African American Progress? A Debate," *New Labor Forum* 15, no. 1 (2006): 69–72.

28. For elaboration of the Census data imputation problem, see chap. 5; and Hattam, "Ethnicity and the American Boundaries of Race." For Serrano's intervention via the appropriations bill, see "Serrano Succeeds in Retaining 'Other' Race Option on Census Form," press release from Rep. José Serrano, November 22, 2004, http://www.house.gov/list/press/ny16_serrano/041122Census.html.

29. For the emergent, see Raymond Williams, *Marxism and Literature* (New York: Oxford University Press, 1977), 123–27.

Chapter 2

1. For broad use of the term *race,* see George W. Stocking, "Lamarckianism in American Social Science, 1890–1915," in *Race, Culture, and Evolution: Essays in the History of Anthropology* (Chicago: University of Chicago Press, 1982); Nicholas Hudson, "From 'Nation' to 'Race': The Origin of Racial Classification in Eighteenth-Century Thought," *Eighteenth Century Studies* 29, no. 3 (1996): 247–64; and Earl W. Count, "The Evolution of the Race Idea in Modern Western Culture during the Period of the Pre-Darwinian Nineteenth Century," *Transactions of the New York Academy of Sciences* 8 (1946): 139–65. Moreover, there was an explicit argument claiming a deep interrelationship among nationality, language, culture, and race through the notion of "affinities" in which scholars explicitly argued for the parallel development of different spheres of life. See William Z. Ripley, "The Racial Geography of Europe: A Sociological Study, V—The Three European Races," *Popular Science Monthly* 15, no. 2 (1897): 192–209; and George W. Stocking, "American Social Scientists and Race Theory: 1890–1915" (PhD diss., University of Pennsylvania, 1960), 326.

2. Social science institutions were established as follows: American Social Science Association, 1865; American Historical Association, 1884; American Economics Association, 1885; American Anthropological Association, 1902; American Political Science Association, 1903; and American Sociological Association, 1905. The first issues of

major journals for each of the social sciences are as follows: *Political Science Quarterly*, 1886; *Quarterly Journal of Economics*, 1886; *American Historical Review*, 1895; *American Anthropologist*, 1888; and *American Journal of Sociology*, 1895. The literature on the formation of the social science disciplines is enormous, but some key works include Dorothy Ross, *The Origins of American Social Science* (New York: Cambridge University Press, 1991); David M. Ricci, *The Tragedy of Political Science: Politics, Scholarship, and Democracy* (New Haven, CT: Yale University Press, 1984); Raymond Seidelman and Peter Novick, *That Noble Dream: The "Objectivity Question" and the American Historical Profession* (New York: Cambridge University Press, 1988); Stocking, *Race, Culture, and Evolution;* George W. Stocking, *The Ethnographer's Magic and Other Essays in the History of Anthropology* (Madison: University of Wisconsin Press, 1992); Martin Bulmer, *The Chicago School of Sociology: Institutionalization, Diversity, and the Rise of Sociological Research* (Chicago: University of Chicago Press, 1984); A. W. Coats, "The First Two Decades of the American Economic Association," *American Economic Review* 50, no. 4 (1960): 555–74; and John B. Parrish, "Rise of Economics as an Academic Discipline: The Formative Years to 1900," *Southern Economics Journal* 34 (July 1967): 1–16.

3. Weismann's critique of natural selection was made visible through his debate with Herbert Spencer, which appeared in a seven-part exchange published in the *Contemporary Review* between February 1893 and October 1894. The specific essays are as follows: Herbert Spencer, "The Inadequacy of 'Natural Selection,'" *Contemporary Review* 63 (February 1893): 153–66; Herbert Spencer, "The Inadequacy of 'Natural Selection (concluded),'" *Contemporary Review* 63 (March 1893): 439–56; Herbert Spencer, "Professor Weismann's Theories," *Contemporary Review* 63 (May 1893): 743–60; Marcus Hartog, "The Spencer-Weismann Controversy," *Contemporary Review* 64 (July 1893): 50–59; August Weismann, "The All-Sufficiency of Natural Selection: A Reply to Herbert Spencer," *Contemporary Review* 64 (September 1893): 309–38; August Weismann, "The All-Sufficiency of Natural Selection: A Reply to Herbert Spencer," *Contemporary Review* 64 (October 1893): 596–610; Herbert Spencer, "A Rejoinder to Professor Weismann," *Contemporary Review* 64 (December 1893): 893–912; Herbert Spencer, "Weismannism Once More," *Contemporary Review* 66 (October 1894): 592–608. Many social scientists writing in the late nineteenth and early twentieth centuries refer back to the debate as they try to sort through the changing views of heredity and race.

4. George Stocking makes a similar point in much of his work, which I draw heavily on throughout this chapter. I have found his extensive research in these areas to have been enormously helpful in understanding late nineteenth- and early twentieth-century writing on race. See Stocking, "American Social Scientists and Race Theory: 1890–1915"; Stocking, *Race, Culture, and Evolution;* Stocking, *The Ethnographer's Magic;* and George W. Stocking, "The Turn-of-the-Century Concept of Race," *Modernism* 1, no. 1 (1993): 4–16.

5. See Hanes Walton Jr., Cheryl M. Miller, and Joseph P. McCormick II, "Race and Political Science: The Dual Traditions of Race Relations Politics and African-American Politics," in *Political Science in History: Research Programs and Political Traditions,* ed. James Farr, John S. Dryzek, and Stephen T. Leonard (New York: Cambridge University Press, 1995). For very different accounts of the origins of political science and race, see Robert Vitalis, "Birth of a Discipline," in *Imperialsim and Internationalism in the Discipline of International Relations,* ed. Brian Schmidt and David Long (Albany: State University of New York Press, 2005), 159–82; and Jessica Blatt, " 'To Bring Out the Best That Is in Their Blood': Race, Reform, and Civilization in the Journal of Race

Development (1910–1919)," *Ethnic and Racial Studies* 27, no. 5 (2004): 691–709. Both work with a more capacious notion of race and are able to document the pervasiveness of colonialism, empire, and discipline formation.

6. See Stocking, "Lamarckianism in American Social Science, 1890–1915."

7. For brief biographical data on these social scientists, see Stocking, "American Social Scientists and Race Theory," appendix C.

8. See William Z. Ripley, "Acclimatization, Second Paper," *Popular Science Monthly* 48 (April 1896): 779. In 1872, Francis A. Walker was appointed professor of political economy and history at Yale, and in 1876 he also became a part-time lecturer at the newly established Johns Hopkins University. For discussion of Walker and the fluidity of movement between the early social science disciplines more generally, see Ross, *The Origins of American Social Science*, chaps. 2–4.

9. For excellent accounts of the influence of Lamarckianism, see Stocking, "Lamarckianism in American Social Science"; and Stocking, "The Turn-of-the-Century Concept of Race." Certainly, Lamarckianism was not all there was to nineteenth-century racial discourse; others have documented the multiple currents in play. For my purposes, however, Lamarckianism, or more precisely the break with Lamarck, is key. It provided the intellectual opening for subsequent figures to craft the notion of ethnicity. The literature on nineteenth-century conceptions of race is enormous; key works include William Stanton, *The Leopard's Spots: Scientific Attitudes Toward Race in America 1815–59* (Chicago: University of Chicago Press, 1960); George M. Fredrickson, *The Black Image in the White Mind: The Debate on Afro-American Character and Destiny, 1817–1914* (New York: Harper & Row, 1972); Stephen Jay Gould, *The Mismeasure of Man* (New York: Norton, 1981); Roy Harvey Pearce, *Savagism and Civilization: A Study of the Indian and the American Mind* (Berkeley: University of California Press, 1988); Thomas F. Gossett, *Race: The History of an Idea in America* (New York: Oxford University Press, 1997); Lee D. Baker, *From Savage to Negro: Anthropology and the Construction of Race, 1896–1954* (Berkeley: University of California Press, 1998); Michael Banton, *Racial Theories* (New York: Cambridge University Press, 1998); Audrey Smedley, *Race in North America: Origin and Evolution of a Worldview* (Boulder, CO: Westview Press, 1999); George M. Fredrickson, *Racism: A Short History* (Princeton, NJ: Princeton University Press, 2002).

10. Stocking, "Turn-of-the-Century Concept of Race," 10 (emphasis in original).

11. Late nineteenth-century social scientists used a number of terms to refer to the division between the *historic* and *natural* races. One can find reference to the *pure*, *true*, and *genuine* races as opposed to *artificial* ones. All of these terms, I am suggesting, referred to the same underlying distinction as that of the *natural* and *historic* races.

12. For an influential account of historic races, see Gustave Le Bon, *The Psychology of Peoples* (originally pub. 1894; New York: Arno Press, 1974); see especially chap. 5.

13. William Z. Ripley, "Acclimatization," *Popular Science Monthly* 48 (March 1896): 662–75; and William Z. Ripley, "Acclimatization, Second Paper," *Popular Science Monthly* 48 (April 1896): 779–93.

14. Ripley, "Acclimatization, Second Paper," 662.

15. Ibid., 781.

16. Ibid., 785, 788.

17. Daniel G. Brinton, "The Factors of Heredity and Environment in Man," *American Anthropologist*, o.s., 11 (September 1898): 271–72.

18. Ibid., 275.

19. See John W. Powell, "The Categories," *American Anthropologist*, n.s., 3, no. 3 (1901): 429. For an excellent discussion of Powell, see Stocking, "American Social Scientists and Race Theory," 325–27. See also J. W. Powell, "Competition as a Factor in Human Evolution," *American Anthropologist*, o.s., 1, no. 4 (1888): 297–323.

20. Joseph Jacobs, "Are Jews Jews?" *Popular Science Monthly* 55, no. 4 (1899): 508. Closer to home, anthropologist W. J. McGee noted in 1899 that the shape of the forehead of American statesmen from the time of George Washington to that of his contemporaries had changed significantly. The changes, McGee argued, were due to "cephalization," by which he meant the changing physical structure of the head due to intensive use of the brain over time. W. J. McGee, "The Science of Humanity," *American Anthropologist* 10, no. 8 (1897): 241–72: W. J. McGee, "The Trend of Human Progress," *American Anthropologist*, n.s., 1, no. 3 (1899): 401–47; W. J. McGee, "Man's Place in Nature," *American Anthropologist*, n.s., 3, no. 1 (1901): 1–13; W. J McGee, "Anthropology and Its Larger Problems," *Science*, n.s., 21, no. 542 (1905): 770–84.

21. See Lester Ward, "Social Differentiation and Social Integration," *American Journal of Sociology* 8, no. 6 (1903): 721–45. For Ward's insistence on the parallel development of organic and social evolution, see 721, 743. See also Carlos Closson, "Social Selection," *Journal of Political Economy* 4, no. 4 (1896): 449–66.

22. I did find a handful of references to the term *ethnic* in discussions of races and peoples. In 1894, for example, Daniel Brinton used the phrases *ethnic anatomy* and *ethnic jurisprudence*, while in 1895, W. I. Thomas referred to *ethnic relationships*. Similarly, William Ripley referred to *ethnic types* in his discussion of the French in part six of "The Racial Geography of Europe." Although scholars occasionally used the term *ethnic*, they did so infrequently and in ways that contrast with our twentieth-century notion of ethnicity. At the turn of the century, little or no distinction is drawn between race and ethnicity; the term *ethnic* was not yet used to refer to immigrants, nor was it reserved for discussion of particular groups. Rather, it was used in a wide-ranging fashion as a adjective in broader discussions of the races in an effort to specify particular racial traits. Brinton referred to *ethnic anatomy* in "Variation in the Human Skeleton and Their Causes," *American Anthropologist*, o.s., 7 (October 1894): 385, 386; for *ethnic jurisprudence*, see Brinton "The 'Nation' as an Element in Anthropology," in *Memoirs of the International Congress of Anthropology*, ed. C. S. Vake (Chicago: Shuttle, 1894), 29; and for W. I. Thomas's reference to *ethnic relationships*, see W. I. Thomas, "The Scope and Method of Folk-Psychology," *American Journal of Sociology* 1 (1896): 440. See also William Z. Ripley, "The Racial Geography of Europe: A Sociological Study, VI—France—The Teuton and the Celt," *Popular Science Monthly* 51, no. 3 (1897): 289.

23. See Ward, "Social Differentiation and Social Integration," 722, 731. For more general discussion of the ranking of races from barbarism to civilization, see Pearce, *Savagism and Civilization*.

24. Stocking, "American Social Scientists and Race Theory," 444–45.

25. For discussion of evolution in Darwin and Lamarckianism, see Stocking, "American Social Scientists and Race," 319–21, 392–93. Darwin himself acknowledged a link between Lamarckianism and his *Origin of the Species*. See Nora Barlow, ed., *The Autobiography of Charles Darwin, 1809–1882* (New York: Norton, 1993), 49. For a merging of Lamarckian and Darwinian notion of heredity, see Brinton, "The Factors of Heredity and Environment in Man," 274.

26. For the rediscovery of Mendelian genetics, see Peter J. Bowler, *The Mendelian Revolution: The Emergence of Hereditarian Concepts in Modern Science and Society* (Baltimore: Johns Hopkins University Press, 1989), especially chap. 6.

27. For Brinton's defense of the heritability of acquired characteristics, see Brinton, "The Factors of Heredity and Environment in Man," 274–75.

28. See Lester F. Ward, "Neo-Darwinism and Neo-Lamarckianism," *Proceeding of the Biological Society of Washington* 6 (1891): 45–50; and Lester F. Ward, "Weismann's Concessions," *Popular Science Monthly* 45 (1894): 175–84.

29. Ripley's "Acclimatization" essays were published in two parts in *Popular Science Monthly* in March and April 1896. See note 13.

30. William Z. Ripley, "The Racial Geography of Europe: A Sociological Study, I—Language, Nationality, and Race," *Popular Science Monthly* 50, no. 4 (1897): 454, 455.

31. William Z. Ripley, "The Racial Geography of Europe: A Sociological Study, XIII—Modern Social Problems," *Popular Science Monthly* 52, no. 4 (1898): 470.

32. Ibid., 471.

33. Ibid. (emphasis added).

34. Ibid., 478. For Ripley's sense of the newness of the social sciences, see William Ripley, "Geography as a Sociological Study," *Political Science Quarterly* 10, no. 4 (1895): 636–55.

35. See William Z. Ripley, *The Races of Europe: A Sociological Study* (New York: Appleton, 1899), 513.

36. W. I. Thomas, "The Scope and Method of Folk-Psychology," 435.

37. Ibid. The phrase *developmental history of mind* is from page 436 in the same essay. See also W. I. Thomas, "The Psychology of Race-Prejudice," *American Journal of Sociology* 9 (March 1904): 593–611.

38. See W. I. Thomas, "On a Difference in the Metabolism of the Sexes," *American Journal of Sociology* 3 (July 1897): 31–63; and W. I. Thomas, "The Mind of Woman and the Lower Races," *American Journal of Sociology* 12 (January 1907): 435–69.

39. Thomas, "On a Difference in the Metabolism of the Sexes," 31.

40. Ibid.

41. Ibid., 62.

42. Thomas, "The Mind of Woman and the Lower Races," 435.

43. Ibid., 437.

44. Ibid., 447, 450.

45. Ibid., 440.

46. Ibid., 441.

47. Ibid., 469.

48. Madison Grant, *The Passing of the Great Race; or, The Racial Basis of European History* (New York: Scribner, 1916), xvii.

49. Ibid., 3.

50. Ibid., 4.

51. Ibid., subtitle of the book.

52. William Z. Ripley, "The Racial Geography of Europe: A Sociological Study, Supplement—The Jews," *Popular Science Monthly* 54, no. 2 (1898): 164 (emphasis added).

53. William Z. Ripley, "The Racial Geography of Europe: A Sociological Study, Supplement—The Jews (continued)," *Popular Science Monthly* 54, no. 3 (1899): 351.

54. Ripley, "The Racial Geography of Europe: A Sociological Study, Supplement—The Jews," 166.

55. Ripley referred five times to Jacobs in his essay. See Ripley, "The Racial Geography of Europe: A Sociological Study, Supplement—The Jews (continued)," 342, 345, 348, 349, 350. Ripley identified Jacobs as president of the Jewish Historical Society in London.

56. See Joseph Jacobs, "Are Jews Jews?" *Popular Science Monthly* 55, no. 4 (1899): 502–11.

57. Ibid., 502.

58. Ibid., 507.

59. Ibid., 511.

60. Ibid., 509.

61. Ibid., 510.

62. Ibid., 510, 511.

63. See Maurice Fishberg, "Physical Anthropology of the Jews, I—The Cephalic Index," *American Anthropologist*, n.s., 4 (1902): 684–706; Maurice Fishberg, "Physical Anthropology of the Jews, II—Pigmentation," *American Anthropologist*, n.s., 5 (1905): 89–106; Maurice Fishberg, "The Jews: A Study of Race and Environment," *Popular Science Monthly* 69 (September 1906): 257–67; Maurice Fishberg, "The Jews: A Study of Race and Environment, II—Marriages," *Popular Science Monthly* 69 (November 1906): 441–50; Maurice Fishberg, "The Jews: A Study of Race and Environment, III—Mixed Marriages between Persons of Different Christian Denominations," *Popular Science Monthly* 69 (December 1906): 502–11; and Maurice Fishberg, "The Jews: A Study of Race and Environment, IV—Mortality," *Popular Science Monthly* 70 (January 1907): 33–47. See also Maurice Fishberg, *The Jews: A Study of Race and Environment* (London: Scott, 1911). For Fishberg's references to Ripley and Jacobs, see Fishberg, "Physical Anthropology of the Jews, I—The Cephalic Index," 684, 698; and Fishberg, "The Jews: A Study of Race and Environment, III—Mixed Marriages between Persons of Different Christian Denominations," 505.

64. Fishberg, "The Jews: A Study of Race and Environment," 257.

65. See Fishberg, "The Jews: A Study of Race and Environment, II—Marriages," 443; Fishberg, "The Jews: A Study of Race and Environment, III—Mixed Marriages between Persons of Different Christian Denominations," 502, 504; and Fishberg, "The Jews: A Study of Race and Environment, IV—Mortality," 35, 45.

66. See Robert Bennett Bean, "The Nose of the Jew and the Quadratus Labi Superioris Muscle," *The Anatomical Record* 7, no. 2 (1913): 47–49; also referred to in a conference report in *American Anthropologist*, n.s., 15 (1913): 106–8. For further discussion on Bean, see Stocking, "American Social Science and Race Theory," 141.

67. Richmond Mayo-Smith, "Assimilation of Nationalities in the United States, I," *Political Science Quarterly* 9, no. 3 (1894): 426. See also Richmond Mayo-Smith, "Assimilation of Nationalities in the United States, II," *Political Science Quarterly* 9, no. 4 (1894): 649–70.

68. See Mayo-Smith, "Assimilation of Nationalities in the United States, I," 426–27, 431, 436.

69. Ibid., 426.

70. For Mayo-Smith's rather romantic account of assimilation, see Mayo-Smith, "Assimilation of Nationalities, I," 431–32; and Mayo-Smith, "Assimilation of Nationalities, II," 651, 669. For another largely abstract discussion of nationality, see Albion W. Small, "The Bonds of Nationality," *American Journal of Sociology* 20 (1915): 609–83.

71. See Marcus L. Hansen, "The History of American Immigration as a Field for Research," *American Historical Review* 32, no. 3 (1927): 500–18.

72. Mayo-Smith, "Control of Immigration, I," *Political Science Quarterly* 3, no. 1 (1888): 53–54.

73. Mayo-Smith, "Assimilation of Nationalities in the United States, I," 436. For additional arguments by Mayo-Smith distinguishing immigrants and slaves, see Richmond Mayo-Smith, "Control of Immigration, II," *Political Science Quarterly* 3, no. 2 (1888): 211–12.

74. See William Z. Ripley, "Race Progress and Immigration," *Annals of the American Academy of Political and Social Science* 34, no. 1 (1909): 134.

75. For lingering Lamarckianism, see John Mitchell, "Immigration and the American Laboring Classes," *Annals of the American Academy of Political and Social Science* 34, no. 1 (1909): 128; Ripley, "Race Progress and Immigration," 131; John R. Commons, *Races and Immigrants in America* (New York: Macmillan, 1916), 12–13, 41, 79. For the new immigration discourse, see text and notes following.

76. For example, see William Bennett's counterarguments about immigration and crime in William S. Bennett, "Immigrants and Crime," *Annals of the American Academy of Political and Social Science* 34, no. 1 (1909): 117–24. See also Commons, *Races and Immigrants in America;* and the first two volumes of the conservative *Immigrants in America Review* published in 1915–16. Several editorials and essays dealt directly with the intersection of immigration and class.

77. See Commons, *Races and Immigrants in America*, chap. 6; Mitchell, "Immigration and the American Laboring Classes," 125–29; and Mayo-Smith, "Control of Immigration, I," 61–77; Mayo-Smith, "Control of Immigration, II," 222–25; Mayo-Smith, "Control of Immigration, III," *Political Science Quarterly* 3, no. 3 (1888): 411, 416–17; and Madison Grant, "America for the Americans," *Forum* 74 (September 1925): 349–50.

78. Mayo-Smith, "Control of Immigration, II," 225.

79. See Mayo-Smith, "Control of Immigration, I," 56, 57–60. See also Mayo-Smith, "Control of Immigration, III," 415, 422.

80. Madison Grant, "America for the Americans," 351.

81. See also John Hawks Noble, "The Present State of the Immigration Question," *Political Science Quarterly* 7, no. 2 (June 1892): 241; and Madison Grant, "Closing the Flood-Gates," in *The Alien in Our Midst, or "Selling Our Birthright for a Mess of Industrial Pottage,"* ed. Madison Grant and Charles Stewart Davidson (New York: Galton, 1930), 17.

82. For reference to Zangwill, see Grant, "America for the Americans," 347–48, 350, 351. The reference to "alien colonies in our midst" is from Grant, "America for the Americans," 351; see also 348. For similar arguments about immigrant colonies, see Mitchell, "Immigration and the American Laboring Classes," 127–28. For disorder, see Noble, "The Present State of the Immigration Question," 232; and for crime, see Grant, "America for the Americans," 352; Bennett, "Immigrants and Crime"; Commons, *Races and Immigrants*, chap. 7; and Hastings H. Hart, "Immigration and Crime," *American Journal of Sociology* 2, no. 3 (1896): 369–77.

Chapter 3

1. For Americanization, see John Higham, *Strangers in the Land: Patterns of American Nativism 1860–1925* (New York: Atheneum, 1963), chaps. 8, 9; John F. McClymer, "The Federal Government and the Americanization Movement," *Prologue*

10 (Spring 1978): 23–41; Gary Gerstle, *Working-Class Americanism: The Politics of Labor in a Textile City, 1914–1960* (New York: Cambridge University Press, 1989); Desmond King, *Making Americans: Immigration, Race, and the Origins of the Diverse Democracy* (Cambridge, MA: Harvard University Press, 2000). For an excellent selection of primary sources, see Philip Davis, ed., *Immigration and Americanization: Selected Readings* (New York: Ginn, 1991); and Frances Kellor, "What Is Americanization?" *Yale Review* 8 (January 1919): 282–99. Kellor was the vice chairman of the National Americanization Committee. For a fascinating account of the anxiety over immigration, see Susan S. Lancer's brilliant reinterpretation of Charlotte Perkins Gilman's *The Yellow Wallpaper* in "Feminist Criticism, 'The Yellow Wallpaper,' and the Politics of Color in America," *Feminist Studies* 15, no. 3 (1989): 415–41.

2. See McClymer, "The Federal Government and the Americanization Movement," 23–26.

3. See Higham, *Strangers in the Land*, chaps. 8, 9; and Roosevelt and Wilson speeches in Davis, ed., *Immigration and Americanization*. For early immigration statutes, see E. P. Hutchinson, *Legislative History of American Immigration Policy 1798–1965* (Philadelphia: University of Pennsylvania Press, 1981); and *United States Immigration Commission* (Washington, DC: Government Printing Office, 1911), volume 39 on "Immigration Legislation." Appendix A contains a very useful synopsis of immigration laws up through 1910.

4. Isaac Berkson refers to "ethnic group[s]," "ethnic identity," "ethnic entity," "ethnic community," "ethnic loyalty," and "loyalty to a minority ethnic group." See Isaac B. Berkson, "A Community Theory of American Life," *Menorah Journal* 6, no. 6 (1920): 311, 313, 314, 316; and Isaac B. Berkson, "The Jewish Right to Live: A Defense of Ethnic Loyalty," *Menorah Journal* 7, no. 1 (1921): 41, 42, 43, 44; and Isaac B. Berkson, *Theories of Americanization: A Critical Study* (New York: Teachers College, Columbia University, 1920), 85, 98, 114, 121, 128, 132. For Drachsler's uses of the term *ethnic*, see "Americanization and Race Fusion," *Menorah Journal* 6, no. 3 (1920): 134, 137, where he also refers to "ethnic groups"; and Julius Drachsler, *Democracy and Assimilation: The Blending of Immigrant Heritages in America* (New York: Macmillan, 1920), x. Horace Kallen refers to "ethnic unity," "ethnic type," "ethnic dualism," "ethnic group[s]," "ethnic and cultural identity," "ethnic differences," and "ethnic diversity." See Horace Kallen "Beyond the Melting Pot: A Study of American Nationality," *Nation*, February 18, 1915, 190–94; and *Nation*, February 25, 1915, 217, 219. See also Horace M. Kallen, *Culture and Democracy in the United States* (New York: Arno Press, 1970), 130, 131, 151, 159, 165, 201. Issues of loyalty arise throughout many sources, but for an extended discussion, see Berkson, *Theories of Americanization*, chap 4.

5. For discussion of the emergence of ethnicity in the 1940s, see Werner Sollors, ed., introduction to *The Invention of Ethnicity* (New York: Oxford University Press, 1991). By focusing on "ethnicity" per se—that is, the appearance of it as a noun—Sollors overlooks the importance of these earlier writers in shaping the category of ethnicity through their discussions of ethnic groups and ethnic loyalties. Sollors subsequently published a more elaborate history of the term *ethnic* in which he identified the nineteenth-century origins of the term. Although more complete, in neither account does Sollors emphasize the 1910s as the critical moment of category formation. See Werner Sollors, ed., *Theories of Ethnicity: A Classic Reader* (New York: New York University Press, 1996).

6. For membership figures of the Harvard Menorah Society, see membership lists in *Minutes*, 1906–8, 1909–15, Menorah Society Archives, Harvard University, General Folder.

7. For founding of the Intercollegiate Menorah Association, see *Report of the Constituent Convention of the Intercollegiate Menorah Association Held at the University of Chicago,* January 1, 2, and 3, 1913 (n.p., n.d.); Henry Hurwitz and I. Leo Sharfman, *The Menorah Movement: For the Study and Advancement of Jewish Ideals, History, Purposes, Activities* (Ann Arbor, MI: Intercollegiate Menorah Association, 1914); and Henry Hurwitz, "The Menorah Movement," *Menorah Journal* 1, no. 1 (1915): 50–55.

In 1915, the following colleges and universities had established Menorah Societies: Boston University, Brown University, Clarke University, College of City of New York, Columbia University, Cornell University, Harvard University, Hunter College, Johns Hopkins University, New York University, Ohio State University, Penn State College, Radcliffe College, Rutgers College, Tufts College, University of California, University of Chicago, University of Cincinnati, University of Colorado, University of Denver, University of Illinois, University of Maine, University of Michigan, University of Minnesota, University of Missouri, University of North Carolina, University of Omaha, University of Pennsylvania, University of Pittsburgh, University of Texas, University of Wisconsin, Valparaiso University, Western Reserve University, and Yale University. See front matter in the *Menorah Journal* 1, no. 1 (1915).

8. See Susanne Klingenstein, *Jews in the American Academy, 1900–1940* (New Haven, CT: Yale University Press, 1991). For a powerful account of the social exclusivity of the general circulation magazines, see the compelling description of Randolph Bourne's first meeting with Ellery Sedgwick, the editor of the *Atlantic Monthly,* in Bruce Clayton, prologue to *Forgotten Prophet: The Life of Randolph Bourne* (Columbia: University of Missouri Press, 1998).

9. Some other scholars have examined the *Menorah Journal.* See Alan M. Wald, *The New York Intellectuals: The Rise and Decline of the Anti-Stalinist Left from the 1930s to the 1980s* (Chapel Hill: University of North Carolina Press, 1987); and Seth Korelitz, "The Menorah Idea: From Religion to Culture, from Race to Ethnicity," *American Jewish History* 85, no. 1 (1997): 75–100. For discussion of early differences among Jews over Zionism, see Naomi Wiener Cohen, "The Maccabaean Message: A Study in American Zionism Until World War I," *Jewish Social Studies* 18 (July 1956): 163–78; and Naomi Wiener Cohen, "The Reaction of Reform Judaism in America to Political Zionism, 1897–1922," *Publications of American Jewish Historical Society* 40 (1950–51): 361–94.

10. For two powerful works that read race and ethnicity together, see Claire Jean Kim, *Bitter Fruit: The Politics of Black-Korean Conflict in New York City* (New Haven, CT: Yale University Press, 2000); and Mae M. Ngai, *Impossible Subjects: Illegal Aliens and the Making of Modern America* (Princeton, NJ: Princeton University Press, 2004).

11. In 1914 membership stood at 7,500, grew to more than 30,000 by 1918, and exploded to 149,000 by 1919. For membership figures, see Evyatar Friesel, "Brandeis' Role in American Zionism Historically Reconsidered," *American Jewish History* 69 (September 1979): 48; and Sarah Schmidt, *Horace M. Kallen: Prophet of American Zionism* (Brooklyn, NY: Carlson, 1995), 51. In its first year, the federation was called the National Federation of American Zionists, but the organization changed its name to Federation of American Zionists in 1889. At the Federation's prewar convention held in June 1914, membership was recorded at a mere 15,000 out of more than the then three million Jews living in the United States. Not only was membership small, but numbers also fluctuated quite dramatically in the prewar years. For example, the number of societies affiliated with the Federation stood at 308 in 1904, fell to 84 in 1910, and rose to 198 by the middle of 1914. In New York City, the Federation had particular trouble getting large numbers of eastern European Jews to join. In 1904 there were 25 Zionist

societies in New York City, 11 in 1911, and only 10 in 1914. See Friesel, "Brandeis' Role in American Zionism Historically Reconsidered," 37–38; and Schmidt, *Horace M. Kallen*, 11. For opposition to Zionism, see Cohen, "The Reaction of Reform Judaism in America to Political Zionism; and Cohen, "The Maccabaean Message"; and Schmidt, *Horace M. Kallen*, 3.

12. See Schmidt, *Horace M. Kallen*, 51–52; Jacob de Haas, *Louis D. Brandeis: A Biographical Sketch, with Special Reference to His Contribution to Jewish and Zionist History* (New York: Bloch, 1929), 161.

13. See Schmidt, *Horace M. Kallen*, 11, 53.

14. There was a vote of no confidence in Brandeis within the Provisional Executive Committee in 1920. Brandeis lost and resigned.

15. For Brandeis and Kallen sources, see text and notes following. For Dewey's arguments for hyphenation, see John Dewey, "Nationalizing Education," *Journal of Education* 84, no. 16 (1916): 426–31; John Dewey, "The Principle of Nationality," *Menorah Journal* 3, no. 4 (1917): 203–8; and John Dewey, "America in the World," *Nation*, March 14, 1918, 287. For Randolph Bourne's defense of transnational identification, see "The Jew and Trans-National America," *Menorah Journal* 2, no. 5 (1916): 277–84; Randolph Bourne, "Trans-National America," *Atlantic Monthly* 118 (July 1916): 86–97. For additional arguments on subnational identification in the United States, see sources in notes 21 and 26.

16. The phrase is from Solomon Schechter, *Zionism: A Statement* (New York: Federation of American Zionists, 1906), 5; and Julian W. Mack, *Americanism and Zionism* (New York: Zionist Organization of America, 1919).

17. "Call to the Educated Jew," *Menorah Journal* 1, no. 1 (1915): 18.

18. Ibid., 18.

19. Louis Brandeis, "The Jewish Problem—How to Solve It," reprinted in De Haas, *Louis D. Brandeis*, 184–85. Part two of the book reprints many of Brandeis's key speeches. See ibid., 179–80.

20. For the whiteness literature, see sources in note 25, chapter 1.

21. For other essays in the *Menorah Journal* emphasizing hyphenated identities, see Henry Hurwitz, "The Menorah Movement," *Menorah Journal* 1, no. 1 (1915): 50–55; Horace M. Kallen, "Nationality and the Hyphenated American," *Menorah Journal* 1, no. 2 (1915): 79–86; Norman Hapgood, "The Jews and American Democracy," *Menorah Journal* 2, no. 4 (1916): 201–5; Bourne, "The Jew and Trans-National America"; Dewey, "The Principle of Nationality"; Israel Zangwill, "The Dilemmas of the Diaspora: A Message to the Menorah Quinquennial Convention," *Menorah Journal* 4, no. 1 (1918): 11–14; Lewis Mumford, "Nationalism or Culturalism? A Search for True Community," *Menorah Journal* 8, no. 3 (1922): 129–33; Ludwig Lewishon, "The Fallacies of Assimilation," *Menorah Journal* 11, no. 5 (1925): 460–65; Sidney Hook, "National Unity and Corporate 'Thinking,'" *Menorah Journal* 30, no. 1 (1942): 61–64.

22. Brandeis, "The Jewish Problem—How to Solve It."

23. For arguments about ethnicity invoking rather essentialized and pure identities, see Werner Sollors, *Beyond Ethnicity: Consent and Descent in American Culture* (New York: Oxford University Press, 1986); and Werner Sollors, "A Critique of Pure Pluralism," in *Reconstructing American Literary History*, ed. Sacvan Bercovitch (Cambridge, MA: Harvard University Press, 1986), 250–79. For a view of ethnicity that explicitly breaks with descent-based arguments, see especially Berkson, *Theories of Americanization*.

24. Louis Brandeis, "The Rebirth of the Jewish Nation," reprinted in De Haas, *Louis D. Brandeis*, 163.

25. See Yonathan Shapiro, "American Jews in Politics: The Case of Louis D. Brandeis," *American Jewish Historical Quarterly* 55 (December 1965): 199–212; Ben Halpern, "Brandeis' Way to Zionism," *Midstream: A Monthly Jewish Review*, October 1971, 3–13; Stuart M. Geller, "Why Did Louis D. Brandeis Choose Zionism?" *American Jewish Historical Quarterly* 62 (June 1973): 383–400; Schmidt, *Horace M. Kallen*, chap. 4.

26. See Dewey, "Nationalizing Education"; and Dewey, "America in the World"; W. E. B. Du Bois, *Souls of Black Folk* (Chicago: McClurg, 1903); Kallen, "Beyond the Melting Pot"; Norman Hapgood, "The Soul of Zionism," *Harper's Weekly*, August 14, 1915, 150–52; Norman Hapgood, "The Future of the Jews in America," *Harper's Weekly*, November 27, 1915, 511–12; Bourne, "Trans-National America"; Schechter, *Zionism: A Statement;* and Mack, *Americanism and Zionism*. See also the classic precursor to pluralist political science, Arthur F. Bentley, *The Process of Government* (Bloomington: Principia, 1935), especially chaps. 22, 23. See also essays in the *Menorah Journal* in note 21.

27. For Kallen's early involvement in the Harvard Menorah Society, see Hurwitz and Sharfman, *The Menorah Movement*, 128.

28. Kallen, Berkson, and Drachsler all extrapolated beyond Jewish particularity in order to formulate more general theories of ethnic politics. See essays in note 4.

29. For recent work drawing on Horace Kallen and cultural pluralism, see Michael Walzer, "What Does It Mean to Be an 'American'?" in *What It Means to Be an American: Essays on the American Experience* (New York: Marsilio, 1996); Rogers M. Smith, *Civic Ideals: Conflicting Visions of Citizenship in U.S. History* (New Haven, CT: Yale University Press, 1997), chap. 12 and epilogue; David Hollinger, *Postethnic America: Beyond Multiculturalism* (New York: Basic Books, 1995); Gary Gerstle, "The Protean Character of American Liberalism," *American Historical Review* 99, no. 4 (1994): 1043–73; Sollors, *Beyond Ethnicity;* William Toll, "Horace Kallen: Pluralism and American Jewish Identity," *American Jewish History* 88 (March 1997): 57–74; Leslie J. Vaughan, "Cosmopolitanism, Ethnicity and American Identity: Randolph Bourne's 'Trans-National America,'" *Journal of American Studies* 25, no. 3 (1991): 443–59; Casey Blake, "'The Cosmopolitan Note': Randolph Bourne and the Challenge of 'Trans-National America,'" *Culturefront* 4 (Winter 1995–96): 25–28.

30. For Kallen's *Menorah Journal* essays, see Horace Kallen, "Nationality and the Hyphenated American," *Menorah Journal* 1, no. 2 (1915): 79–86; Horace Kallen, "Facing the Facts of Palestine," *Menorah Journal* 7, no. 3 (1921): 133–42, and 7, no. 4 (1921): 238–43; Horace Kallen, "Can Judaism Survive in the United States?" *Menorah Journal* 11, no. 2 (1925): 101–13, and *Menorah Journal* 11, no. 6 (1925): 544–59; Horace Kallen, "A Contradiction in Terms," *Menorah Journal* 13, no. 5 (1927): 479–86; Horace Kallen, "Spinoza: Three Hundred Years After," *Menorah Journal* 31, no. 1 (1945): 1–15.

Kallen published several other interesting essays on these same themes in other general circulation magazines. For example, see Horace M. Kallen, "Zionism and the Struggle Towards Democracy," *Nation*, September 23, 1915, 379–80; Horace M. Kallen, "The Meaning of Americanism," *Immigrants in America Review*, January 1916, 12–19; Horace M. Kallen, "The Issues of the War and the Jewish Position," *Nation*, November 24, 1917, 590–92; Horace M. Kallen, "Zionism: Democracy or Prussianism," *New Republic*, April 5, 1919, 311–13.

31. Kallen, "Can Judaism Survive in the United States?" *Menorah Journal* 11, no. 2 (1925): 109, 112; and *Menorah Journal* 11, no. 6 (1925): 552, 557–58. For discussion of

the "Judaistic economy," see ibid., 547–48. For discussion of rabbinical training, see ibid., 552–55.

32. Kallen, "Democracy versus the Melting Pot," *Nation*, February 25, 1915, 217.

33. For a powerful version of Kallen's anti-assimilationist politics and his dread of "sameness," see Kallen, "Zionism: Democracy or Prussianism," 311. For reference to "force" and "cultural imperialism," see Horace Kallen, "Democracy, Nationality, and Zionism," *Maccabaean*, July 1918, 187; and Kallen, "Zionism: Democracy or Prussianism," 312.

34. Kallen, "Democracy Versus the Melting Pot," *Nation*, February 25, 1915, 220.

35. Ibid., 220.

36. Ibid., 192–93. Kallen frequently bemoaned the tyranny of mass production, lamenting "cheap newspapers," "cheap novels," vaudeville, and movies, all of which standardized the mind of immigrant cultures.

37. Kallen explicitly challenge Teddy Roosevelt's Americanization theories in the opening page of his "Can Judaism Survive in the United States?" *Menorah Journal* 11, no. 6 (1925): 544.

38. For a favorable assessment of Kallen's legacy, see Walzer, "What Does It Mean to Be an 'American'?" For critiques, see John Higham, *Send These to Me: Jews and Other Immigrants in Urban America* (New York: Atheneum, 1975), chap. 10; and Sollors, "A Critique of Pure Pluralism."

39. Kallen, Culture and Democracy, 218.

40. For powerful critiques of Kallen, see Higham, *Send These to Me*, chap. 10; and Sollors, "A Critique of Pure Pluralism," both of which address Kallen's inattention to African Americans.

41. Kallen, "Democracy versus the Melting Pot," *Nation*, February 18, 1915, 192.

42. Ibid., 191 (italics in the original).

43. Ibid., 192.

44. Ibid.

45. See Berkson, "A Community Theory of American Life"; and Berkson, "The Jewish Right to Live."

46. For references to "the East" and "last two decades," see ibid., 191; and *Nation*, February 25, 1915, 218.

47. Kallen, "Democracy versus the Melting Pot," *Nation*, February 18, 1915, 194. For further discussion of nationality and class, see ibid., 192–94.

48. Kallen never dispensed with class altogether since much of his work presumes an interest in forging a more effective class-based politics for the Left by preserving American democracy from the ravages of industrialization. Ethnic groups and their respective immigrant cultures provide one such refuge for Kallen, thereby allowing for the possibility that class and ethnic difference might be aligned.

49. For comments that immigrants cannot change their grandfathers, see Kallen, "Democracy versus the Melting Pot," *Nation*, February 18, 1915, 194; and *Nation*, February 25, 1915, 220. For the quotation comparing class versus nationality, see also Kallen, "Democracy versus the Melting Pot," *Nation*, February 18, 1915, 194. For phrases linking nationality and ancestry, see Kallen, "Democracy versus the Melting Pot," *Nation*, February 18, 1915, 191, 194; and *Nation*, February 25, 1915, 217.

50. See Sollors, *Beyond Ethnicity*.

51. Kallen, "Democracy versus the Melting Pot," *Nation*, February 25, 1915, 220. For an additional statement about immigrants not changing their grandfathers, see Kallen, "Democracy versus the Melting Pot," *Nation*, February 18, 1915, 194.

52. Kallen, "Democracy versus the Melting Pot," *Nation*, February 18, 1915, 194 (emphasis in original).

53. See Kallen, "Democracy versus the Melting Pot," *Nation*, February 25, 1915, 217.

54. Ibid., 217.

55. For contact with Americans as source of ethnic identification, see ibid. Interestingly, many subsequent ethnicity theorists have taken up this notion of retrospective ethnicity. See, for example, Nathan Glazer, "Ethnic Groups in America," in *Freedom and Control in Modern Society*, ed. Morroe Berger, Theodore Abel, and Charles H. Page (New York: Octagon Books, 1978), 166–69; and Alejandro Portes and Ruben G. Rumbaut, *Immigrant America: A Portrait* (Berkeley: University of California Press, 1996), chap. 4.

56. Kallen, "Democracy versus the Melting Pot," *Nation*, February 25, 1915, 218 (italics in the original).

57. Ibid., 218.

58. William Ripley's "Racial Geography of Europe" series in *Popular Science Monthly* contained two supplemental essays on the Jews and race published in December 1898 and January 1899. These essays prompted an extended scholarly discussion of the question both in this and other journals. For discussion and references to this debate, see chapter 2.

59. For a wonderful biography of Kroeber, see Theodora Kroeber, *Alfred Kroeber: A Personal Configuration* (Berkeley: University of California Press, 1970), 6–26.

60. Kroeber, *Alfred Kroeber: A Personal Configuration*, 46–48. Personal communication with Clifford Geertz, Institute for Advanced Study, May 12, 2001.

61. A. L. Kroeber, "Are the Jews a Race?" *Menorah Journal* 3, no. 5 (1917): 290.

62. Ibid., 291.

63. Ibid.

64. Ibid.

65. Ibid.

66. Ibid., 292 (emphasis added).

67. For an early critique of racial classification of all kinds, see W. I. Thomas, "The Mind of Women and the Lower Races," *American Journal of Sociology* 12, no. 4 (1907): 435–69.

68. Kroeber, "Are the Jews a Race?" 294.

69. See Franz Boas, "The Instability of Human Types," in *Papers on Interracial Problems Communicated to the First Universal Races Congress Held at the University of London, July 26–29, 1911*, ed. Gustav Spiller (London: King, 1911); Franz Boas, *Changes in the Bodily Form of Descendants of Immigrants, Final Report, Immigration Commission*, vol. 38 (Washington, DC: Government Printing Office, 1911); Franz Boas, *Changes in the Bodily Form of Descendants of Immigrants* (New York: Columbia University Press, 1912); Franz Boas, "Changes in the Bodily Form of Descendants of Immigrants," *American Anthropologist*, n.s., 14, no. 3 (1912): 530–62; Franz Boas, "The Head-Form of the Italians as Influenced by Heredity and Environment," *American Anthropologist*, n.s., 15, no. 2 (1913): 163–88; Franz Boas, "Effects of Environment on Immigrants and Their Descendants," *Science* 84 (1936): 522–25; Franz Boas, "Changes

in Bodily Form of Descendants of Immigrants," *American Anthropologist*, n.s., 42, no. 2, pt. 1 (1940): 183–89. See also Leonard Glick, "Types Distinct from Our Own: Franz Boas on Jewish Identity and Assimilation," *American Anthropologist*, n.s., 84, no. 3 (1984): 545–65.

70. Fishberg was born in Russia in 1872, came to the United States in 1890, received his M.D. from New York University in 1897, and was appointed clinical professor of medicine at the University and Bellevue Hospital Medical College. For his writings on the Jews and race, see Maurice Fishberg, "The Jews: A Study of Race and Environment," *Popular Science Monthly* 69 (September 1906): 257–67; Maurice Fishberg, "The Jews: A Study of Race and Environment, II—Marriages," *Popular Science Monthly* 69 (November 1906): 441–50; Maurice Fishberg, "The Jews: A Study of Race and Environment, III—Mixed Marriages between Persons of Different Christian Denominations," *Popular Science Monthly* 69 (December 1906): 502–11; Maurice Fishberg, "Physical Anthropology of the Jews, I—The Cephalic Index," *American Anthropologist*, n.s., 4 (1902): 684–706; Maurice Fishberg, "Physical Anthropology of the Jews II—Pigmentation," *American Anthropologist*, n.s., 5 (1905): 89–106; Maurice Fishberg, *The Jews: A Study of Race and Environment* (New York: Scott, 1911); and Maurice Fishberg, "Assimilation: A Statement of Facts by a Scientist," *Menorah Journal* 6, no. 1 (1920): 25–37.

71. Fishberg, "Assimilation." The quote and brief biography are taken from the insert on the front page of the essay.

72. Ibid., 26-27, 32.

73. Ibid., 36.

74. Ibid.

75. In contrast with Kroeber and Fishberg, Kallen, Berkson, and Drachsler all extrapolated beyond particular ethnic groups in order to formulate more general theories of ethnic politics. Kallen introduced the term *cultural pluralism* as a catch phrase for his theory in 1924; see Kallen, *Culture and Democracy*, 3, 35. Berkson, while drawing directly from the Jewish experience, explicitly claimed that his was a general theory of ethnic groups not just Jews. See Berkson, *Theories of Americanization*. See also Julius Drachsler, *Democracy and Assimilation: The Blending of Immigrant Heritages in America* (New York: Macmillan, 1920).

76. For numerous references to the war and to the "present condition of society," see Berkson, "The Jewish Right to Live," 45-46. He referred explicitly to the League of Nations in both of his *Menorah Journal* essays; see ibid., 46; "A Community Theory of American Life," 318. The specter of war can also be seen clearly in many of Randolph Bourne's essays. For a useful collection in that regard, see Carl Resek, ed., *Randolph S. Bourne: War and the Intellectual, Collected Essays, 1915–1919* (Indianapolis: Hackett, 1999).

77. I am indebted to discussions with Carl Schorske for the impact of World War I on the shift from nationality to ethnicity.

78. Berkson, "A Community Theory of American Life," 311–12 (emphasis added).

79. Berkson, "The Jewish Right to Live," 45, 51.

80. Ibid., 45.

81. Berkson, "A Community Theory of American Life," 316.

82. For an extended discussion of the importance of education as a means of sustaining ethnic identity, see Berkson, *Theories of Americanization*, chaps. 5, 6.

83. Quoted from Kallen, *Culture and Democracy*, 6–7. For the specter of the war, see ibid., 4–8.

84. Ibid., 4.

85. Ibid., 13–14. See also ibid., 4, 9, 15.

86. Ibid., 25–26.

87. Ibid., 28.

88. See Sarah Schmidt, "A Conversation with Horace M. Kallen: The Zionist Chapter of His Life," *Reconstructionist* 41 (November 1975): 28–33.

89. Ibid., 29.

90. For Kallen and Locke at Harvard, see Schmidt, "A Conversation with Horace M. Kallen"; and Sollors, "A Critique of Pure Pluralism." For Locke's inclusion in the Kallen-Hook volume, see Horace M. Kallen and Sidney Hook, *American Philosophy Today and Tomorrow* (New York: Furman, 1935). For Locke's participation in the Kallen feschrift, see Alain Locke, "Pluralism and Ideological Peace," in *Freedom and Experience: Essays Presented to Horace M. Kallen*, ed. Sidney Hook and Milton R. Konvitz (Ithaca, NY: Cornell University Press, 1947).

91. Sollors, "A Critique of Pure Pluralism," 270.

92. For Kallen's reference to Boas, see *Culture and Democracy*, 177. For Bourne taking a class with Boas, see F. H. Matthews, "The Revolt Against Americanism: Cultural Pluralism and Cultural Relativism," *Canadian Review of American Studies* 1, no. 1 (1970): 16. For Kallen and the NAACP panel on Africa, see Horace Meyer Kallen and James Weldon Johnson, *Africa in the World Democracy* (New York: NAACP, 1919). See also interview with Louise Rosenblatt, 11 Cleveland Lane, Princeton, NJ, June 3, 2001. Rosenblatt was a member of an informal "methods" seminar held at the New School for Social Research for "several decades." Alain Locke, Franz Boas, John Dewey, and Horace Kallen also participated in the seminar.

Chapter 4

1. See Hasia Diner, *Lower East Side Memories: A Jewish Place in America* (Princeton, NJ: Princeton University Press, 2000); Hasia Diner, *Jews in America* (New York: Oxford University Press, 1999); Deborah Dash Moore, *At Home in America: Second Generation New York Jews* (New York: Columbia University Press, 1981); and Arthur Goren, *New York Jews and the Quest for Community: The Kehillah Experiment, 1908–1922* (New York: Columbia University Press, 1970).

2. See Marian L. Smith, "Race, Nationality, and Reality: INS Administration of Racial Provisions in US Immigration and Nationality Law Since 1898," *Immigration Daily*, June 16, 2003, http://www.ilw.com; and Marian Smith " 'Other Considerations at Work': The Question of Mexican Eligibility to US Naturalization before 1940" (paper prepared for presentation at the Organization of American Historians Annual Meeting, Memphis, Tennessee, April 3, 2003); Patrick Weil, "Races at the Gate: A Century of Racial Distinctions in American Immigration Policy," *Georgetown Immigration Law Journal* 15, no. 4 (2001): 625–48.

3. See Claudette Bennett, "Racial Categories Used in the Decennial Censuses, 1790 to the Present," *Government Information Quarterly* 17, no. 2 (2000): 161–80; Sharon M. Lee, "Racial Classifications in the US Census: 1890–1900," *Ethnic and Racial Studies* 16, no. 1 (1993): 75–94; Melissa Nobles, *Shades of Citizenship: Race and the Census in Modern Politics* (Stanford, CA: Stanford University Press, 2000); Margo Anderson and Stephen E. Fienberg, *Who Counts? The Politics of Census-Taking in Contemporary America* (New York: Russell Sage Foundation, 1999); Kenneth Prewitt, "The Census Counts, the Census Classifies," in *Not Just Black and White: Historical and Contemporary Perspectives on Immigration, Race, and Ethnicity in the United States*, ed. Nancy Foner and

George M. Fredrickson (New York: Russell Sage Foundation, 2004); Joel Perlmann and Mary C. Waters, eds., *The New Race Question: How the Census Counts Multiracial Individuals* (New York: Russell Sage Foundation, 2002).

4. For other work on ethnicity and the U.S. census, see Reynolds Farley, "The New Census Question about Ancestry: What Did it Tell US?," *Demography* 28, no. 3 (1991): 411–29; see also Ira Rosenwaike, "Ancestry in the United States Census, 1980–1990," *Social Science Research* 22 (1993): 383–90; Charles Hirshman, "How to Measure Ethnicity: An Immodest Proposal," in *Challenges of Measuring an Ethnic World: Science, Politics and Reality*, Proceedings of the Joint Canada-U.S. Conference on the Measurement of Ethnicity, Ottawa, Canada, April 1–3, 1992 (Washington, DC: Government Printing Office, 1993); Jose Hernandez, Leo Estrada, and David Alvirez, "Census Data and the Problem of Conceptually Defining the Mexican American Population," *Social Science Quarterly* 53, no. 4 (1973): 671–87; Ira S. Lowry, "The Science and Politics of Ethnic Enumeration," in *Ethnicity and Public Policy*, Winston A. Van Horne (Madison: University of Wisconsin Press, 1982), 42–61; Theodore W. Allen, "'Race' and 'Ethnicity': History and the 2000 Census," *Cultural Logic* 3, no. 1 (1999); Harvey M. Choldin, "Statistics and Politics: The 'Hispanic Issue' in the 1980 Census," *Demography* 23, no. 3 (1986): 403–18; Nancy Bates, Elizabeth A. Martin, Teresa J. DeMaio, and Manuel de la Puente, "Questionnaire Effects on Measurement of Race and Spanish Origin," *Journal of Official Statistics* 11, no. 4 (1995): 433–59; David J. Fein, "Racial and Ethnic Differences in U.S. Census Omission Rates," *Demography* 27, no. 2 (1990): 285–302; David E. Hayes-Bautista and Jorge Chapa, "Latino Terminology: Conceptual Bases for Standardized Terminology," *AJPH* 77, no. 1 (1987): 61–68; and William Petersen, "Politics and the Measurement of Ethnicity," in *The Politics of Numbers*, William Paul Starr (New York: Russell Sage Foundation, 1987).

5. For a complete history of census questions and instructions to enumerators, see U.S. Census Bureau, *Measuring America: The Decennial Censuses from 1790 to 2000* (Washington, DC: Government Printing Office, 2002). For other examples of census responsiveness, consider 1870, when the census refers explicitly to passage of the Fifteenth Amendment, and similarly in 1930, when questions about work and employment proliferated.

6. See Henry Cabot Lodge, "Lynch Law and Unrestricted Immigration," *North American Review* 152, no. 414 (1891): 602–12; Henry Cabot Lodge, "The Restriction of Immigration," *North American Review* 152, no. 410 (1891): 27–36; Madison Grant, *The Passing of the Great Race, or The Racial Basis of European History* (New York: Scribner, 1916); Madison Grant, "Closing the Flood-Gates," in *The Alien in Our Midst, or "Selling Our Birthright for a Mess of Industrial Pottage,"* ed. Madison Grant and Charles Stewart Davidson (New York: Galton, 1930). For an overview of racism and immigration in the late nineteenth and early twentieth centuries, see John Higham, *Strangers in the Land: Patterns of American Nativism, 1860–1925* (New York: Atheneum, 1963).

7. For the number of immigrants entering the United States by decade, see appendix A. Wolf protested possible classification of Jews by race or religion prior to the 1900 census. He conveyed his opposition first to Frank P. Sargent, then commissioner-general of immigration, and then to his successor, Terrence V. Powderly. See Simon Wolf, "Testimony before the United States Industrial Commission," 1901, in which he refers to his earlier protests. His testimony is reprinted in Simon Wolf, ed., *Selected Addresses and Papers of Simon Wolf* (Cincinnati: Union of American Hebrew Congregations, 1926), 234. See also Simon Wolf, *The Presidents I Have Known from 1860–1918* (Washington, DC: Adams, 1918), 238; Union of American Hebrew Organi-

zation, "Report of Board of Delegates on Civil and Religious Rights," Washington, DC, November 14, 1899, 4121–22, in which Wolf reports on his efforts to oppose classification of Jews by religion, in *Twenty-Sixth Annual Report of the Union of American Hebrew Organization* (1899); *United States Immigration Commission* (Washington, DC: Government Printing Office, 1911), 41:269; and Weil, "Races at the Gate," 639, 640–41. For Jewish opposition to census classification of Jews as a race in the 1910 census, see Joel Perlmann, "'Race or People': Federal Race Classifications for Europeans in America, 1898–1913," Working Paper Number 320 (Levy Economics Institute, Bard College, January 2001), 35–36; and Wolf, *The Presidents I Have Known from 1860–1918,* 236–65. For a fascinating account of Jewish opposition to the INS list of "races and peoples" devised at Ellis Island in 1898, see Smith, "Race, Nationality, and Reality."

8. I am indebted to Joel Perlmann's work on the Dillingham Commission and his generosity in sharing his material with me. See Perlmann, "'Race or People.'"

9. For a useful discussion of the Commission's composition, see Lawrence H. Fuchs, "Immigration Reform in 1911 and 1981: The Role of Select Commissions," *Journal of American Ethnic History* 3, no. 1 (1983): 58–89. Commission members were as follows: Senator William P. Dillingham, chairman; Senator Henry Cabot Lodge; Senator Asbury C. Latimer (died February 20, 1908; replaced by Senator Anselm J. McLaurin, died Dec. 22, 1909; replaced by Senator Le Roy Percy); Representative Benjamin F. Howell; Representative William S. Bennett; Representative John L. Bennett; Mr. Charles P. Neil; Mr. Jeremiah W. Jenks; and Mr. William R. Wheeler.

10. A complete list of Commission reports is contained in the front matter of each volume. See *United States Immigration Commission* (Washington, DC: Government Printing Office, 1911), vols. 1–42 (hereafter cited as *USIC*).

11. See Perlmann, "'Race or People,'" 17–18.

12. See *USIC,* vol. 5, *Dictionary of Races or Peoples,* 5 (hereafter cited as *Dictionary of Races or Peoples*). The *Dictionary* was compiled for the Commission by Dr. Daniel Folkmar, assisted by Dr. Elnora C. Folkmar. See *Dictionary of Races or Peoples,* Letter of Transmittal.

13. Ibid., 73.

14. Ibid., 74.

15. See sources in note 7.

16. For transcripts of the testimonies, see *USIC,* vol. 41.

17. See Max J. Kohler and Abram I. Elkus, "Brief for the Petitioner in the Matter of Hersch Skuratowski," *USIC,* 41:180; and Wolf testimony, *USIC,* 41:267.

18. *USIC,* 41:267.

19. Simon Wolf, *Report of the Board of Delegates on Civil and Religious Rights,* 1904. Extracts are also reprinted in *USIC,* 41:286–87.

20. *USIC,* 41:270, 274. The Poles, too, are discussed as yet another example of the increasing disjunction between nations and peoples; see, for example, *USIC,* 41:278.

21. *USIC,* 41:273. See also *USIC,* 41:275.

22. *USIC,* 41:266.

23. For explicit reference to the dangers of anti-Semitism, see *USIC,* 41:178, 273, 274, 277. But even when not discussed directly, the threat of anti-Semitism informs Wolf and Mack's objection to state classification of Jews as a race.

24. I am indebted to Aristide Zolberg for pointing out the importance of Chinese exclusion in framing discussions of how to classify immigrant Jews. See also Kohler,

Elkus Petition, *USIC*, 41:178; Commissioner Bennett's remarks during Louis Marshall's testimony, *USIC*, 41:216, 217, 218; and Aristide Zolberg, *A Nation by Design* (Cambridge, MA: Harvard University Press, 2006).

25. See Toni Morrison, "Unspeakable Things Unspoken: The Afro American Presence in American Literature," *Michigan Quarterly Review* 28, no. 1 (1989): 1–34; Cheryl I. Harris, "Whiteness as Property," *Harvard Law Review* 106, no. 8 (1993): 1709–91; and David Roediger, *The Wages of Whiteness: Race and the Making of the American Working Class* (New York: Verso, 1991).

26. See *USIC*, vol. 1, where the Commission spells out the classificatory scheme that had been adopted by the Bureau of Immigration in 1899 and which the Commission had endorsed as the path to follow. The taxonomy identified forty-one different races and peoples that the Commission felt should be used both to classify immigrants entering the United States and should provide the basis of census classification as well. See *USIC*, 1:17. The Commission's list of races and peoples was as follows: African (Black); Armenian; Bohemian and Moravian; Bulgarian, Servian, and Montenegrin; Chinese; Croatian and Slovenian; Cuban; Dalmatian, Bosnian, and Herzegovinian; Dutch and Flemish; East Indian; English; Finnish; French; German; Greek; Hebrew; Irish; Italian, North; Italian, South; Japanese; Korean; Lithuanian; Magyar; Mexican; Pacific Islander; Polish; Portuguese; Roumanian; Russian; Ruthenian (Russniak); Scandinavian; Scotch; Slovak; Spanish; Spanish-American; Syrian; Turkish; Welsh; West Indian (except Cuban); All other peoples.

27. See sources in note 7.

28. *USIC*, 41:271. See also *USIC*, 41:269.

29. U.S. Census Bureau, *Measuring America*, 49.

30. For the instructions to enumerators for mother tongue, see U.S. Census Bureau, *Measuring America*, 48–50. For a complete list of the forty-one principal foreign languages spoken in the United States, see ibid., 50. From 1910–1940, both Hebrew and Yiddish were included on the Bureau's mother tongue list. After 1940, Hebrew was dropped. See also E. A. Goldenweiser, "The Mother Tongue Inquiry in the Census of Population," *Publications of the American Statistical Association* 13, no. 104 (1913): 648–55.

31. U.S. Census Bureau, *Measuring America*, 50.

32. For Lodge's discussion of "scientific races" or the "grand divisions," see *USIC*, 41:269.

33. For 1848 territorial expansion, see Jeffrey B. Morris and Richard B. Morris, *Encyclopedia of American History*, 7th ed. (New York: HarperCollins, 1996), 231–32.

34. For the legacy of conquest and the Treaty of Guadalupe Hidalgo, see David Gutiérrez, *Walls and Mirrors: Mexican Americans, Mexican Immigrants, and the Politics of Ethnicity* (Berkeley: University of California Press, 1995), chap. 1; David Montejano, *Anglos and Mexicans in the Making of Texas, 1836–1986* (Austin: University of Texas Press, 1987); and Mae Ngai, *Impossible Subjects: Illegal Aliens and the Making of Modern America* (Princeton, NJ: Princeton University Press, 2004), chap. 1. On racial prerequisites for U.S. citizenship, see Ian Haney López, *White by Law: The Legal Construction of Race* (New York: New York University Press, 1996); and Smith, "Other Considerations at Work"; Rogers Smith, *Civic Ideals: Conflicting Visions of Citizenship in U. S. History* (New Haven, CT: Yale University Press, 1997).

35. *In re Rodriguez*, 81 F. 337 (W.D. Tex. 1897).

36. Haney López, *White by Law*, 61.

37. To situate *Rodriguez* in the context of other prerequisite cases, see Haney López, *White by Law*, 61–62; for analysis of the interplay of imperial expansion and racial exclusion in *Rodriguez*, see Ngai, *Impossible Subjects*, 53–55; and Smith, "Other Considerations at Work."

38. *In re Rodriguez*, 349.

39. Ibid., 348–52.

40. Ibid., 350.

41. Ibid., 352.

42. See George J. Sánchez, *Becoming Mexican American: Ethnicity, Culture and Identity in Chicano Los Angeles, 1900–1945* (New York: Oxford University Press, 1993); Ngai, *Impossible Subjects*, chap. 2.

43. House Committee on Immigration and Naturalization, Hearings on Immigration from Countries of the Western Hemisphere, Feb. 21, 24, 25, 27–29; March 1, 2, 7; April 5, 1928 (Washington, DC: Government Printing Office, 1928). Small farmers were usually at odds with larger agricultural producers since they were hurt economically by the large-scale use of cheap labor. See also Ngai, *Impossible Subjects*, chaps. 2, 4.

44. For key immigrant statutes in the first quarter of the twentieth century, see Immigration Act of March 3, 1903, *U.S. Statutes at Large* 32 (1903): 1213; Immigration Act of 1907, *USIC*, 39:85–86, 94; Immigration Act of February 5, 1917, Public Law 64-301, *U.S. Statutes at Large* 39 (1917): 874; Immigration Act of May 19, 1921, Public Law 67-5, *U.S. Statutes at Large* 42 (1921): 5; and Immigration Act of May 26, 1924, Public Law 68-139, *U.S. Statutes at Large* 43 (1924): 153.

45. For immigration legislation, see E. P. Hutchinson, *Legislative History of American Immigration Policy, 1798–1965* (Philadelphia: University of Pennsylvania Press, 1981); and *USIC*, vol. 39, "Immigration Legislation." Appendix A of *USIC*, volume 39, contains a useful synopsis of immigration laws up through 1910.

46. See table 1 in appendix A.

47. Exemptions were always granted to Mexicans and Canadians in these early immigration statutes, and at times also included persons from Cuba, Guam, Puerto Rico, and Hawaii.

48. Immigration Act of March 3, 1903, *U.S. Statutes at Large* 32 (1903): pt. 1, reprinted in *USIC*, 102–10. See also *USIC*, 39:39, appendix A.

49. *USIC*, 39:108–9.

50. The statute stated: "That the said tax shall not be levied upon aliens who shall enter the United States after an uninterrupted residence of at least one year, immediately preceding such entrance, in the Dominion of Canada, Newfoundland, the Republic of Cuba, or the Republic of Mexico, nor upon otherwise admissible residents of any possession the United States." *USIC*, 39:110. For easier border crossing between Mexico and the United States in the 1907 Act, see section 32, *USIC* 39:118.

51. See Immigration Act of 1924, section 4c, *U.S. Statutes at Large* 43 (1924): 153.

52. Two of the most sophisticated accounts of issues of race and nationality in this period, Ngai, *Impossible Subjects*, and Smith, "Other Considerations at Work," do address this issue of Western Hemisphere exemptions, but I think that more needs to be done to explain the ambiguous location of Mexican immigration within American immigration policy. For example, Ngai states, "It was ironic that Mexicans became so associated with illegal immigration because, unlike Europeans, they were not subject to numerical quotas and, unlike Asiatics, they were not excluded as racially ineligible to citizenship." Ngai, *Impossible Subjects*, 71. If I read Ngai correctly, her explanation

of U.S. immigration policy toward Mexicans rests to a considerable degree on the disjunction between formal legislative exemption and racial practice in implementation of the law and intense class pressures for cheap labor. In contrast, I see the ambiguity of Mexicans' racial location as rooted in the changing conceptions of race and the emergence of the category ethnicity as a means of securing the unsteady racial taxonomy in the early twentieth century.

53. See Sánchez, *Becoming Mexican American*, chap 2.

54. See Ngai, *Impossible Subjects*, 68.

55. Ibid., 72–75. See also George J. Sánchez, "Disposable People, Expendable Neighborhoods: Repatriation, Internment, and Other Population Removals," paper presented at Organization of American Historians, Washington, DC, April 19–22, 2006.

56. Agricultural workers were not covered by the National Labor Relations Act, 1935; the Social Security Act, 1935; or the Fair Labor Standards Act of 1938. See Melvin L. Oliver and Thomas M. Shapiro, *Black Wealth, White Wealth: A New Perspective on Racial Inequality* (New York: Routledge, 1997); George Lipset, *The Possessive Investment in Whiteness: How White People Profit from Politics* (Philadelphia: Temple University Press, 1998), chap. 1; Robert Lieberman, *Shifting the Color Line: Race and the American Welfare State* (Cambridge, MA: Harvard University Press, 1998); Michael Brown, *Race, Money, and the American Welfare State* (Ithaca, NY: Cornell University Press, 1999); Dalton Conley, *Being Black, Living in the Red: Race, Wealth, and Social Policy in America* (Berkeley: University of California Press, 1999); and Ira Katznelson, *When Affirmative Action Was White* (New York: Norton, 2005).

57. The literature here is extensive, but for discussion of housing, school, and cultural segregation in the Southwest, see Charles M. Wollenberg, *All Deliberate Speed: Segregation and Exclusion in California Schools, 1855–1975* (Berkeley: University of California Press, 1976); José F. Morena, ed., *The Elusive Quest for Equality: 150 Years of Chicano/Chicana Education* (Cambridge, MA: Harvard Educational Review, 1999); Carlos Kevin Blanton, *The Strange Career of Bilingual Education in Texas, 1836–198* (College Station: Texas A & M University Press, 2004); Linda Gordon, *The Great Arizona Orphan Abduction* (Cambridge, MA: Harvard University Press, 2001); Sánchez, *Becoming Mexican American;* Ngai, *Impossible Subjects.*

58. For exemptions or special accommodations for Mexican immigrants in the 1903 and 1907 immigrations statutes, see *USIC*, 39:85–8, 94. For the exemptions or accommodations to the 1917 Immigration Act, see *U.S. Statutes at Large* 39 (1917): 875, 892; to the 1921 Immigration Act, see *U.S. Statutes at Large* 42 (1921): 5; and to the 1924 Immigration Act, see *U.S. Statutes at Large* (1924): 155, 163.

59. Several bills sought to change the Western Hemisphere exemption. For example, see H.R. 6465; H.R. 8523; H.R. 8530; H.R. 8702; H.R. 10343; H.R. 12382. For discussion of these bills and the Western Hemisphere exemptions more generally, see House Committee on Immigration and Naturalization, *Immigration from Countries of the Western Hemisphere: Hearings before the Committee on Immigration and Naturalization,* statement of James H. Patten, 70th Cong., 1st sess., March 7, 1927 (Washington, DC: Government Printing Office, 1927); House Committee on Immigration and Naturalization, *Immigration from Countries of the Western Hemisphere: Hearings before the Committee on Immigration and Naturalization,* 70th Cong., 1st sess., February 21 to April 5, 1928 (Washington, DC: Government Printing Office, 1928); House Committee on Immigration and Naturalization, *Western Hemisphere Immigration: Hearings before the Committee on Immigration and Naturalization,* 71st Cong., 2d sess. (Wash-

ington, DC: Government Printing Office, 1930); House Committee on Immigration and Naturalization, *Report, Immigration from Countries of the Western Hemisphere*, 71st Cong., 2d sess., March 13, 1930 (Washington, DC: Government Printing Office, 1930) (hereafter cited as *Report, Immigration from the Western Hemisphere*); House Committee on Immigration and Naturalization, *Immigration from Mexico: Hearings before the Committee on Immigration and Naturalization*, 71st Cong., 2d sess., May 15, 1930 (Washington, DC: Government Printing Office, 1930) (hereafter cited as *Immigration from Mexico: Hearings*).

60. *Report, Immigration from the Western Hemisphere*, 3.

61. For other references to the Mexican Revolution as an impetus to Mexican immigration into the U.S., see *Immigration from Mexico: Hearings*, 6–7; and *Report, Immigration from the Western Hemisphere*, 2.

62. *Report, Immigration from the Western Hemisphere*, 4.

63. Ibid., 12.

64. For other parallels drawn between Mexicans and Negroes, see House Committee on Immigration and Naturalization, *Immigration from Countries of the Western Hemisphere: Hearings before the Committee on Immigration and Naturalization*, 70th Cong., 1st sess., March 7, 1927 (Washington, DC: Government Printing Office, 1928), 753.

65. Quoted from *Report, Immigration from the Western Hemisphere*, 5.

66. Ibid., 7 (emphasis added). While the Minority Committee opposed passage of H.R. 10343, it did not do so because it considered Mexican to be white, nor because it welcomed Mexicans into the United States on what we might now describe as multicultural grounds. Rather, those favoring continuation of the Western Hemisphere exemption did so largely on economic grounds because they wanted to protect, as they willingly acknowledged, the needs of "American industry." Cheap Mexican labor was understood as central to the southwestern economic growth, leading those endorsing the Minority Committee report to oppose the introduction of national origin quotas on Mexicans.

67. *Report, Immigration from the Western Hemisphere*, 4.

68. *Immigration from Mexico: Hearings*, 5–6.

69. See Lee, "Racial Classifications in the US Census," 78.

70. U.S. Bureau of the Census, *U.S. Census of Population: 1950*, vol. 1V, *Special Reports*, pt. 3, chap. C, *Persons of Spanish Surname* (Washington, DC: Government Printing Office, 1953), 4 (hereafter cited as *U.S. Census of Population: 1950*).

71. Ibid.

72. For references to the Mexican Revolution of 1917 and to political instability more generally as generating increased immigration flows in the Southwest, see *Immigration from Mexico: Hearings*, 6–7; and *Report, Immigration from the Western Hemisphere*, 2, 4. For provisions excluding anarchists, see Immigration Act of 1917, *U.S. Statutes at Large* 39 (1917): 889.

73. For more on the contestation of classification of Mexicans as a race, see Smith, "Other Considerations at Work"; Thomas A. Guglielmo, "Fighting for Caucasian Rights: Mexicans, Mexican Americans, and the Transnational Struggle for Civil Rights in World War II Texas," *Journal of American History* 92, no. 4 (2006): 1212–37; Ngai, *Impossible Subjects*, 160. For 1970 instructions to Census enumerators, see Lee, "Racial Classifications in the U.S. Census," 78.

74. See George Lockwood, George Vanson, and Clerk Josephine Ortiz, *Manual of Immigration Spanish* (Washington, DC: Commissioner of Immigration and Naturalization, 1936).

75. See John G. Friar and George W. Kelley, *A Practical Spanish Grammar for Border Patrol Officers* (Washington, DC: Government Printing Office, 1946), ii.

76. See Lockwood et al., *Manual of Immigration Spanish,* 1. For a fascinating discussion of earlier classification of immigrants by races or peoples, see Weil, "Races at the Gate."

77. I have not been able to locate a copy of the Spanish Surname Supplement to date, but several Census Bureau documents refer explicitly to it when describing how the Bureau began to collect Spanish name data. For example, see U.S. Bureau of the Census, *U.S. Census of Population: 1950,* 4–5; U.S. Census Bureau, *Data Access Descriptions No. 41: Data on the Spanish Ancestry Population, Available from the 1970 Census of Population and Housing* (Washington, DC: Social and Economic Statistics Administration, 1975), 3, n. 3. Also subsequent Spanish surname lists updating the original supplement are readily available. For example, see U.S. Bureau of the Census, *Census of Population: 1970, Subject Reports,* PC(2)-1D, *Persons of Spanish Surname* (Washington DC: Government Printing Office, 1973); U.S. Department of Justice, *Immigration and Naturalization Service, Spanish Name Book,* M-153 (Washington DC: U.S. Department of Justice, 1973); and David L. Word and Colby Perkins Jr., "Building a Spanish Surname List for the 1990's—A New Approach to an Old Problem," Technical Working Paper No. 13 (U.S. Census Bureau, March 1996), appendix A.

78. See Campbell Gibson and Kay Jung, "Historical Census Statistics on Population Totals by Race, 1790 to 1990, and by Hispanic Origin, 1970 to 1990, for the United States, Regions, Divisions, and States," Working Paper Series No. 56 (Washington, DC: U.S. Bureau of the Census, Population Division, September 2002), esp. tables 6, 8, available at http://www.census.gov/population/www/documentation/twps0056.html.

79. See U.S. Bureau of the Census, *U.S. Census of Population: 1950.* Vol. IV, *Special Reports,* pt. 3, chap. C, *Persons of Spanish Surname* (Washington, DC: Government Printing Office, 1953), 5.

80. See Gibson and Jung, "Historical Census Statistics on Population Totals," table 1.

81. For discussion of Lockwood and the Spanish surname list, see U.S. Bureau of the Census, *U.S. Census of Population: 1950,* 5.

82. *The 1950 Censuses—How They Were Taken: Procedural Studies of the 1950 Censuses, No. 2 Population, Housing, Agriculture, Irrigation, Drainage* (Washington, DC: U.S. Department of Commerce, 1955), 51.

83. For migration of the INS Spanish name list to the Census Bureau, see U.S. Bureau of the Census, *U.S. Census of Population: 1950,* 4–5; and U.S. Bureau of the Census, *Data Access Descriptions No. 41,* 3.

Chapter 5

1. When OMB adopted the "Race and Ethnic Standards for Federal Statistics and Administrative Reporting" on May 12, 1977, the standards were not yet known as Statistical Policy Directive 15. Rather, the Race and Ethnic Standards were a revision of an earlier document, Circular No. A-46 on Standards and Guidelines for Federal Statistics, issued by the Bureau of the Budget (a predecessor to OMB) on March 28, 1952. The circular contained standards and guidelines for conducting surveys and releasing and publishing federal statistics. —Exhibit F from the circular dealt specifically with data on race and ethnicity. For the original notification of "Race and Ethnic Standards for

Federal Statistics and Administrative Reporting." In October 1977 the statistical policy function was transferred from OMB to the Department of Commerce, where it was housed in the newly established Office of Federal Statistical Policy and Standards. The individual standards and guidelines were reissued as statistical policy directives and published in the *Federal Register* in May 1978. The race and ethnic standards were reissued as Statistical Policy Directive No. 15. I am especially grateful to Suzann Evinger from OMB for clarifying this complex history. See *Federal Register* 43, no. 87 (May 4, 1978): 19269–70 (hereafter cited as Directive 15). For the Directive's history, see "Standards for the Classification of Federal Data on Race and Ethnicity," in *Federal Register* 59, no. 110 (June 9, 1994): 29831–35; Barry Edmonston, Joshua Goldstein, Juanita Tamayo Lott, eds., *Spotlight on Heterogeneity: The Federal Standards for Racial and Ethnic Classification* (Washington, DC: National Academy Press, 1996); Katherine K. Wallman, "Data on Race and Ethnicity: Revising the Federal Standard," *American Statistician* 52, no. 1 (1998): 31–33; and Juanita Tamayo Lott, *Asian Americans: From Racial Category to Multiple Identities* (New York: Alta Mira Press, 1998), chap. 2.

2. For useful secondary sources on the Directive, see Michael Omi, "Racial Identity and the State: The Dilemmas of Classification," *Law and Inequality: A Journal of Theory and Practice* 25, no. 1 (1997): 7–23; Margo J. Anderson and Stephen E. Fienberg, *Who Counts? The Politics of Census-Taking in Contemporary America* (New York: Russell Sage Foundation, 1999); David Hollinger, postscript to *Postethnic America: Beyond Multiculturalism* (New York: Basic Books, 2000); Melissa Nobles, *Shades of Citizenship: Race and the Census in Modern Politics* (Palo Alto: Stanford University Press, 2000); Clara E. Rodriguez, *Changing Race: Latinos, the Census, and the History of Ethnicity in the United States* (New York: New York University Press, 2000); Peter Skerry, *Counting on the Census: Race, Group Identity, and the Evasion of Politics* (Washington, DC: Brookings Institution Press, 2000); and Darryl Fears, "The Roots of 'Hispanic': 1975 Committee of Bureaucrats Produced Designation," *Washington Post*, October 15, 2003, A21.

3. Directive 15, 19269. See also Elizabeth Grieco and Rachael C. Cassidy, "Overview of Race and Hispanic Origin: Census 2000 Brief" (Washington, DC: U.S. Department of Commerce, Economics and Statistics Administration, U.S. Census Bureau, 2001), 1.

4. I use the term *Latino* throughout, even though OMB used *Hispanic* until it added *Latino* alongside of *Hispanic* in the 1997 revisions. See "Revisions to the Standards for the Classification of Data on Race and Ethnicity," *Federal Register* 62, no. 280 (October 30, 1997).

5. See Directive 15, 19269.

6. Ibid.

7. Ibid.

8. Ibid.

9. Ibid.

10. See Lott, *Asian Americans*, 44–47. For testimony during the review process, see House Committee on Government Reform and Oversight, *Federal Measures of Race and Ethnicity and the Implications for the 2000 Census: Hearings before the Subcommittee on Government Management, Information, and Technology of the Committee on Government Reform and Oversight*, 105th Cong., 1st sess., April 23, May 22, and July 25, 1997 (Serial No. 105-57) (Washington, DC: Government Printing Office, 1998).

11. See *Federal Register* 59, no. 110 (June 9, 1994): 29832; Edmonston et al., eds., *Spotlight on Heterogeneity*; Barry Edmonston and Charles Schultze, eds., *Modernizing the U. S. Census* (Washington, DC: National Academy Press, 1995). For an excellent

account of the mixed-race movement and pressure to revise Directive 15, see Kim M. Williams, *Mark One or More: Civil Rights in Multiracial America* (Ann Arbor: University of Michigan Press, 2006).

12. For testimony during the extended review process, see House Committee on Post Office and Civil Service, *Review of Federal Measures of Race and Ethnicity: Hearings before the Subcommittee on Census, Statistics and Postal Personnel of the Committee on Post Office and Civil Service*, 103d Cong., 1st sess., April 14, June 30, July 29, November 3, 1993 (Washington, DC: Government Printing Office, 1994). See especially testimony by Sonia Perez (La Raza); Steven Carbo (MALDEF); Juanita Tamayo Lott; Susan Graham (Project RACE).

13. Grieco and Cassidy, "Overview of Race and Hispanic Origin: Census 2000 Brief," 1. The post-1997 race categories are as follows: American Indian or Alaska Native, Asian, Black or African American, Native Hawaiian or Other Pacific Islander, and White. See "Revisions to the Standards for the Classification of Data on Race and Ethnicity," *Federal Register* 62, no. 280 (October 30, 1997). For an overview of the revision, see Suzann Evinger, "How Shall We Measure Our Nation's Diversity?" *Chance* 8, no. 1 (1995): 7–14.

14. The report on *Higher Education for Chicanos, Puerto Ricans, and American Indians* was never published. See preface and background to *Report of the Ad Hoc Committee on Racial and Ethnic Definitions* (Washington, DC: U.S. Department of Health, Education, and Welfare, National Institute of Education, 1975) (hereafter cited as *Report of the Ad Hoc Committee*). For the most detailed account of the meeting and formation of the Ad Hoc Committee on Racial and Ethnic Definitions, see Fears, "The Roots of 'Hispanic.'"

15. See *Report of the Ad Hoc Committee*, 8.

16. For a list of the Committee members, see ibid., 5.

17. Ibid., 8–9.

18. Ibid., 9.

19. Ibid., 10–11.

20. Ibid., 17–18.

21. The working group made recommendations to the committee as a whole on problem areas and helped draft the final report. Johnson appointed three people from HEW to the working group: John Hodgon from the Office of Civil Rights at HEW, Juanita Lott from the Office of Asian American Affairs at HEW, and Frank Weil from the Office for Civil Rights at HEW.

22. Darryl Fears has provided the most detailed insight into the discussions via his interviews with both Grace Flores and Abdin Noboa-Rios. See Fears, "The Roots of 'Hispanic.'" See also my interview with Juanita Tamayo Lott, June 23, 2004, at the Census Bureau, Washington, DC. Lott was a member of the Ad Hoc Committee on Racial and Ethnic Definitions, served on the working group for the ad hoc committee, and is now at the Human Resources Division at the Census Bureau.

23. Fears, "The Roots of 'Hispanic.'"

24. Ibid.

25. Ibid.

26. See interview with Tamayo Lott June 23, 2004. Lott remarked on the national and racial heterogeneity of the Hispanic members of the ad hoc committee.

27. See *Report of the Ad Hoc Committee*, 20.

28. The original posting was in *Federal Register, Notices* 43, no. 87 (May 4, 1978): 19269–70.

29. The Subcommittee on Minority Education produced a report in 1973 that called for the creation of common definitions of racial and ethnic groups, which Caspar Weinberger took up for further action. See *Federal Register* 59, no. 110 (June 9, 1994): 29831. See also *Lau v. Nichols*, 414 U.S. 563 (1974). For an overview of language policy, see Ronald Schmidt, *Language Policy and Identity Politics in the United States* (Philadelphia: Temple University Press, 2000).

30. For the context of bilingual education in the early 1970s, see the Supreme Court decision in *Lau v. Nichols*, 414 U.S. 563 (1974); Schmidt, *Language Policy and Identity Politics in the United States;* John D. Skrentny, *The Minority Rights Revolution* (Cambridge, MA: Harvard University Press, 2002), chap. 7.

31. See Public Law 94-311, *U.S. Statutes at Large* 90 (1976): 688. The quotation is from Katherine K. Wallman, "Statistics for Americans of Spanish Origin or Descent," *Statistical Reporter* (February 1978): 148. See also Jeanne E. Griffith, "Update on Statistics for Americans of Spanish Origin or Descent," *Statistical Reporter* (September 1980): 401–5. See also meeting with Katherine Wallman, chief statistician of the U.S. government, at OMB, Washington, DC, Monday, April 5, 2004.

32. See the U.S. Commission on Civil Rights, *Toward Quality Education for Mexican Americans*, Report 6: *Mexican American Education Study* (Washington, DC: Government Printing Office, 1974).

33. For the U.S. Commission on Civil Rights' Mexican American Education Study reports, see U.S. Commission on Civil Rights, *Employment*, Report 3 (1961); U.S. Commission on Civil Rights, *Toward Quality Education for Mexican Americans;* U.S. Commission on Civil Rights, *To Know or Not to Know: Collection and Use of Racial and Ethnic Data in Federal Assistance Programs* (Washington, DC: Government Printing Office, 1973). For the Commission's critique of the 1970 census, see U.S. Commission on Civil Rights, *Counting the Forgotten: The 1970 Census Count of Persons of Spanish Speaking Background in the United States* (Washington, DC: Government Printing Office, 1974). See also Inter-Agency Committee on Mexican American Affairs, *The Mexican American: A New Focus on Opportunity: Testimony Presented at the Cabinet Committee Hearings on Mexican American Affairs*, El Paso, Texas, October 26–28, 1967 (Washington, DC: Government Printing Office, 1967).

34. See Executive Order 8802 (signed June 25, 1941), *Federal Register* 6 (June 27, 1941): 3109; Executive Order 9346 (signed May 27, 1943), *Federal Register* 8 (May 29, 1943): 7183; Executive Order 9980 (signed July 26, 1948), *Federal Register* 13 (July 28, 1948): 4311; Executive Order 9981 (signed July 26, 1948), *Federal Register* 13 (July 28, 1948): 4313; Executive Order 10308 (signed January 3, 1951), *Federal Register* 16 (January 4, 1951): 12303; Executive Order 10479 (signed August 13, 1953), *Federal Register* 18 (August 18, 1953): 4899; Executive Order 10925 (signed March 6, 1961), *Federal Register* 26 (March 8, 1961): 1977; Executive Order 11246 (signed September 24, 1965), *Federal Register* 30 (September 28, 1965): 12319. See also the report of President Truman's Committee on Civil Rights, *To Secure These Rights: The Report of the President's Committee on Civil Rights* (Washington, DC: Government Printing Office, 1947), which also operates with a broad conception of discrimination.

35. This view of antidiscrimination policy embraces a capacious conception of race from the outset and differs from that offered by John Skrentny and Hugh Davis Graham. Both Skrentny and Graham argue that civil rights reform was initially nar-

rowly framed for African Americans and only subsequently expanded to immigrants as a result of what Skrentny calls "the minority rights revolution." Their view both misspecifies the history of American racism and distorts present-day political opportunities. The problem is a two-step-one in which they initially ignore other racialized groups by focusing almost exclusively on the legacy of slavery and Jim Crow and ignoring the many other manifestations of American racism. This narrow account of the past then distorts their view of the post–civil rights era in which they generally equate other racialized groups with "new immigration." Immigrants are then seen as having benefited undeservedly from civil rights reforms that had been intended for African Americans. See Skrentny, *The Minority Rights Revolution*, chap 4; and Hugh Davis Graham, *Collision Course: The Strange Convergence of Affirmative Action and Immigration Policy in America* (New York: Oxford University Press, 2002). From my point of view, antidiscrimination policy as evident in early executive orders, civil rights laws, and federal bureaucratic categories always operated with the knowledge that American racism had been inflicted on many. For a more extended critique of Skrentny, see Victoria Hattam, "The 1964 Civil Rights Act: Narrating the Past, Authorizing the Future," *Studies in American Political Development* 18, no. 1 (2004): 60–69; and John Skrentny's response in the same issue.

36. For example, Anthony Chen, "'The Hitlerian Rule of Quotas': Racial Conservatism and the Politics of Fair Employment Legislation in New York State, 1941–1945," *Journal of American History* 92 (March 2006): 1238–64; and Matthew Gritter, "Unfulfilled Promise? Latinos and the Origins of Anti-Discrimination Policy" (paper presented at Race and U.S. Political Development, University of Oregon, Eugene, Oregon, May 11–12, 2006).

37. See Marian Smith, "Race, Nationality, and Reality: INS Administration of Racial Provisions in US Immigration and Nationality Law Since 1898," http://www.ilw.com; and Marian Smith "'Other Considerations at Work': The Question of Mexican Eligibility to US Naturalization before 1940" (paper prepared for presentation at the Organization of American Historians Annual Meeting, Memphis, Tennessee, April 3, 2003); Patrick Weil, "Races at the Gate: A Century of Racial Distinctions in American Immigration Policy," *Georgetown Immigration Law Journal* 15, no. 4 (2001): 625–48; and Joel Perlmann, "'Race or People': Federal Race Classifications for Europeans in America, 1898–1913," Working Paper Number 320 (Levy Economics Institute, Bard College, January 2001).

38. See Martha E. Gimenez, "Latino/'Hispanic'—Who Needs a Name? The Case Against a Standardized Terminology," *International Journal of Health Services* 19, no. 3 (1989): 557–71. For creation of the category Hispanic/Latino, see Geoffrey Fox, *Hispanic Nation: Culture, Politics, and the Construction of Identity* (Tucson: University of Arizona Press, 1996), chap. 2.

39. For evidence of increased pan-ethnic identification among the children of immigrants, see Michael Jones-Correa and David L. Leal, "Becoming 'Hispanic': Secondary Panethnic Identification Among Latin American-Origin Populations in the United States," *Hispanic Journal of the Behavioral Sciences* 18, no. 2 (1996): 214–54; and Alejandro Portes and Rubén G. Rumbaut, *Legacies: The Story of the Immigrant Second Generation* (Berkeley: University of California Press, 2001), chap. 7. For the lack of generational differences in pan-ethnic identification rates, see Pew Hispanic Center/Kaiser Family Foundation, *2002 National Survey of Latinos: Summary of Findings* (Menlo Park, CA: Henry J. Kaiser Family Foundation, 2002), section 2, 28, Table 2.5.

40. See Pew Hispanic Center/Kaiser Family Foundation, *National Survey of Latinos: The Latino Electorate* (Washington, DC: Pew Hispanic Center and Henry J. Kaiser

Family Foundation, 2002), 24–33. The Pew/Kaiser poll was released in December 2002. The survey was conducted by telephone between April 4 and June 11, 2002; 4,213 adults were interviewed, 18 years or older, selected at random. Of those interviewed, 2,929 self-identified as Hispanic or of Latin origin or descent, and 1,329 of Hispanics/Latinos interviewed self-reported as registered voters.

41. See Rodriguez, *Changing Race;* North American Congress on Latin America, "The Social Origins of Race: Race and Racism in the Americas, Part 1," *NACLA: Report on the Americas* 34, no. 6 (2001); North American Congress on Latin America, "Crossing Borders: Race and Racism, Part II," *NACLA: Report on the Americas* 35, no. 2 (2001); North American Congress on Latin America, "Racial Politics, Racial Identities: Race and Racism in the Americas, Part III," *NACLA: Report on the Americas* 35, no. 6 (2002); North American Congress on Latin America, "The Politics of Race and Globalization: Part 1: Changing Identities," *NACLA: Report on the Americas* 38, no. 2 (2004); Ian Haney López, "Hispanics and the Shrinking White Majority," *Daedalus* (Winter 2005): 42–52.

42. See Grieco and Cassidy, "Overview of Race and Hispanic Origin: Census 2000 Brief," 3, 10.

43. For changes in numbers selecting "some other race," see Nancy M. Gordon, "Race and Ethnicity Testing: Update and Discussion" (handout distributed at Census Bureau's Race and Ethnic Advisory Committee meetings, Washington, DC, May 2004), 3–4.

44. Note these are percentages of the total population, not the Hispanic population, as in the preceding paragraphs. See Gordon, "Race and Ethnicity Testing," 4.

45. The Census Bureau was actively pursuing dropping "some other race" when Representative Serrano added a rider to the appropriations bill, thereby ensuring continuation of "some other race" for the next appropriations cycle. But the problem will not go away, and what to do with "some other race" has only been deferred, not solved. For Serrano's rider on the appropriations bill, see "Serrano Succeeds in Retaining 'Other' Race Option on Census Form," press release from Rep. José Serrano, November 22, 2004, http://www.house.gov/list/press/ny16_serrano/041122Census.html.

46. The operational definition of the 1990 90 percent rule was to use the unallocated race responses cross-tabulated for respondents who reported a single ancestry. If 90 percent or more respondents who gave a specific ethnic response to the question on race also reported a specific ethnic group in the question on ancestry, but did not check a specific race-response category in the race question, then all such ethnic entries were reassigned to the specified race group. For example, if 93 percent of the ethnic write-in entries of "French" in the question on ancestry reported white only in the question on race, then all write-in entries of French in the question on race, in the absence of checking a race-response category, were coded to the white population. White and Black national origin groups not meeting the 90 percent rule and some generic responses, such as "interracial" and so forth, remained in the "some other race" category. My thanks to Claudette Bennett from the Bureau of Census for clarifying the 90 percent rule.

47. For the Bureau's own account of this reallocation around same-sex marriage, see Jason M. Fields and Charles L. Clark, "Unbinding the Ties: Edit Effects of Marital Status on Same Gender Couples" U.S. Census Bureau, Population Division Working Paper No. 34 (April 1999).

48. The Race and Ethnicity Advisory Committee meetings began on the afternoon of May 4. I attended on May 5 and 6.

49. Initially, the committees were known as Race Advisory Committees and later became the Race and Ethnic Advisory Committees. For an account of the Seale incident,

see Barbara Milton and David Pemberton, "Oral History Interview with Vincent P. Barabba," August 7, 1989, 28–30. A transcript of the interview is available from the Census Bureau.

50. Membership lists of REACs are made public by the Census Bureau. Transcripts of the advisory committee meetings are also available, though many transcripts from past years have been lost.

51. For the Census Bureau pretest report, see Elizabeth Martin, David Sheppard, Michael Bentley, and Claudette Bennett, "Results of 2003 National Census Test of Race and Hispanic Questions," (Washington, DC: U.S. Census Bureau, 2003). For pretests planned for 2005 and 2006, see "Cognitive Questions," April 27, 2004, distributed by Nancy Gordan at the REAC meetings, May 5–7, 2004.

52. Carlos Chardón, chair of the Hispanic advisory committee, voiced his opposition to the removal of "some other race" in a recent *New York Times* article. See Rachael L. Swarns, "Hispanics Debate Census Plan to Change Racial Grouping," *New York Times,* October 24, 2004, A21.

53. Quotes are from the Hispanic advisory committee discussions, REAC meetings, Crystal City, Virginia, May 5–6, 2004.

54. See Orlando Patterson, "Race by the Numbers," Op Ed section, *New York Times,* May 8, 2001; and National Association for the Advancement of Caucasian Latinos, http://www.whitehispanic.com.

Chapter 6

1. Antonio Villaraigosa did win the 2005 election on May 17, 2005, becoming the first Latino mayor of Los Angeles in over a century. For commentary touting the emergence of Black-Brown coalitions in New York City and Los Angeles in 2001, see Héctor Tobar, "Intensity Fuels Consensus Builder's Rapid Rise," *Los Angeles Times,* March 16, 2001; Matea Gold, "New Coalitions Forged in an Upbeat L.A.," *Los Angeles Times,* April 11, 2001; Hector Tobar and Carla Hall, "Villaraigosa's Backers Revel in His Historic feat," *Los Angeles Times,* April 11, 2001; Dexter Filkins, "In Bid for Unity, Black and Hispanic Politicians Make Pledge to Back Ferrer," *New York Times,* August 18, 2001, Metro section, B2; and Michael Finnegan and Richard Fausset, "Latino-Black Alliance Seems to be Forming," *Los Angeles Times,* April 30, 2005.

2. I distinguish between Latinos becoming white and white ethnics as follows: those who identify as white assimilate into a white racial identification, making race their principal point of identification. In contrast, the official classificatory system in the United States designates Latinos to be ethnic group and not a race. While Latino ethnicity often has gone hand in hand with white racial identification, it need not always do so. It is precisely the racial status of ethnicity that is currently being reconfigured.

3. For discussion of Latinos and Republican Party electoral fortunes, see Tamar Jacoby, "Republicans and Their Amigos: GOP No Longer for the Gringos-Only Party," *Weekly Standard,* November 25, 2002; and Mireya Navarro, "Pataki's Success Among Latinos Worries Some Democrats," *New York Times,* November 9, 2002, Metro section, B1; Will Lester, "Political Parties Court Hispanic Vote," Associated Press, March 14, 2003; Jordan Rau, "Gov Eyes More Latino Support, but Budget Plans Spark Major Debate," *Newsday,* March 9, 2003, A23. For the ambiguity of Latino racial and political identifications, see Lizette Alvarez, "Hispanic Voters Hard to Profile, Poll Finds: Mixture of Beliefs Helps Make Latinos an Attractive Swing Bloc," *New York Times,* October 4, 2002, National section, A20; Matt Barreto, Rodolfo O. de la Garza, Jongho Lee, Jaesung Ryu, and Harry P. Pachon, "Latino Voter Mobilization in 2000: A Glimpse

into Latino Policy and Voting Preferences" (Claremont, CA: Tomas Rivera Policy Institute, n.d.); Domenico Maceri, "Bush and Latinos: Beyond Espanol?" *Hispanicvista,* January 27, 2003; Erica Werner, "Hispanic Voters Rush to Polls," Associated Press, November 9, 2000; and Peter Skerry, *Mexican Americans: The Ambivalent Minority* (Cambridge, MA: Harvard University Press, 1993).

4. See Barreto et al., "Latino Voter Mobilization in 2000," 1.

5. For a powerful critique of the category Hispanic, see Martha E. Giminez, "Latino/ 'Hispanic'—Who Needs a Name? The Case Against a Standardized Terminology," *International Journal of Health Services* 19, no. 3 (1989): 557–71.

6. For history of low naturalization rates and depressed political turnout among Latinos, see Michael Jones-Correa, *Between Two Nations: The Political Predicament of Latinos in New York City* (Ithaca, NY: Cornell University Press, 1998); and Paula D. McClain and John A. García, "Expanding Disciplinary Boundaries: Black, Latino, and Racial Minority Group Politics in Political Science," in *Political Science: The State of the Discipline,* ed. Ada W. Finifter (Washington, DC: American Political Science Association, 1993), 261–62; Rodolfo O. de la Garza, Louis DeSipio, F. Chris Garcia, John García, and Angelo Falcón, *Latino Voices: Mexican, Puerto Rican, and Cuban Perspectives on American Politics* (Boulder, CO: Westview Press, 1992), chaps. 8, 9; and F. Chris Garcia, ed., *Pursuing Power: Latinos and the Political System* (South Bend, IN: University of Notre Dame Press, 1997).

7. For different conceptions of race in Latin America and the United States, see Clara Rodriguez, *Changing Race: Latinos, the Census, and the History of Ethnicity in the United States* (New York: New York University Press, 2000); Clara Rodriguez and Héctor Cordero-Guzmán, "Placing Race in Context," *Ethnic and Racial Studies* 15, no. 4 (1992): 523–42; and the excellent series of essays in "Race and Racism in the Americas, I-III," *NACLA: Report on the Americas* 34, no. 6 (2001); 35, no. 2 (2001); 35, no. 6 (2002).

8. Latinos are now said to be the largest minority in the United States, at 12.5 percent of the population nationally and a larger percentage in major metropolitan areas. See Elizabeth M. Grieco and Rachel C. Cassidy, *Overview of Race and Hispanic Origin: Census 2000 Brief* (Washington, DC: U.S. Department of Commerce, Economics and Statistics Administration, U.S. Census Bureau, 2001). For a fascinating accounts of recent party identification broken down by race, see K. Conie Kang, "Asian Americans Lean to Democrats, Poll Says," *Los Angeles Times,* November 10, 2000. The article reports data from two exit polls, one conducted by the Asian Pacific American Legal Center, the other by the *Los Angeles Times.*

9. See Rodolfo de la Garza and Louis DeSipio, ed., *Awash in the Mainstream: Latino Politics in the 1996 Election* (Bolder, CO: Westview Press, 1999); and David L. Neal, Matt A. Barreto, Jongho Lee, and Rodolfo O. de la Garza, "The Latino Vote in the 2004 Election," *PS* (January 2005): 41-49.

10. Latinos are now the largest minority in twenty-three of the fifty states. See Barreto et al., "Latino Voter Mobilization in 2000," 1.

11. See Julie Mason, "Hispanic Vote Called a Toss-Up: Neither Party Has Lock, Latino Coalition's Poll Indicate," *Houston Chronicle,* September 19, 2002, http://www .chron.com; and Lori Rodriguez, "Hispanic Voters Cool So Far to Dream Team," *Houston Chronicle,* September 23, 2002, http://www.chron.com.

12. See Pew Hispanic Center/Kaiser Family Foundation, *National Survey of Latinos: The Latino Electorate* (Washington, DC: Pew Hispanic Center and Henry J. Kaiser Family Foundation, 2002), charts 5-7. Party identification figures do not add to one hun-

dred as some selected something else or "don't know." See also Barreto et al., "Latino Voter Mobilization in 2000"; and Jacoby, "Republicans and Their Amigos."

13. For primary and runoff results, see Michael Cooper, "Ferrer and Green Divide the Spoils of Their Rivals," *New York Times*, September 27, 2001, Metro section, D5; "Gotbaum Victorious, Virtually Assuring Election," *New York Times*, October 12, 2001, Metro section, D10.

14. For ethnic and racial coalition building as a means of Democratic Party rejuvenation, see Rufus Browning, Dale Rogers Marshall, and David Tabb, eds., *Protest Is Not Enough* (Berkeley: University of California Press, 1984); and Rufus P. Browning, Dale Rogers Marshall, and David H. Tabb, eds., *Racial Politics in American Cities* (New York: Longman, 1997). For ethnic and racial coalition building in New York City politics, see John H. Mollenkopf, *Phoenix in the Ashes: The Rise and Fall of the Koch Coalition in New York City Politics* (Princeton, NJ: Princeton University Press, 1992); Phillip J. Thompson, "The Election and Governance of David Dinkins as Mayor of New York," in *Race, Politics, and Governance in the United States*, ed. Huey L. Perry (Gainesville: University Press of Florida, 1996), 65–81; J. Phillip Thompson, "David Dinkins' Victory in New York City: The Decline of the Democratic Party Organization and the Strengthening of Black Politics," *PS: Political Science and Politics* 23, no. 2 (1990): 145–48.

15. See John Mollenkopf, "New York: The Great Anomaly," in Browning, Marshall, and Tabb, eds., *Racial Politics in American Cities*; Rufus P. Browning, Dale Rogers Marshall, and Raphael J. Sonenshein, "The Prospects for Multiracial Coalitions: Lessons from America's Three Largest Cities," in Browning, Marshall, and Tabb, eds., *Racial Politics in American Cities*.

16. National Public Radio, *All Things Considered*, September 5, 2001 (transcript in possession of author), 3. See also "Mayoral Campaign Announcement Speech: Remarks by Hon. Fernando Ferrer, Fox Street, Bronx," June 27, 2001 (transcript in possession of author).

17. "The Race for Mayor: First Televised Mayoral Debate, August 21, 2001," reprinted in *Gotham Gazette*, available at http://www.gothamgazette.com/searchlight2001/debate.1.html (transcript in possession of author).

18. For example, see Tom Robbins, "Up from Fox Street: Ferrer Campaigns for the 'Other New York,'" *Village Voice*, August 1–7, 2001, Citystate section; and "Mayoral Campaign Announcement Speech."

19. Lincoln Anderson, "Mayoral Hopefuls Speak at Village Forum," *Villager*, February 12, 2001; transcript of Ferrer's remarks reprinted in *Gotham Gazette*, Searchlight on Campaign 2001, "Ferrer Transcript," available at http://www.gothamgazette.com/searchlight2001/ferrer_transcript.html (transcript in possession of author).

20. For discussion of the "racial subtext" of Ferrer's campaign, see Greg Sargent, "Was Freddy Fingered? Or Was Ferrer Caught in Own Sharpton Trap?" *New York Observer*, May 21, 2001, 1. For accusations of Ferrer running a racially divisive campaign, see Pete Hamill, "Freddy Will Pick Own Top Cop," *New York Daily News*, October 10, 2001; Josh Benson, "It's Mean Mark Green: Former Front Runner Jostles Freddy Ferrer," *New York Observer*, October 15, 2001, 1; Peter Noel, "Take It or Leave It, Mark Green: Brooklyn Assemblyman Roger Green's Challenge to a Turncoat Liberal," *Village Voice*, October 31–November 6, 2001, Citystate section; Jill Nelson, "Race Counts: White Voters Play the Race Card, Again," *Village Voice*, October 24–30, 2001, Citystate section.

21. For the classic discussion of Republican racial coding in the 1980s, see Thomas Byrne and Mary D. Edsall, *Chain Reaction: The Impact of Race, Rights, and Taxes on American Politics* (New York: Norton, 1991).

22. The persistence of the color line within the New Deal can be seen, for example, in the exclusion of domestic servants and agricultural workers from Social Security. See Michael K. Brown, *Race, Money, and the American Welfare State* (Ithaca, NY: Cornell University Press, 1999); Michael K. Brown, "Race in the American Welfare State: The Ambiguities of 'Universalistic' Social Policy Since the New Deal," in *Without Justice for All*, ed. Adolph Reed Jr. (Boulder, CO: Westview Press, 1999); Dennis R. Judd, "Symbolic Politics and Urban Policies: Why African Americans Got So Little from the Democrats," in Reed, ed., *Without Justice for All*; Larry Bennett and Adolph Reed Jr., "The New Face of Urban Renewal: The Near North Redevelopment Initiative and the Cabrini-Green Neighborhood," in Reed., ed., *Without Justice for All*; Robert Lieberman, *Shifting the Color Line: Race and the American Welfare State* (Cambridge, MA: Harvard University Press, 1998); Daniel Kryder, *Divided Arsenal: Race and the American State During World War II* (New York: Cambridge University Press, 2000); Suzanne Mettler, *Soldiers to Citizens: The GI Bill and the Making of the Greatest Generation* (New York: Oxford University Press, 2005); and Ira Katznelson, *When Affirmative Action Was White: An Untold History of Racial Inequality in Twentieth-Century America* (New York: Norton, 2005).

23. See Fernando Ferrer, "Help Schools Connect with Their Communities," *Newsday*, May 14, 2002, Viewpoints, A30.

24. See Sargent, "Was Freddy Fingered?"

25. Abner Louima, a Haitian immigrant, was brutalized by several New York Police Department officers in the bathroom of the 70th precinct's station house on August 9, 1997. Officer Justin Volpe received a thirty-year jail term. Amadou Diallo was a West African immigrant who was mistakenly shot forty-one times by members of NYPD's Special Crimes Unit on February 4, 1999. Officers in the Diallo case were acquitted. Racial profiling and police brutality were not included in Ferrer's thirteen campaign positions on his official Web site, but he did raise them during his announcement speech delivered in the Bronx on June 27, 2001, and discussed them during the debates on August 21 and August 28, 2001. However, neither police brutality nor racial profiling were given the highest priority by Ferrer.

26. The thirteen issues identified on Ferrer's official Web site were children, domestic violence, economic development, educational opportunity, energy and environment, health care, homelessness, housing, justice and safety, lesbian/gay/bisexual/transgender issues, senior citizens, transportation, and welfare. Each of these issues was followed by a brief paragraph explaining Ferrer's views on the subject. Although questions of racial inequality and discrimination intersected many of these concerns, it is somewhat surprising that his supposedly racially divisive campaign had nothing explicit to say about issues of race and racism. See Dexter Filkins, "Ferrer the Campaigner Offers an Old-Style Approach," *New York Times*, August 30, 2001. When asked whom he would support in a hypothetical three-way race among Mayor Rudolph Giuliani and former mayors Ed Koch and David Dinkins, Ferrer became flustered and never clearly supported Dinkins, the first African American mayor of New York City. See Sargent, "Was Freddy Fingered?"

27. For liberal critics of Ferrer, see, for example, Michael Tomasky, "Liberal Crack-Up; Polarization in New York's Mayoral Contest," *American Prospect*, November 20, 2001; and criticisms by former governor Mario Cuomo and U.S. Representative Jerrold Nadler in Benson, "It's Mean Mark Green."

28. Many scholars continue to advance arguments that assume immigrants will seek to distance themselves from Blacks. The assumption is that racial identification always carries with it negative associations and, as such, is always avoided if possible.

For example, see Mary Waters, *Black Identities: West Indian Immigrant Dreams and American Realities* (Cambridge, MA: Harvard University Press, 2000); Mary C. Waters, "Ethnic and Racial Identities of Second-Generation Black Immigrants in New York City," *The New Second Generation,* ed. in Alejandro Portes (New York: Russell Sage Foundation, 1996); M. Patricia Fernández-Kelley and Richard Schauffler, "Divided Fates: Immigrant Children and the New Assimilation," in Portes, ed., *The New Second Generation;* and Jennifer Hochschild, "From Nominal to Ordinal: Reconceiving Racial and Ethnic Hierarchy in the United States," in *The Politics of Democratic Inclusion,* ed. Christina Wolbrecht and Rodney Hero (Philadelphia: Temple University Press, 2005). For a powerful critique of such arguments, see Laura S. Miller, "The Language of Group Hierarchy: Keeping Ethnics and Immigrants Away from American Blacks" (MA portfolio, Department of Political Science, New School for Social Research, Fall 2002).

29. For Rangel et al. endorsement, see Dexter Filkins, "In Bid for Unity, Black and Hispanic Politicians Make Pledge to Back Ferrer," *New York Times,* August 18, 2001, B2.

30. For evidence of the change in momentum during the primary, see Charles Rangel's and Dennis Rivera's change of heart in endorsing Ferrer. Initially, Rangel and Rivera had said they would support Ferrer only if they thought he had a chance of winning rather than as an act of unconditional solidarity. Hence, when they eventually supported Ferrer, it was understood that Ferrer's position had changed. See Wayne Barrett, "Coalition Confusion: McCall Crowns Ferrer, but Sharpton, Rivera, Rangel Skip the Coronation," *Village Voice,* February 27, 2001; and Sargent, "Was Freddy Fingered?" For other sources noting the shift in momentum to Ferrer, see Adam Nagourney, "Political Memo: Ferrer Gains Sudden Momentum in Latest Twist of the Campaign," *New York Times,* October 3, 2001.

31. For exit poll data on the primary, see "Voters' Survey: Democratic Primary Voters," *New York Times,* September 27, 2001, Metro section, D5. See also "The New York Primary: Turnout and Turnover," *New York Times,* September 27, 2001, Metro section, D6; and Adam Nagourney, "Ferrer's Choice: Appeal to Pride, or Embrace All," *New York Times,* September 27, 2001, Metro section, D1, D4.

32. The phrase "mean Mark Green" is from Benson, "It's Mean Mark Green."

33. For Green's longtime reliance on white advisers, see Wayne Barrett, "The Kid from Great Neck," *Village Voice,* August 8–14, 2001. For Green's equivocation on Sharpton, see "The Race for Mayor: Run-Off Debate," 5–6 (transcript available at *Gotham Gazette,* http://www.gothamgazette.com/searchlight2001/debate.3.html). For the Green ad attacking Ferrer as irresponsible, see Adam Nagourney, "Political Memo; Heated Race Revisited, Amid Claims of Racism," *New York Times,* October 16, 2001; and Jill Nelson, "Race Counts: White Voters Play the Race Card Again," *Village Voice,* Citystate section, October 24–30, 2001.

34. For claims that Green supporters circulated the *Daily News* cartoon and arranged for automated phone calls touting the dangers of Al Sharpton running city hall, see Jonathan P. Hicks, "Green's Campaign Angers Backers of Ferrer," *New York Times,* October 13, 2001, D3; and Dean E. Murphy and Michael Cooper, "Bloomberg Sees Race Overtones in Final Days of Green Effort," *New York Times,* October 17, 2001, Metro section, D1, D3. For more recent acknowledgment that the Green campaign circulated the cartoons, see Diane Cardwell, "Racial Politics of 2001; Unhealed Wounds in 2005," *New York Times,* May 6, 2005, Metro section, 33, 36. For text of the automated phone calls, see Nelson, "Race Counts."

35. The reporter, Peter Noel, suggested that Green initially made the comment on the television channel New York 1, and that Green's campaign manager, Rich Schrader,

repeated the remark during the reconciliation meeting. However the meeting actually went, two sources actually quoted the Green remark, and it was widely known that the meeting did not go well and that Ferrer backers had little or no enthusiasm for getting out Black and Latino voters for Green. See Noel, "Take It or Leave It, Mark Green"; and Juan Gonzalez, "Mark Must Take Blame," *Daily News*, November 8, 2001, 44. See also Wayne Barrett, "Is the Peace Real? Probing Green's Shaky Rapprochement with the Ferrer Camp," *Village Voice*, October 24–30, 2001, Citystate section. The phrase "Great White Hope" as applied to Green is also taken from Noel, "Take It or Leave It, Mark Green." Noel's article documents rifts within the New York Democratic Party between Black Brooklyn Assemblyman Roger Green and the white liberal, Mark Green. For accounts of Green's arrogance, see Ciro Scotti, "Bloomberg's Secret Weapon: Green," BusinessWeek Online, November 9, 2001, which quotes former mayor Ed Koch describing Green as "obnoxious."

36. Gonzalez, "Mark Must Take Blame."

37. White liberals were very skittish about supporting Ferrer, with only 17 percent joining his coalition in the runoff election. Given the very small margin of victory, even a small increase in white support might have made the difference.

38. For the specter of Sharpton hanging over the campaign, see Adam Nagourney, "Squirming in Sharpton's Embrace; Fidgeting Without It," *New York Times*, October 5, 2001; Dexter Filkins and Adam Nagourney, "Courting Blacks and Latinos, Ferrer Is Walking a Fine Line," *New York Times*, September 6, 2001, A1; Jennifer Steinhausser and Dexter Filkins, "In Courting Black Voters, Candidates Try Ubiquity," *New York Times*, September 8, 2001, Metro section, B5; Harold Meyerson, "Race Conquers All: In New York as in L.A., Racial Politics Thwarts a Rebirth of Urban Liberalism," *American Prospect*, December 3, 2001; Zev Chafets, "The Race Is about Race: In a Divided City, the Gulf is Expressed at the Polls," *Daily News*, September 9, 2001, 41. For references to the Dinkins years, see above, as well as Michael Kramer, "Ghosts of 1989 Could Haunt Mayoral Primary," *Daily News*, September 9, 2001, 4–5. For excellent accounts of the Crown Heights riots and the Red Apple boycott, see Anna Deavere Smith, *Fires in the Mirror* (Bera Video, 1992); and Clair Jean Kim, *Bitter Fruit: The Politics of Black-Korean Conflict in New York City* (New Haven, CT: Yale University Press, 2000).

39. For anxieties over whether Al Sharpton would have a veto over the next police commissioner, see Hamill, "Freddy Will Pick Own Top Cop."

40. A series of cartoons appeared almost daily in the *New York Post* the week prior to the Green-Ferrer runoff. See *New York Post*, October 3, 4, 5, 7, 10, and 11.

41. See Wayne Barrett, "The Giuliani Dilemma: How Freddy and Mark Used Rudy to Define Themselves," *Village Voice*, October 9, 2001, Citystate section, 21.

42. For acknowledgment that the Green campaign circulated the cartoons, see Cardwell, "Racial Politics of 2001."

43. For the cartoon of Sharpton as a Joker, see Jim Sleeper, "The Joker," Salon.com, February 28, 2002.

44. For the makeover of Al Sharpton, see *Village Voice*, April 16–22, 2003, cover. I am grateful to Keith Bolland for pointing out that the Stanley Martucci and Cheryl Greisbach image of Sharpton getting a makeover reworks an earlier image of Richard Nixon getting a makeover that appeared on the cover of *Esquire* magazine for the May issue in 1968. The parallels are stunning. The Nixon image is reproduced in David Greenberg, *Nixon's Shadow: The History of an Image* (New York: Norton, 2003). For innovative work on the intersection of sexual and racial taxonomies, see Jennifer Terry, *An American Obsession: Science, Medicine, and Homosexuality in Modern Society* (Chicago: University of Chicago Press, 1999); Roderick Ferguson, "The Nightmares of

the Heteronormative," *Cultural Values* 4, no. 4 (2000): 419–44; and Siobhan B. Somerville, *Queering the Color Line: Race and the Invention of Homosexuality in American Culture* (Durham, NC: Duke University Press, 2000).

45. Howard Beach, a largely white neighborhood, made headlines in 1986 and 1987 when three African Americans were attacked by a group of white youth wielding baseball bats. One of the African Americans, Michael Griffith, ran onto the Shore Parkway to escape the attackers and was killed by an oncoming car. Three of the white youth were tried, convicted, and sentenced to five to thirty years in jail. Later in 1987, fifteen-year-old Tawana Brawley claimed she had been raped by six white men in Wappingers Falls, New York. Sharpton quickly stepped in to champion her case. A grand jury was called and heard testimony from 180 witnesses. The case became a media sensation. In October 1988, the grand jury dismissed the case, claiming lack of evidence. It became apparent to many that Brawley had invented the story, though she still maintained that she was telling the truth, and Sharpton continues to support Brawley to this day. Sharpton and two supporting attorneys were later sued for defamatory statements made during the case and ordered to pay $345,000 in damages. The Brawley episode is still regularly bought up whenever Sharpton is interviewed.

46. Scott Sherman, "He Has a Dream," *Nation,* April 16, 2001, 15.

47. For classic profiles of Sharpton, see Martin Gottlieb with Dean Baquet, "Street-Wise Impresario: Sharpton Calls the Tunes, and Players Take their Cues," *New York Times,* December 19, 1991, Metro section, B1; Mike Sager, "The Sharpton Strategy," *Esquire,* January, 1991, 23–24, 112–114, 119; M. A. Farber, "A 'New' Sharpton: Maturing of a Maverick?" *New York Times,* January 21, 1991, B1; Catherine S. Manegold, "The Reformation of a Street Preacher: Al Sharpton Tries on the Power of 166,000 Votes," *New York Times Magazine,* January 24, 1993, 18; Jim Sleeper, "A Man of Too Many Parts," *New Yorker,* January 25, 1993, 55–67; Michael Tomasky, "Regarding Al," *Village Voice,* July 12, 1994, 17; Craig Horowitz, "The Anti-Sharpton," *New York Magazine,* January 26, 1998; Craig Horowitz, "30th Anniversary Issue/Al Sharpton: The Rev," *New York Magazine,* April 6, 1998; Peter Noel, "Should Al Sharpton Apologize? The Racial Politics of Reconciliation in New York," *Village Voice,* July 28, 1998, 55–57; Richard Lowry, "Disrespecting Sharpton," *National Review,* September 14, 1998; David Plotz, "Al Sharpton: How Al Charlatan became Al Kingmaker," *Slate,* March 3, 2000; Jay Nordlinger, "Power Dem," *National Review,* March 20, 2001; Scott Sherman, "He Has a Dream," *Nation,* April 16, 2001, 11–19; Kevin Chappell, "The 'New' Al Sharpton Talks about the 'Old' Al Sharpton and the New Threats to Black Americans," *Ebony,* July 2001, 124–29; Richard Goldstein, "Al Sharpton's Jewish Problem," *Village Voice,* November 20, 2001, 36–38; Michael Tomasky, "The Untouchable," *New York Magazine,* December 3, 2001; "The Dangerous Quest of Al Sharpton," *Economist,* January 19, 2002, 29; Elizabeth Kolbert, "The People's Preacher," *New Yorker,* February 18 & 25, 2002, 156–67; Sleeper, "The Joker"; Rod Dreher, "Al on Al: Reverend Sharpton's Pre-Campaign Treatise," *National Review,* October 8, 2002; Garance Franke-Ruta, "Let's Get Ready to Rumble! Al Sharpton Gears Up to Take on the Dems," *American Prospect,* February 2003; Ta-Nehisi Coates, "The Makeover of Al Sharpton: How the Presidential Candidate Can Woo Democrats," *Village Voice,* April 16–22, 2003; and Margaret Carlson, "The Rev's Big Shakedown," *Gentlemen's Quarterly,* May 2003, 117–18.

48. In January 1988, in the midst of the Tawana Brawley case, *New York Newsday* ran a series of articles accusing Sharpton of being an FBI informant. See Bob Drury, Robert E. Kessler, and Mike McAlary, "The Minister and the Feds," *New York Newsday,* January 20, 1988; Bob Drury, Robert E. Kessler, and Mike McAlary, "Black Leader:

Probe FBI," *New York Newsday*, January 21, 1988, and 2–3, 24–25; Bob Drury et al., "The Minister and the Mob: Feds' Data Ties Sharpton to Reputed Crime Figures," *New York Newsday*, January 22, 1988; William Bastone, Joe Conason, Jack Newfield, and Tom Robbins, "The Hustler: How Al Sharpton Conned the Movement, the Media, and the Government," *Village Voice*, February 2, 1988; and Ron Howell, "The Minister and the Fugitive: Sharpton Tried to Trap Chesimard for Feds in 1983, Activists Charge," *New York Newsday*, October 21, 1988. See also Robert D. McFadden et al., *Outrage: The Story Behind the Tawana Brawley Hoax* (New York: Bantam Books, 1990), 112–13; and Michael Klein, *The Man Behind the Sound Bite: The Real Story of the Rev. Al Sharpton* (New York: Castillo, 1991), chaps. 11, 13.

49. For a more sympathetic view of Sharpton's FBI and Mob connections, see Klein, *The Man Behind the Sound Bite*, chaps. 11, 13, esp. 180–83.

50. For a description of Sharpton as "charlatan," see Sleeper, "A Man of Too Many Parts," 67; and Sherman, "He Has a Dream," 20; for a depiction of Sharpton as a "clown," see the cartoon in the *New York Post*, October 3, 2001, 36; for Sharpton as the "joker," see Sleeper, "The Joker," and accompanying graphic, 1; for reference to Sharpton as "showman," see "The Dangerous Quest of Al Sharpton"; and Michael Meyers of the New York Civil Rights Coalition called Sharpton a "racial buffoon," quoted in Kolbert, "The People's Preacher," 64. For claims that Sharpton is politically ineffective, see Sleeper, "The Man of Too Many Parts," 62; Sherman, "He Has a Dream," 17; "The Dangerous Quest of Al Sharpton"; and Sleeper, "The Joker," 1, 4, 5.

51. For reference to "inflatable hair do" and "considerable girth," see Jesse Drucker, "The Making of a Boogeyman," Salon.com, March 30, 2000; and for reference to "gaudy gold medallions," see "The Dangerous Quest of Al Sharpton"; and Kevin Chappell, "The 'New' Al Sharpton Talks about the 'Old' Al Sharpton and the New Threats to Black Americans," *Ebony*, July 2001, 129.

52. For discussion of Sharpton being awarded the Martin Luther King medal and for promising to keep his hairdo until Brown died, see Michael Klein, *The Man Behind the Sound Bite: The Real Story of the Rev. Al Sharpton* (New York: Castillo International, 1991), 123; and Chappell, "The 'New' Al Sharpton Talks about the 'Old' Al Sharpton," 129.

53. Kevin Chappell, "The 'New' Al Sharpton Talks about the 'Old' Al Sharpton," 129.

54. See Ta-Nehisi Coates, "A Campaign Plan for Making Al Sharpton Matter: From Sideshow to Big Tent," *Village Voice*, April 16–22, 2003. The Joseph Salina illustration that accompanied the article is reproduced here.

55. For reference to "race baiting," see Sleeper, "The Joker," 1; for "one-note racial analysis," see Kolbert, "The People's Preacher," 165; for Sharpton as "hatemonger," see Sherman, "He Has a Dream," 13; for "politics of protest and victimhood," see "The Dangerous Quest of Al Sharpton"; and Sleeper, "The Joker", 2; for Sharpton promoting "racial violence," see Drucker, "The Making of a Boogeyman"; for Sharpton as "rabble-rouser," and "agent provocateur," see Alicia Montgomery, "Brothers Under the Skin," Salon.com, March 15, 2001.

56. For comparison of Sharpton with bin Laden, see Noel, "Take It or Leave It, Mark Green."

57. For Sharpton as a "racial arsonist," see Niger Innis, National Review Online, November 28, 2001. For the Republican National Committee "backgrounder" on Sharpton and Matalin's remarks on *Crossfire*, see Drucker, "The Making of a Boogeyman," 1. For other sources signaling racial division via Sharpton, see Heather MacDonald, "Al Sharpton Just Won't Let Racial Wounds Heal," *Wall Street Journal*, August 31, 2000; William Mayer, "Doing the Harlem Shuffle: Al Sharpton's Traveling Minstrel Show,"

Ether Zone, January 14, 2002; Sleeper, "The Joker"; "The Dangerous Quest of Al Sharpton"; and Jonathan P. Hicks, "Green's Campaign Angers Backers of Ferrer," *New York Times*, October 13, 2001, D3.

58. Sleeper, "The Joker."

59. "The Dangerous Quest of Al Sharpton."

60. For equation of the Tawana Brawley case with Chappaquiddick, see Sherman, "He Has a Dream," 5.

61. Sleeper, "A Man of Too Many Parts," 58.

62. For advocacy of "interracial dialogue," see ibid. See also Sleeper's claim that Sharpton prevents "honest racial dialogue," in Sleeper, "The Joker," 2.

63. Kolbert, "The People's Preacher," 167.

64. Ibid.

65. For an interesting poll concerning views of Sharpton for different racial groups, see "The Impact of Al Sharpton Endorsement," New York-WABC, August 17, 2001, 7online.com. The poll asked: "The Reverend Al Sharpton will make an endorsement in the New York city mayor's race. Would Sharpton's endorsement make you more likely or less likely to vote for a candidate?" Forty-three percent of Black respondents said "more likely," 14 percent said "less likely," 35 percent said "no impact," and 8 percent answered "not sure." There were five hundred respondents overall, but unfortunately the report does not specify the number of Black respondents. For Sharpton approval ratings over time but not broken down by race, see Quinnipiac polls, which show Sharpton's favorables ranging from a low of 9 percent on February 11, 1997, to a high of 25 percent on March 15, 2000. See Quinnipiac University, New York City Trends, available at http://www.quinnipiac.edu (hard copy in possession of author).

66. Ramirez is quoted in Nagourney, "Political Memo; Heated Race Revisited, Amid Claims of Racism"; and Barrett, "Is the Peace Real?"

67. For Lynch's criticism of Green and the Democratic Party, see Jill Nelson interview with Lynch, "A View from Behind the Scenes: The Race Factor," *Village Voice*, October 24–30, 2001; and also Benson, "It's Mean Mark Green."

68. "The Dangerous Quest of Al Sharpton."

69. Axelrod is quoted in Nagourney, "Political Memo; Heated Race Revisited, Amid Claims of Racism."

70. The quotation describing the attack ad is taken from Matea Gold, James Rainey, and Jeffrey L. Rabin, "Final Debate an Angry One," *LA Times*, June 1, 2001, home edition, A1. For additional accounts of Hahn's racial attacks on Villaraigosa, see George Skelton, "Black Affection for Hahn a Hurdle Villaraigosa Couldn't Vault," *LA Times*, June 7, 2001, home edition, California section, B7; Steve Lopez, "Villaraigosa Was Ill-Prepared for Letter Bomb," *LA Times*, June 6, 2001, home edition, A21.

71. Harry Pachon quoted in Skelton, "Black Affection for Hahn."

72. Villaraigosa did not run Spanish-language media commercials and held few public events in the Eastside or in other heavily Latino communities. In general, Villaraigosa deemphasized his own ethnicity in order to broaden his political reach. For Villaraigosa's "balancing act" when it comes to race and ethnicity, see James Rainey and Matea Gold, "Mayor's Race Avoids Ethnic Schisms: Tests Loom," *LA Times*, April 16, 2001; Patrick J. McDonnell, "Ethnicity Issue Mixed Blessing for Villaraigosa," *LA Times*, May 28, 2001, home edition, A1; Matea Gold, "Villaraigosa Lets Others Court Latinos," *LA Times*, June 2, 2001, home edition, A1; and James Rainey and Greg Krikorian, "Hahn Won on His Appeal to Moderates, Conservatives," *LA Times*, June 7, 2001, home edition, A1.

73. For classic backlash arguments about the sixties, see Thomas Edsall and Mary Edsall, *Chain Reaction: The Impact of Race, Rights and Taxes on American Politics* (New York: Norton, 1991); Jim Sleeper, *The Closest of Strangers: Liberalism and the Politics of Race in New York* (New York: Norton, 1990); Todd Gitlin, *Twilight of Common Dreams: Why America Is Wracked by Culture Wars* (New York: Holt, 1995). See also Norman Podhoretz, "My New York: An Intellectual Considers His City, from LaGuardia to Giuliani and Beyond," *National Review* 51, no. 11 (1999).

74. See Anthony Downs, *An Economic Theory of Democracy* (New York: Harper, 1957).

75. See Diane Cardwell and Jonathan P. Hicks, "Ferrer Takes Defensive After Comments on Diallo Killing," *New York Times*, March 17, 2005, Metropolitan Desk. For New York leaders backing away from Ferrer and throwing their support to Fields, see Diane Cardwell and Michael Slackman, "Diallo Remarks Haunt Ferrer at Convention," *New York Times*, April 9, 2005, Metropolitan Desk; Diane Cardwell, "Political Memo; Ferrer Tries to Shift the Debate, and It Shoves Back," *New York Times*, April 24, 2005, Metropolitan Desk.

76. For the lack of traction to Ferrer's campaign, see Nicholas Confessore (Patrick D. Healy contributed), "Fund-Raising for Ferrer Gets Off to a Slow Start," *New York Times*, September 24, 2005, Metropolitan Desk; Patrick D. Healy and Diane Cardwell, "Political Memo; Ferrer Being Hurt by Self-Inflicted Wounds," *New York Times*, September 30, 2005, Metropolitan Desk; and Diane Cardwell, "Ferrer Camp Finds City's Deep Pockets Sewed Up," *New York Times*, October 11, 2005, A1.

77. For an excellent assessment of the 2005 Los Angeles mayoral election, see Robert Gottlieb, Regina Freer, Mark Vallianatos, and Peter Dreier, *The Next Los Angeles: The Struggle for a Livable City* (Berkeley: University of California Press, 2005). They offer a substantially more favorable assessment of Villaraigosa's win. Once in power he will be able to appoint movement people and thereby secure a progressive agenda without making it explicit. Even if this assessment is correct, I think failing to contest public discourse on issues of racism and inequality creates enormous long-term problems and ultimately constrains real possibilities for progressive change.

Chapter 7

1. See Jo Craven McGinty, "Breaking Down Hate Crime," *New York Times*, July 24, 2005, Metro section, 25.

2. For estimate of number of rallies held on May 1, see Randal C. Archibold, "Immigrants Take to U.S. Streets in Show of Strength," *New York Times*, May 2, 2006.

3. For text of H.R. 4437, see http://www.govtrack.us/congress/billtext.xpd?bill =h109-4437.

4. For a general overview of the rallies, see http://www.may1/info.

5. For splits within the Republican coalition, see Arnold Schwarzenegger's refusal to send California National Guard troops to patrol the border. See Peter Nicholas, "Gov. Refuses Bush Request for Border Troops," *Los Angeles Times*, June 24, 2006; Morton M. Kondracke, "Pence-Hutchinson Bill Creates Hope on Immigration," *Roll Call*, July 27, 2006, 6. Divisions within Republican ranks were accommodated in part by holding numerous hearings on immigration in which regional differences could be voiced. In August, Republican leaders in the House of Representatives planned nineteen sets of hearings across twelve states and eight separate congressional committees. See Lara Jakes Jordan, "Border Security Plans Criticized: Both Parties Say They Doubt Measures Will Work Effectively," Associated Press, July 27, 2006. See also divisions in recent congressional hearings in the Northeast and Southwest. For tensions over

immigration within Democratic Party ranks, see debates over Stephen Steinberg's essay on race and immigration in both *New Politics* and *New Labor Forum*. See Stephen Steinberg, "Immigration, African Americans, and Race Discourse," *New Politics* 10, no. 3 (2006); and "Do Immigrants Block African American Progress? A Debate," *New Labor Forum* 15, no. 1 (2006); and Rachael L. Swarns, "Growing Unease for Some Blacks on Immigration," *New York Times*, May 4, 2006, A1.

6. For Sensenbrenner and undocumented workers, see Mark Leibovich, " 'Pit Bull' of the House Latches on to Immigration," *New York Times*, July 11, 2006, A1, A16. For discussion of the boycott, see Kristin Kloberdanz, "The Immigrants' Dilemma: To Boycott or Not to Boycott? A Split Is Growing over How Militant the Upcoming 'Day Without Immigrants' Should Be," *Time*, April 18, 2006.

7. See Gus Kim, "Yes, We Can: A Firsthand Account of A Day Without Immigrants," *New Magazine*, May 1, 2006, http://www.fnewsmagazine.com/spotlight.

8. A transcript of Jesse Jackson's speech at the May Day rally at Union Square on May 1, 2006, was available on the RainbowPush Web site, "Immigration Dignity Day Statement," May 1, 2006, New York, NY, http://www.rainbowpush.org (transcript in possession of author). For others linking immigrant rallies and civil rights protest, see Nathaniel Hernandez, "Chicago Protest Draws Diverse Support," *Chicago Defender*, May 1, 2006; and the New York Committee for May 1 Boycott, which refers directly to Rosa Parks. See http://leftshift.org.

9. For the phrase "show of strength," see Archibold, "Immigrants Take to U.S. Streets."

10. Jarrett Murphy, "Under One Flag: City's Melting Pot Reaches the Boiling Point: Inside the Immigrant Uprising," *Village Voice*, April 19–25, 2006, Citystate section, 15.

11. Logan is quoted in Michael Muskal, "Immigration Dissent Sweeps L.A. and the Nation," *Los Angeles Times*, May 1, 2006; Powell is quoted in Kim, "Yes, We Can." See also Archibold, "Immigrants Take to U.S. Streets"; and Gregory Rodriguez, "Can-Do Spirit Fuels Immigrants," *Los Angeles Times*, May 7, 2006.

12. For reference to immigrants coming out of the "shadows," see Arnold Schwarzenegger, "Next Step for Immigration," *Los Angeles Times*, March 28, 2006, Op Ed section; Gustavo Arellano, "O.C. Can You Say . . . 'Anti-Mexican'? *Los Angeles Times*, May 8, 2006; and Swarns, "Growing Unease for Some Blacks on Immigration." For division among immigrants over the May Day rallies, see Kloberdanz, "The Immigrants' Dilemma"; and Michelle O'Donnell, "Thousands Turn Out, but Support Is Mixed Among New York's Immigrants," *New York Times*, May 2, 2006.

13. For reference to the patchwork multinational flag in Los Angeles, see Andre Herndon, Gene C. Johnson Jr., and Marisela Santana, "Latinos Draw Multi-ethnic Support on May Day," *Wave Newspapers*, May 5, 2006. For the many national flags being waved at New York rallies, see Sarah Ferguson, "A Day without White People: On May Day, the Masses Rose Up in New York, But Where Were the White Peaceniks?" *Village Voice*, May 2, 2006.

14. Jackson, "Immigration Dignity Day Statement."

15. Ibid.

16. Jackson has long advocated a broad "rainbow coalition." For earlier efforts to link immigration politics and civil rights, see the Immigrant Freedom Rides held in the fall of 2003. For accounts of the 2003 Immigration Freedom Rides, see Stephen Greenhouse, "Immigrant Rally in City, Seeking Rights," *New York Times*, October 5, 2003; Jose Antonio Vargas, "Immigrant Freedom Rides Hold Rally in City Hall in S.F. Immigrant Workers to Bus Across Nation," http://sfgate.com, September 21, 2003; Maya

Raquel Anderson, "Retracing the 1960s Freedom Rides Through the Deep South," American Friends Service Committee, http://www.afsc.org/immigrants-rights/news/ retracing.htm.

17. Al Sharpton, "Immigrants, Blacks Must March as One," *New York Daily News*, Ideas and Opinions section, May 10, 2006. See also the very measured account of the May Day rallies on the front page of the *Amsterdam News*. See Ashley Tusan, "We the People: Local, National Immigrant Protest Sets New Tone," *New York Amsterdam News*, May 4–May 10, 2006, 1.

18. See Van Jones, "Shout 'Viva!' Anyhow: On Being Black at a Latino March," *New America Media*, May 4, 2006, http://news.ncmonline.com/news/view_article.html, July 5, 2006; and Erin Aubry Kaplan, "What Was Lost in the Crowd," *Los Angeles Times*, May 3, 2006. For powerful engagements with issues of loss and identification, see David Eng and Shinhee Han, "A Dialogue on Racial Melancholia," in *Loss*, ed. David L. Eng and David Kazanjian (Berkeley: University of California Press, 2003), 343–71.

19. See Jones, "Shout 'Viva!' Anyhow."

20. For one of the most elegant accounts for identification across difference, see Lisa Lowe, *Immigrant Acts: On Asian American Cultural Politics* (Durham, NC: Duke University Press, 1996), chap. 3.

21. The Drum Major Institute for Public Policy is a progressive think tank in New York City headed up by Fernando Ferrer. The Institute did release an important study of H.R. 4437. See Amy M. Traub, *Principles for an Immigration Policy to Strengthen and Expand the American Middle Class: A Primer for Policymakers and Advocates* (New York: Drum Major Institute for Public Policy, 2005), http://www.drummajorinstitute .org/library/report.php?ID=21.

22. "U.S. Prepares for 'Day without Immigrants,'" Associated Press, May 1, 2006.

23. This is a paraphrase of Villaraigosa's remarks and not a direct quote. See Sam Quinones and Arin Gencer, "Fox Makes Rounds for Immigration," *Los Angeles Times*, May 27, 2006.

BIBLIOGRAPHY

Ackerman, Bruce. "The Broken Engine of Progressive Politics." *American Prospect,* May/June 1998.

Alba, Richard D. *Ethnic Identity: The Transformation of White America*. New Haven, CT: Yale University Press, 1990.

Alba, Richard, and Victor Nee. *Remaking the American Mainstream: Assimilation and Contemporary Immigration*. Cambridge, MA: Harvard University Press, 2003.

———. "Rethinking Assimilation Theory for a New Era of Immigration." *International Migration Review* 31, no. 4 (1997): 826–74.

Alcoff, Linda. "Cultural Feminism Versus Poststructuralism: The Identity Crisis in Feminist Theory." *Signs* 13, no. 3 (1988): 405–36.

Alexander, Hartley Burr. "The Hebrew Contribution to the Americanism of the Future." Menorah Pamphlets No.1. New York: Intercollegiate Menorah Association, 1923.

Allen, Theodore W. "'Race' and 'Ethnicity': History and the 2000 Census." *Cultural Logic* 3, no. 1 (1999). http://clogic.eserver.org/3-1&2/allen.html.

Alvarez, Lizette. "Hispanic Voters Hard to Profile, Poll Finds: Mixture of Beliefs Helps Make Latinos an Attractive Swing Bloc." *New York Times*, October 4, 2002, A20.

Anderson, Lincoln. "Mayoral Hopefuls Speak at Village Forum." *Villager*, February 12, 2001.

Anderson, Margo J., and Stephen E. Fienberg. *Who Counts? The Politics of Census-Taking in Contemporary America*. New York: Russell Sage Foundation, 1999.

Anderson, Maya Raquel. "Retracing the 1960s Freedom Rides Through the Deep South." American Friends Service Committee. http://www.afsc.org.

Anzaldúa, Gloria. *Borderlands = La Frontera: The New Mestiza*. San Francisco: Aunt Lute Books, 1987.

Appiah, Anthony. "The Uncompleted Argument: Du Bois and the Illusion of Race." In *"Race," Writing, and Difference*, edited by Henry Louis Gates Jr. Chicago: University of Chicago Press, 1986.

Archibold, Randal C. "Immigrants Take to U.S. Streets in Show of Strength." *New York Times*, May 2, 2006.

Arellano, Gustavo. "O.C. Can You Say . . . 'Anti-Mexican'?" *Los Angeles Times*, May 8, 2006.

Arendt, Hannah. "We Refugees." *Menorah Journal* 31, no. 1 (1943): 69–77.

———. "Zionism Reconsidered." *Menorah Journal* 33, no. 2 (1945): 162–96.

Arteaga, Luis M., Chione Flegal, and Guillermo Rodriguez. *Latino Vote 1998: The New Margin of Victory*. San Francisco: Latino Issues Forum, 1998.

Bailyn, Bernard. *The Ideological Origins of the American Revolution*. Cambridge, MA: Harvard University Press, 1967.

Baker, Lee D. *From Savage to Negro: Anthropology and the Construction of Race, 1896–1954*. Berkeley: University of California Press, 1998.

———. "The Location of Franz Boas within the African-American Struggle." *Critique of Anthropology* 14, no. 2 (1994): 199–217.

Baldwin, James. "On Being White. And Other Lies." *Essence*, April 1984, 10–12.

Banton, Michael. *Racial Theories*. New York: Cambridge University Press, 1998.

Barkan, Joanne. "Clinton and the Left." *Dissent* 40 (1993): 5–8.

Barlow, Nora, ed. *The Autobiography of Charles Darwin, 1809–1882*. New York: Norton, 1993.

Barreto, Matt, Rodolfo O. de la Garza, Jongho Lee, Jaesung Ryu, and Harry P. Pachon. *Latino Voter Mobilization in 2000: A Glimpse into Latino Policy and Voting Preferences*. Claremont, CA: Tomas Rivera Policy Institute, September 2002.

Barreto, Matt A., Gary M. Segura, and Nathan D. Woods. "The Mobilizing Effect of Majority-Minority Districts on Latino Turnout." *American Political Science Review* 98, no. 1 (2004): 65–75.

Barrett, Wayne. "Coalition Confusion: McCall Crowns Ferrer, but Sharpton, Rivera, Rangel Skip the Coronation." *Village Voice*, February 27, 2001.

———. "The Giuliani Dilemma: How Freddy and Mark Used Rudy to Define Themselves." *Village Voice*, October 9, 2001.

———. "Is the Peace Real? Probing Green's Shaky Rapprochement with the Ferrer Camp." *Village Voice*, October 24–30, 2001.

———. "The Kid from Great Neck." *Village Voice*, August 8–14, 2001.

Bastone, William, Joe Conason, Jack Newfield, and Tom Robbins. "The Hustler: How Al Sharpton Conned the Movement, the Media, and the Government." *Village Voice*, February 2, 1988.

Bates, Nancy, Elizabeth A. Martin, Teresa J. DeMaio, and Manuel de la Puenta. "Questionnaire Effects on Measurement of Race and Spanish Origin." *Journal of Official Statistics* 11, no. 4 (1995): 433–59.

Bean, Robert Bennett. "The Nose of the Jew and the Quadratus Labi Superioris Muscle." *Anatomical Record* 7, no. 2 (1913): 47–49.

Bennet, William S. "Immigrants and Crime." *Annals of the American Academy of Political and Social Science* 34, no. 1 (1909): 117–24.

Bennett, Claudette. "Racial Categories Used in the Decennial Censuses, 1790 to the Present." *Government Information Quarterly* 17, no. 2 (2000): 161–80.

Bennett, Larry, and Adolph Reed Jr. "The New Face of Urban Renewal: The Near North Redevelopment Initiative and the Cabrini-Green Neighborhood." In *Without Justice for All*, edited by Adolph Reed Jr. Boulder, CO: Westview Press, 1999.

Benson, Josh. "It's Mean Mark Green: Former Front Runner Jostles Freddy Ferrer." *New York Observer*, October 15, 2001.

Bentley, Arthur F. *The Process of Government*. Bloomington: Principia Press, 1935.

Berchovitch, Sacvan. *Reconstructing American Literary History*. Cambridge, MA: Harvard University Press, 1986.

Berkson, Isaac B. "A Community Theory of American Life," *Menorah Journal* 6, no. 6 (1920): 311–21.

———. "The Jewish Right to Live: A Defense of Ethnic Loyalty." *Menorah Journal* 7, no. 1 (1921): 41–51.

———. *Theories of Americanization: A Critical Study*. New York: Arno Press, 1920.

Biondi, Martha. *To Stand and Fight: The Struggle for Civil Rights in Postwar New York City*. Cambridge, MA: Harvard University Press, 2003.

Blake, Casey. "'The Cosmopolitan Note': Randolph Bourne and the Challenge of 'Trans-National America.'" *Culturefront* 4 (Winter 1995–96): 25–28.

Blanton, Carlos Kevin. *The Strange Career of Bilingual Education in Texas, 1836–1981*. College Station: Texas A & M University Press, 2004.

Blatt, Jessica. "'To Bring Out the Best That Is in Their Blood': Race, Reform, and Civilization in the Journal of Race Development, 1910–1919." *Ethnic and Racial Studies* 27, no. 5 (2004): 691–709.

Boas, Franz. *Changes in the Bodily Form of Descendants of Immigrants*. New York: Columbia University Press, 1912.

———. *Changes in the Bodily Form of the Descendants of Immigrants*. Final Report, U.S. Immigration Commission. Washington, DC: Government Printing Office, 1911.

———. "Changes in the Bodily Form of Descendants of Immigrants." *American Anthropologist*, n.s., 14, no. 3 (1912): 530–62.

———. "Changes in the Bodily Form of Descendants of Immigrants." *American Anthropologist*, n.s., 42, no. 2 (1940): 183–89.

———. "Effects of Environment on Immigrants and Their Descendants." *Science* 84 (1936): 522–25.

———. "The Head-Form of the Italians as Influenced by Heredity and Environment." *American Anthropologist*, n.s., 15, no. 2 (1913): 163–88.

———. "The Instability of Human Types." In *Papers on Interracial Problems Communicated to the First Universal Races Congress Held at the University of London, July 26–29, 1911*, edited by Gustav Spiller. London: King, 1911.

———. "What Is a Race?" *Nation*, January 28, 1925, 89–91.

Bourke, Paul F. "The Status of Politics 1909–1919: The New Republic, Randolph Bourne, and Van Wyck Brooks." *American Studies* 8, no. 2 (1969–70): 171–202.

Bourne, Randolph. "The Jew and Trans-National America." *Menorah Journal* 2, no. 5 (1916): 277–84.

———. *The Radical Will: Selected Writings, 1911–1918*. Berkeley: University of California Press, 1992.

———. "Transnational America." *Atlantic Monthly*, July 1916, 86–97.

———. *War and the Intellectuals: Collected Essays, 1915–1919*, edited by Carl Resek. Indianapolis: Hackett, 1999.

———. *War and the Intellectuals: Essays, 1915–1919,* edited by Carl Resek. New York: Harper Torchbooks, 1964.

Bowler, Peter J. *The Mendelian Revolution: The Emergence of Hereditarian Concepts in Modern Science and Society.* Baltimore: Johns Hopkins University Press, 1989.

Bradley, Phillips. "Political Aspects of Cultural Pluralism." *Journal of Educational Sociology* 12, no. 8 (1939): 492–98.

Brandeis, Louis. "Call to the Educated Jew." *Menorah Journal* 1, no. 1 (1915): 13–19.

———. "The Jewish Problem." In *Louis D. Brandeis: A Biographical Sketch, with Special Reference to His Contribution to Jewish and Zionist History,* edited by Jacob de Haas. New York: Block, 1929.

———. "The Rebirth of the Jewish Nation." In *Louis D. Brandeis: A Biographical Sketch, with Special Reference to His Contribution to Jewish and Zionist History,* edited by Jacob de Haas. New York: Block Publishing Company, 1929.

Brinton, Daniel G. "The Factors of Heredity and Environment in Man." *American Anthropologist* 11 (1898): 271–77.

———. "The 'Nation' as an Element in Anthropology." In *Memoirs of the International Congress of Anthropology,* edited by C. S. Vake. Chicago: Shuttle, 1894.

———. "Variation in the Human Skeleton and Their Causes." *American Anthropologist* 7 (October 1894): 385–86.

Brown, Michael K. "Race in the American Welfare State: The Ambiguities of 'Universalistic' Social Policy since the New Deal." In *Without Justice for All,* edited by Adolph Reed Jr. Boulder, CO: Westview Press, 1999.

———. *Race, Money, and the American Welfare State.* Ithaca, NY: Cornell University Press, 1999.

Browning, Rufus P., Dale Rogers Marshall, and Raphael J. Sonenshein. "The Prospects for Multiracial Coalitions: Lessons from America's Three Largest Cities." In *Racial Politics in American Cities,* edited by Rufus P. Browning, Dale Rogers Marshall, and David Tabb. New York; Longman, 1997.

Browning, Rufus P., Dale Rogers Marshall, and David Tabb, eds. *Protest Is Not Enough.* Berkeley: University of California Press, 1984.

———. *Racial Politics in American Cities.* New York: Longman, 1997.

Broyard, Anatole. *Kafka Was the Rage: A Greenwich Village Memoir.* New York: Vintage Books, 1993.

Bulmer, Martin. *The Chicago School of Sociology: Institutionalization, Diversity, and the Rise of Sociological Research.* Chicago: University of Chicago Press, 1984.

Burstein, Paul. *Discrimination, Jobs, and Politics: The Struggle for Equal Employment Opportunity in the United States Since the New Deal.* Chicago: University of Chicago Press, 1985.

Butler, Judith. *Bodies That Matter: On the Discursive Limits of Sex.* New York: Routledge, 1993.

———. *Gender Trouble: Feminism and the Subversion of Identity.* New York: Routledge, 1990.

Byrne, Thomas, and Mary D. Edsall. *Chain Reaction: The Impact of Race, Rights, and Taxes on American Politics.* New York: Norton, 1991.

Cardwell, Diane. "Ferrer Camp Finds City's Deep Pockets Sewed Up." *New York Times,* October 11, 2005, A1.

———. "Political Memo; Ferrer Tries to Shift the Debate, and It Shoves Back." *New York Times*, April 24, 2005, Metropolitan Desk.

———. "Racial Politics of 2001; Unhealed Wounds in 2005." *New York Times*, May 6, 2005, Metro section, 33, 36.

Cardwell, Diane, and Jonathan P. Hicks. "Ferrer Takes Defensive After Comments on Diallo Killing." *New York Times*, March 17, 2005, Metropolitan Desk.

Cardwell, Diane, and Michael Slackman. "Diallo Remarks Haunt Ferrer at Convention." *New York Times*, April 9, 2005, Metropolitan Desk.

Carlson, Margaret. "The Rev's Big Shakedown." *Gentlemen's Quarterly* (May 2003): 117–18.

Chafets, Zev. "The Race Is About Race: In a Divided City, the Gulf Is Expressed at the Polls." *Daily News*, September 9, 2001.

Chappell, Kevin. "The 'New' Al Sharpton Talks about the 'Old' Al Sharpton and the New Threats to Black Americans." *Ebony*, July 2001, 124–29.

Chen, Anthony. "'The Hitlerian Rule of Quotas': Racial Conservatism and the Politics of Fair Employment Legislation in New York State, 1941–1945." *Journal of American History* 92 (March 2006): 1238–64.

Choldin, Harvey M. "Statistics and Politics: The 'Hispanic Issue' in the 1980 Census." *Demography* 23, no. 3 (1986): 403–18.

Clayton, Bruce. *Forgotten Prophet: The Life of Randolph Bourne*. Columbia: University of Missouri Press, 1998.

Closson, Carlos. "Social Selection." *Journal of Political Economy* 4, no. 4 (1896): 449–66.

Coates, Ta-Nehisi. "A Campaign Plan for Making Al Sharpton Matter: From Sideshow to Big Tent." *Village Voice*, April 16–22, 2003.

———. "From Sideshow to Big Tent: A Campaign Plan for Making Al Sharpton Matter." *Village Voice*, April 16–22, 2003.

———. "The Makeover of Al Sharpton: How the Presidential Candidate Can Woo Democrats." *Village Voice*, April 16–22, 2003.

Coats, A. W. "The First Two Decades of the American Economic Association." *American Economic Review* 50, no. 4 (1960): 555–74.

Cockburn, Alexander. "Obama: As He Rises, He Falls." *Nation*, May 8, 2006, 9.

———. "They Should Have Hissed Barack Obama." *Nation*, April 24, 2006, 10.

"Cognitive Questions." Distributed as a handout by Nancy Gordon at the REAC meetings, May 5–7, 2004. Washington, DC: U.S. Bureau of the Census, April 27, 2004.

Cohen, Cathy. *The Boundaries of Blackness: AIDS and the Breakdown of Black Politics*. Chicago: University of Chicago Press, 1999.

Cohen, Joshua, and Joel Rogers. "After Liberalism." *Boston Review* (April/May 1995).

Cohen, Naomi Wiener. "The Maccabaean Message: A Study in American Zionism until World War I." *Jewish Social Studies* 18 (July 1956): 163–78.

———. "The Reaction of Reform Judaism in America to Political Zionism (1897–1922)." *Publications of American Jewish Historical Society* 40 (1950–51): 361–94.

Commons, John R. *Races and Immigrants in America*. New York: Macmillan, 1916.

Confessore, Nicholas. "Fund-Raising for Ferrer Gets Off to a Slow Start." *New York Times*, September 24, 2005, Metropolitan Desk.

Conley, Dalton. *Being Black, Living in the Red: Race, Wealth, and Social Policy in America*. Berkeley: University of California Press, 1999.

Connolly, William E. *The Ethos of Pluralization.* Minneapolis: University of Minnesota Press, 1995.

"Controversy: Race, Liberalism, and Affirmative Action." *American Prospect* 3, no. 9 (1992): 116–28.

"Controversy: Race, Liberalism, and Affirmative Action." *American Prospect* 3, no. 10 (1992): 86–97.

"Controversy: Race, Liberalism, and Affirmative Action." *American Prospect* 3, no. 11 (1992): 11–16.

Cooper, Michael. "Ferrer and Green Divide the Spoils of Their Rivals." *New York Times,* September 27, 2001, Metro section, D5.

Count, Earl W. "The Evolution of the Race Idea in Modern Western Culture During the Period of the Pre-Darwinian Nineteenth Century." *Transactions of the New York Academy of Sciences* 8 (1946): 139–65.

Crenshaw, Kimberle Williams. "Sharp Tongues for Sharpton." *Nation,* August 6, 2004.

Cresce, Arthus R., and Roberto R. Ramirez. "Analysis of General Hispanic Responses in Census 2000." Working Paper No. 72 (Washington, DC: U.S. Census Bureau, 2003).

"The Dangerous Quest of Al Sharpton." *Economist,* January 19, 2002, 29.

Daniels, Roger. "The Bureau of the Census and the Relocation of the Japanese Americans: A Note and a Document." *Amerasia* 9, no. 1 (1982): 101–5.

Davis, James F. *Who Is Black? One Nation's Definition.* University Park, PA: Pennsylvania State University Press, 1991.

Davis, Philip, ed. *Immigration and Americanization: Selected Readings.* Boston: Ginn, 1920.

Dawson, Michael C. *Black Visions: The Roots of Contemporary African-American Political Ideologies.* Chicago: University of Chicago Press, 2003.

Deavere Smith, Anna. *Fires in the Mirror.* Bera Video, 1992.

"A Debate on the New Party." *Boston Review,* January/February 1993.

De Haas, Jacob. *Louis D. Brandeis: A Biographical Sketch, with Special Reference to His Contribution to Jewish and Zionist History.* New York: Bloch, 1929.

Dewey, John. "America in the World." *Nation,* March 14, 1918, 287.

———. *Education Today.* New York: Putnam, 1940.

———. "Interpretation of Savage Mind." *Psychological Review* 9, no. 3 (1902): 217–30.

———. "The Jewish Problem." In *Louis D. Brandeis: A Biographical Sketch,* edited by Jacob de Haas, 184–85. New York: Bloch, 1929.

———. "Nationalizing Education." *Journal of Education* 84, no. 16 (1916): 426–31.

———. "The Principle of Nationality." *Menorah Journal* 3, no. 4 (October 1917): 203–08.

———. "Racial Prejudice and Friction." *Chinese Social and Political Science Review* 6, no. 1 (1921): 1–17.

Diner, Hasia. *Jews in America.* New York: Oxford University Press, 1999.

———. *Lower East Side Memories: A Jewish Place in America.* Princeton, NJ: Princeton University Press, 2000.

Dionne, E. J. "Back from the Dead: Neoprogressivism in the 90s." *American Prospect* 7, no. 28 (1996): 24–32.

Downs, Anthony. *An Economic Theory of Democracy.* New York: Harper, 1957.

Drachsler, Julius. "Americanization and Race Fusion." *Menorah Journal* 6, no. 3 (1920): 131–38.

———. "The Blending of Immigrant Cultures." *Menorah Journal* 6, no. 2 (1920): 80–88.

———. *Democracy and Assimilation: The Blending of Immigrant Heritages in America.* New York: Macmillan, 1920.

Dreher, Rod. "Al on AL: Reverend Sharpton's Pre-Campaign Treatise." *National Review,* October 8, 2002.

Drucker, Jesse. "The Making of a Boogeyman." *Salon.com,* March 30, 2000. http://archive.salon.com/politics2000/feature/2000/03/30/sharpton/index.html.

Drury, Bob, Robert E. Kessler, Bob Liff, Mike McAlary, Paul Moses, and Manny Topol. "The Minister and the Mob: Feds' Data Ties Sharpton to Reputed Crime Figures." *New York Newsday,* January 22, 1988.

Drury, Bob, Robert E. Kessler, and Mike McAlary. "Black Leader: Probe FBI." *New York Newsday,* January 21, 1988.

———. "The Minister and the Feds." *New York Newsday,* January 20, 1988.

Du Bois, W. E. B. *Souls of Black Folk.* Chicago: McClurg, 1903.

Dugger, Ronnie. "Race, Class, and the Democrats." *Boston Review* (Summer 1995). http://bostonreview.net/BR20.3/dugger.html.

Dyer, Richard. "White." *Screen* 29, no. 4 (1988): 44–65.

Edmonston, Barry, Joshua Goldstein, and Juanita Tamayo Lott, eds. *Spotlight on Heterogeneity: The Federal Standards for Racial and Ethnic Classification.* Washington, DC: National Academy Press, 1996.

Edmonston, Barry, and Charles Schultze, eds. *Modernizing the U.S. Census.* Washington, DC: National Academy Press, 1995.

Edsall, Thomas, and Mary Edsall. *Chain Reaction: The Impact of Race, Rights and Taxes on American Politics.* New York: Norton, 1991.

Eliot, Charles W. "The Potency of the Jewish Race." *Menorah Journal* 1, no. 3 (1915): 141–44.

Enda, Jodi. "Great Expectations." *American Prospect* 17, no. 2 (2006): 23–27.

Eng, David, and Shinhee Han. "A Dialogue on Racial Melancholia." In *Loss,* edited by David L. Eng and David Kazanjian, 343–71. Berkeley: University of California Press, 2003.

Eng, David, and David Kazanjian, eds. *Loss: The Politics of Mourning.* Berkeley: University of California Press, 2002.

Equal Employment Opportunity Commission. *First Annual Report.* Washington, DC: Equal Employment Opportunity Commission, 1967.

Escobar, Edward J. *Race, Police, and the Making of Political Identity: Mexican Americans and the Los Angeles Police Department, 1900–1945.* Berkeley: University of California Press, 1999.

Evinger, Suzann. "How Shall We Measure Our Nation's Diversity." *Chance* 8, no. 1 (1995): 7–14.

———. "Update on OMB's Review of Directive No. 15," *Chance* 10, no. 2 (1997): 57.

Executive Order 8802. *Federal Register* 6, no. 12 (June 27, 1941): 3109.

Executive Order 9346. *Federal Register* 8 (May 29, 1943): 7183.

Executive Order 9980. *Federal Register* 13 (July 28, 1948): 4311.

Executive Order 9981. *Federal Register* 13 (July 28, 1948): 4313.

Executive Order 10308. *Federal Register* 16 (January 4, 1951): 12303.

Executive Order 10479. *Federal Register* 18 (August 18, 1953): 4899.

Executive Order 10925. *Federal Register* 26 (March 8, 1961): 1977.

Executive Order 11246. *Federal Register* 30 (September 28, 1965): 12319.

Farber, M. A. "A 'New' Sharpton: Maturing of a Maverick?" *New York Times,* January 21, 1991, B1.

Farley, Reynolds. "The New Census Question About Ancestry: What Did It Tell Us?" *Demography* 28, no. 3 (1991): 411–29.

Fears, Darryl. "The Roots of 'Hispanic' 1975 Committee of Bureaucrats Produced Designation." *Washington Post,* October 15, 2003, A21.

Federal Interagency Committee on Culture and Education. *Report of the Ad Hoc Committee on Racial and Ethnic Definitions.* U.S. Department of Health, Education and Welfare, National Institute of Education, April 1975.

Fein, David J. "Racial and Ethnic Differences in U.S. Census Omission Rates." *Demography* 27, no. 2 (1990): 285–302.

Ferguson, Roderick. "The Nightmares of the Heteronormative." *Cultural Values* 4, no. 4 (2000): 419–44.

Ferguson, Sarah "A Day without White People: On May Day, the Masses Rose Up in New York, But Where Were the White Peaceniks?" *Village Voice,* May 2, 2006.

Fernández-Kelley, M. Patricia, and Richard Schauffler. "Divided Fates: Immigrant Children and the New Assimilation." In *The New Second Generation,* edited by Alejandro Portes. New York: Russell Sage Foundation, 1996.

Ferrer, Fernando. "Help Schools Connect with Their Communities." *Newsday,* May 14, 2002, A30.

Fields, Jason M., and Charles L. Clark. "Unbinding the Ties: Edit Effects of Marital Status on Same Gender Couples." Population Division Working Paper No. 34. Washington, DC: U.S. Bureau of the Census, Fertility and Family Statistics Branch, Population Division, April 1999.

Filkins, Dexter. "Ferrer the Campaigner Offers an Old-Style Approach." *New York Times,* August 30, 2001.

———. "In Bid for Unity, Black and Hispanic Politicians Make Pledge to Back Ferrer." *New York Times,* August 18, 2001, B2.

Filkins, Dexter, and Adam Nagourney. "Courting Blacks and Latinos, Ferrer Is Walking a Fine Line." *New York Times,* September 6, 2001, A1.

Finnegan, Michael, and Richard Fausset. "Latino-Black Alliance Seems to Be Forming." *Los Angeles Times,* April 30, 2005.

Fishberg, Maurice. "Assimilation: A Statement of Facts by a Scientist." *Menorah Journal* 6, no. 1 (1920): 25–37.

———. "Physical Anthropology of the Jews. I—the Cephalic Index." *American Anthropologist,* n.s., 4 (1902): 684–706.

———. "Physical Anthropology of the Jews. II—Pigmentation." *American Anthropologist,* n.s., 5 (1905): 89–106.

———. *The Jews: A Study of Race and Environment.* London: Walter Scott, 1911.

———. "The Jews: A Study of Race and Environment." *Popular Science Monthly* 69 (September 1906): 257–67.

———. "The Jews: A Study of Race and Environment, II—Marriages." *Popular Science Monthly* 69 (November 1906): 441–50.

———. "The Jews: A Study of Race and Environment, III—Mixed Marriages between Persons of Different Christian Denominations." *Popular Science Monthly* 69 (December 1906): 502–11.

———. "The Jews: A Study of Race and Environment, IV—Mortality." *Popular Science Monthly* 70 (January 1907): 33–47.

Flacks, Richard. "Reflections on Strategy in a Dark Time: Radical Democracy—A Relic of the 60s, or an Idea Whose Time Has Come?, with Thirteen Responses." *Boston Review* (February/March 1996). http://bostonreview.net/BR20.6/flacks.html.

Foner, Nancy, and George M. Fredrickson., eds. *Not Just Black and White: Historical and Contemporary Perspectives on Immigration, Race, and Ethnicity in the United States.* New York: Russell Sage Foundation, 2004.

"Four More Years." *Dissent* 32 (1985): 5–25.

Fox, Geoffrey. *Hispanic Nation: Culture, Politics, and the Construction of Identity.* Tucson: University of Arizona Press, 1996.

Franke-Ruta, Garance. "Let's Get Ready to Rumble! Al Sharpton Gears Up to Take on the Dems." *American Prospect*, February 2003.

Fredrickson, George. *The Black Image in the White Mind: The Debate on Afro-American Character and Destiny, 1817–1914.* New York: Harper & Row, 1972.

———. *Racism: A Short History.* Princeton, NJ: Princeton University Press, 2002.

Friar, John G., and George W. Kelley. *A Practical Spanish Grammar for Border Patrol Officers.* Washington, DC: Government Printing Office, 1946.

Friesel, Evyatar. "Brandeis' Role in American Zionism Historically Reconsidered." *American Jewish History* 69 (September 1979): 34–59.

Fuchs, Lawrence H. "Immigration Reform in 1911 and 1981: The Role of Select Commissions." *Journal of American Ethnic History* 3, no. 1 (1983): 58–89.

Fuss, Diana. *Identification Papers.* New York: Routledge, 1995.

Garcia, F. Chris, ed. *Pursuing Power: Latinos and the Political System.* South Bend: University of Notre Dame Press, 1997.

Garza, Rodolfo O. de la, and Louis DeSipio, eds. *Awash in the Mainstream: Latino Politics in the 1996 Election.* Bolder, CO: Westview Press, 1999.

Garza, Rodolfo O. de la, Louis DeSipio, F. Chris Garcia, John Garcia, and Angelo Falcon. *Latino Voices: Mexican, Puerto Rican, and Cuban Perspectives on American Politics.* Boulder, CO: Westview Press, 1992.

Geller, Stuart M. "Why Did Louis D. Brandeis Choose Zionism?" *American Jewish Historical Quarterly* 62 (June 1973): 383–400.

Gerstle, Gary. *American Crucible: Race and Nation in the Twentieth Century.* Princeton, NJ: Princeton University Press, 2001.

———. "Liberty, Coercion, and the Making of Americans." *Journal of American History* 84, no. 2 (1997): 524–58.

———. "The Power of Nations." *Journal of American History* 84, no. 2 (1997): 576–80.

———. "The Protean Character of American Liberalism." *American Historical Review* 99, no. 4 (1994): 1043–73.

———. "Race and the Myth of the Liberal Consensus." *Journal of American History* (September 1995): 579–586.

———. "Theodore Roosevelt and the Divided Character of American Nationalism." *Journal of American History* 86, no. 3 (1999): 1280–1307.

———. *Working-Class Americanism: The Politics of Labor in a Textile City, 1914–1960.* Princeton, NJ: Princeton University Press, 1989.

———. "The Working Class Goes to War." *Mid-America: A Historical Review* 75, no. 3 (1993): 303–22.

———. "Working-Class Racism: Broaden the Focus." *International Labor and Working-Class History* 44 (Fall 1993): 33–40.

Gibson, Campbell J., and Kay Jung. "Historical Census Statistics on Population Totals by Race, 1790 to 1990, and by Hispanic Origin, 1970 to 1990, for Large Cities and Other Urban Places in the United States." Working Paper Series No. 76. Washington, DC: U.S. Bureau of the Census, Population Division, February 2005.

———. "Historical Census Statistics on Population Totals by Race, 1790 to 1990, and by Hispanic Origin, 1970 to 1990, for the United States, Regions, Divisions, and States." Working Paper Series No. 56. Washington, DC: U.S. Bureau of the Census, Population Division, September 2002.

Gibson, Campbell J., and Emily Lennon. "Historical Census Statistics on the Foreign-born Population of the United States: 1850–1990." Population Division Working Paper No. 29. Washington, DC: U.S. Bureau of the Census, Population Division, February 1999.

Gilroy, Paul. *The Black Atlantic: Modernity and Double-Consciousness.* Cambridge, MA: Harvard University Press, 1993.

———. "Ethnic Absolutism." In *Small Acts: Thoughts on the Politics of Black Cultures,* edited by Paul Gilroy. New York: Serpents Tail, 1994.

Gimenez, Martha E. "Latino/'Hispanic'—Who Needs a Name? The Case against a Standardized Terminology." *International Journal of Health Services* 19, no. 3 (1989): 557–71.

Gitlin, Todd. *Twilight of Common Dreams: Why America Is Wracked by Culture Wars.* New York: Holt, 1995.

Glazer, Nathan. "Ethnic Groups in America." In *Freedom and Control in Modern Society,* edited by Morroe Berger, Theodore Abel, and Charles H. Page. New York: Octagon Books, 1978.

Glazer, Nathan, and Daniel Patrick Moynihan. *Beyond the Melting Pot.* Cambridge, MA: MIT Press, 1963.

———. *Ethnic Dilemmas, 1964–1982.* Cambridge, MA: Harvard University Press, 1983.

Glick, Leonard. "Types Distinct from Our Own: Franz Boas on Jewish Identity and Assimilation." *American Anthropologist,* n.s., 84 (1984): 545–65.

Gold, Matea. "New Coalitions Forged in an Upbeat L.A." *Los Angeles Times,* April 11, 2001.

———. "Villaraigosa Lets Others Court Latinos." *Los Angeles Times,* June 2, 2001, home edition, A1.

Gold, Matea, James Rainey, and Jeffrey L. Rabin. "Final Debate an Angry One." *Los Angeles Times,* June 1, 2001, A1.

Goldenweiser, Alexander A. "Concerning 'Racial Differences.'" *Menorah Journal* 8, no. 5 (1922): 309–16.

Goldenweiser, E. A. "The Mother Tongue Inquiry in the Census of Population." *Publications of the American Statistical Association* 13, no. 104 (1913): 648–55.

Goldstein, Richard. "Al Sharpton's Jewish Problem." *Village Voice,* November 20, 2001, 36–38.

Gomez, Laura E., "The Birth of the 'Hispanic' Generation: Attitudes of Mexican-American Political Elites toward the Hispanic Label." *Latin American Perspectives* 19, no. 4 (1992): 45–58.

Gonzalez, Juan. "Mark Must Take Blame." *Daily News,* November 8, 2001.

Gordon, Linda. *The Great Arizona Orphan Abduction.* Cambridge, MA: Harvard University Press, 2001.

Gordon, Milton. *Assimilation in American Life: The Role of Race, Religion, and National Origins.* New York: Oxford University Press, 1964.

Gordon, Nancy M. "Race and Ethnicity Testing: Update and Discussion." Handout distributed at the REAC Meetings, May 5–7, 2004, Washington, DC.

Goren, Arthur. *New York Jews and the Quest for Community: The Kehillah Experiment, 1908–1922.* New York: Columbia University Press, 1970.

Gossett, Thomas F. *Race: The History of an Idea in America.* New York: Oxford University Press, 1997.

"Gotbaum Victorious, Virtually Assuring Election." *New York Times,* October 12, 2001, Metro section, D10.

Gotlieb, Martin. "Street-Wise Impresario: Sharpton Calls the Tunes, and Players Take Their Cues." *New York Times,* December 19, 1991, B1.

Gottlieb, Robert, Regina Freer, Mark Villianatos, and Peter Dreier. *The Next Los Angeles: The Struggle for a Livable City.* Berkeley: University of California Press, 2005.

Gould, Stephen Jay. *The Mismeasure of Man.* New York: Norton, 1981.

Graham, Hugh Davis. *The Strange Convergence of Affirmative Action and Immigration Policy in America.* New York: Oxford University Press, 2002.

Grant, Madison. "America for the Americans." *Forum* 74 (September 1925): 346–55.

———. "Closing the Flood-Gates." In *The Alien in Our Midst or "Selling Our Birthright for a Mess of Industrial Pottage,"* edited by Madison Grant and Charles Stewart Davidson. New York: Galton, 1930.

———. *The Passing of the Great Race: or, the Racial Basis of European History.* New York: Scribner's, 1916.

Grant, Madison, and Charles Stewart Davidson, eds. *The Alien in Our Midst or "Selling Our Birthright for a Mess of Industrial Pottage."* New York: Galton, 1930.

Greenberg, David. *Nixon's Shadow: The History of an Image* (New York: Norton, 2003).

Greenhouse, Stephen. "Immigrant Rally in City, Seeking Rights." *New York Times,* October 5, 2003.

Grieco, Elizabeth, and Rachael C. Cassidy. "Overview of Race and Hispanic Origin. Census 2000 Brief." U.S. Department of Commerce, Economics and Statistics Administration, U.S. Census Bureau, 2001.

Griffith, Jeanne E. "Update on Statistics for Americans of Spanish Origin or Descent." *Statistical Reporter* (September 1980): 401–5.

Gritter, Matthew. "Unfulfilled Promise? Latinos and the Origins of Anti-Discrimination Policy." Paper presented at Race and U.S. Political Development, University of Oregon, Eugene, OR, May 11–12, 2006.

Guglielmo, Thomas A. "Fighting for Caucasian Rights: Mexicans, Mexican Americans, and the Transnational Struggle for Civil Rights in World War II Texas." *Journal of American History* 92, no. 4 (2006): 1212–37.

Gutiérrez, David. *Walls and Mirrors: Mexican Americans, Mexican Immigrants, and the Politics of Ethnicity.* Berkeley: University of California Press, 1995.

Halberstam, Judith. *Female Masculinity.* Durham, NC: Duke University Press, 1998.

Hall, G. Stanley. "Yankee and Jew." *Menorah Journal* 1, no. 2 (1915): 87–90.

Halladjian, In re. 174 F. 834 (C.C.D. Mass. 1909).

Halpern, Ben. "Brandeis' Way to Zionism." *Midstream: A Monthly Jewish Review* (October 1971): 3–13.

Hamill, Pete. "Freddy Will Pick Own Top Cop." *New York Daily News*, October 10, 2001.

Hammond, Maurice S. "Some Experiments in Cultural Pluralism." *Journal of Educational Sociology* 12, no. 8 (1939): 476–81.

Haney López, Ian. "Hispanics and the Shrinking White Majority." *Daedalus* 134, no. 1 (2005): 42–52.

———. *Racism on Trial: The Chicano Fight for Justice.* Cambridge, MA: Belknap/Harvard University Press, 2003.

———. *White by Law: The Legal Construction of Race.* New York: New York University Press, 1996.

Hansen, Marcus L. "The History of American Immigration as a Field for Research." *American Historical Review* 32, no. 3 (1927): 500–18.

Hapgood, Norman. "The Future of the Jews in America." *Harper's Weekly,* November 27, 1915, 511–12.

———. "The Jews and American Democracy." *Menorah Journal* 2, no. 4 (1916): 201–5.

———. "The Jews and American Democracy." *Menorah Journal* 2, no. 5 (1916): 277–84.

Harris, Cheryl. "Whiteness as Property." *Harvard Law Review* 106, no. 8 (1993): 1709–91.

Hart, Hastings H. "Immigration and Crime." *American Journal of Sociology* 2, no. 3 (1896): 369–77.

Hartog, Marcus. "The Spencer-Weismann Controversy." *Contemporary Review* 64 (July 1893): 50–59.

Hattam, Victoria. "Ethnicity and the American Boundaries of Race." *Daedalus* 134, no. 1 (2005): 61–69.

———."The 1964 Civil Rights Act: Narrating the Past, Authorizing the Future." *Studies in American Political Development* 18, no. 1 (2004): 60–69.

———. "Whiteness: Theorizing Race, Eliding Ethnicity." *International Race and Working Class History* 60 (Fall 2001): 61–68.

Hattam, Victoria, and Joseph Lowndes. "Ground Beneath Our Feet: Language, Culture and Political Change." In *Formative Acts: American Politics in the Making,* edited by Stephen Skowronek and Matthew Glassman. Philadelphia: University of Pennsylvania Press, 2007.

Hayes-Bautista, and Jorge Chapa. "Latino Terminology: Conceptual Bases for Standardized Terminology," *AJPH* 77, no. 1 (1987): 61–68.

Healy, Patrick D., and Diane Cardwell. "Political Memo; Ferrer Being Hurt by Self-Inflicted Wounds." *New York Times*, September 30, 2005, Metropolitan Desk.

Herford, R. Travers. "The Truth about the Pharisees." Menorah Pamphlets No. 3. New York: Intercollegiate Menorah Association, 1925.

Hernandez, Jose, Leo Estrada, and David Alvirez. "Census Data and the Problem of Conceptually Defining the Mexican American Population." *Social Science Quarterly* 53, no. 4 (1973): 671–87.

Hernandez, Nathaniel. "Chicago Protest Draws Diverse Support." *Chicago Defender,* May 1, 2006.

Herndon, Andre, Gene C. Johnson Jr., and Marisela Santana. "Latinos Draw Multiethnic Support on May Day." *Wave Newspapers*, May 5, 2006.

Hicks, Jonathan P. "Green's Campaign Angers Backers of Ferrer." *New York Times*, October 13, 2001, D3.

Higham, John. *Send These to Me: Jews and Other Immigrants in Urban America*. New York: Atheneum, 1975.

———. *Strangers in the Land: Patterns of American Nativism, 1860–1925*. New York: Atheneum, 1963.

Hirschman, Charles. "How to Measure Ethnicity: An Immodest Proposal." In *Challenges of Measuring an Ethnic World: Science, Politics and Reality*. Proceedings of the Joint Canada-U.S. Conference on the Measurement of Ethnicity, Ottawa, Canada, April 1–3, 1992. Washington, DC: Government Printing Office, 1993.

Hirschman, Charles, Philip Kasinitz, and Josh De Wind, eds. *The Handbook of International Migration: The American Experience*. New York: Russell Sage Foundation, 1999.

Hochschild, Jennifer. *Facing Up to the American Dream: Race, Class, and the Soul of Nation*. Princeton, NJ: Princeton University Press, 1995.

———. "From Nominal to Ordinal: Reconceiving Racial and Ethnic Hierarchy in the United States." In *The Politics of Democratic Inclusion*, edited by Christina Wolbrecht and Rodney Hero. Philadelphia: Temple University Press, 2005.

———. *What's Fair: American Beliefs About Distributive Justice*. Cambridge, MA: Harvard University Press, 1981.

Hollinger, David A. *In the American Province*. Bloomington: Indiana University Press, 1985.

———. "National Solidarity at the End of the Twentieth Century: Reflections on the United States and Liberal Nationalism," *Journal of American History* 84, no. 2 (1997): 559–69.

———. "The One Drop & the One Hate Rule." *Daedalus* 134, no. 1 (2005): 18–28.

———. "Postethnic America," *Contention* 2, no. 1 (1992): 79–96.

———. *Postethnic America: Beyond Multiculturalism*. New York: Basic Books, 1995.

Hook, Sidney. "National Unity and Corporate 'Thinking.'" *Menorah Journal* 30, no. 1 (1942): 61–68.

Horowitz, Craig. "The Anti-Sharpton." *New York Magazine*, January 26, 1998.

———. "30th Anniversary Issue/Al Sharpton: The Rev." *New York Magazine*, April 6, 1998.

House Committee on Government Reform and Oversight. *Federal Measures of Race and Ethnicity and the Implications for the 2000 Census: Hearings before the Subcommittee on Government Management, Information, and Technology*. 105th Cong., 1st sess. April 23, May 22, and July 25, 1997. Serial No. 105–57. Washington, DC: Government Printing Office, 1998.

House Committee on Immigration and Naturalization. *Immigration from Countries of the Western Hemisphere: Hearings before the House Committee on Immigration and Naturalization*. February 21, 24, 25, 27–29; March 1, 2, 7; April 5, 1928. Washington, DC: Government Printing Office, 1928.

———. *Immigration from Countries of the Western Hemisphere: Hearings before the House Committee on Immigration and Naturalization*. Statement of James H. Patten. 70th Cong., 1st sess. March 7, 1927. Washington, DC: Government Printing Office, 1927.

———. *Immigration from Countries of the Western Hemisphere: Report*. 71st Cong., 2nd sess. March 13, 1930. Washington, DC: Government Printing Office, 1930.

———. *Immigration from Mexico: Hearings before the Committee on Immigration and Naturalization*. 71st Cong., 2nd sess. May 15, 1930. Washington, DC: Government Printing Office, 1930.

House Committee on Post Office and Civil Service. *Review of Federal Measures of Race and Ethnicity: Hearings before the Subcommittee on Census, Statistics, and Postal Personnel*. 103rd Cong., 1st sess. April 14, June 30, July 29, and November 3, 1993. Washington, DC: Government Printing Office, 1994.

Howell, Ron. "The Minister and the Fugitive: Sharpton Tried to Trap Chesimard for Feds in 1983, Activists Charge." *New York Newsday*, October 21, 1988.

Hsu, Ruth Y. "Will the Model Minority Please Identify Itself? American Ethnic Identity and Its Discontents." *Diaspora* 5, no. 1 (1996): 37–63.

Hudson, Nicholas. "From 'Nation' to 'Race': The Origin of Racial Classification in Eighteenth-Century Thought." *Eighteenth Century Studies* 29, no. 3 (1996): 247–64.

Hull, Gloria T., Patricia Bell Scott, and Barbara Smith. *All the Women Are White, All the Blacks Are Men, but Some of Us Are Brave: Black Women's Studies*. New York: Feminist Press, 1982.

Hurwitz, Henry. "The Menorah Movement." *Menorah Journal* 1, no. 1 (1915): 50–56.

Hurwitz, Henry, and Leo I. Sharfman. *The Menorah Movement: For the Study and Advancement of Jewish Culture and Ideals*. Ann Arbor, MI: Intercollegiate Menorah Association, 1914.

Hutchinson, Edward P. *Legislative History of American Immigration Policy 1798–1965*. Philadelphia: University of Pennsylvania Press, 1981.

Ignatiev, Noel. *How the Irish Became White*. New York: Routledge, 1995.

Immigration Act of March 3, 1903. *U.S. Statutes at Large* 32 (1903): 1213.

Immigration Act of 1907. *United States Immigration Commission*, 39:85–86, 94. Washington, DC: Government Printing Office, 1911.

Immigration Act of February 5, 1917. Public Law 64-301. *U.S. Statutes at Large* 39 (1917): 874.

Immigration Act of May 19, 1921. Public Law 67-5. *U.S. Statutes at Large* 42 (1921): 5.

Immigration Act of May 26, 1924. Public Law 68-139. *U.S. Statutes at Large* 43 (1924): 153.

"The Impact of Al Sharpton Endorsement." New York-WABC. *7Online.com*, August 17, 2001.

Inter-Agency Committee on Mexican Affairs. *The Mexican American: A New Focus on Opportunity*. Testimony presented at the Cabinet Committee Hearings on Mexican American Affairs, El Paso, TX, October 26–28, 1967. Washington, DC: Government Printing Office, 1967.

Jacobs, Joseph. "Are Jews Jews?" *Popular Science Monthly* 55, no. 4 (1899): 502–11.

———. "The Jews in the War." *Menorah Journal* 1, no. 1 (1915): 23–25.

———. "Liberalism and the Jew." *Menorah Journal* 1, no. 5 (1915): 298–308.

Jacobson, Matthew Frye. *Whiteness of a Different Color: European Immigrants and the Alchemy of Race*. Cambridge, MA: Harvard University Press, 1998.

Jacoby, Tamar. "Republicans and Their Amigos: GOP No Longer for the Gringos-Only Party." *Weekly Standard*, November 25, 2002.

Johnson, Lyndon B. "Commencement Address," June 4, 1965.

———. "Special Message to the Congress: The American Promise. March 15, 1965." In *Public Papers of the Presidents of the United States, Lyndon B. Johnson, Containing the Public Messages, Speeches, and Statements of the President, 1965, Book 1—January 1 to May 31, 1965.* Washington, DC: Government Printing Office, 1966.

Jones, Van. "Shout 'Viva!' Anyhow: On Being Black at a Latino March." *New America Media*, May 4, 2006.

Jones-Correa, Michael. *Between Two Nations: The Political Predicament of Latinos in New York City.* Ithaca, NY: Cornell University Press, 1998.

Jones-Correa, Michael, and David L. Leal. "Becoming 'Hispanic': Secondary Panethnic Identification among Latin American-Origin Populations in the United States." *Hispanic Journal of the Behavioral Sciences* 18, no. 2 (1996): 214–54.

Jordan, Lara Jakes. "Border Security Plans Criticized: Both Parties Say They Doubt Measures Will Work Effectively." Associated Press, July 27, 2006.

Jordan, Winthrop D. *The White Man's Burden: Historical Origins of Racism in the United States.* New York: Oxford University Press, 1974.

Judd, Dennis R. "Symbolic Politics and Urban Policies: Why African Americans Got So Little from the Democrats." In *Without Justice for All*, edited by Adolph Reed Jr. Boulder, CO: Westview Press, 1999.

Judis, John B., and Ruy Teixeira. *The Emerging Democratic Majority.* New York: Scribner, 2002.

Kallen, Horace M. "Beyond the Melting Pot: A Study of American Nationality." *Nation*, February 18, 1915, 190–94.

———. "Can Judaism Survive in the United States?" *Menorah Journal* 11, no. 2 (1925): 101–13.

———. "Can Judaism Survive in the United States?" *Menorah Journal* 11, no. 6 (1925): 544–59.

———. "A Contradiction in Terms." *Menorah Journal* 13, no. 5 (1927): 479–86.

———. *Culture and Democracy in the United States.* New York: Boni & Liveright, 1924.

———. "Cultural Pluralism." Text of speech delivered at the Jewish Frontier Anniversary Dinner, Hotel Commodore. February 12. No year given.

———. "Democracy, Nationality, and Zionism." *Maccabaean*, July 1918, 175–76, 227.

———. "Democracy versus the Melting Pot." *Nation*, February 18, 1915, 190–98.

———. "Democracy versus the Melting Pot." *Nation*, February 25, 1915, 217–20.

———. "The Ethics of Zionism." *Maccabaean* 11, no. 2 (1906): 61–71.

———. "Facing the Facts of Palestine," *Menorah Journal* 7, no. 3 (1921): 133–42.

———. "Facing the Facts of Palestine," *Menorah Journal* 7, no. 4 (1921): 238–43.

———. "The Issues of the War and the Jewish Position." *Nation*, November 24, 1917, 590–92.

———. "The Meaning of Americanism." *Immigrants in America Review*, January 1916, 12–19.

———. "Nationality and the Hyphenated American." *Menorah Journal* 1, no. 2 (1915): 79–86.

———. "National Solidarity and the Jewish Minority." *Annals of the American Academy of Political and Social Science* 223 (September 1942): 17–28.

———. "Pluralism and American Jewish Identity." *American Jewish History* 88 (March 1997): 57–74.

———. "Spinoza: Three Hundred Years After," *Menorah Journal* 31, no. 1 (1945): 1–15.

———. "The Struggle for Jewish Unity." An Address by Horace M. Kallen before the Eleventh Annual Session of the American Jewish Congress, Washington, DC, May 21, 1933. New York: AD Press, n.d.

———. *What I Believe and Why—Maybe: Essays for the Modern World.* Edited by Alfred J. Marrow. New York: Horizon Press, 1971.

———. "Zionism and the Struggle Towards Democracy." *Nation,* September 23, 1915, 379–80.

———. "Zionism: Democracy or Prussianism." *New Republic,* April 5, 1919, 311–13.

Kallen, Horace, M., and James Weldon Johnson. *Africa in the World Democracy.* New York: National Association for the Advancement of Colored People, 1919.

Kallen, Horace, M., and Sidney Hook, eds. *American Philosophy Today and Tomorrow.* New York: Lee Furman, 1935.

Kang, K. Conie. "Asian Americans Lean to Democrats, Poll Says." *Los Angeles Times,* November 10, 2000.

Kaplan, Erin Aubry. "What Was Lost in the Crowd." *Los Angeles Times,* May 3, 2006.

Kaplan, Mordecai M., "The Future of Judaism." *Menorah Journal* 2, no. 3 (1916): 160–72.

———. "How May Judaism Be Saved." *Menorah Journal* 2, no. 1 (1916): 34–44.

———. "Judaism and Christianity." *Menorah Journal* 2, no. 2 (1916): 105–15.

———. "Judaism as a Civilization: Religion's Place in It." *Menorah Journal* 15, no. 6 (1928): 501–14.

———. "A Program for the Reconstruction of Judaism." *Menorah Journal* 6, no. 4 (1920): 181–96.

———. "Toward a Reconstruction of Judaism." *Menorah Journal* 13, no. 2 (1927): 113–30.

———. "Toward a Reconstruction of Judaism." Menorah Pamphlets No. 4. New York: Intercollegiate Menorah Association, 1927.

———. "What Is Judaism?" *Menorah Journal* 1, no. 5 (1915): 309–18.

———. "What Judaism Is Not." *Menorah Journal* 1, no. 4 (1915): 208–16.

———. "Where Does Jewry Really Stand Today?" *Menorah Journal* 4, no. 1 (1918): 33–43.

Kaplowitz, Craig. "A Distinct Minority: Lulac, Mexican American Identity, and Presidential Policymaking, 1965–1972." *Journal of Policy History* 15, no. 2 (2003): 192–222.

Kasfir, Nelson. "Explaining Ethnic Political Participation." *World Politics* 31, no. 1 (1979): 5–16.

Kasinitz, Philip. *Caribbean New York: Black Immigrants and the Politics of Race.* Ithaca, NY: Cornell University Press, 1992.

Katznelson, Ira. *Black Men, White Cities: Race, Politics, and Migration in the United States, 1900–30, and Britain, 1948–68.* Chicago: University of Chicago Press, 1973.

———. *City Trenches: Urban Politics and the Patterning of Class in the United States.* New York: Pantheon, 1981.

———. *When Affirmative Action Was White: An Untold History of Racial Inequality in Twentieth-Century America.* New York: Norton, 2005.

Katznelson, Ira, and Aristide Zolberg, eds. *Working Class Formation: Nineteenth Century Patterns in Western Europe and the United States.* Princeton, NJ: Princeton University Press, 1985.

Kazal, Russell A. "Revisiting Assimilation: The Rise, Fall, and Reappraisal of a Concept in American Ethnic History." *American Historical Review* 100, no. 2 (1995): 437–71.

Kellor, Frances. "What Is Americanization?" *Yale Review*, January 1919, 282–99.

Kim, Claire Jean. *Bitter Fruit: The Politics of Black-Korean Conflict in New York City.* New Haven, CT: Yale University Press, 2000.

———. "Playing the Racial Trump Card: Asian Americans in Contemporary U.S. Politics." Paper presented at the annual meeting of the American Political Science Association, Atlanta, September 2–5, 1999.

———. "The Racial Triangulation of Asian Americans." *Politics and Society* 27, no. 1 (1999): 105–38

Kim, Gus. "Yes, We Can: A Firsthand Account of a Day Without Immigrants." *F Newsmagazine*, May 2, 2006.

King, Desmond. *The Liberty of Strangers: Making the American Nation.* New York: Oxford University Press, 2005.

———. *Making Americans: Immigration, Race, and the Origins of the Diverse Democracy.* Cambridge, MA: Harvard University Press, 2000.

King, Desmond, and Rogers Smith. "Racial Orders in American Political Development." *American Political Science Review* 99 (2005): 75–88.

Klein, Joe. "Why Barack Obama Could Be the Next President." *Time*, October 23, 2006, 44–49.

Klein, Michael. *The Man Behind the Sound Bite: The Real Story of the Rev. Al Sharpton.* New York: Castillo International, 1991.

Klingenstein, Susanne. *Jews in the American Academy, 1900–1940.* New Haven, CT: Yale University Press, 1991.

Kloberdanz, Kristin "The Immigrants' Dilemma: To Boycott or Not to Boycott? A Split Is Growing over How Militant the Upcoming 'Day Without Immigrants' Should Be." *Time*, April 18, 2006.

Kohler, Max J., and Abram I. Elkus. "Brief for the Petitioner in the Matter of Hersch Skuratowski." In *United States Immigration Commission*, 41:267. Washington, DC: Government Printing Office, 1911.

Kolbert, Elizabeth. "The People's Preacher." *New Yorker*, February 18 & 25, 2002, 156–67.

Kondracke, Morton M. "Pence-Hutchinson Bill Creates Hope on Immigration." *Roll Call*, July 27, 2006, 6.

Korelitz, Seth. "The Menorah Idea: From Religion to Culture, from Race to Ethnicity." *American Jewish History* 85, no. 1 (1997): 75–100.

Kramer, Michael. "Ghosts of 1989 Could Haunt Mayoral Primary." *Daily News*, September 9, 2001, 4–5.

Kroeber, Alfred L. "Are the Jews a Race?" *Menorah Journal* 3, no. 5 (1917): 290–94.

Kroeber, Theodora. *Alfred Kroeber: A Personal Configuration.* Berkeley: University of California Press, 1970.

Kryder, Daniel. *Divided Arsenal: Race and the American State During World War II.* New York: Cambridge University Press, 2000.

Kuttner, Robert. "Up from 1994." *American Prospect* 6, no. 20 (1995).

Laclau, Ernesto. *Emancipation(s)*. New York: Verso, 1996.

Lancer, Susan S. "Feminist Criticism, 'The Yellow Wallpaper,' and the Politics of Color in America." *Feminist Studies* 15, no. 3 (1989): 415–41.

Lau v. Nichols. 414 U.S. 563 (1974).

Lauretis, Teresa de. *The Practice of Love: Lesbian Sexuality and Perverse Desire*. Bloomington: Indiana University Press, 1994.

Le Bon, Gustave. *The Psychology of Peoples*. New York: Arno Press, 1974.

Lehman, Irving. "Our Duty as Americans." *Menorah Journal* 4, no. 1 (1918): 6–10.

———. "Our Spiritual inheritance." *Menorah Journal* 1, no. 5 (1915): 277–81.

Lee, Sharon M. "Racial Classifications in the U.S. Census: 1890–1990." *Ethnic and Racial Studies* 16, no. 1 (1993): 75–94.

Leibovich, Mark. " 'Pit Bull' of the House Latches on to Immigration." *New York Times*, July 11, 2006, A1, A16.

Lesser, Jeff H. "Always 'Outsiders': Asians, Naturalization, and the Supreme Court." *Amerasia Journal* 12, no. 1 (1985–86): 83–100.

Lester, Will. "Political Parties Court Hispanic Vote." Associated Press, March 14, 2003.

Lewishon, Ludwig. "The Fallacies of Assimilation." *Menorah Journal* 11, no. 5 (1925): 460–68.

Lieberman, Robert. *Shifting the Color Line: Race and the American Welfare State*. Cambridge, MA: Harvard University Press, 1998.

Lipsitz, George. *The Possessive Investment in Whiteness: How White People Profit from Identity Politics*. Philadelphia: Temple University Press, 1998.

Locke, Alain. "Pluralism and Ideological Peace." In *Freedom and Experience*, edited by Sidney Hook and Milton R. Konvitz, 63–69. Ithaca, NY: Cornell University Press, 1947.

———. "Values and Imperatives." In *American Philosophy Today and Tomorrow*, edited by Horace Kallen and Sidney Hook, 312. New York: Furman, 1935.

Lockwood, George, George Vanson, and Clerk Josephine Ortiz. *Manual of Immigration Spanish*. Washington, DC: U.S. Commissioner of Immigration and Naturalization, 1936.

Lodge, Henry Cabot. "Lynch Law and Unrestricted Immigration." *North American Review* 152, no. 414 (1891): 602–12.

———. "The Restriction of Immigration." *North American Review* 152, no. 410 (1891): 27–36.

Lopez, Steve. "Villaraigosa Was Ill-Prepared for Letter Bomb." *Los Angeles Times*, June 6, 2001, home edition, A-21.

Lorde, Audre. *Sister Outsider: Essays and Speeches by Audre Lorde*. Freedom, CA: Crossing Press, 1984.

Lott, Eric. *Love and Theft: Blackface Minstrelsy and the American Working Class*. New York: Oxford University Press, 1995.

Lott, Juanita Tamayo. *Asian Americans: From Racial Category to Multiple Identities*. New York: Alta Mira/Rowman & Littlefield, 1998.

Lowe, Lisa. *Immigrant Acts: On Asian American Cultural Politics*. Durham: Duke University Press, 1996.

Lowndes, Joseph. "The Southern Origins of Modern Conservatism: 1945–1976." PhD diss., New School for Social Research, 2003.

Lowry, Ira S. "The Science and Politics of Ethnic Enumeration." In *Ethnicity and Public Policy*, edited by Winston A. Van Horne, 42–61. Madison: University of Wisconsin Press, 1982.

Lowry, Richard. "Disrespecting Sharpton." *National Review*, September 14, 1998.

MacDonald, Heather. "Al Sharpton Just Won't Let Racial Wounds Heal." *Wall Street Journal*, August 31, 2000.

Maceri, Domenico. "Bush and Latinos: Beyond Espanol?" *Hispanicvista*, January 27, 2003.

Mack, Julian W. *Americanism and Zionism*. New York: Zionist Organization of America, 1919.

———. "Jewish Hopes at the Peace Table." *Menorah Journal* 5, no. 1 (1919): 1–7.

Manegold, Catherine S. "The Reformation of a Street Preacher: Al Sharpton Tries on the Power of 166,000 Votes." *New York Times Magazine*, January 24, 1993, 18.

Martin, Douglas. "In Brooklyn, Two Worlds on an Edge: At the Scene of a Bias Beating, a Line Divides Red Hook and Carroll Gardens." *New York Times*, September 28, 1977, Metropolitan Desk, 35, 38.

Martin, Elizabeth, David Sheppard, Michael Bentley, and Claudette Bennett. *Results of 2003 National Census Test of Race and Hispanic Questions*. Washington, DC: U.S. Bureau of the Census, 2003.

Mason, Julie. "Hispanic Vote Called a Toss-Up: Neither Party Has Lock, Latino Coalition's Poll Indicate." *Houston Chronicle.com*, September 19, 2002.

Matthews, F. H. "The Revolt against Americanism: Cultural Pluralism and Cultural Relativism." *Canadian Review of American Studies* 1, no. 1 (1970): 4–31.

Mayer, William. "Doing the Harlem Shuffle: Al Sharpton's Traveling Minstrel Show." *Ether Zone*, January 14, 2002.

Mayo-Smith, Richmond. "Assimilation of Nationalities in the United States—I." *Political Science Quarterly* 9, no. 3 (1894): 426–44.

———. "Assimilation of Nationalities in the United States—II." *Political Science Quarterly* 9, no. 4 (December 1894): 649–70.

———. "Control of Immigration—I." *Political Science Quarterly* 3, no. 1 (1888): 46–77.

———. "Control of Immigration—II." *Political Science Quarterly* 3, no. 2 (1888): 197–225.

———. "Control of Immigration—III." *Political Science Quarterly* 3, no. 3 (1888): 409–24.

McClain, Paula D., and John A. Garcia. "Expanding Disciplinary Boundaries: Black, Latino, and Racial Minority Group Politics in Political Science." In *Political Science: The State of the Discipline*, edited by Ada W. Finifter, 247–79. Washington, DC: APSA, 1993.

McClymer, John F. "The Federal Government and the Americanization Movement." *Prologue* 10, no. 1 (1978): 23–41.

McDonnell, Patrick J. "Ethnicity Issue Mixed Blessing for Villaraigosa." *Los Angeles Times*, May 28, 2001, home edition, A-1.

McFadden, Robert D., Ralph Blumenthal, M. A. Farber, E. R. Shipp, Charles Strum, and Craig Wolff. *Outrage: The Story Behind the Tawana Brawley Hoax*. New York: Bantam Books, 1990.

McGee, W. J. "Anthropology and Its Larger Problems." *Science*, n.s., 21, no. 542 (1905): 770–84.

———. "Man's Place in Nature." *American Anthropologist*, n.s., 3, no. 1 (1901): 1–13.

———. "The Science of Humanity." *American Anthropologist* 10, no. 8 (1897): 241–72.

———. "The Trend of Human Progress." *American Anthropologist*, n.s., 1, no. 3 (1899): 401–47.

McGinty, Jo Craven. "Breaking Down Hate Crime," *New York Times*, July 24, 2005, Metro section.

McWilliams, Carey. *North from Mexico: The Spanish-Speaking People of the United States.* New York: Praeger, 1990.

Mehta, Uday Singh. *Liberalism and Empire: A Study in Nineteenth-Century British Liberal Thought.* Chicago: University of Chicago Press, 1999.

Menorah Journal. "Census of Jewish Students." *Menorah Journal*, 2, no. 4 (1916): 260–62.

———. "Census of Jewish Students." *Menorah Journal* 3, no. 4 (1917): 252–53.

———. *Third of a Century Index, 1915–1948.* New York: Menorah Association, 1948.

Menorah Society Archives. *Minutes*, 1906–8, 1909–15. Harvard University, General Folder.

Mettler, Suzanne. *Soldiers to Citizens: The GI Bill and the Making of the Greatest Generation.* New York: Oxford University Press, 2005.

Meyerson, Harold. "Clinton Proposes, We Respond." *Dissent* 40, no. 2 (1993): 137–65.

———. "Race Conquers All: In New York as in L.A., Racial Politics Thwarts a Rebirth of Urban Liberalism." *American Prospect* 12, no. 21 (2001).

Miles, Jack. "Blacks vs. Browns: The Struggle for the Bottom Rung." *Atlantic Monthly*, October 1992, 41–68.

Miller, Laura S. "The Language of Group Hierarchy: Keeping Ethnics and Immigrants Away from American Blacks," MA portfolio, Department of Political Science, New School for Social Research, Fall 2002.

Milton, Barbara, and David Pemberton. "Oral History: Interview with Vincent P. Barabba." Available from the U.S. Bureau of the Census, August 7, 1989, 28–30.

Mitchell, John. "Immigration and the American Laboring Classes." *Annals of the American Academy of Political and Social Science* 34, no. 1 (1909): 125–29.

Mitchell, Timothy. "The Limits of the State." *American Political Science Review* 85, no. 1 (1991): 77–96.

Mollenkopf, John. "New York: The Great Anomaly." In *Racial Politics in American Cities*, edited by Rufus P. Browning, Dale Rogers Marshall, and David Tabb. New York: Longman, 1997.

———. *A Phoenix in the Ashes: The Rise and Fall of the Koch Coalition in New York City Politics.* Princeton, NJ: Princeton University Press, 1992.

Molyneaux, Guy. "Putting the Middle Class First." *Dissent* 40, no. 2 (1993): 133–36.

Montejano, David. *Anglos and Mexicans in the Making of Texas, 1836–1986.* Austin: University of Texas Press, 1987.

Montgomery, Alicia. "Brothers under the Skin." *Salon.com*, March 15, 2001. http://archive.salon.com/news/feature/2001/03/15/horowitz/.

Moore, Deborah Dash. *At Home in America: Second Generation New York Jews.* New York: Columbia University Press, 1981.

Moraga, Cherríe L., and Gloria Anzaldúa. *This Bridge Called My Back: Writings by Radical Women of Color.* Watertown, MA: Persephone Press, 1981.

Morena, José F., ed. *The Elusive Quest for Equality: 150 Years of Chicano/Chicana Education*. Cambridge, MA: Harvard Educational Review, 1999.

Morris, Jeffrey B., and Richard B. Morris. *Encyclopedia of American History*. 7th edition. New York: HarperCollins, 1996.

Morrison, Toni. "On the Backs of Blacks." In *Arguing Immigration: Are New Immigrants a Wealth of Diversity. Or a Crushing Burden?* edited by Nicholas Mills. New York: Simon & Schuster, 1994.

———. *Playing in the Dark: Whiteness in the Literary Imagination*. New York: Vintage, 1993.

———. "Unspeakable Things Unspoken: The Afro American Presence in American Literature." *Michigan Quarterly Review* 28, no. 1 (1989): 1–34.

Morton, William E. "U.S. Bureau of the Census List of Spanish Surnames." Revised as of October 20, 1967. Oregon: University of Oregon Medical School, 1968.

Mumford, Lewis. "Nationalism or Culturalism? A Search for True Community." *Menorah Journal* 8, no. 3 (1922): 129–33.

Munoz, Jose. *Disidentification: Queers of Color and the Performance of Politics*. Minneapolis: University of Minnesota Press, 1999.

Murphy, Dean E., and Michael Cooper. "Bloomberg Sees Race Overtones in Final Days of Green Effort." *New York Times*, October 17, 2001, D1, D3.

Murphy, Jarrett. "Under One Flag: City's Melting Pot Reaches the Boiling Point: Inside the Immigrant Uprising." *Village Voice*, April 19–25, 2006, Citystate section, 15.

Muskal, Michael. "Immigration Dissent Sweeps L.A. and the Nation." *Los Angeles Times*, May 1, 2006.

Nagourney, Adam. "Ferrer's Choice: Appeal to Pride, or Embrace All." *New York Times*, September 27, 2001, D1 & D4.

———. "Political Memo; Ferrer Gains Sudden Momentum in Latest Twist of the Campaign." *New York Times*, October 3, 2001, Metro section.

———. "Political Memo; Heated Race Revisited, Amid Claims of Racism." *New York Times*, October 16, 2001.

———. "Squirming in Sharpton's Embrace; Fidgeting without It." *New York Times*, October 5, 2001.

Navarro, Mireya. "Pataki's Success among Latinos Worries Some Democrats." *New York Times*, November 9, 2002, B1.

Neal, David L., Matt A. Barreto, Jongho Lee, and Rodolfo O. de la Garza. "The Latino Vote in the 2004 Election." *PS* (January 2005): 41–49.

Nelson, Jill. "Race Counts: White Voters Play the Race Card, Again." *Village Voice*, October 30, 2001.

———. "The Race Factor: A View from Behind the Scenes." *Village Voice*, October 30, 2001.

"The New York Primary: Turnout and Turnover." *New York Times*, September 27, 2001, D6.

Ngai, Mae M. "The Architecture of Race in American Immigration Law: A Reexamination of the Immigration Act of 1924." *Journal of American History* 86, no. 1 (1999): 67–92.

———. "Illegal Aliens and Alien Citizens: United States Immigration Policy and Racial Formation, 1924–1945." PhD diss., Columbia University, 1998.

———. *Impossible Subjects: Illegal Aliens and the Making of Modern America.* Princeton, NJ: Princeton University Press, 2004.

Nicholas, Peter. "Gov. Refuses Bush Request for Border Troops." *Los Angeles Times,* June 24, 2006.

The 1950 Censuses—How They Were Taken: Procedural Studies of the 1950 Censuses, No. 2 Population, Housing, Agriculture, Irrigation, Drainage. Washington, DC: U.S. Department of Commerce, 1955.

Noble, John Hawks. "The Present State of the Immigration Question." *Political Science Quarterly* 7, no. 2 (1892): 232–43.

Nobles, Melissa. *Shades of Citizenship: Race and the Census in Modern Politics.* Stanford: Stanford University Press, 2000.

Noel, Peter. "Should Al Sharpton Apologize? The Racial Politics of Reconciliation in New York." *Village Voice,* July 28, 1998, 55–57.

———. "Take It or Leave It, Mark Green: Brooklyn Assemblyman Roger Green's Challenge to a Turncoat Liberal." *Village Voice,* October 31–November 6, 2001.

Nordlinger, Jay. "Power Dem." *National Review,* March 20, 2001.

North American Congress on Latin America. "Crossing Borders: Race and Racism, Part II." *NACLA: Report on the Americas* 35, no. 2 (2001).

———. "The Politics of Race and Globalization: Part 1: Changing Identities." *NACLA: Report on the Americas* 38, no. 2 (2004).

———. "Racial Politics, Racial Identities: Race and Racism in the Americas, Part III." *NACLA: Report on the Americas* 35, no. 6 (2002).

———. "The Social Origins of Race: Race and Racism in the Americas, Part 1." *NACLA: Report on the Americas* 34, no. 6 (2001).

Norton, Anne. *Alternative Americas: A Reading of Antebellum Political Culture.* Chicago: University of Chicago Press, 1986.

———. *Leo Strauss and the Politics of American Empire.* New Haven, CT: Yale University Press, 2004.

———. *95 Theses on Politics, Culture, and Method.* New Haven, CT: Yale University Press, 2004.

———. *Reflections on Political Identity.* Baltimore: Johns Hopkins University Press, 1988.

———. *Republic of Signs: Liberal Theory and American Popular Culture.* Chicago: University of Chicago Press, 1993.

O'Donnell, Michelle "Thousands Turn Out, but Support Is Mixed among New York's Immigrants." *New York Times,* May 2, 2006.

Oboler, Suzanne. *Ethnic Labels, Latino Lives: Identity and the Politics of (Re)Presentation in the United States.* Minneapolis: University of Minnesota Press, 1995.

Office of Management and Budget. Circular No. A-46. Revised. May 3, 1974.

———. Circular No. A-46. Revised Exhibit F. May 12, 1977.

———. Directive No. 15. "Race and Ethnic Standards for Federal Statistics and Administrative Reporting." *Federal Register* 43, no. 87 (May 4, 1978): 19269–70.

———. Recommendations from the Interagency Committee for the Review of Racial and Ethnic Standards to the Office of Management and Budget Concerning Changes to the Standards for Classification of Federal Data on Race and Ethnicity; Notice. *Federal Register* 62, no. 131 (July 9, 1997): 36874–6946.

———. "Revisions to the Standards for the Classification of Data on Race and Ethnicity; Notices." *Federal Register* 62, no. 210 (October 30, 1997): 58781–90.

———. "Standards for the Classification of Federal Data on Race and Ethnicity." *Federal Register* 59, no. 110 (June 9, 1994): 29831–35.

———. "Standards for the Classification of Federal Data on Race and Ethnicity; Notice." *Federal Register* 60, no. 166 (August 28, 1995): 44674–93.

Ogunnika, Olu. "Inter-Ethnic Tension: Management and Control in a Nigerian City." *Politics, Culture, and Society* 1, no. 4 (1988): 519–37.

Okamura, Jonathan Y. "Situational Ethnicity." *Ethnic and Racial Studies* 4, no. 4 (1981): 452–65.

Oliver, Melvin L., and Thomas M. Shapiro. *Black Wealth, White Wealth: A New Perspective on Racial Inequality.* New York: Routledge, 1997.

Omi, Michael. "Racial Identity and the State: The Dilemmas of Classification." *Law and Inequality: A Journal of Theory and Practice* 25, no. 1 (1997): 7–23.

Orozco, Jose Clemente. *An Autobiography.* Translated by Robert C. Stephenson Mineola. New York: Dover, 1962.

Orren, Karen, and Stephen Skowronek. "Beyond the Iconography of Order: Notes for a 'New Institutionalism.' " In *Dynamics of American Politics: Approaches and Interpretations*, edited by Lawrence C. Dodd and Calvin Jillson. Boulder, CO: Westview Press, 1994.

———. *The Search for American Political Development.* New York: Cambridge University Press, 2004.

Pace, David. "Latino Numbers More Impressive in Census Than Ballot Box." *Los Angeles Times*, September 9, 2001.

Padilla, Felix M. *Latino Ethnic Consciousness: The Case of Mexican Americans and Puerto Ricans in Chicago.* South Bend, IN: University of Notre Dame Press, 1986.

———. "On the Nature of Latino Ethnicity." *Social Science Quarterly* 65, no. 2 (1984): 651–64.

Parrish, John B. "Rise of Economics as an Academic Discipline: The Formative Years to 1900." *Southern Economics Journal* 34 (July 1967): 1–16.

Patterson, Orlando. "Race by the Numbers." *New York Times*, May 8, 2001, A27.

Pearce, Roy Harvey. *Savagism and Civilization: A Study of the Indian and the American Mind.* Berkeley: University of California Press, 1988.

Perlmann, Joel. " 'Race or People': Federal Race Classifications for Europeans in America, 1898–1913." Working Paper Number 320. New York: Levy Economics Institute, Bard College, January 2001.

Perlmann, Joel, and Mary C. Waters, eds. *The New Race Question: How the Census Counts Multiracial Individuals.* New York: Russell Sage Foundation, 2002.

Persons, Stow. *Ethnic Studies at Chicago, 1905–45.* Urbana: University of Illinois Press, 1987.

Petersen, William. "Politics and the Measurement of Ethnicity." In *The Politics of Numbers*, edited by William Alonso Paul Starr. New York: Russell Sage Foundation, 1987.

Pew Hispanic Center/Kaiser Family Foundation. *National Survey of Latinos: The Latino Electorate.* Washington, DC: Pew Hispanic Center and Henry J. Kaiser Family Foundation, 2002.

———. *2002 National Survey of Latinos: Summary of Findings.* Menlo Park, CA: Henry J. Kaiser Family Foundation, 2002.

Plotz, David. "Al Sharpton: How Al Charlatan Became Al Kingmaker." *Slate*, March 3, 2000.

Pocock, John Greville Agard. *The Machiavellian Moment: Florentine Political Thought and the Atlantic Republican Tradition.* Princeton, NJ: Princeton University Press, 1975.

———. *Politics, Language, and Time: Essays on Political Thought and History.* Chicago: University of Chicago Press, 1989.

———. *Virtue, Commerce, and History: Essays on Political Thought and History, Chiefly in the Eighteenth Century.* Cambridge: University of Cambridge Press, 1985.

Podhoretz, Norman. "My New York: An Intellectual Considers His City, from Laguardia to Giuliani and Beyond." *National Review,* June 14, 1999.

Portes, Alejandro, and Rubén G. Rumbaut. *Immigrant America: A Portrait.* Berkeley: University of California Press, 1996.

———. *Legacies: The Story of the Immigrant Second Generation.* Berkeley: University of California Press, 2001.

Portes, Alejandro, and Richard Schauffler. "Language and the Second Generation: Bilingualism Yesterday and Today." *International Migration Review* 28, no. 4 (1994): 640–61.

Posnock, Ross. *Color and Culture: Black Writers and the Making of the Modern Intellectual.* Cambridge, MA: Harvard University Press, 1998.

Powell, John Wesley. "The Categories." *American Anthropologist,* n.s., 3, no. 3 (1901): 404–30.

———. "Competition as a Factor in Human Evolution." *American Anthropologist* 1, no. 4 (1888): 297–323.

Prewitt, Kenneth. "The Census Counts, the Census Classifies." In *Not Just Black and White: Historical and Contemporary Perspectives on Immigration, Race, and Ethnicity in the United States,* edited by Nancy Foner and George M. Fredrickson. New York: Russell Sage Foundation, 2004.

———. "Racial Classification in America." *Daedalus* 134 (Winter 2005): 5–17.

Public Law 94-311. 90 Stat. 688 (1976).

Pycior, Julie Leininger. *LBJ and Mexican Americans: The Paradox of Power.* Austin: University of Texas Press, 1997.

Quadagno, Jill. *The Color of Welfare: How Racism Undermined the War on Poverty.* New York: Oxford University Press, 1996.

Quinones, Sam, and Arin Gencer. "Fox Makes Rounds for Immigration." *Los Angeles Times,* May 27, 2006.

"Race and Racism in the Americas, I." *NACLA: Report on the Americas,* 34, no. 6 (2001).

"Race and Racism in the Americas, II." *NACLA: Report on the Americas,* 35, no. 2 (2001).

"Race and Racism in the Americas, III." *NACLA: Report on the Americas,* 35, no. 6 (2002).

Rainey, James, and Matea Gold. "Mayor's Race Avoids Ethnic Schisms: Tests Loom." *Los Angeles Times,* April 16, 2001.

Rainey, James, and Greg Krikorian. "Hahn Won on His Appeal to Moderates, Conservatives." *Los Angeles Times,* June 7, 2001, home edition, A-1.

Rau, Jordan. "Gov Eyes More Latino Support, but Budget Plans Spark Major Debate." *Newsday*, March 9, 2003, A23.

Reed, Adolph, Jr., ed. *Without Justice for All*. Boulder, CO: Westview Press, 1999.

Report of the Constituent Convention of the Intercollegiate Menorah Association Held at the University of Chicago, January 1, 2, and 3, 1913 (n.p., n.d.).

Ricci, David M. *The Tragedy of Political Science: Politics, Scholarship, and Democracy*. New Haven, CT: Yale University Press, 1984.

Riley, Denise. *Feminism and the Category of "Women" in History*. Minneapolis: University of Minnesota Press, 1988.

Ripley, William Z. "Acclimatization." *Popular Science Monthly* 48 (March 1896): 662–75.

———. "Acclimatization, Second Paper." *Popular Science Monthly* 48 (April 1896): 779–93.

———. "Geography as a Sociological Study." *Political Science Quarterly* 10, no. 4 (1895): 636–55.

———. "Race Progress and Immigration." *Annals of the American Academy of Political and Social Science* 34, no. 1 (1909): 130–38.

———. *The Races of Europe: A Sociological Study*. (New York: Appleton, 1899).

———. "The Racial Geography of Europe: A Sociological Study, I—Language, Nationality, and Race." *Popular Science Monthly* 50, no. 4 (1897): 454–68.

———. "The Racial Geography of Europe: A Sociological Study, Supplement—the Jews." *Popular Science Monthly* 54, no. 2 (1898): 163–75.

———. "The Racial Geography of Europe: A Sociological Study, Supplement—the Jews (Continued)." *Popular Science Monthly* 54, no. 3 (1899): 338–51.

———. "The Racial Geography of Europe: A Sociological Study, XIII—Modern Social Problems." *Popular Science Monthly* 52, no. 4 (1898): 469–86.

———. "The Racial Geography of Europe: A Sociological Study, V—The Three European Races." *Popular Science Monthly* 51, no. 2 (1897): 192–209.

———. "The Racial Geography of Europe: VI—France—The Teuton and the Celt." *Popular Science Monthly* 51, no. 3 (1897): 289–307.

Rischin, Moses. *The Spirit of the Ghetto: Hutchins Hapgood*. Cambridge, MA: Belknap Press of Harvard University Press, 1967.

Robbins, Tom. "Up from Fox Street: Ferrer Campaigns for the 'Other New York.'" *Village Voice*, August 1–7, 2001.

Rodriguez, In re, 81 F. 337 (W.D. Tex. 1897).

Rodriguez, Clara. *Changing Race: Latinos, the Census, and the History of Ethnicity in the United States*. New York: New York University Press, 2000.

Rodriguez, Clara, and Hector Cordero-Guzman. "Placing Race in Context." *Ethnic and Racial Studies* 15, no. 4 (1992): 523–42.

Rodriguez, Gregory. "Can-Do Spirit Fuels Immigrants." *Los Angeles Times*, May 7, 2006.

Rodriguez, Lori. "Hispanic Voters Cool So Far to Dream Team." *Houston Chronicle .com*, September 23, 2002.

Rodriguez, Nancy. "Race and Ethnicity Testing: Update and Discussion." Distributed at the REAC Meetings, May 5–7, 2004. Washington, DC: U.S. Bureau of the Census, 2004.

Roediger, David. "Getting into the White House Southern and Eastern Europeans." Talk delivered at the New School for Social Research, April 22, 2004.

———. *Towards the Abolition of Whiteness: Essays on Race, Politics, and Working Class History.* New York: Verso, 1994.

———. *The Wages of Whiteness: Race and the Making of the American Working Class.* New York: Verso, 1991.

———. *Working Toward Whiteness: How America's Immigrants Became White, The Strange Journey from Ellis Island to the Suburbs.* New York: Basic Books, 2005.

Rogin, Michael. *Blackface, White Noise: Jewish Immigrants in the Hollywood Melting Pot.* Berkeley: University of California Press, 1996.

———. *Ronald Reagan, the Movie: And Other Episodes of Political Demonology.* Berkeley: University of California Press, 1988.

Rosenwaike, Ira. "Ancestry in the United States Census, 1980–1990." *Social Science Research* 22 (1993): 383–90.

Ross, Dorothy. *The Origins of American Social Science.* New York: Cambridge University Press, 1991.

"Roundtable: Hanging Separately." *Salon.com,* November 12, 1995. http://www.salon.com/12nov1995/feature/race.html.

Rumbaut, Rubén G., and Alejandro Portes, eds. *Ethnicities: Children of Immigrants in America.* Berkeley: University of California Press; New York: Russell Sage Foundation, 2001.

Sacks, Karen Brodkin. "How Did Jews Become White Folks?" In *Race,* edited by Stephen Gregory and Roger Sanjek. New Brunswick, NJ: Rutgers University Press, 1994.

Sager, Mike. "The Sharpton Strategy." *Esquire,* January 1991, 23–24, 112–19.

Saito, Leland T. "Asian Americans and Multiracial Political Coalitions: New York City's Chinatown and Redistricting, 1990–1991." In *Asian Americans and Politics: Perspectives, Experiences, Prospects,* edited by Gordon Chang. Washington, DC: Woodrow Wilson Center Press; Stanford: Stanford University Press, 2001.

———. *Race and Politics: Asian Americans, Latinos, and Whites in a Los Angeles Suburb.* Urbana: University of Illinois Press, 1998.

Saito, Leland T., and John Horton. "The New Chinese Immigration and the Rise of Asian American Politics in Monterey Park, California." In *The New Asian Immigration in Los Angeles and Global Restructuring,* edited by Paul Ong, Edna Bonacich, and Lucie Cheng. Philadelphia: Temple University Press, 1994.

———. "The Sedimentation of Political Inequality: Charter Reform and Redistricting in New York City's Chinatown, 1989–1991." *UCLA Asian Pacific American Law Journal* 8, no. 1 (2002): 123–45.

Salins, Peter. *Assimilation American Style.* New York: Basic Books, 1997.

Sánchez, George J. *Becoming Mexican American: Ethnicity, Culture and Identity in Chicano Los Angeles, 1900–1945.* New York: Oxford University Press, 1993.

———. "Disposable People, Expendable Neighborhoods: Repatriation, Internment, and Other Population Removals." Paper presented at Organization of American Historians, Washington, DC, April 19–22, 2006.

Sapir, Edward. "Racial Superiority." *Menorah Journal* 10, no. 3 (1924): 200–12.

Saragoza, Alex M., Concepcion R. Juarez, Abel Valenzuela Jr., and Oscar Gonzalez. "History and Public Policy: Title VII and the Use of the Hispanic Classification." *La Raza Law Journal* 5 (1992): 1–27.

Sargent, Greg. "Was Freddy Fingered? Or Was Ferrer Caught in Own Sharpton Trap?" *New York Observer,* May 21, 2001.

Sawyer, Thomas C. "Measuring Race and Ethnicity: Meeting Public Policy Goals." *American Statistician* 52, no. 1 (1998): 34–35.

Schechter, Solomon. *Zionism: A Statement.* New York: Federation of American Zionists, 1906.

Schmidt, Ronald, Sr. *Language Policy and Identity Politics in the United States.* Philadelphia: Temple University Press, 2000.

Schmidt, Sarah. "A Conversation with Horace M. Kallen: The Zionist Chapter of His Life." *Reconstructionist* 41 (November 1975): 28–33.

———. *Horace M. Kallen: Prophet of American Zionism.* Brooklyn: Carlson, 1995.

Schwarzenegger, Arnold. "Next Step for Immigration." *Los Angeles Times,* March 28, 2006, Op Ed section.

Scott, James C. *Domination and the Arts of Resistance: Hidden Transcripts.* New Haven, CT: Yale University Press, 1990.

Scott, Joan. "Fantasy Echo: History and the Construction of Identity." *Critical Inquiry* 27 (Winter 2001): 284–304.

———. *Gender and the Politics of History.* New York: Columbia University Press, 1999.

Scotti, Ciro. "Bloomberg's Secret Weapon: Green." *BusinessWeek.com,* November 9, 2001.

Seidelmam, Raymond, and Peter Novick. *That Noble Dream: The "Objectivity Question" and the American Historical Profession.* New York: Cambrige University Press, 1988.

"Serrano Succeeds in Retaining 'Other' Race Option on Census Form." Press release from Rep. José Serrano, November 22, 2004, http://www.house.gov/list/press/ny16_serrano/041122Census.html.

Shapiro, Yonathan. "American Jews in Politics: The Case of Louis D. Brandeis." *American Jewish Historical Quarterly* 55 (December 1965): 199–212.

Sharpton, Al. "Immigrants, Blacks Must March as One." *New York Daily News,* May 10, 2006.

Sheridan, Clare. "'Another White Race': Mexican Americans and the Paradox of Whiteness in Jury Selection." *Law and History Review* 21, no. 1 (2003): 109–37.

Sherman, Scott. "He Has a Dream." *Nation,* April 16, 2001, 11–19.

Silverstein, Ken. "Barack Obama Inc: The Birth of a Washington Machine." *Harper's,* November 2006, 31–40.

Skelton, George. "Black Affection for Hahn a Hurdle Villaraigosa Couldn't Vault." *Los Angeles Times,* June 7 2001, home edition, California section, B-7.

Skerry, Peter. *Counting on the Census: Race, Group Identity, and the Evasion of Politics.* Washington, DC: Brookings Institution Press, 2000.

———. *Mexican Americans: The Ambivalent Minority.* Cambridge, MA: Harvard University Press, 1993.

Skinner, Quentin. "Meaning and Understanding in the History of Ideas." *History and Theory* 8, no. 1 (1969): 3–53.

Skowronek, Stephen. "The Reassociation of Ideas and Purposes: Racism, Liberalism, and the American Political Tradition." *American Political Science Review* 100, no. 3 (2006): 385–401.

Skrentny, John D., ed. *Color Lines: Affirmative Action, Immigration, and Civil Rights Options for America.* Chicago: University of Chicago Press, 2001.

————. *The Minority Rights Revolution.* Cambridge, MA: Harvard University Press, 2002.

————. "Policy Making Is Decision Making: A Response to Hattam." *Studies in American Political Development* 18 (Spring 2004): 70–80.

Sleeper, Jim. *The Closest of Strangers: Liberalism and the Politics of Race in New York.* New York: Norton, 1990.

————. "The Joker." *Salon.com,* February 28, 2002.

————. *Liberal Racism: How Fixating on Race Subverts the American Dream.* New York: Penguin Books, 1997.

————. "A Man of Too Many Parts." *New Yorker,* January 25, 1993, 55–67.

Small, Albion W. "The Bonds of Nationality." *American Journal of Sociology* 20 (1915): 609–83.

Smedley, Audrey. *Race in North America: Origin and Evolution of a Worldview.* Bolder, CO: Westview Press, 1999.

Smith, Marian. "'Other Considerations at Work': The Question of Mexican Eligibility to U.S. Naturalization before 1940." Paper prepared for presentation at the Organization of American Historians Annual Meeting, Memphis, TN, April 3, 2003.

————. "Race, Nationality, and Reality: INS Administration of Racial Provisions in U.S. Immigration and Nationality Law Since 1898." *Immigration Daily,* June 16, 2003, http://www.ILW.com.

Smith, Robert. *Mexican New York: Transnational Lives of New Immigrants.* Berkeley: University of California Press, 2006.

Smith, Rogers M. *Civic Ideals: Conflicting Visions of Citizenship in U.S. History.* New Haven, CT: Yale University Press, 1997.

Snitow, Ann. "Pages from a Gender Diary." *Dissent* 36, no. 2 (1989): 205–24.

Sollors, Werner. *Beyond Ethnicity: Consent and Descent in American Culture.* New York: Oxford University Press, 1986.

————. "A Critique of Pure Pluralism." In *Reconstructing American Literary History,* edited by Sacvan Bercovitch. Cambridge, MA: Harvard University Press, 1986.

————. "Introduction." In *The Invention of Ethnicity,* edited by Werner Sollors. Oxford: Oxford University Press, 1991.

————., ed. *The Invention of Ethnicity.* Oxford: Oxford University Press, 1991.

————., ed. *Theories of Ethnicity: A Classical Reader.* New York: New York University Press, 1996.

Somerville, Siobhan B. *Queering the Color Line: Race and the Invention of Homosexuality in American Culture.* Durham, NC: Duke University Press, 2000.

Sovern, Michael I. *Legal Restraints on Racial Discrimination in Employment.* New York: Twentieth Century Fund, 1966.

Spencer, Herbert. "The Inadequacy of 'Natural Selection.'" *Contemporary Review* 63 (February 1893): 153–66.

————. "The Inadequacy of 'Natural Selection' (concluded)." *Contemporary Review* 63 (March 1893): 439–56.

————. "Professor Weismann's Theories." *Contemporary Review* 63 (May 1893): 743–60.

————. "A Rejoinder to Professor Weismann." *Contemporary Review* 64 (December 1893): 893–912.

———. "Weismannism Once More." *Contemporary Review* 66 (October 1894): 592–608.

Stallybrass, Peter. "Marx and Heterogeneity: Thinking the Lumpenproletariat." *Representations* 31 (Summer 1990): 69–95.

Stanton, William. *The Leopard's Spots: Scientific Attitudes Toward Race in America, 1815–59.* Chicago: University of Chicago Press, 1960.

Starr, Paul. "Liberalism after Clinton." *American Prospect* 11, no. 19 (2000).

———. *The Politics of Numbers.* New York: Russell Sage Foundation, 1987.

Stavrakakis, Yannis. *Lacan and the Political.* New York: Routledge, 1999.

Steinberg, Stephen. "Do Immigrants Block African American Progress? A Debate." *New Labor Forum* 15, no. 1 (2006): 69–72.

———. "Immigration, African Americans, and Race Discourse." *New Politics* 10, no. 3 (2005): 1–14.

Steinhausser, Jennifer, and Dexter Filkins. "In Courting Black Voters, Candidates Try Ubiquity." *New York Times,* September 8, 2001, B5.

Stocking, George W. "American Social Scientists and Race Theory: 1890–1915." PhD diss., University of Pennsylvania, 1960.

———. *The Ethnographer's Magic and Other Essays in the History of Anthropology.* Madison: University of Wisconsin Press, 1992.

———. "Lamarckianism in American Social Science, 1890–1915." In *Race, Culture, and Evolution: Essays in the History of Anthropology,* edited by George W. Stocking. Chicago: University of Chicago Press, 1982.

———., ed. *Race, Culture, and Evolution: Essays in the History of Anthropology.* Chicago: University of Chicago Press, 1982.

———. "The Turn-of-the-Century Concept of Race." *Modernism* 1, no. 1 (1993): 4–16.

Sundquist, James. *Dynamics of the Party System: Alignment and Realignment of Political Parties in the United States.* Washington, DC: Brookings Institute, 1973.

Swarns, Rachael L. "Growing Unease for Some Blacks on Immigration." *New York Times,* May 4, 2006, A1.

———. "Hispanics Debate Census Plan to Change Racial Grouping." *New York Times,* October 24, 2004, A21.

"A Symposium: The Left 40 Years Later." *Dissent* 41, no. 1 (1994): 7–17.

Takaki, Ronald. *A Different Mirror: A History of Multicultural America.* Boston: Little, Brown, 1993.

Terry, Jennifer. *An American Obsession: Science, Medicine, and Homosexuality in Modern Society.* Chicago: University of Chicago Press, 1999.

"Thinking About the Election." *Dissent* 31 (1984): 389–414.

Tienda, Marta, and Vilma Ortiz. "'Hispanicity' and the 1980 Census." *Social Science Quarterly* 67, no. 1 (1986): 3–20.

Thomas, William I. "The Mind of Woman and the Lower Races." *American Journal of Sociology* 12, no. 4 (1907): 435–69.

———. "On a Difference in the Metabolism of the Sexes." *American Journal of Sociology* 3, no. 1 (1897): 31–63.

———. "The Psychology of Race-Prejudice." *American Journal of Sociology* 9, no. 5 (1904): 593–611.

———. "The Scope and Method of Folk-Psychology." *American Journal of Sociology* 1, no. 4 (1896): 434–45.

Thompson, Phillip. J. "David Dinkins' Victory in New York City: The Decline of the Democratic Party Organization and the Strengthening of Black Politics." *PS: Political Science and Politics* 23, no. 2 (1990): 145–48.

———. "The Election and Governance of David Dinkins as Mayor of New York." In *Race, Politics, and Governance in the United States*, edited by Huey L. Perry, 65–81. Gainesville: University Press of Florida, 1996.

———. "The Untouchable." *New York Magazine*, December 3, 2001.

Tobar, Héctor. "Intensity Fuels Consensus Builder's Rapid Rise." *Los Angeles Times*, March 16, 2001.

Tobar, Héctor, and Carla Hall, "Villaraigosa's Backers Revel in His Historic Feat." *Los Angeles Times*, April 11, 2001.

Toll, William. "Horace M. Kallen: Pluralism and American Jewish Identity." *American Jewish History* 88 (March 1997): 57–74.

Tomasky, Michael. "Liberal Crack-Up; Polarization in New York's Mayoral Contest." *American Prospect*, November 20, 2001.

———. "Regarding Al." *Village Voice*, July 12 1994, 17.

To Secure These Rights: The Report of the President's Committee on Civil Rights. Washington, DC: Government Printing Office, 1947.

Traub, Amy M. *Principles for an Immigration Policy to Strengthen and Expand the American Middle Class: A Primer for Policymakers and Advocates.* New York: Drum Major Institute for Public Policy, 2005.

Tusan, Ashley. "We the People: Local, National Immigrant Protest Sets New Tone." *New York Amsterdam News*, May 4–May 10, 2006, 1.

Union of American Hebrew Organization. "Report of Board of Delegates on Civil and Religious Rights." In *Twenty-Sixth Annual Report of the Union of American Hebrew Organization*, 4121–22. (Washington, DC: Union of American Hebrew Organization, 1899).

U.S. Bureau of the Census. "American Fact Finder." Available at http://www.census.gov.

———. *Data Access Descriptions No. 41: Data on the Spanish Ancestry Population,* Available from the 1970 Census of Population and Housing. Washington, DC: Social and Economic Statistics Administration, 1975.

———. *Measuring America: The Decennial Censuses from 1790 to 2000.* Washington, DC: Government Printing Office, 2002.

———. *The 1950 Censuses—How They Were Taken.* Washington, DC: Government Printing Office, 1955.

———. *U.S. Census of Population: 1950.* Vol. IV, *Special Reports*, pt. 3, chap. C. *Persons of Spanish Surname.* Washington, DC: Government Printing Office, 1953.

———. *U.S. Census of Population: 1960. Subject Reports, Final Report PC(2)-1B. Persons of Spanish Surname.* Washington, DC: Government Printing Office, 1963.

———. *U.S. Census of Population: 1970. Subject Reports, PC(2)-1D. Persons of Spanish Surname.* Washington DC: Government Printing Office, 1973.

———. *U.S. Census of Population and Housing: 1970. Procedural History, PHC(R)-11. Advance Issuance of Chapters 1 and 2.* Washington, D C Government Printing Office, 1976.

U.S. Commission on Civil Rights. *Counting the Forgotten: The 1970 Census Count of Persons of Spanish Speaking Background in the United States.* Washington, DC: Government Printing Office, 1974.

————. *Employment*. Report 3. Washington, DC: Government Printing Office, 1961.

————. *To Know or Not to Know: Collection and Use of Racial and Ethnic Data in Federal Assistance Programs*. Washington, DC: Government Printing Office, 1973.

————. *Toward Quality Education for Mexican Americans*. Report 6: *Mexican American Education Study*. Washington, DC: Government Printing Office, 1974.

————. *The Unfinished Education: Outcomes for Minorities in the Five Southwestern States*. Mexican American Education Series 11. Washington, DC: Government Printing Office, 1971.

U.S. Department of Commerce. "Data on the Spanish Ancestry Population." Available from the 1970 Census of Population and Housing, DAD No. 41. Washington, DC: Government Printing Office, May 1975.

————. "Subject Reports: Persons of Spanish Surname." 1970 Census of Population, PC(2)-1D. Washington, DC: Government Printing Office, June 1973.

U.S. Department of Justice, Immigration and Naturalization Service. *Spanish Name Book (M-153)*. Washington, DC: Government Printing Office, 1973.

U.S. Department of Labor. *Annual Report of the Commissioner General of Immigration*. Washington, DC: Government Printing Office, 1921.

————. *Annual Report of the Commissioner General of Immigration*. Washington, DC: Government Printing Office, 1922.

————. *Annual Report of the Commissioner General of Immigration*. Washington, DC: Government Printing Office, 1923.

————. *Annual Report of the Commissioner General of Immigration*. Washington, DC: Government Printing Office, 1924.

————. *Annual Report of the Commissioner General of Immigration*. Washington, DC: Government Printing Office, 1925.

————. *Annual Report of the Commissioner General of Immigration*. Washington, DC: Government Printing Office, 1926.

————. *Annual Report of the Commissioner General of Immigration*. Washington, DC: Government Printing Office, 1927.

————. *Annual Report of the Commissioner General of Immigration*. Washington, DC: Government Printing Office, 1928.

————. *Annual Report of the Commissioner General of Immigration*. Washington, DC: Government Printing Office, 1929.

U.S. Equal Employment Opportunity Commission. "Equal Employment Opportunity Report No. 1: Job Patterns for Minorities and Women in Private Industry, 1966." Washington DC: Government Printing Office, 1966.

U.S. Immigration Commission. Vols. 1–42. Washington, DC: Government Printing Office, 1911.

————. *Dictionary of Races and Peoples*. Washington, D. C.: Government Printing Office, 1911.

"U.S. Prepares for 'Day Without Immigrants,'" Associated Press, May 1, 2006.

Vargas, Jose Antonio. "Immigrant Freedom Rides Hold Rally in City Hall in S.F. Immigrant Workers to Bus Across Nation." *SFGate.com*, September 21, 2003.

Vaughan, Leslie J. "Cosmopolitanism, Ethnicity and American Identity: Randolph Bourne's 'Trans-National America.'" *Journal of American Studies* 25, no. 3 (1991): 443–59.

Vitalis, Robert. "Birth of a Discipline." In *Imperialism and Internationalism in the Discipline of International Relations*, edited by David Long and Brian Schmidt. Albany: State University of New York Press, 2005.

"Voters' Survey: Democratic Primary Voters." *New York Times*, September 27, 2001, Metro section, D5.

Wald, Alan M. *The New York Intellectuals: The Rise and Decline of the Anti-Statist Left from the 1930s to the 1980s*. Chapel Hill: University of North Carolina Press, 1987.

Waite, Jay. Presentation by the associate director of the Decennial Census at the meeting of the Prewitt Working Group, held at the Russell Sage Foundation, New York City, June 20, 2005.

Wallman, Katherine K. "Data on Race and Ethnicity: Revising the Federal Standard." *American Statistician* 52, no. 1 (1998): 31–33.

———. "Statistics for Americans of Spanish Origin or Descent." *Statistical Reporter* 78, no. 5 (1978): 148–52.

Wallman, Katherine K., Suzann Evinger, and Susan Schechter. "Measuring Our Nation's Diversity: Developing a Common Language for Data on Race/Ethnicity." *American Journal of Public Health* 90, no. 11 (2000): 1705–8.

Walton, Hanes, Jr., Cheryl M. Miller, and Joseph P. McCormick II. "Race and Political Science: The Dual Traditions of Race Relations Politics and African-American Politics." In *Political Science in History: Research Programs and Political Traditions*, edited by James Farr, John S. Dryzek, and Stephen T. Leonard. New York: Cambridge University Press, 1995.

Walzer, Michael. "Blacks and Jews: A Personal Reflection." In *Struggles in the Promised Land: Toward a History of Black-Jewish Relations in the United States*, edited by Jack Salzman and Cornel West. New York: Oxford University Press, 1997.

———. "What Does It Mean to Be an 'American'?" *Social Research* 57, no. 3 (1990): 591–614.

———. *What It Means to Be an American: Essays on the American Experience*. New York: Marsilio, 1996.

Ward, Lester F. "Neo-Darwinism and Neo-Lamarckianism." *Proceeding of the Biological Society of Washington* 6 (1891): 45–50.

———. "Social Differentiation and Social Integration." *American Journal of Sociology* 8, no. 6 (1903): 721–45.

———. "Weismann's Concessions." *Popular Science Monthly* 45 (1894): 175–84.

Warner, Michael, ed. *Fear of a Queer Planet: Queer Politics and Social Theory*. Minneapolis: University of Minnesota Press, 1993.

———. *The Trouble with Normal: Sex, Politics, and the Ethics of Queer Life*. Cambridge, MA: Harvard University Press, 1999.

Waters, Mary C. *Black Identities: West Indian Immigrant Dreams and American Realities*. Cambridge, MA: Harvard University Press, 2000.

———. "Ethnic and Racial Identities of Second-Generation Black Immigrants in New York City." In *The New Second Generation*, edited by Alejandro Portes. New York: Russell Sage Foundation, 1996.

———. *Ethnic Options: Choosing Identities in America*. Berkeley: University of California Press, 1990.

Weil, Patrick. "Races at the Gate: A Century of Racial Distinctions in American Immigration Policy." *Georgetown Immigration Law Journal* 15, no. 4 (2001): 625–48.

Weismann, August. "The All-Sufficiency of Natural Selection: A Reply to Herbert Spencer." *Contemporary Review* 64 (September 1893): 309–38.

———. "The All-Sufficiency of Natural Selection: A Reply to Herbert Spencer." *Contemporary Review* 64 (October 1893): 596–610.

Werner, Erica. "Hispanic Voters Rush to Polls." Associated Press, November 9, 2000.

Williams, Kim. "Boxed In: The United States Multiracial Movement." PhD diss., Cornell University, 2001.

———. *Mark One or More: Civil Rights in Multiracial America.* Ann Arbor: University of Michigan Press, 2006.

Williams, Raymond. *Keywords: A Vocabulary of Culture and Society.* New York: Oxford University Press, 1985.

———. *Marxism and Literature.* New York: Oxford University Press, 1977.

Wolf, Simon. *The Presidents I Have Known from 1860–1918.* Washington, DC: Byron S. Adams, 1918.

———. "Report of the Board of Delegates on Civil and Religious Rights," 1904. Reprinted in Vol. 41, edited by United States Immigration Commission. Washington, DC: Government Printing Office, 1911.

———. "Testimony before the United States Industrial Commission." In *Selected Addresses and Papers of Simon Wolf,* edited by Simon Wolf, 215–39. Cincinnati: Union of American Hebrew Congregations, 1926.

Wolfson, Harry Austryn. "Escaping Judaism." Menorah Pamphlets No. 2. New York: Intercollegiate Menorah Association, 1923.

Wollenberg, Charles M. *All Deliberate Speed: Segregation and Exclusion in California Schools, 1855–1975.* Berkeley: University of California Press, 1976.

Word, David L., and Colby Perkins Jr., "Building a Spanish Surname List for the 1990's— A New Approach to an Old Problem." Technical Working Paper No. 13, Appendix A. Washington, DC: U.S. Bureau of the Census, Population Division, March 1996.

Zangwill, Israel. "Chosen Peoples: The Hebraic Ideal versus the Teutonic." *Menorah Journal* 4, no. 5 (1918): 255–76.

———. "The Dilemmas of the Diaspora: A Message to the Menorah Quinquennial Convention." *Menorah Journal* 4, no. 1 (1918): 11–14.

———. "The Fate of Palestine: 'The Center of the World's Desire.' " *Menorah Journal* 3, no. 4 (1917): 196–202.

Zerilli, Linda. "Doing without Knowing: Feminism's Politics of the Ordinary." *Political Theory* 26, no. 4 (1998): 435–58.

———. *Feminism and the Abyss of Freedom.* Chicago: University of Chicago Press, 2005.

Zizek, Slavoj. *The Sublime Object of Ideology.* New York: Verso, 1989.

Zolberg, Aristide. "Moments of Madness." *Politics and Society* 2, no. 2 (1972): 183–207.

———. *A Nation by Design.* Cambridge, MA: Harvard University Press, 2005.

INDEX

Page numbers followed by an *f* or a *t* refer to figures and tables, respectively.

213n30; "A Day Without Immigrants" rally participation, 163–67; impact on immigrants, 13–15, 213–14n35; Mississippi Freedom Summer, 4; protected minority status, 112–15; "race, creed, color, or national origins" language, 120–21; rhetorical themes of, 4–9, 12; "some other race" category, 122–25, 126, 215nn44–45, 216n52; Statistical Policy Directive No. 15 of the OMB, 111–15, 119–21

Clinton, Bill, 133

Commons, John R., 40, 41–42

"Comparative Classification of Immigrant Races or Peoples" table, 82, 83*f*

Cotton, Joseph P., 104–5

Crenshaw, Kimberly, 5

cultural pluralism, 54–62, 68–69, 73–76, 202n75. *See also* discourses on ethnicity

Culture and Democracy (Kallen), 56, 61–62, 71–73, 75

"Culture and the Ku Klux Klan" essay (Kallen), 71–73

Cuomo, Mario, 137–38, 219n27

Darwin, Charles, 28

Davenport, Charles, 80

"A Day Without Immigrants" rallies, 160–68

De Haas, Jacob, 47, 53

Delonas, Sean, 140–46, 162*f*

"Democracy versus the Melting Pot: A Study of American Nationality" essay (Kallen), 55–59, 71–73

Democratic Leadership Council, 133

Democratic Party, 130–32; African American members of, 4–5; Black racial polarization in, 133, 148–51; class-based racial pluralism in, 133–40, 153–55; Convention of 2004 speeches, 4–9, 163; defense of race-based reform by, 130; gubernatorial races of 2002, 132; Latino members of, 11–12, 132, 187–88nn17–18, 217n12; New Deal, 100, 120–21, 136, 208n56; racial identification of the Left wing of, 151–55; splits over immigration policy, 160–61, 225–26n5; white liberal racism in, 133, 150–51, 153–55.

See also Los Angeles mayoral races; New York mayoral races

Dewey, John, 18, 47, 50, 53

Diallo, Amadou, 137, 155

Dictionary of Races or Peoples (Dillingham Commission), 82, 84–95, 104–5, 109, 205n10, 205n12; "Comparative Classification of Immigrant Races or Peoples" table, 82, 83*f*; textual entry for Jews, 84–86

Dillingham, William P., 82, 86–91, 93–94

Dillingham Immigration Commission, 9, 66, 82–95, 109, 158; Chinese exclusion discussions by, 92; classification system of, 82–84, 206n26; "Comparative Classification of Immigrant Races or Peoples" table, 82, 83*f*; Jewish classification debates by, 84–95, 204–5n7; "mother tongue" classification, 93–95, 206n30; omission of consideration of African Americans, 92–93

Diner, Hasia, 77

Dinkins, David, 133, 137

Directive 15 of the OMB. *See* Statistical Policy Directive No. 15 of the OMB

discourses on ethnicity, xi, 1–3, 8, 10–13; Berkson's community theory of ethnic groups, 68–71, 202n76; Brandeis's views of anti-assimilationist nationalism, 50–54; census classification methods (*see* census classification system); contrasts with race of, 1–3, 9–11, 56–59, 68, 157–60, 186n4; disappearance of references to slavery and race in, 41, 71–73, 92–93; in discourses on nationality, 71–73; elision of racial inequality in, 12–15; emergence of ethnicity as social formation in, 18, 42–43, 45–48, 196nn4–5; ethnic pluralism and hyphenated identities in, 46, 48, 50, 52–54; exclusion of African Americans from, 13, 14–15, 41, 56, 92–93, 163, 219–20n28; focus on assimilation and incorporation of, 12–15, 51–52; Kallen's theories of cultural pluralism, 54–62, 68–69, 73–76, 199nn36–37; in mayoral races of 2001, 152–55; nineteenth-century emergence of, 17–18, 21, 42–43, 192n22; Obama's language of ethnicity, 4–9,